Magadan

Yakut
ASSR

60°

DERATED          SOCIALIST          REPUBLIC          Khabarovsk
Kray

Krasnoyarsk
Kray

Amur

Tomsk

Irkutsk          Buryat-
Mongol
ASSR          50°

Kemerovo
osibirsk          LAKE
BAIKAL

Altay Kray

·Tuva AO

y-
n

40°

# Christian Religion
# in the Soviet Union

# Christian Religion in the Soviet Union

*A sociological study*

*by*
CHRISTEL LANE

STATE UNIVERSITY OF NEW YORK PRESS
ALBANY 1978

Published by
State University of New York Press
Albany, New York 12246

© 1978 George Allen & Unwin (Publishers) Ltd.

Printed and made in the United Kingdom

**Library of Congress Cataloging in Publication Data**

Lane, Christel.
  Christian religion in the Soviet Union.

  Bibliography: p.
  Includes index.
  1. Sociology, Christian–Russia.
  2. Sects–Russia.
I. Title
BR933.L36      301.5'8      77–801

ISBN 0-87395-327-4

*For Julie and Christopher*

# Acknowledgements

I am indebted to the SSRC, whose research grant made this work possible, to Professor David Martin of the LSE, who read and advised me on several chapters, and to the staff at the Centre for the Study of Religion in Communist Society in Keston, Kent, who gave me full access to their extensive collection of *samizdat* (self-printed) and other sources on the subject of religion in the USSR. Lastly, I would like to thank those Soviet scholars who discussed my work with me when I visited the USSR in 1973.

# A Note on Abbreviations

The following abbreviations have been used throughout this book.

| | |
|---|---|
| *KSISRiOAV* | *Konkretno-sotsiologicheskoe izuchenie sostoyaniya religioznosti i opyta ateisticheskogo vospitaniya* |
| *KISRV* | *Konkretnye izucheniya sovremennykh religioznykh verovanii* |
| RSFSR | Russian Soviet Federated Socialist Republic |
| ASSR | Autonomous Soviet Socialist Republic |

# Contents

|  |  | page |
|---|---|---:|
| Acknowledgements | | 9 |
| Abbreviations | | 9 |
| 1 | Introduction | 13 |
| | Methodological considerations – theoretical perspectives – historical antecedents | |
| 2 | The Russian Orthodox Church I | 30 |
| | The Church in the sixties and seventies – socio-demographic distribution and social composition of membership – organisational structure and religious functionaries | |
| 3 | The Russian Orthodox Church II | 55 |
| | Dimensions of religious commitment among contemporary Russian Orthodox – some explanations for the persistence of Orthodox religion | |
| 4 | Orthodox Sects of the Soviet Period | 80 |
| | True Orthodox Christians | |
| 5 | The Old Russian Sects | 91 |
| | The Khlysts – the Skoptsy – the Dukhobors – the Molokans | |
| 6 | Old Believers | 112 |
| | Historical development and present trends – socio-political responses of Old Believers – the social composition of Old Believers – the nature of religious commitment among Old Believers | |
| 7 | Baptists | 138 |
| | Sect membership – 'sect'-like and 'denominational' tendencies – the schism in 1961 and the emergence of the Initsiativniks – the socio-demographic distribution and social composition of Baptists – the socio-demographic distribution and social composition of the Initsiativnik sect – explanations of the schism – the moral community | |
| 8 | The Smaller Sects of Western Origin | 167 |
| | Seventh Day Adventists – Pentecostalists – Jehovah's Witnesses | |
| 9 | Religion and Nationality I | 192 |
| | Lutherans and Mennonites | |
| 10 | Religion and Nationality II | 207 |
| | The Roman Catholic Church – the Lithuanian Catholic Church | |

11  Conclusion                                                    218
    Types of religious collectivities and their development
    – the incidence and social distribution of religiosity in
    Soviet   society – qualitative   changes   in   religious
    ideology, organisation and individual religiosity

Appendix A                                                        235
    List 1: Registered urban congregations of the AUCECB
    List 2: Geographical distribution of Initsiativniks

Appendix B                                                        240
    The organisational strength of the Roman Catholic
    Church in the Soviet Union (except Lithuania)

References                                                        241

Index                                                             251

# Chapter 1

# Introduction

This book is addressed mainly to sociologists of religion. But it is hoped that it will offer something also to students of Soviet society and to all those who are interested in the relationship between the Christian religion and communism. Despite the use of some sociological terminology, the book should be easily understood by non-sociologists. It brings together and analyses a wide range of data on most Christian religious organisations in the present-day USSR, many of which have never been studied by any Western researcher. Soviet area specialists will find that the study of the religious situation throws light on more general social and political processes in Soviet society and on the way these have had an impact on the lives of different groups of Soviet citizens. Christians, one hopes, will want to read the book to find out how their fellow Christians in the Soviet Union practise their faith in the social context of a socialist and militantly atheist society and how the various Christian denominations have been affected by this social system.

Sociologists of religion seeking to hypothesise in a general way about religion in modern industrial society have up to now confined themselves to the framework of Western society. The debate on types of religious collectivities and the religiosity of their members, on their relation to each other and to structures and processes in the wider society, is based almost exclusively on studies carried out in Western society ranging from the late medieval pre-capitalist to the industrial capitalist type. A few attempts to encompass non-Christian religious collectivities in the Eastern world have been made. But up to now there has been a complete absence of studies of Christian religious organisations and believers in the framework of a communist and militantly atheist society. Consequently, there has been no attempt to test the appropriateness of some of the basic theoretical assumptions of the sociology of religion in this rather different societal framework. Moreover, the analyses of the dynamic aspects of religious collectivities, having been conducted in a pluralist society, have tended to see religious collectivities as largely autonomous organisations and have concentrated predominantly on processes within them. Such studies have neglected to investigate the impact of state and social order on the religious organisation and the ways in which they have determined religious change.

In addition to trying to fill this serious gap in the sociological literature, the present work is motivated by the conviction that a militantly atheist society represents one of the rare socio-historical mixtures of circumstances which make it easier for the sociologist of religion to uncover important characteristics of religion and religious collectivities which might otherwise remain hidden. In a social situation where religious collectivities and believers are under continual pressure and religion is reduced to a closely circumscribed sphere, it is more likely that phenomena and processes hitherto unnoticed become revealed.

This introductory first chapter is intended to fulfil three tasks: to make clear the methodological considerations which have guided the work; to outline the theoretical perspectives adopted in the presentation and analysis of the empirical data; and, lastly, to provide a very short and compressed account of those social and political developments since the 1917 Revolution which have shaped the contemporary religious scene. This last section is addressed to readers not familiar with the evolution of Soviet society and does not offer anything new to the area specialist. Chapters 2 to 10 will each deal with one major or several smaller related religious organisations. The Russian Orthodox Church, being the most important religious organisation, will be covered in some detail in two chapters (2 and 3). The three succeeding chapters will be devoted to sects and dissenters in the Orthodox tradition: Chapter 4 will deal with schismatic groups of the Soviet period, Chapter 5 with the Russian sects of pre-revolutionary origin, and Chapter 6 with the various branches of Old Believers. The next two chapters describe and analyse the Protestant sects which have come to Russia from the West. The most important of them, the Evangelical Christian Baptists, is covered in a separate chapter (7), while the smaller sects (except for the Mennonites) are dealt with in Chapter 8. The last two chapters are concerned with those religious organisations which are the focus of both religious and nationalist sentiments. Chapter 9 looks at the national Lutheran churches of Latvia and Estonia, and at the German Lutherans. The Mennonites, although a sect of Western origin, are also included in this chapter because of their pronounced German cultural heritage. Then follows a chapter devoted to the Lithuanian Catholic Church. The conclusion to the book draws together and discusses the theoretical findings.

## METHODOLOGICAL CONSIDERATIONS

The Soviet Union has been selected for study because it represents a polar case of a communist, militantly atheist society of more than fifty years' duration and because a very wide range of religious collectivities – in terms of time of genesis, Christian tradition and sociological type – can be found there. The book concentrates chiefly on religious change during the period from 1959 to 1974. Earlier historical developments relevant to this period have also been considered, though necessarily in a very condensed and general form. It is assumed that the historical development and present general theological positions of the religious organisations which came to Russia from the West are known in broad outline to the reader. More space is devoted to the history and teachings of the indigenous Russian sects and churches which are largely unfamiliar to Western readers. The 1959–74 period was selected because it witnessed both an intensive anti-religious campaign (1959–64) and a period of relative religious toleration.

The work is firmly based on a selective analysis of empirical data on Christian religious organisations in Soviet society during the time under consideration. Data have been obtained from a number of sources. First, and most extensively, from empirical studies conducted by Soviet social scientists and, to a lesser degree, militant atheists. These have ranged from work on one local branch of a religious collectivity and studies of one organisation on a nationwide scale to analyses of several organisations in one geographical region. The extremely large volume of such work since 1959 has ensured a good supply of data on many aspects of Christian religious organisations in all the various geographical areas of the Soviet Union, but such information is uneven in the quality of coverage for different religious groups. In general, the data are better and more plentiful on the large, legal organisations. Descriptions of the smaller illegal sects by Soviet writers are hampered by their lack of easy access to these organisations, as well as by their more emotional approach to them. The methodological implications of relying intensively on this type of source will be discussed in detail below. Secondly, Soviet newspaper reports have been utilised. Thirdly, information issued by the religious organisations themselves has been considered. This falls into two categories: (*a*) information officially issued on the pages of their journals (such information is available only for the Russian Orthodox Church and the Union of Evangelical Christian Baptists) and (*b*) information issued illegally in the underground press (Russ. *samizdat*) by civil rights groups, by individuals or groups of Christians from legally recognised organisations, or by illegal religious collectivities. Fourthly, use has been made of reports by Western religious organisations or individual churchmen who have been in close contact with their Soviet counterparts. Fifthly, the author's own conversations with social scientists, churchmen and ordinary Russian people during two visits to the Soviet Union in 1970 and 1973 gave some limited impressionistic information, while observation of services in Orthodox and Baptist churches provided a useful check of data given in the Soviet sociological literature. It is impossible for Western researchers to conduct independent surveys of any kind.

It is worth noting that the political authorities are in possession of the general statistics on the number of local religious organisations and their believers, as registration with the local authority is compulsory, and all those organisations which do not comply with this regulation render themselves illegal. Yet the political authorities do not issue any statistics on religious organisations and their believers because, according to the legal position, religion is a private matter.

The reliability of the data utilised in this book depends to a large extent on the soundness of the methodology of Soviet scholars. Apart from the work of 'religious sociologists', Western sociology pursues the understanding of religious phenomena as an end in itself. In the Soviet Union, however, understanding is still sought to further the eradication of religion from the social life of a socialist society, while at the same time its social scientists subscribe to the same methods as Western scholars and, like them, aspire to 'scientific objectivity'. Soviet sociologists are further hampered in their research by the dictates of the fairly rigid ideological and methodological framework given by Marxism–Leninism, which cannot easily be ignored. This restricts the number of questions raised in an inquiry. Individual sociologists pursuing empirical research are thus faced with the formidable task of preventing the intrusion of their ideological orientations into their field studies by being as objective as possible.

By and large Soviet sociologists are fairly successful in this endeavour.* They not only attempt to keep ideological polemics out of their interviews but also try to compensate for any ideological bias that inevitably remains associated with

* For discussions of methodological aspects of Soviet empirical sociological work on religion, see Pivovarov, 1974, pp. 191*f*., or Alekseev, 1967, pp. 131*f*.

their work by employing methods to check the reliability of their results. Thus surveys by interview or questionnaire are supplemented by prolonged observation and consultation with key informants and by reference to documentary evidence. The vast resources poured into such empirical research into religion in the Soviet Union assist the researcher in this endeavour. He is also helped in striving to minimise ideological bias by the low level of sophistication among a large section of believers, who are often elderly and poorly educated. To a large extent these respondents are unaware of the purpose of the research in which they are participating. A pretence of ideological neutrality is, however, harder to maintain effectively when the respondents belong to more educated strata or to religious organisations hostile to the Soviet regime and zealous in the political education of their members, such as the smaller illegal sects. In these latter cases the methods outlined above probably cannot overcome the ideological bias and some socially vulnerable or politically hostile respondents will probably give a false response or no response at all. But many of the best researchers do not base their results solely on respondents' answers and have several other research techniques to check the reliability of their survey results, particularly consultation of key informants and prolonged observation of religious life. Often a social scientist is at the same time an active militant atheist who has lived and worked in the area of study for years and has the co-operation of local officials in the Party, officers in local government, and workers in education, factories, collective farms, libraries and similar institutions. The study by Teplyakov (1972) of the religious life of Voronezh region, for example, gives the impression that it is well informed of everything that goes on in the religious sphere and that religious commitment with any kind of social manifestation is impossible to conceal in a social context where the ideological cohesion of elites is great.

In some studies, however, an unintended bias in the sample or the responses of respondents may have remained. Measures have been taken by the present author to exclude its intrusion into the book as far as possible. Checks have continually been made, first by viewing all the results with such a bias in mind, secondly by consulting a wide range of Soviet studies on certain aspects to counter-check them with each other, and thirdly by using Western and underground *samizdat* material to gauge the reliability of information. While such measures can deal with unintentional bias in the Soviet sources to a large extent, they cannot overcome it completely, especially when this bias has led to such gaps in the data as described above. As such inadequacies are particularly likely to occur as far as quantitative data on membership are concerned we are consequently restricted in our own dealing with this aspect of the subject. It must be made clear that, on the whole, quantitative data in this study constitute only rough approximations, and emphasis has been put on comparing the strength and activity of one organisation in relation to others and, more positively, much qualitative information has been analysed. Although this admittedly constitutes a limitation in our work it must be considered far less of a shortcoming than the highly impressionistic and speculative nature of the studies presented by earlier, usually religiously committed, writers in this field.

While bias resulting from ideological orientations is stronger in Soviet than in Western sociological research on religion, evidence of intended bias due to manipulation of research methods or misrepresentation of results is infrequent in Soviet studies. They are generally of high quality though usually less sophisticated in the use of methods and techniques and in theoretical perspective. These short-comings are partly compensated for by the much greater volume of research in the sociology of religion and its wide scope.

Throughout the study a comparative approach is adopted. The findings on religion in the USSR will, wherever possible, be compared and contrasted with what is known about religion in Western capitalist society. This will serve to put into perspective, and to highlight, marked divergencies in the pattern of religious change between these two types of society.

The countries of the capitalist West are not, of course, homogeneous as regards religion, and one needs to distinguish between the American and the Western European pattern. Even then generalisations remain at a very high level and inevitably gloss over many intra- and international peculiarities. The Soviet Union has experienced some social processes in common with Europe, while others it shares only with the USA. Like Europe, it had a feudal and peasant past and a state-supported religious monopoly. Like the USA, it has experienced exceptionally rapid processes of industrialisation and urbanisation, as well as extensive internal migration and something like the American frontier in the settlement of the east and central Asia. As regards industrial development, the Soviet Union is, of course, at an earlier stage than the leading Western societies. All these historical, social and economic differences make a comparison between the Soviet and the Western patterns of religious change very difficult and must inevitably result in a highly general and somewhat oversimplified picture.

THEORETICAL PERSPECTIVES

Having dealt with the methodological problems of the study we may now move on to discuss the theoretical issues that will be raised. The main objective of the book is to analyse religious change both within individual religious organisations and at the general societal level under the impact of various processes in Soviet society. The general theoretical framework adopted is that of the 'sect-church' typology and the related 'sect-to-church' hypothesis. The ideal types of 'church', 'sect' and 'denomination' are mental constructs which each unite the elements of empirically found religious groupings into an internally consistent system of relationships. As such they do not correspond to any religious organisations actually found in society but serve as theoretical tools to analyse such organisa-tions. Detailed definitions of each type will be given below. The 'sect-to-church' hypothesis refers to the empirically testable proposition that religious organisa-tions undergo a development along a continuum from 'sect' to 'church'. The typology will serve as a heuristic device for the analysis of data and will be applied only loosely. The choice of number of types and their characteristics has been informed by consideration both of previous work in the field and of the special context provided by a communist and militantly atheist society. Rather than adopting a great number of sub-types (as does Yinger, 1957), it is considered preferable to point to the presence of conflicting religious orientations within each type (see detailed discussion below).

The three types of 'church', 'sect' and 'denomination' will be adopted. Each type has been defined by several rather than one or two characteristics. These have been chosen by utilising the insights of Troeltsch (1931, Vol. I) and, more extensively, those of Wilson (1970), and have in turn been modified in the light of the peculiarities of Soviet society. In contrast to the Troeltschian typology, collectivities are defined partly in relation to each other and partly according to their response to the Soviet order and communist ideology. This approach is based on the conclusion that each religious collectivity in the Soviet Union is shaped by affirmation of, or opposition to, the dictates of both a particular Christian heritage and the social and political order in which they exist. The latter is deemed a more powerful influence.

Troeltsch's typology, although having provided the basis and inspiration for much subsequent work in the field, has also come under heavy criticism from many quarters (e.g. Johnson, 1963 and 1970; the contributions to a symposium on the subject in the *Journal for the Scientific Study of Religion*, 1967; Wilson, 1970, pp. 22*ff*) and has received several amendments and alterations. In the present work the validity of these criticisms is examined in the light of evidence derived from the study of a communist and militantly atheist modern industrial society. It will be shown that, while most of the basic criticisms also apply in this particular social context, some are too narrowly conceived in relation to Western capitalist society. It will further be demonstrated how some of the more recent amendments to and developments of the 'church-sect' thesis can be applied to overcome the shortcomings of the 'church-sect' typology and be utilised to give a satisfying explanation of religious change in one type of modern industrial society.

The types utilised have been defined in the following way.

### The 'church' type
Unlike Troeltsch's 'sect' type, his 'church' type may be utilised in this study with little amendment. Following Troeltsch, the church is defined as a body which:

(a) bestows saving grace through the dispensation of the sacraments;
(b) postulates a religious division of labour and a hierarchical religious status order;
(c) emphasises its permanence and transcendance over individual members and society;
(d) claims as members everyone born in the surrounding society;
(e) generates among its membership a relatively shallow religious commitment;
(f) is integrated into the world and is allied with the ruling class, acting as its agency of social control. (Troeltsch, 1931, Vol. I, pp. 328–82)

While traits (a), (b) and (c) are not generally questioned, those described under (d), (e) and (f) have come under considerable criticism.

Some critics argue that the 'church' type is becoming irrelevant to the study of religion in modern industrial society. Referring to point (d), they point out that there are few contemporary Western societies where the church enjoys the regular support of most of the population (e.g. Johnson, 1963, p. 541; Wilson, 1970, p. 74). But such an observation, while generally true, defines the problem far too narrowly. It is not crucial whether people support their church regularly or not, but whether the church still *aspires* to represent the nation it is placed in and continues to *claim* its citizens as members by birth.

It is also said that (e) constitutes a value judgement and does the church an injustice. Church members, it is held by these critics, show as much variation of religious commitment as members of other religious collectivities (e.g. Johnson, 1971, p. 131). Of course, there is variation in the depth of religious commitment in all religious organisations. The crucial point is, however, that in the 'church' type of religious collectivity members with a weakly developed religious commitment predominate. To counter the accusation that such a statement is based on a value judgement I shall examine in some detail the nature of religiosity of church members, utilising Glock and Stark's theoretical framework (1965, 1968).

It is further contended that few churches today enjoy a politically protected religious monopoly and that one can no longer speak of an alliance between the ruling classes and the church. This view is based on a one-sided interpretation of facts. First, one can ignore constitutionally fixed relations and concentrate on identifying the extensive *actual* privileges most national churches enjoy over other religious organisations. Thus the Soviet state, although in theory holding to the thesis of the eventual demise of all religious organisations, has in practice accorded the Russian Orthodox Church limited privileges, raising its status in Soviet society above that of other religious organisations (see Chapter 2). Secondly, even if one cannot always speak of an alliance between church and state based on *mutual* support, one must not discount the church's unilateral declaration of national loyalty and of support for the dominant ideology and the political status quo as well as for established social mores. These latter characteristics must be stressed particularly in the context of a militantly atheist society (see Chapter 2).

## The 'sect' type

The Troeltschian definition of the 'sect', although also still suggestive, has needed more change than that of the 'church'. A particularly cogent and useful redefinition of the type is that by Bryan Wilson (1959, 1970). Most, though not all, of his redefinition forms the basis for our 'sect' type. Like Wilson, we see the sect as:

(a) a voluntary body, entrance to which is by conscious adult choice;
(b) granting membership after a test of merit and withdrawing it from those deemed unworthy by expulsion.
(c) possessing a strong sense of self-identity;
(d) demanding from its members exclusive allegiance;
(e) fostering an elite conception. This manifests itself in a belief in the superiority of sect teachings and in exclusive access to salvation, or at least to superior blessings. It also implies a degree of hostility to other religious organisations and their members and precludes ecumenical striving.

    One can agree with Wilson that Troeltsch's characterisation of the sect as appealing principally to the lower classes and espousing the idea of poverty is no longer apposite. Unlike Wilson, I have retained some other traits of the Troeltschian 'sect' type in a slightly modified form or given them more emphasis. It is considered necessary to include the description of the sect as
(f) a small community which shares the fellowship of love. 'Small community' might refer to the sect as a whole, as Troeltsch meant it, or it might refer to the local branch. I consider the local community the most important unit, i.e. the most influential in shaping members' consciousness. Members may have

an awareness of the existence of a large bureaucratic network but it is only of secondary relevance to them as long as their local independence is safeguarded to a large degree. It is deemed particularly important to include this character-istic in the 'sect' type because the realisation of most of the other charac-teristics depends on the existence of a relatively small and intimate face-to-face society. A further important characteristic is

(g) an emphasis on religious equality, a minimisation of the distinction between clergy and lay. Again religious equality at the *local* level is the decisive factor;
(h) being in tension with and/or apart from the world. The separation from and/or opposition to the world will differ in the range of areas affected as well as in the degree of disaffection involved.

Following Wilson, a distinction between sects with different responses to the world will be made. This will test the applicability of Wilson's typology of sects in the context of Soviet society. I shall try to explain why certain of the sect types Wilson specifies have taken firm root in Soviet society and why others are either rare or non-existent.

We have seen that some of the characteristics of the 'sect' type are still mean-ingful in the social context of Soviet society. This is due to the fact that, in contrast to Western societies, Soviet society resembles late medieval society in some important aspects, despite the general radical difference between the two types of society. The basic antagonism between religious and political ideology and the resulting religious intolerance of the Soviet state, coupled with a monopoly of coercive power, may be likened to the ideological stance of the medieval Catholic Church *vis-à-vis* dissenters. The position of *all* religious organisations in the Soviet Union (with some degree of variation) resembles that of the persecuted sects in pre-industrial Europe. Another aspect of Soviet society also renders the Troeltschian sect type useful. Being composed of areas with highly discrepant levels of economic and social development, Soviet society has given rise to an extremely wide range of religious collectivities. At one end of this range we find sects which do not differ very much from those late medieval ones depicted by Troeltsch (see Chapters 4, 5 and 6).

But besides these similarities between a militantly atheist and a quasi-theocratic society there are also, of course, obvious differences between the two. Like other modern industrial societies, the Soviet Union is now socially and occupationally highly differentiated and has become increasingly devoid of class polarisation. Such a social structure has become difficult to reconcile with an intransigent religious intolerance by the state, and it has minimised religious divisions based on class divisions. Consequently, movement from 'sect' to 'denomination' as well as from 'church' to 'denomination' has become notable in recent decades, and the adoption of the 'denominational' type has become necessary for the analysis of the contemporary Soviet religious scene. But in contrast to its appropriateness as a research tool in the analysis of religion in the West, this type is useful mainly for analysing *developmental tendencies* rather than *faits accomplis*.

*'The denomination'*
Although the 'denomination' is largely defined in relation to the 'sect' and the 'church', it is not seen as just a halfway point between them. Study of the definition given by Wilson (1966) suggests the following traits as characteristic: it

(*a*) grants membership on demand;
(*b*) is tolerant of heterodoxy;
(*d*) demanding from its members exclusive allegiance;
(*e*) fostering an elite conception. This manifests itself in a belief in the superiority
    worship;
(*e*) has accommodated itself to the ethical standards of the larger society;
(*f*) accepts the political status quo.


    After this discussion and definition of the three types of religious collectivities, which are to serve as analytical tools throughout the study, we may now proceed to a review of the debate among sociologists on change in religious organisations. This book is not primarily concerned with establishing types or discussing the merits of typologies of religious organisations but merely utilises such a typology in the examination of religious change.

    A realisation of the importance of change in religious collectivities is considered a significant advance in the analysis of the religious scene of a rapidly changing society. The contributions on this subject by Niebuhr (1929), Wilson (1959, 1970), Schwartz (1970) and Isichei (1964) have all provided different valuable insights for this study. Niebuhr's merit consists in drawing attention to the impact of changes in the wider society on religious collectivities and to the constant interplay between the social and the religious sectors. His shortcomings, as Wilson (1959) has so succinctly stated, are the one-sided emphasis of this fact and the neglect of the internal dynamics of religious collectivities. Wilson's own work on sect development has clearly demonstrated that factors internal to the sect can either prevent or encourage movement towards a denominational position. Although Wilson's classification of sects according to their response to the world implies a consideration of both general societal factors and factors internal to the sect as relevant to change, his work in practice gives undue emphasis to the latter. Furthermore, these internal characteristics are considered at a very general and abstract level, disregarding the social significance of the finer aspects of doctrine or secular ethic as they are apprehended by rank-and-file members. The recent work of Schwartz (1970) shows that a less abstract review of sects' teachings may yield valuable findings about members' responses to the world. Isichei's insight that a sect may change its response to the world at different points of its history and that sect development must not be viewed as a linear process but rather as an oscillation between 'sect'- and 'church'-like tendencies constitutes a further theoretical refinement in the analysis of religious change.

    The analysis of religious change made in the following chapters will build on the contributions of the above-mentioned sociologists and will attempt to overcome their individual theoretical shortcomings. Although their findings were formulated in relation only to sect development it has been found profitable to utilise some of their conclusions in the analysis of *all* religious collectivities. Throughout the study, changes in response to the world as well as less general doctrinal or organisational shifts will be related to the impact of state and society. At the same time Wilson's typology of sects has alerted us to the fact that characteristics internal to religious organisations can mediate this impact in various ways. It will be shown, however, that the radically different nature of the Soviet order has sometimes influenced the development of religious organisations in ways unforeseen by a typology conceived of in the context of Western society.

We have attempted to go beyond the image of the organisation conveyed by the leadership of the collectivity and have also taken account of 'responses to the world' by rank-and-file members on various aspects of their social environment.

Religious change is perceived in terms of movement between the three types of religious collectivities outlined above. Although theoretically movement may occur all the way from 'sect' to 'church' and vice versa, it will be shown that, as in other modern industrial societies, movement is predominantly from the two extreme types to the denominational type in the middle. Like Isichei (1964), we have not assumed that development is always linear but have tried to identify processes of oscillation between 'sect'- and 'church'-like tendencies within organisations.

Another criticism of a typology of religious collectivities arises from its inability to deal with variation in religious orientations within individual collectivities. This is implied most strongly in the work of Dynes (1955) and Demerath (1965). They have brought out the fact that different religious orientations may be present simultaneously in a collectivity and have identified this coexistence of religious orientations not only in sects but in *all* types of religious collectivity. Both authors take the nature of members' religiosity as an index of the type of religious orientation held. The authors also found that a 'sect'-like orientation is related to low socio-economic status and a 'church'-like one to high status.

Like Dynes and Demerath I shall identify 'sect'- and 'church'-like tendencies within collectivities by making inferences about the nature of members' religiosity. The collectivity will then be loosely assigned to a type according to the predominant tendency within it at the time of investigation. In general, it will be more useful to distinguish between the great empirical variety of religious collectivities in terms of dominant religious orientations rather than assigning them rigidly to a certain type or sub-type. It will be shown that the many diverse aspects of Soviet society – its industrial-developmental, socialist and militantly atheist character – often influence religious collectivities in ways which result in incongruous mixtures of religious orientations within collectivities. It will be demonstrated how these can often be contained within one collectivity in coexistence for some length of time and how, at other times, they lead to schism and the reassertion of the sectarian tendency in a separate collectivity. This is demonstrated in some detail on the example of the Initsiativniks (see Chapter 7).

I do not maintain, as do Dynes and Demerath, that those people having a 'sect'-like orientation have a lower socio-economic status than those with a 'church'-like orientation, but I shall argue that more complex relations than this exist between social status and religious orientation. A wide range of data on social characteristics of members of the various religious collectivities will be reviewed, and emerging differences will be highlighted and explained. This will involve establishing a relation between social characteristics and religious orientations.

In addition to such an analysis of religious change in terms of a shifting balance between religious orientations I shall raise more general, though related, theoretical issues. Questions as to which social strata believers in Soviet society are concentrated in, and how this social distribution of believers as well as any changes in the nature of their religiosity are related to the nature of Soviet society, will be answered. The ways in which these processes differ from those in Western capitalist society will be highlighted. I shall distinguish, where possible, between three different kinds of influence on religion. First, the impact of a rapidly developing modern industrial society – of the processes of industrialisation, urbanisation and cultural and technological advance – will be considered. Secondly, an assessment of the effect of communist ideology and social order will be made. Special attention will be paid to the ways in which religious ideology and practice are affected by, and adapt themselves to, the former. Variations in response by the different types of religious collectivities will be highlighted. I shall show that although there is generally far greater conflict between political ideology and practice and religion in Soviet than in Western capitalist society, there are also certain facets of ideology and social order which harmonise with, and therefore either reinforce or cancel out, religious objectives much more than is the case in Western capitalist society. Thirdly, I shall examine the impact of militant atheism on religious believers and organisations and their different capacities to resist this onslaught. In practice, of course, these three analytically separate areas of impact are often closely intertwined and thus difficult to separate. Lastly, it must be borne in mind that these various effects were mediated by the scope and character of religion itself before these processes began. The existence of a strongly established and widely influential national church, as well as of a plethora of extremely varied, embattled and vigorous sects, and a history of conflict between radical secularist and religious groups, will all be considered as intervening factors.

In addition to relating processes in the wider society to general religious change, I shall determine their impact on the religious orientations of individual believers. I shall examine how these social processes have created tensions and aroused aspirations which are expressed or satisfied through religion. The following aspirations will be identified: (a) for clear and firm moral standards, (b) for communality, (c) for various psychological gratifications and (d) for the expression of political dissent of varying degrees and kinds. These individual aspirations are then linked to a particular religious orientation.

As is made clear in the title and the preceding introductory section of the book, we are dealing only with the impact of Soviet society on religion and not with the relationship in reverse. This is not because of a crude Marxist view that ideology is merely the reflex of other more basic social forces and that the impact of religion on society is therefore sociologically a non-problem. The complete neglect of this issue is simply due to the fact that this question is a different subject from that studied here, though a most important one.

HISTORICAL ANTECEDENTS

Before we proceed to the more detailed discussion of the development of individual religious organisations, the reader not familiar with Soviet society needs to be acquainted with some aspects of the social and political framework in which they are located. Since the Bolshevik Revolution of October 1917 the processes which have decisively shaped religious change in the Soviet Union are:

(1) the rapid and large-scale economic and social development of a modern industrial society of a socialist, politically authoritarian type;
(2) militant atheist legislation and activity.

*Economic development and political change*

At the beginning of the twentieth century Russia was still a backward, pre-dominantly agrarian society with a small privileged aristocratic elite and a large mass of poor and mostly illiterate peasants, ruled over by the Tsarist autocracy. But Russia was not stagnating in its backwardness and important changes were beginning to take place in all areas of society. Large-scale advanced industrial development, based largely on Western technology and capital, was well under way by the end of the nineteenth century. The hierarchical social structure was becoming undermined by the new social strata emerging out of the industrialisa-tion process as well as by the many transformations which had followed in the wake of the 1861 Emancipation of the Serfs. Urbanisation and the increased availability of education were gradually reducing the backward sector of Russian society. From 1905, the Tsar's autocratic rule had been weakened by the establishment of the Duma and political parties which, despite their limited influence, challenged the sanctity of the Tsar's rule and the inviolability of the social status quo. Many of these changes were accelerated by the First World War, and in 1917 the Russian people were confronted by two revolutions, the second of which, in October, began the most drastic transformation of all aspects of their society.

The immediate post-revolutionary period of War Communism (1918–21) was characterised by political and economic change and great social upheaval. (The following account is based on Carr, 1959, Vol. 5; Nutter, 1962; Conquest, 1968; Nove, 1969; and Lane, 1970.) In 1918 the key industries were nationalised, and in 1920 these were followed by all enterprises using either more than five men aided by mechanised power or more than ten men. The impact of these measures, however, was greatly muted by the disruption of the Civil War. Instead of economic development, chaos and recession ruled. Output fell to only 20 per cent of the 1913 volume, trade was disrupted and inflation was high. In the countryside, peasants had spontaneously seized the large estates and divided them among themselves.

The New Economic Policy (NEP) period of 1921–8 saw the reversal of some of these economic measures and a return to some measure of normality and economic recovery. All except the key industries were temporarily returned to private ownership. By 1926 the gross value of industrial production had just sur-passed the 1913 level.

The really drastic economic changes and severe political controls came only with the beginning of the First Five Year Plan in 1928. Not only did this Plan help to achieve in a very short space of time extremely rapid economic develop-ment without outside help, but it also created an advanced industrial economy based on the latest modern technology. The rate of this development is well illustrated by the fact that the Soviet rate of economic growth during various time-spans between 1928 and 1955 surpassed that of the USA during comparable periods of rapid growth (see Bergson, 1961, p. 264).

Industrialisation was accompanied by a sweeping process of manpower reallocation resulting in urbanisation, migration from west to east, and great educational advances. Between 1926 and 1955 the non-agricultural workforce increased from 10 to 45 million (i.e. twice as quickly as the same increase was achieved in the USA), the urban population rose from 19 per cent of the total population in 1929 to 33 per cent in 1940, and migration to the east and central

Asia, both voluntary and forced, involved many millions of Soviet citizens. To appreciate the immensity of the social dislocation involved in the industrialisation process it must be called to mind that, whereas the USA could rely to a large extent on migrants with a European urban background, the USSR could only draw on the educationally and technologically extremely backward rural sector. According to the 1897 census, only 19·6 per cent of the rural population were then literate. The overall percentage of those who were literate rose from 24 per cent in 1897 to 81·2 per cent in 1939. The most spectacular advances were made in higher education, where the number of enrolled students increased from 127,400 in 1914 to 3,500,000 in 1964–5.

This process of industrialisation was paralleled by an equally sweeping transformation of the rural sector of Soviet society. Rapid and ruthless collectivisation of agriculture was carried out between 1929 and 1933. In that period the percentage of collectivised homesteads rose from 3·9 per cent to 93·5 per cent, with 25 million peasant homesteads being merged into 250,000 collective farms. The collectivisation drive was carried out with great ruthlessness, especially as far as the richer farmers, the *kulaks*, were concerned. They were deprived of all their property and many were either killed or deported to the camps in the East. For the poorer peasants the consequences of collectivisation were less drastic but even for them it meant the destruction of a familiar rhythm and method of work and of a whole way of life. The complete disruption of the countryside resulted in a severe famine in 1932 which still haunts the memories of survivors.

The centralisation of economic power was paralleled by a greater concentration of political power which partly contributed to the next big social upheaval – the purges of the late thirties. Beginning among the top echelons of the political apparatus, they swept right through society, claiming, according to some commentators, several million victims. The large-scale and apparently indiscriminate way in which they were carried out threw the whole population into fear and terror. After only a short respite, the Soviet population was again subjected to fear and misery by the German invasion accompanied by immense destruction and loss of life estimated at 20 million dead during the Second World War.

In the face of the great social dislocation attendant on geographical and social mobility and a complete change of work culture and technological environment, one must not lose sight of the many positive consequences brought about by these processes. Here we can only hint at the many ways in which the quality of life was enhanced for a large majority of Soviet citizens. Better public and social services and, since the fifties, great increases in the standard of personal consumption, greater equality in economic and social status, increased social security and personal dignity and wider social and cultural horizons are among the many positive achievements of the Soviet pattern of development inspired by the ideology of communism.

Since the end of the fifties the pace of change has slowed down, and economic, social and political stability have brought a new equilibrium to Soviet society. But the effects of decades of great social upheaval still linger on for many Soviet citizens, for whom they often constituted the formative life experience. For those born or growing up since the war, the developmental aspects of Soviet society have greatly receded in importance as determinants of social consciousness, while various aspects of communist ideology and social order have retained their influence, though a less powerful one, in shaping a general world-view.

*State–church relations*

Militant atheist policies and activity have developed relatively independently from other social changes and have, despite some fluctuations, been a remarkably constant phenomenon of the Soviet social scene. Here we shall consider them historically in their manifestation in state–church relations. For the sake of comparison, a brief review will be made of the position of organised religion on the eve of the Revolution.

Before the Revolution the religious scene was dominated by the Russian Orthodox Church. The Orthodox Church was the established state church and counted as its members the vast majority of Russians. Its established status brought the Church great privileges but also considerable disadvantages. The Tsarist autocracy fostered a close union between state and church with the Tsar being the God-given ruler of Holy Russia. The Orthodox Church was openly considered as a force binding the people in reverence and obedience to its worldly rulers. Up to the tolerance edict of 1905, all other religious organisations were legally proscribed, and all Russians were nominally church members. After 1905, Old Believers and the sects of Orthodox or Western Protestant origin gained more ground but never seriously challenged the monopoly position of the Orthodox Church. The Lutheran and Catholic Churches were tolerated as churches of foreign nationals and were not perceived as competitors or disruptive influences.

On the debit side, the close connection between Church and state meant a strict supervision and circumscription of Church policy and affairs by the autocracy. The most powerful man in the Church was a secular official appointed by the Tsar. Consequently, the Church had little independence and merely echoed and exalted the social and political concerns of the autocracy, reinforcing the reactionary policies of the state in many areas of Russian society. Although the Church counted around 90 per cent of Russians as its members, its claim on the Russian population was not generally accepted and its hold was not evenly deep. The small but influential Russian intelligentsia was almost completely alienated from the Church. Large sections of the mercantile and rising industrial strata had also abandoned the Church in favour of the Old Believers, the indigenous Russian sects and the rising sects of Western origin. Unlike the majority of Orthodox clergy and lay members, many of these dissenters and sectarians had pronounced sympathies for the liberal and socialist political parties. Although all these groups formed only a small percentage of the population (i.e. about 20 million out of 180 million inhabitants) and were no serious challenge to the supremacy of the Church, they were a thorn in its flesh; their growth and influence were continually being restricted and their members were at times cruelly persecuted.

Soon after the 1917 Revolution church–state relations were radically changed, and the whole religious scene was dramatically transformed. The Bolshevik Party, which had come to power during the Revolution, not only adhered to Marxist principles in the restructuring of socio-political relations but had also adopted Marx's views on religion. Marx's views were interpreted in a harsh and uncompromising form, as the following quotation from Lenin illustrates:

'Every religious idea, every idea of God, even of flirting with the idea of God, is unutterable vileness . . . vileness of the most dangerous kind, "contagion" of the most abominable kind. Millions of sins, filthy deeds, acts of violence and physical "contagions" . . . are far less dangerous than the subtle, spiritual idea of a God decked out in the smartest "ideological" costumes. . . . Every defence or justification of the idea of God, even the most refined, the best intentioned, is a justification of reaction.' (Lenin, 1959, pp. 89–90 and 93)

Like Marx, the Bolsheviks believed that with the abolition of economic exploitation of man by man, religion would gradually wither away. But, realising that the forces of reaction would remain at work in Soviet society during the early years of socialist construction, they thought it necessary to adopt measures to hasten the dying out of religion. These measures included the withdrawal of all social support from religion and the vigorous dissemination of scientific-educational and anti-religious propaganda. In 1918, a decree on religion reflecting this policy was published. It specified the position of religious organisations and believers in Soviet society in a fundamental way and has provided guidance for anti-religious legislation and activity ever since. The main provisions of the 1918 decree are as follows:

(1) separation of the church from the state;
(2) establishment of freedom of conscience for individuals with a heavy emphasis on the rights of atheists rather than believers;
(3) separation of the church from schools;
(4) religion decreed to be an entirely private matter, and its practice not to interfere with the rights of other people or citizens' other obligations;
(5) no money to be taken from believers except voluntary donations;
(6) all religious property to be made public and buildings to be let to religious organisations at the discretion of the political authorities.

None of these points was elaborated in great detail and the various regulations could be stretched and interpreted in many ways. Future developments showed that this was often done at great cost to the religious organisations. (For a detailed account of the legal position of religious organisations and believers, see Rothenberg, 1971, and Beeson, 1974, Chapter 2.)

The provisions of this decree dealt a serious blow to the Orthodox Church which lost all its extensive privileges. They were initially advantageous to the sects which, for the first time in Russian history, had equal status with the Church. In general, believers of all faiths were left free to practise their religion as long as they kept it an individual and private act. Efforts to stamp out religion were mainly concentrated on creating the social and economic conditions believed to be conducive to the liberation of the working classes from a religious world-view. It was realised that coercion would hinder rather than help this process of liberation. Besides these ideological considerations, purely pragmatic ones prevented a more drastic course of action. The chaos and uncertainty of this time channelled energies into more urgent tasks than the destruction of religion.

This period of relative religious tolerance ended in 1928 when Stalin amended the 1918 Laws. The most significant provisions of this decree were the following: there was a requirement for religious organisations to register with the local authority by putting forward the names of twenty initiators (Russ. *dvadtsatka*); the authorities became empowered to remove persons from executive positions in religious organisations; children were to be excluded from any activity connected with a religious organisation; organisations were not permitted to organise any activities of a social, cultural or welfare kind; religious functionaries were restricted to the geographical area in which their organisation was located. These changes enabled the state further to constrict the sphere of influence of religious organisations and to extend its own control over religious affairs.

During the late twenties and thirties either these new regulations were harshly applied, or believers and churchmen were treated with complete disregard for any of the laws on religion.

This bleak period for organised religion lasted until the Second World War, when the threat from outside demanded the creation of the greatest possible unity among the people and loyalty to the state. The law on religion was interpreted more liberally, and a degree of toleration was extended to most religious organ- isations. A great revival of religion during the war occurred, partly as a con- sequence of this newly-given relative religious freedom, and partly because the tremendous misery and upheaval inflicted upon the Soviet people by their enemy made large numbers return to religion.

In 1959 a new anti-religious campaign was mounted under Khrushchev's leadership. During this campaign, which lasted until 1964, the 1928 Law was again stringently applied and often manipulated in ways which permitted a large- scale destruction of religious networks. The campaign was aimed at all religious organisations but affected the Russian Orthodox Church more seriously than all other organisations. The most disruptive changes of policy were the implementa- tion in 1961 of new restrictive regulations for the Russian Orthodox Church and the Evangelical Christian Baptists (see Chapter 2, pp. 37–81 and Chapter 7, p. 146).

In addition to this policy of directly restricting and controlling the activities of religious organisations and their members, there is another important element in the militant atheist campaign, namely, atheist propaganda and education. Although this element has always been a part of the campaign it has been applied with varying degrees of intensity during the Soviet period. Sometimes atheist propaganda and education are addressed specifically to religious believers. At other times they are meant for the general population, either aimed at enlisting their help in the atheist campaign and providing the knowledge to conduct it or intended as preventive measures, particularly among children and young people. During the 1959–74 period the ideas of atheism have been disseminated widely both through the utilisation of the mass media and by individualist approaches. The most widely used channels are probably books and pamphlets of varying degrees of sophistication, but radio, television, film and visual arts have also been brought into service. Lectures on atheist themes are another favoured means. To give some impression of the scope of this atheist propaganda work I quote the following statistics for Voronezh region of the RSFSR (2,511,000 inhabitants): in 1965–6, 101 *new* books on atheist topics appeared on the shelves of book shops and libraries, two atheist popular journals had 25,000 subscriptions, local radio stations had regular programmes on atheist themes, and in 1970 alone 222,620 popular lectures were given on the subject (Teplyakov, 1972, pp. 93*f*.). Atheist education figures prominently in the general education of children and is gaining ground in higher education. Lastly, in recent years efforts have been increased to 'convert' believers to atheism through one-to-one encounters. Here the atheist fieldworker tries to establish a personal relationship with a believer, investing a lot of time and effort to bring about the 'conversion'. Taken together, all the above measures constitute a propaganda campaign of immense cost and scope. It appears as if the effectiveness of the mass undertakings is not in proportion to this effort. The main reasons for their lack of impact and sometimes counter-productiveness is the low level of sophistication of some and the difficulty encountered in actually reaching believers. The individualist approaches have been more successful. Also the consistent indoctrination of children must have had some impact on their world-view, although this would be difficult to measure.

The cumulative impact of all these social processes and political measures on the different religious collectivities and their members will be examined in detail in the various chapters of the book which follow.

# Chapter 2

# The Russian Orthodox Church I

The Russian Orthodox Church (hereafter ROC) has undergone many changes, some hardly perceptible to the outsider, and others more drastic, in all aspects of its life since its disestablishment after the 1917 Revolution. Although most observers would hold that its most recent history has not been marked by any momentous transformations, a close study of developments in the Church's social, political and religious teachings, and in its organisation of its membership as well as in the nature of members' religiosity during the 1959–74 period will reveal that very significant changes in all these areas have occurred and are still occurring. These many formal and informal changes are best understood if viewed socio-logically as both departures from, and approximations to, the 'church' type of organisation. They are most profitably regarded as the efforts of a one-time typical 'church'-like institution to cope with its disestablishment and generally precarious status in a communist and militantly atheist society. This study intends to show that such efforts to survive in a hostile political environment may lead a national church to assume a highly incongruous mixture of traditional 'church'-type characteristics together with features deviating strongly from that type.

To show that 'church'-type characteristics cannot only be identified at the level of the religious organisation and its leadership but also among ordinary believers, their social and political responses as well as the nature of their reli-giosity will be analysed. To appreciate the nature and the extent of all these changes in the contemporary Church a brief outline is necessary of its history in the period prior to the major concern of this book.

Up to 1917 the ROC was an archetypal established church enjoying all the privileges and disadvantages of such a position. The Church fully supported the social and political policies of the autocracy, asserted the God-given nature of tsardom, and inculcated in the masses a respect for the claim to social and political superiority by the ruling groups. But Church policy was also closely supervised and extensively directed by members of the political administration. In some ways, Church activities in the nineteenth and twentieth centuries were as circumscribed by the state as they are now under the Soviet regime, although then the ROC enjoyed immense concessions in return.

Church membership was automatically acquired by birth on Russian soil, and even after the tolerance edict of 1905 over 95 per cent of the population were considered members of the ROC. In 1914, the ROC had 54,174 churches and 23,592 chapels (*Ezhegodnik Rossii za 1914*, p. 99). Religious values were tightly woven into the general culture and continually reinforced by compulsory religious education in schools of which a majority were run by the Church. Church expansion into newly-gained or opened-up territory to the east of the Urals was fully encouraged. On top of all these privileges the Church was allowed to amass immense wealth and was a landowner of considerable magnitude.

Organisation was strictly hierarchical, and performance of religious ceremonies by laymen only permissible in emergencies. Great emphasis was laid on the immutability of Church organisation, dogma and ritual, and its ancient traditions were highly revered. Individual priests, however, were generally not very highly esteemed.

Individual Church members, though influenced by, and under the hold of, Orthodox dogma and ritual, always regarded their religion as one of several facets of their life rather than organising all their thought and activity according to religious precepts. Even before the Revolution, ritual was a more dominant aspect of Church life than dogma, and pagan magic and folk beliefs held equal sway with Orthodox precepts of faith.

After the assumption of power by the Bolsheviks in 1917, the status of the Orthodox Church in Russian society became radically altered. The Church was disestablished, and any connection with Orthodox religion and Church now became a stigma for the members of the political elite. The Church lost its privileged status and most of its wealth. Individual ecclesiastical or religious associations within the Church lost the right to be a legal entity. Clergymen and their children were socially ostracised by having withdrawn their rights as citizens. Bolshevik intolerance *vis-à-vis* Orthodox activity and belief was fully reciprocated by hostility to Bolshevik political goals and ideology on the part of the majority of religious functionaries.

Although membership in the ROC by birth was no longer legally enforced and both atheism and other religious organisations freely developed for the first time, a close identification of Russianness and Orthodoxy continued in fact in the consciousness of the majority of Soviet citizens during the twenties.

An important event in the life of the ROC in the early twenties was the emergence of the Renewal movement or 'Living Church'. Encouraged by the spirit of the time, the socially more progressive and theologically more modernist, though somewhat opportunistic, elements in the ROC asserted themselves. The Renewal movement's aim was to bring the Church into step with the new developments in the wider society, and its suggested reforms were far-reaching and drastic. It sought to re-establish a relation between state and church which cast the church into the same supportive and acclamatory role that it had held *vis-à-vis* the Tsarist regime and which, although not securing re-establishment, would at least make the state more favourably disposed towards the church. The Renewalists' other reforms were far more drastic as they attacked the very essence of the 'church' type. They envisaged the abolition of the strictly hierarchical organisational structure and the introduction of greater participatory rights for the lower clergy and laymen. Besides, they argued for far-reaching changes in dogma, ritual and secular ethic. The ancient tradition and immutability of these aspects of Church life had up to then been regarded as the main distinguishing feature of the Orthodox Church.

The Renewal movement carried a large minority of the upper and lower clergy with it and enjoyed the support of the regime. Utilising the disarray in the Church, whose head, Patriarch Tikhon, was in prison, it gained ascendancy for a while and established the 'Living Church' as the true Orthodox Church. Estimates of its sphere of influence in 1923 range from a following of 15,000 parishes, i.e. less than a third of the total number (Titov, 1967, p. 116), to more than half of all parishes (Sheinman, 1966, p. 58). But the reforms implemented by the 'Living Church' were too radical for the majority of the clergy and simple peasant parishioners, and it was unable to gain enough grass-roots support. Also their leaders have been widely accused of having been unprincipled careerists and generally unworthy of support. From 1923 onwards the 'Living Church' gradually fell apart, and the conservative main body of the church regained power. In 1923, the imprisoned Patriarch succumbed to state pressure and issued a declaration in which he regretted the Church's hostile attitude to the state and promised benevolent neutrality. Significantly, Tikhon was not prepared to commit his church to a position of full and active support for the new regime and its policies. After his death in 1925, his *locum tenens* Sergei not only upheld Tikhon's more conciliatory policy towards the state but also reaffirmed the Church's and his own loyalty.

Although these measures received support from a wide spectrum of clergy and laymen and helped to secure the survival of the ROC as an organisation at this critical stage, it also evoked disappointment and bitter resentment among some sections of Orthodox. In the eyes of the latter the support pledged to the Soviet regime and the implied surrender of the principle of the God-given nature of the Tsarist autocracy constituted the abandonment of a central tenet of Orthodox faith and prejudiced chances of salvation. These oppositional factions within the Church would not be reconciled to a violation of its political creed and went into schism (Gordienko, 1968, pp. 94–5). It is from 1923 onwards that groups of clergy and laymen split off from the Church to form the many small sects of the Soviet period we shall discuss in Chapter 4.

Disillusionment with the hierarchy became even greater when this political volte-face did not even gain the Church any privileges from the state. On the contrary, in 1929 new legislation on church–state relations made its position in Soviet society more precarious than ever. The decade or so following that legislation was probably the hardest for the Orthodox Church, although slight relaxation took place in 1936 when some new laws on religion were passed. It lost thousands of churches and religious functionaries, and millions of believers. But although its position in Soviet society became immeasurably weakened during those years, the ROC gave up little of its 'church' essence.

A significant change in church–state relations came about when the Soviet Union was threatened by the German invasion in the Second World War. This threat to land and people prompted the Church to offer to the regime sincere loyalty and active support. This support, it must be underlined, was called forth by the deep national feelings nourished by the ROC rather than by political sympathies based on ideological agreement. It was accepted and rewarded by Stalin who granted the ROC significant privileges not offered on the same scale to any of the other religious organisations. In 1943 Sergei became Patriarch at last. The Church was able to restart the publication of its journal (Gordienko, 1968, p. 69), and from 1944 onwards it reopened theological academies and seminaries in several towns as well as reopening many of its closed churches. During the war and immediate postwar period the Church also regained many of the old members who had left it during the late twenties and thirties. In that period the Church also started to conduct church foreign policy on a wide scale. The three basic goals pursued were (and still are) to spread the influence of the Moscow patriarchate among foreign autocephalous and exarch Orthodox churches in step with the designs of the state's foreign policy, to gain status in international church circles for the Soviet Union and the broad outlines of its foreign policy, and to portray the political authorities as tolerant in religious matters.

This period of relative calm and security was to last until 1959 when a new wave of legal restrictions and persecution threw church life once more into jeopardy. An unprecedentedly harsh interpretation of the 1929 laws on religion and a complete disregard by some local officials for any legislation safeguarding church rights led to the complete abolition of organised church life in some areas and to a serious disruption of it in other localities. Around 10,000 churches are said to have been closed in the 1959–64 period (Simon, 1970, p. 95).

In the year 1961 a synod of bishops accepted the Patriarch's proposal that parish priests should be deprived of any vote or even voice in the administration of their churches and parishes by the church council. The head of this council became the *starosta* or churchwarden who received far-reaching competences and could, as soon became clear, throw church life into disarray. (See, for example, the description of the *starosta*'s subversive activities in Father Shpiller's Moscow church given by Bourdeaux, 1969, pp. 305*f.*) When pressure from the political authorities on the ROC subsided towards the beginning of 1965, protest from within the Church, involving several individual clergymen and parish groups, began to arise (for details see p. 34). It is the impact of these more recent events, as well as the cumulative effect of forty-nine years of existence in a socialist, militantly atheist society on *all* aspects of church life, which we shall now examine in some detail.

THE CHURCH IN THE SIXTIES AND SEVENTIES

*Approximation to the 'church'-type*
Most members of state apparatus and Church hierarchy would assert that the contemporary ROC is strictly divided from the state and has completely departed from Troeltsch's ideal type in so far as the latter is characterised by mutually supportive arrangements. While this is certainly true as far as membership and formal interaction is concerned, the relation is much more complex than the formula about the division of the Church from the state implies. There is, of course, no interlocking membership, and ideological distance between members of the clergy and the political apparatus must be considerable. It would also be ludicrous to describe the political posture adopted towards the ROC as supportive, but one must note that the ROC does receive distinctly more favourable treatment than other religious organisations. Viewed historically, the Soviet regime has always given active support to politically loyal groups inside the Church. Thus it has supported the Renewal movement against the Tikhonite Church in the early twenties, the official Church against the dissenting breakaway groups in the late twenties, and the efforts of the ROC to incorporate the Ukrainian Eastern Rite Church. Since the war, the ROC, unlike the other churches, has enjoyed a wide, though reduced network of churches all over the Soviet Union and a well-

functioning organisation on a national and international level. Compared with the most privileged sectarian organisation – the Union of Baptists and Evangelical Christians – it has better facilities for training and publishing religious literature as well as more generous support for diplomatic relations with foreign churches at the top level of the hierarchy. Orthodox hierarchs are occasionally honoured with invitations to formal social gatherings, and in 1967 Patriarch Alexei was even decorated with the Red Banner of Labour, presumably for his services as unofficial propagandist and diplomat.

The approximation to the 'church' type, however, is closest when we focus on the Church's relation to the political apparatus. At the end of the fifties a clear change became discernible from benevolent political neutrality mixed with ardent patriotism to a more active ideological and political support (see e.g. Gordienko, 1968, p. 102). Despite the continuing intransigent state attitude on religion in general, important sections within the Orthodox Church have been striving for a closer union with the political apparatus and for fuller integration into socialist society. They try to achieve it by giving acclaim to, and actively supporting, the social and political goals of socialism at home and abroad as well as giving tacit agreement to selective anti-religious policies. Furthermore, they strive for greater congruence between religious and political ideology by consciously adjusting the Church's teachings to the officially held principles of socialism and a materialist philosophy.

While church support for the social and political objectives of a regime has always been an important feature of the 'church' type, the sanctioning of anti-religious policy by the church hierarchy is a new element in an accommodative attitude. Although the ROC has avoided confrontations with the political apparatus since Patriarch Sergei's capitulation in 1927, individual members of the Church hierarchy, until the forties, did continue to express their protest at measures they considered harmful to their church. The best reminder of this is the number of bishops who died in penal camps in the 1917–40 period (see Struve, 1967, pp. 354–7). In the early years of the period under consideration here, however, such measures as the large-scale closure of churches, the dismissal of priests, the introduction of such rules as registration of baptisms and other ritual services with the local political authorities, and the exclusion of the priest from the church council have not, with some notable exceptions, excited any open protest from leading members of the Church hierarchy. These exceptions have been Archbishops Ermogen of Kaluga, Venyamin of Irkutsk and Pavel of Novosibirsk who are known to have exposed the disruptive consequences for the Church of the 1961 amendment to section four of the Church statutes (see Bourdeaux and Matchett, 1975, pp. 48–9). The period of Khrushchev's anti-religious campaign (1959–64) is notable for the virtual absence of arrests among members of the Orthodox hierarchy, while over a hundred dissident Baptist leaders went into labour camps during the same period (see my statistics on this in Chapter 7 below). This fact is also noted by Simon (1969, p. 25) when he says: 'Far more serious for the situation within the Church was the fact that the bishops remained untouched although the Council for the Affairs of the ROC in most cases demanded from them a sanctioning of repressions.' Sometimes violation of the laws on religion would even be justified by the hierarchy in religious terms. When for example, the civil rights campaigner V. N. Chalidze took up the cause of believers in Naro-Fominsk/Moscow region who wanted a church reopened, a spokesman for the patriarchate gave him the following reply: 'If the authorities will not agree to open a church, it means that God does not wish it, so a blessing would be inappropriate.' (Quoted by Bourdeaux in the *Church Times*, 11 June 1971.) Similarly, in Gorky/RSFSR Archbishop Flavian condemned from the pulpit the independent efforts of believers to get a new church opened (*Religion und Atheismus in der UdSSR*, 9, 47, 1971, p. 4).

Parish priests, with the notable exceptions of Fathers Eshliman, Yakunin, Shpiller and Zheludkov, also kept silent. (The full text of the open protest letters to the Patriarch, the political authorities, and the press by priests Eshliman and Yakunin in 1965 and the more spontaneous expressions of protest from Fathers Shpiller and Zheludkov are given in Bourdeaux, 1969, pp. 798*f*, 304*f*.) Significantly, the voices of protest were most numerous among Orthodox laymen. Various Orthodox intellectuals as well as whole parish groups voiced their anger and sorrow about recent developments in the ROC and sometimes accused the hierarchy in no uncertain terms of connivance in the execution of policies dangerously weakening the ROC at local level (for details of such protests see Bourdeaux, 1969, pp. 125*f*.). Such attempts at revolt from below is a new phenomenon in the ROC. The strictly hierarchical structure of the Church, coupled with traditional lack of co-ordination between lay activists of different parishes, served to contain these protests and prevented the formation of an opposition movement.

We have noted that the second way of putting the influence of the Orthodox Church into the service of the political regime is to support and acclaim its social and political objectives. This propaganda function of the ROC has become both more general and more pronounced during the period at present under consideration. Socialist values are not only propagated by members of the hierarchy for an international audience, but they have also become well embedded in the secular ethic pronounced from the pulpit and are echoed by wide sections of ordinary believers. They have also had some impact on dogma and ritual, though to a much lesser extent. Let us consider in turn developments in each of these areas and at the different levels of the church.

Church foreign policy has been strictly aligned to, and in the service of, that of the government. At the international level in encounters with other Orthodox churches in East and West or with member churches of the World Council of Churches (WCC) and the Prague Peace Conference (PPC), representatives of the ROC regularly emphasise the religious tolerance and humanitarianism in general of the Soviet Union (e.g. *Zhurnal Moskovskoi Patriarkhii* (*ZhMP*), 1, 1963, p. 43). The Church urges support for the following particular policies of the regime: the establishment of world peace, the abolition of race and class difference as well as of the economic exploitation entailed by the colonial system (see, for example, *ZhMP*, 12, 1962, p. 78). More specifically, it supported the Czechoslovak invasion (*ZhMP*, 10, 1968, pp. 1–3) and condemned US aggression in Vietnam as well as the Greek dictatorship (*ZhMP*, 5, 1968, p. 32). Recently a high-ranking member of the Church hierarchy, Metropolitan Seraphim, joined the political authorities in denouncing A. Solzhenitsyn (*The Times*, 1 March 1974). He dissociated the Church from a man who had publicly aligned himself with the ROC and had stood up to defend it during a difficult time. In addition members of the hierarchy sometimes act as diplomats for the Soviet government. Thus, two hierarchs used a recent visit to Israel to conduct political talks with Israeli ministers on behalf of their government exploring possible ways out of the Soviet–Israeli political deadlock (*Sunday Times*, 27 April 1975). These political stances, it seems, are on the whole confined to members at the top of the hierarchy and are, to a large extent, prompted by political prudence.

The position is somewhat different, however, where social and political issues at home are concerned. From the beginning of the sixties an interest in social questions has grown in the ROC. The ROC sees itself as helping the state in creating the new social order: 'Orthodoxy . . . sees its basic social task in creating a deep unity with the people, in giving support to the people's effort at creating a flourishing and harmoniously developing society . . .' (*ZhMP*, 10, 1966, p. 70). There is a widespread conviction in the Church that communism and Christianity are very closely connected, or even that the former is derived from the latter. Thus Soviet Orthodox theologians advocate a 'Communist Christianity' or talk about a 'theology of revolution' or a 'theology of peace'. They argue that the atheist Soviet regime, although denying God's will, carries it out in creating a new just society.

Among the social values and attitudes endorsed by the Church are a greater involvement in the life of Soviet society, concern for the suffering of the oppressed and exploited people of other countries, collectivism and positive attitudes towards labour.

The following extracts from the *ZhMP*, for example, emphasise the need for greater social involvement and accommodation to current values by Church members.

'Christians must not close themselves off from the world, withdraw into their own form of ghetto. They must not ignore historical reality . . . such great events as the October Revolution which changed the social system in many countries . . . nor the fact that a whole number of governments are building a new social structure.' (*ZhMP*, 11, 1962, p. 47)

'Christians do not live in a vacuum, in isolation from the rest of humanity. Entering not only into the body of the church but also into the body of the state and the society in which they live, they cannot be estranged from mankind with its needs, sufferings and ailments. (*ZhMP*, 3, 1963, p. 23)

Metropolitan Nikodim before an international audience argued against 'extreme spiritualisation of the ROC' and acknowledged 'the church's duty to society and state' (Nikodim, 1968, p. 54). The training programme for new priests, too, stresses the need to raise problems of contemporary social life in sermons (see Andrianov, Lopatkin and Pavlyuk, 1966, p. 210).

With regard to work attitudes the Church now stresses the collectivist aspect, the duty to society rather than to God, and has quietly dropped the idea that work is God's punishment for man. Instead, the dictum 'he who does not work shall not eat', which is a major component of the communist moral code, is given great emphasis (Andrianov *et al.*, 1966, p. 116; Yankova, 1963, pp. 91–2). Many priests intersperse sermons to rural believers with admonitions of their work obligations on religious holidays, such as the following:

'How lamentable and how painful it is to see, at a time when the rich grain is ripening in the fields and every minute is dear, that there are people, who under the pretext of a feast day established by the holy Church, spend their time in revelry and drunkenness . . . Such people forget about the citizen's duty to his motherland, family and society . . .'

and

'Do not spend costly time in vain, try with all your might to gather the ripe corn more quickly in order that our prayer will be one of honest, conscientious toilers.' (Quoted by Andrianov *et al.*, 1966, p. 117)

At parish level, the majority of both priests and laymen accept the social and political goals of their socialist environment and wish to be integrated into Soviet society as full citizens. One author even reports believers as thinking that the Church assists the state and that the state approves of the ROC and is only hostile to sects (Chernyak, 1965, p. 49). While older priests are sometimes said to be less forthcoming in expressing their political loyalty, one rarely meets comments branding them as political enemies, the label frequently given to sectarian leaders. Rank-and-file believers are usually described as loyal citizens. It is less easy to know the political attitudes of Orthodox intellectuals whose existence is rarely acknowledged by fieldworkers. From *samizdat* documents we know that those who challenge the political authorities over their anti-religious policies are nevertheless supporters of a socialist political order (excepting only Talantov), although they want it in a more humane form. Significantly, they demand the religious rights guaranteed by the Leninist 1918 legislation on religion. The only politically hostile and active circle of Orthodox laymen to become known is the now defunct Berdyaev Circle of the early sixties (for details, see Osipov, 1972, pp. 153*ff.*; *The Times*, 18 April 1968).

For a long time the espousing of socialist morality could be regarded as the mere adoption of socialist jargon which was neither based on theological argument nor touched Orthodox clergy and lay members at the parish level. From the beginning of the sixties, however, the situation has become slightly more complex. Although the syllabus at Orthodox seminaries and academies is still very narrowly focused on purely theological issues and concentrates on their internalisation rather than critical discussion (for details of the syllabus see Struve, 1967, pp. 125*ff.* and Oppenheim, 1974, p. 8), some members of the hierarchy and of the staff of training institutes have begun to make attempts to achieve a greater congruence of Orthodox teaching with principles of socialist ideology. Since 1959 the church publication of *Theological Works* (Russ. *Bogoslovskie Trudy*) affords theologians an opportunity to express their ideas on both theological and social and moral themes (Gordienko, 1968, p. 69).

Among those furthering a new course on the relation between Orthodoxy and socialism are said to be Metropolitan Nikodim, Professors-Archpriests Borovoi and Voronov, Archpriest Sokolovsky, Professor of Theology Zabolotsky and a few others (Kurochkin, 1971, p. 168). They must have support from, and influence over, a wider circle of the Church elite, as they are permitted to express their views on the pages of the Church's official mouthpiece, the *ZhMP*, but it is impossible to gauge exactly the political mood in the hierarchy.

While concessions to the values of the dominant ideology have thus gone some way and are not just ideological window dressing but have been absorbed by, and express the sentiments of, a large number of the clergy and lay, changes in dogma and ritual have been less striking and the notion of change in these areas still evokes hostile reactions from some members of the Church.

Up to the end of the fifties it had been held that the very essence of Orthodoxy is its long unbroken tradition going back to the holy apostles themselves. 'Even today when theological thinking changes to an amazing extent, Orthodoxy, in its structure, spiritual quality, in its prayer and dogmatic consciousness, is identical at the very least with the Church of the Seventh Ecumenical Council (787), with the *Una Sancta* before any schism . . .' (Evdokimov, 1967, p. 62). Up to then any mention even of modernisation in this field had been regarded as sacrilegious. The beginning of the sixties has been notable for the opening up of a discussion about whether fundamentals of Orthodox faith are immutable, or whether some basic adjustments to dogma and ritual have become necessary. Yet at the present time opposition to basic changes is still strong at all levels of the Church. This steadfast conservatism is based on the conviction that the permanency of Orthodoxy has been psychologically needed amidst all the social and cultural upheaval, both by the majority of Orthodox believers at home as well as in the many *émigré* churches in the West. Also the memory of the disastrous 'Living Church' attempt at modernisation has dampened any great zeal in this area. The following two extracts from pronouncements on this subject by Orthodox theologians in 1947 and 1957 serve well to illustrate this position of the Moscow patriarchate:

'We Orthodox are distinguished from other Christian faiths by the fact that we preserve strictly the teaching of the Christian Church still from those times when there were no divisions in it, when there were neither Lutherans nor Catholics, when all believed together. And we have put ourselves the task to preserve this faith unchanged, neither to add to it nor to take anything away from it but to preserve strictly and exactly. In this consists our task, our advantage, and also our honour.' (Quoted by Gordienko, 1968, p. 102)

'Everything not in accordance with the original teaching in the sermons of the apostles, simply because it is different and new, must not be accepted . . . Every newly-introduced teaching, which is not in accordance with the apostolic faith, is a heresy.' (*ZhMP*, 9, 1957, p. 48)

While this position was still being defended in the 1960s as, for instance, by Metropolitan Nikodim in 1968, when addressing the plenum of the Ecumenical Council of Churches (Metropolit Nikodim, 1968, pp. 49, 53), advocates of change could now for the first time be heard. The necessity for basic Christian rethinking of long-established positions was suddenly acknowledged (see, for example, *ZhMP*, 8, 1964, pp. 44f.).

At parish level, among priests and believers, opposition to any changes of fundamentals of Orthodox faith was still strong, although there were minorities in support of modernisation. Among priests, especially the younger ones, who were trained since the Second World War, many favoured the new course, while bitter resentment against it was expressed by the older clergy (Nosovich, 1962, p. 19; Gordienko, 1968, p. 112). This latter attitude is well expressed in the following statement made to a Soviet sociologist:

'Any novelty disturbs and weakens the spirit of prayer. The Orthodox Church must not bow to any side – neither towards the ecumenical, nor the political, neither towards time-serving nor to servility. She must to the end of the century stand only on the one divine truth and neither add any new matters, nor take away anything, for she is founded on the very stone of Jesus Christ . . .' (A respondent, quoted by Kurochkin, 1971, p. 112)

Parishioners are said to understand even less the need for any corrections to Orthodox faith which for them is something absolute. As far as fundamentals of faith are concerned, the Church hierarchy has thus resisted pressures to accommodate to the modernising spirit of the wider society and has preserved the 'churchly' principle of objective sanctity of religious traditions.

Although no fundamental changes have thus been made as far as basic dogma is concerned, many minor adjustments have been carried out. Aspects of dogma, ritual and secular ethic have been reinterpreted, expanded or omitted in accordance with the sensibilities of the wider society and demands of the regime. Thus Bible sections which are in opposition to socialist values, such as the subordination of women, miracle tales or hostile references to secular power, are dropped from sermons and texts, while those congruent with communist ideology are emphasised (Yankova, 1963, p. 84). When discussing the figure of Christ, for example, contemporary theologians play down the royal, 'King of David' side and emphasise his proletarian origin and honest attitude to work: 'during the course of his whole life he was poor, lived the life of a poor provincial worker, of an artisan' (*ZhMP*, 1, 1964, p. 58). Special emphasis is given to the early period of Christendom, likening the communitarian social organisation of that time to that in Soviet society.

Among the changes in ritual we shall note here only those which have been consciously effected to bring the Church into line with contemporary attitudes and leave until later the discussion of adjustments necessitated by the imposition of restrictions by the political authorities. The Church abandoned all those rituals which have become outdated by a change-over to collective ownership and the adoption of advanced technology in agriculture as well as all those religious practices which have a strong element of magic in them or are liable to be condemned by the political authorities as damaging to believers' health. Thus it is no longer in general practice among priests to bless new houses, wells, or cattle being driven out to pasture, to arrange communal prayer for protection against adverse climatic conditions, nor to attempt to heal the sick, renew worn icons and drive out the devil (Chernyak, 1965, p. 54; Andrianov *et al.*, 1966, p. 209; Gordienko, 1968, p. 90). On the other hand, these practices are by no means completely extinct (see Krasnikov, 1968, pp. 95, 96). The mass manufacture of miracle-working icons and holy relics has stopped, and officially arranged processions with miracle-working icons have been abandoned (Krasnikov, 1968, p. 91; Andrianov *et al.*, 1966, p. 209). Out of consideration for believers' health the traditional Orthodox prolonged prayer and incessant genuflections are no longer required (see *ZhMP*, 4, 1964, p. 60). Infant baptism is now done by sprinkling water on the child's forehead rather than by the traditional immersion, and it takes place in separate, well-heated rooms to avoid the dangers of catching cold and infection (Chernyak, 1965, p. 30). Priests have been advised to introduce their services with a short sermon in Russian (rather than in the traditional Church-Slavonic) designed to explain Bible texts and even the meaning of individual rites (see *ZhMP*, 9, 1960, p. 50).

On the preceding pages we have shown how the ROC in the sixties made attempts to adjust all aspects of its life to its socialist environment and the demands of its political masters. However, we have to qualify this statement somewhat and draw attention to the fact that the tendency to seek accommodation varies in intensity over different aspects of church life. At all levels of the Church the drive to adapt is weakest in the area of dogma and ritual and strongest as far as the social teachings of the Church are concerned. But even those Orthodox who go out of their way to express their loyalty to the social and political values of their society and stress the great similarity between the social and moral ideals of Christianity and communism do not postulate an identity between Orthodox and communist morals but imply that their religion is more effective in this respect. In communist society, they argue, Christian ideals are only partly realised and some spiritual requirements of man remain unsatisfied. Also, unlike some Western Christian socialists, Orthodox theologians of 'Communist Christianity' do not belittle the saving function of the church (Kurochkin, 1971, p. 205). Parish priests, when giving sermons on moral issues, do also often imply that Orthodox Christians are better equipped than atheists to lead a morally exemplary life, that atheists do not know a higher meaning of life, or even that shortcomings in Soviet society are the result of lack of morals among unbelievers (Yankova, 1963, pp. 86, 88).

The question arises why trends towards modernisation and accommodation to the Soviet authorities and to Marxist–Leninist ideology have become more pronounced from the beginning of the sixties. One answer is that during this period several key posts in the hierarchy were given to young churchmen (Gordienko, 1968, p. 111). Thus bishops invested between 1958 and 1968 had an average age of 46 years, several being only in their thirties (Kurochkin, 1971, p. 109). Having grown up under the Soviet political order and having had no experience of the traumatic events during the 'Living Church' period, they have not been burdened by the memories of old political hostilities and destructively radical religious modernism and thus have been more open to contemporary political and religious ideas. At parish level, a new generation of young and well-educated priests, trained since 1945, is also beginning to make its weight felt. Unlike the older priests, they are said to be more active, committed and imaginative (Kurochkin, 1971; *Prichiny* . . ., 1965, pp. 93, 189 and 190). Believers, however, are not benefiting from a relatively large influx of young and eager newcomers but have, as a body, a high average age (see details below).

All these conscious adjustments by the ROC to the reality of its socialist environment have to be viewed as an effort to achieve as close a union with the state as is possible for a disestablished church in a militantly atheist society. Although the exigencies of existence in the USSR do not allow the establishment of mutually supportive church-state relations as implied by the 'church'-type, the ROC's unilateral striving for such relations brings to mind 'churchly' characteristics.

Other changes in the ROC, which can also be viewed as the result of efforts to keep the Church alive in a hostile political environment, have, however, endowed the Church with characteristics which are completely removed from those implied by the 'church' type. Unlike the changes discussed above, these adjustments were not consciously initiated or fostered by the hierarchy but arose as spontaneous responses by priests and parishioners in their struggle for the survival of their local churches or, at least, of an environment in which their religious needs could be satisfied.

*Deviation from the 'church'-type*

From the 1930s onwards a number of adaptive developments have occurred in the ROC to overcome the increasing restriction of, and control over, church life and believers. In areas where the stock of churches was only depleted, priests and parishioners reorganised their religious activities to exploit the available facilities to their fullest. Whereas in the past Orthodox believers organised themselves strictly on a parish basis and the church was a community church, social community and church constituency are now no longer coterminous. Instead believers from churchless areas have to travel to places where functioning churches may be visited. Thus one village church in Gorky region, for example, in 1966 catered for only 70 believers from its original parish and for 430 from other, churchless, villages (Pivovarov, 1968, pp. 138, 143). Whereas believers used to perform church rituals spaced out over the year when the need was felt, they now 'save them up' for those occasions when circumstances permit travel to areas where a church is functioning. While this change in religious practice permits believers a minimum of religious need satisfaction, it deprives both priests and believers of that stable religious community still possessed by many sects which strengthens religiosity. Furthermore, it puts a greater burden on the remaining priests who now have to cater for increased numbers.

To cope with the increased demand on church facilities and priests' services and to satisfy the needs of those who will not or cannot travel for some reason, various adaptive practices have developed. Thus two or three daily celebrations of the Eucharist are widely held instead of one, and vigils are sometimes duplicated to accommodate more people and to fit the requirements of Soviet working life (Chernyak, 1965, p. 54; Andrianov *et al.*, 1966, p. 214; Krasnikov, 1968, p. 113). Confession is mostly held communally, participants being told to confess the 'standard sins' (Yankova, 1963, p. 78; Gordienko, 1968, p. 92).

Another important development to overcome the shortage of priests is the introduction of funeral rites conducted 'by correspondence' (Russ. *zaochno*). The relatives of the deceased send by post to the priest some earth from the grave, and the priest blesses it *in absentia* and returns it the same way. The following data illustrate how widespread this practice has become. In 1963 funeral rites performed 'by correspondence' amounted to 46·8 per cent of all funeral rites in Alma-Ata region of Kazakhstan (Chernyak, 1965, p. 32), to over 75 per cent in Vladimir region during 1966–7 (Nosova, 1969, p. 19), to between 63 and 89 per cent in different parishes of Ivanovo region (Andrianov *et al.*, 1966, p. 213), and to over half of all funerals in 1963 in Krasnoyarsk, Gorky and Pskov regions. Since then, these percentages have increased even more (Krasnikov, 1968, p. 130). One study points out the great increase in such funerals in the Altai region after several churches had been closed there in the early sixties (*Stroitel'stvo kommunizma . . .*, 1966, p. 223).

A change of a different kind was introduced to overcome the shortage of ancillary church servants. Whereas before the Revolution canon law required that these church employees always be male because no woman is allowed near the altar, the small representation of men among believers now makes it imperative to employ women as church servants. Thus it is widespread practice in the present time for women to serve at the altar, sing in the choir, or serve as *starosta* (elder), sexton or on the church council (Andrianov *et al.*, 1966, p. 214; Gordienko, 1968, p. 92).

Many new practices in the ROC have come about to allow believers to satisfy their religious requirements in anonymity, or to shelter them from discrimination and ridicule at work or in educational establishments. Many believers avoid going to church and fulfil their religious needs either 'by correspondence' or by letting elderly relatives run 'spiritual errands' for them. Thus prayers and blessings by the priest are ordered and paid for by post, and wedding rings are sent for blessing (Kiselev, 1967, p. 87). One author states that in 1960 in one Ryazan region church 30 per cent of church income was obtained from such services (Yankova, 1963, p. 80). The increased popularity of funerals 'by correspondence' could also partly be due to a desire for secrecy by younger relatives of the deceased. Older or occupationally less exposed relatives buy and burn candles or have special blessings said for members of their family and bring them home some blessed bread (Kiselev, 1967, p. 65; Krasnikov, 1968, p. 132).

In areas completely deprived of working churches a particularly interesting phenomenon has occurred. Believers have helped themselves by establishing 'domestic churches'. Between ten and twenty people meet more or less regularly in private houses or secluded places, and religiously knowledgeable women perform regular or occasional services, or only rites of passage. Such 'domestic churches' are mentioned as existing in the Komi ASSR (Gagarin, 1971, p. 74), in Vladimir region (Nosova, 1969, p. 16), in Orel region (Alekseev, 1967, p. 138), and in the Altai region (Basilov, 1967, p. 154). A particularly detailed study of the religious life in one Russian region mentions 482 unregistered groups of Orthodox (Teplyakov, 1972, p. 169). This practice is probably as prevalent in other areas and is not mentioned in the sociological literature as the disclosure of its existence implies the need for more churches. Many churchless villages also have a group of active believers (mostly old women) who make it their task to watch over the maintenance of religious mores (e.g. keeping of icons) and the spreading of a minimum of religious information, such as reminding villagers of impending religious holidays (Andrianov *et al.*, 1966, p. 24). Often these women execute religious functions in a way which is far removed from official Orthodox practice or spread religious information at variance with official teaching. This is not surprising as they have for decades tried to keep religious mores and traditions alive without assistance from the official Church. They are aware of, but not worried about, their unorthodox activities. 'It is the intention and not the form which matters to God,' they say (Basilov, 1967, p. 157).

Another development is the insertion of religious actions into ceremonies which were originally performed by the Church but have now become civil affairs. Thus, a pair to be married are often blessed before departing to the state wedding palace and are received with icons on their return, and the customs of kissing the icons and crossing oneself still form a part of many otherwise secular wedding festivities (Anokhina and Shmeleva, 1966, p. 122). Also at funerals conducted without a priest some elements of religious ritual, such as reading psalms and putting a cross into the grave, are still observed (Anokhina and Shmeleva, 1966, p. 123).

All these adaptive developments, but especially the formation of domestic churches and the permanent performance of rites by laymen, form a departure from the 'churchly' principles of organisation in general and those of the Orthodox Church in particular. The former stipulate that salvation can only be gained through the offices of the church and that a strict division between clergy and lay must be observed during the administering of sacraments. The Orthodox Church in addition also emphasises the inviolability of its ancient traditions of dogma and ritual and, in theory, views aberration from them as heresy. In practice, however, the Church tolerates and even encourages these rather 'sectarian' practices as emergency measures designed at least to maintain the influence of Orthodox religion in some measure, and such acceptance does not seem to diminish its 'churchly' character. However, as the continuing restriction on the training of new priests will eventually reduce the availability of professional priests to a dangerously low level, the assumption of religious functions by laymen may reach a level where it will seriously weaken the 'church' status of the ROC.

Two further characteristics of a 'church'-type organisation stated in the introductory chapter are that membership is inclusive and acquired at birth and that it manifests itself more in outward religious observance separated from other life activities than in inner-directed piety permeating the individual's whole existence. In the following, we will therefore present and analyse data on Orthodox Church members and religious functionaries as well as describe the nature of their religiosity.

## SOCIO-DEMOGRAPHIC DISTRIBUTION AND SOCIAL COMPOSITION OF MEMBERSHIP

Precise knowledge of the size and nature of Orthodox Church membership during the last decade is impossible to gain, and nothing more than vague and partial impressions can be recorded. While similar difficulties were encountered when sectarian membership at all-Union level was measured, we encountered little confusion over the definition of membership and could ascertain a whole number of local membership figures. When a membership figure was last stated in 1961 by the Orthodox Church itself on the occasion of its joining the WCC, the figure of 30 million was given, while on other occasions the figures of 40 or 50 million have been mentioned (see Struve, 1967, p. 179, for details of calculating these figures). Definition of membership is usually based on the criterion of church attendance. The method of compilation of such membership figures is, however, left very vague. It is based on the capacity of the larger churches while many churches are now quite small, often being former cemetery chapels. Also it is not made explicit how attenders are counted and whether ordinary Sunday or feastday attendance is considered. In any case, it would present a fairly committed rather than just a nominal membership. Soviet sociologists do not attempt to estimate membership of the whole church but merely follow developments in local membership.

Here I shall consider the evidence on how many people become nominal members of the Church at a given time, i.e. baptism statistics; and data on how many people actually feel themselves to be Orthodox believers, i.e. self-identified believers in the central tenets of Orthodox faith stated in sociological investigations.

While a newly born Russian infant no longer becomes a member of the ROC as a matter of course, the percentage of children baptised in the ROC is still very high at the present time and seems to have been stabilising or even increasing. In one town in Kazakhstan, for example, the number of baptisms doubled from 1965 to 1966 (*Kazakhstanskaya Pravda*, 20 July 1966, p. 4). Only two sociological writers (Yankova, 1963, p. 80; Chernyak, 1965, p. 29) make this stability explicit. But it may be inferred from the fact that a decline in the number of baptisms is rarely mentioned, and Soviet sociologists never fail to stress a decline for any index of religiosity. The remark by Anokhina and Shmeleva (1966, p. 119), that many parents who have had their children baptised were never themselves baptised, also supports this conclusion. A few sociologists, however, do report a decline in the number of baptisms in certain areas (Chernyak, 1965, p. 29; Aptekman, 1965, p. 89; Gagarin, 1971, p. 88). Whereas before the Revolution baptism occurred within a few days of birth, there now seems to be no socially prescribed period, but baptism takes place at the most convenient time for parents, sometimes a considerable time after birth. Even adult baptism is not unusual now.

A survey of a wide range of statistics on baptism (Aptekman, 1965, p. 83; *Agitator*, 23 December 1966, p. 42; Sapronenko, 1969, p. 5; Nosova, 1969, p. 18; Andrianov *et al.*, 1966, p. 206; Mukhin, 1969, p. 6; Duluman, 1973, p. 3) tells us that in most rural areas of the USSR around 50 per cent of children have been baptised, while the percentage for urban areas is somewhat lower. An attempt to assess the Church's general influence at the beginning of the sixties put the proportion of baptised among infants as being between 40 and 50 per cent in a whole number of regions (*Stroitel'stvo kommunizma . . .*, 1966, p. 221). This percentage is thus not much lower than the 55·4 per cent and 49 per cent of live births baptised in the Church of England in 1960 and 1968 respectively (statistics quoted in Pickering, 1974, p. 64). Although baptism is most frequently requested by parents in the lower social and educational groups, it is prevalent among all social strata (see Aptekman, 1965, p. 84; Kobetskii, 1969, p. 171), and among all educational groups (Aptekman, 1965, p. 84; Zelenkov, 1968, p. 95). Viewed against the background of strong pressure against baptism from the official side and of the practical difficulties of obtaining one in churchless areas, these figures are impressive. It has to be emphasised, however, that we cannot deduce from this high level of participation in the baptismal rite an equally high level of religiosity nor even the continuation of membership by these new citizens at later stages of their life-cycles. The first point will be discussed in detail below, and the second point is immediately relevant to our discussion of church membership.

While the 'church' type implies that nominal membership, once acquired, is reaffirmed at later critical points in the life-cycle of the individual, no such assumption can be made for all those baptised in the contemporary ROC. The fact that young people under 18 are by law excluded from all religious instruction and activity outside the family prevents the development of ties to the church and leaves their church membership latent for a long and important period of their lives. When, as young adults, an opportunity does arise for them to express their allegiance to the Church publicly, a very small percentage take it. Unlike the rite of baptism, the wedding rite is now only performed for a small proportion of couples. Many of these nominal members may not have any contact with the Church again until the time that their relatives arrange a church funeral for them. (For data on wedding and funeral rites, see below.) Parents, on the whole, do not feel that baptism of their children obliges them to bring them up in a religious way (Kiselev, 1967). Even believers will rarely instruct their children in their religion. In a Ukrainian sample 84 per cent of Orthodox, as against only 52 per cent among Baptists, did not attempt to impart a religious education to their children or grandchildren (Duluman, Lubovik and Tancher, 1970, p. 94). Most parents baptising their children are not primarily expressing support for the Orthodox Church as a religious organisation but are giving allegiance to it as an institution embodying cherished cultural values and being closely associated with Russianness (see, for example, the findings of Shevchenko, 1966, p. 35 and Zelenkov, 1968, p. 96). This identification of Orthodoxy with Russianness becomes especially strong in areas of mixed ethnic-religious composition, as in the republics where Moslems predominate (see Aptekman, 1965, p. 87; Chernyak, 1969, p. 132; Lawrence, 1973, p. 21). All those motivated in this way are thus still acknowledging a crucial fact implied by the 'church' type, namely, that birth in a certain country means entry into the church, even if later commitments arising from this acknowledgement are not honoured.

Let us now turn to consider church membership defined as self-professed allegiance to Orthodox faith and established by sociological surveys. Soviet sociologists differ in the way they identify believers and then classify them according to strength of belief. While the majority define as believers all those who have a minimal commitment in the form of a belief in God, a few stipulate also adherence to further central Christian beliefs (e.g. in life beyond death) or commitment to some aspect of practice. But *active* participation in church life is never taken as a criterion of membership. Some of these passive Orthodox believers are unable to take part in church life because of physical distance from a functioning church. Others may be unwilling to participate actively for various reasons and yet continue to regard themselves as part of the Orthodox tradition. Most Soviet sociologists go beyond dividing respondents into believers and non-believers and classify them according to the strength of their commitment. While there is some difference in the complexity of classification schemes used, nearly all speak of believers, waverers and non-believers. 'Waverers', as the word implies, are no longer certain in their faith but they have maintained some connection with the Orthodox Church by engaging in episodic religious practice. In the statistics given below on Orthodox believers as a percentage of the population in various regions of the USSR, waverers have not been included. It is likely that many of those who confess to wavering in their faith in the Soviet social context would have called themselves believers in Western society where religious belief is still a cultural norm.

Thus the problem of the researcher into the prevalence of religious belief in Soviet society is exactly the opposite of that facing those working in the context of Western society. While in Western society profession of atheism is still considered as being socially non-conformist and reprehensible and religious belief is consequently grossly over-reported, in general exactly the opposite is true in the Soviet social context. But even here public opinion is not of one piece. In the cities and among the more educated strata public opinion tends to correspond closely to state ideology on religion. In the countryside, however, among ordinary collective farmers, the climate of opinion is more tolerant and, in some areas, even supportive of religion. The following statistics on the percentage of believers in various socio-geographical areas will have to be interpreted with these reservations about the accuracy of data in mind.

Unlike the sects, the ROC has its support overwhelmingly in the countryside (Gaidurova, 1969, p. 26; Lebedev, 1970, pp. 142, 144; Gagarin, 1971, p. 76). It has somewhat less support in the small old towns, and relatively little following in most of the large industrial towns. During the sixties, Orthodox believers as a percentage of the population amounted to between 20 and 40 per cent in various rural regions. Statistics on urban Orthodox are much more scanty. Probably between 5 and 16 per cent in urban areas came into this category during this time (Alekseev, 1967, p. 149; Safronov, 1967, p. 69; Pechnikov, 1968, p. 63; Arutyunyan, 1968, p. 75n; Sapronenko, 1969, p. 4; Arutyunyan, 1970, p. 157; Alekseev, 1970, p. 232; Gagarin, 1971, p. 76). Figures collected for the Penza region of the RSFSR illustrate well the differences in church support in different socio-demographic areas. Thus in districts of rural Penza region Orthodox believers constituted between 23·3 (Lebedev, 1970, pp. 142, 143, 144) and 28·4 per cent (Kurochkin, 1971, p. 92) of the population, in small towns 14 per cent and in one industrial district of Penza town only 11·2 per cent (Lebedev, 1970).

Looking at the geographical distribution of Orthodox believers one finds the following pattern. Predictably, membership is still large in those areas of the Soviet Union where the Church has its longest tradition, in the south-western, north-western and central regions of the RSFSR. Here Orthodox are strong in absolute numerical terms as well as relative to the sects. Thus surveys in Orel region and Penza town showed that 99 per cent and 98 per cent respectively of all believers were Orthodox (Alekseev, 1970, p. 232; Lebedev, 1970, p. 140). The Orthodox Church also seems to be strong in the western republics, particularly in the Ukraine where churches are more abundant than anywhere else in the USSR. Here church life was less disturbed as the western parts of these republics were incorporated very late into the USSR. The eastern parts were occupied by the Germans who are said to have reopened many of the previously closed churches. In the Ukraine alone there were estimated to have been around 5,000 parishes, organised into nineteen dioceses in the late 1960s (figures quoted by Mykula, 1969, p. 24). However, one cannot automatically deduce a large membership from this fact. It is noteworthy that the sects of western origin have a much greater relative weight in these republics than in the RSFSR and have gained new members from the OC. In the central Asian republics adherence to Orthodox faith is, generally, in proportion to the size of the European population. The Orthodox Church has the weakest support in the eastern and north-eastern areas of the USSR which were settled very late, and where western settlers never revived the Orthodox traditions of their homeland to any significant extent.

All these figures and facts about self-professed allegiance to the ROC or faith, though somewhat discrepant and not strictly comparable, tell us at least that a substantial proportion of the Soviet population – between 20 and 25 per cent – still regard themselves as Orthodox believers. How does the figure of between 20 and 25 per cent compare with statistics given for earlier periods? Again, no straightforward answer can be given as the available data are very inadequate, and decline has been measured in various ways. Sometimes a decrease in the number of believers is noted; at other times a decline in the number of churches is taken as an indicator of general loss of influence by the Orthodox Church. This latter method has to be viewed with caution as it is well known that thousands of churches were closed against believers' wishes, especially during the thirties and the 1959–64 period. This index is not totally unreliable though, as the number of believers is said to be significantly lower in churchless areas (Ul'yanov, 1971, p. 222), even if only as a result of church closure. There are no overall figures on the number of Orthodox believers over time which would enable us to measure membership trends. We have to infer such trends indirectly from figures on the total number of religious in the population and from data on sect development. Both point towards a substantial decline in membership of the ROC from the late twenties onwards. If we accept that in the middle twenties around 80 per cent of the population were religious (Congress notes by Lunacharkii in 1930, quoted by Kobetskii, 1973, p. 126), and that the bulk of these have always been Orthodox believers, then we have, approximately, a threefold decline in believers over the last fifty years.

Figures on sect recruitment, showing a steady stream of defection from the ROC to the sects but none vice versa (Prokoshchina *et al.*, 1969, p. 48), would bear out the incidence of a reduction in the number of Orthodox believers over time. These isolated data are not sufficient to permit any definite general conclusion about the extent of decline in the number of Orthodox believers and the above estimate must be taken only as a rough approximation. The matter is complicated by the fact that one index of church support, income derived from the sale of cultic objects, the performance of rites, and from donations, has not declined but may even have grown for some churches during the sixties (Yankova, 1963, p. 80; Chernyak, 1965, p. 35; Eryshev, 1969, p. A41). Let us now turn to examine the social composition of the membership of the ROC.

The data on social characteristics of members have been mainly collected by Soviet sociologists in surveys among self-identified believers. They are supplemented by impressions from personal and other Western visitors' observations in churches. Survey data collected during the late sixties show that an overwhelming majority of self-identified Orthodox believers are female and elderly. Thus women constituted between 76 and 86 per cent of believers in various regions of the USSR, and those over 50 years of age ranged from 43 to 92 per cent (Basilov, 1967, p. 155; Pivovarov, 1968, p. 143; Eryshev, 1969, p. A39; Pashkov, 1969, p. 50; Sapronenko, 1969, p. 4; Nosova, 1970, p. 354; Gagarin, 1970, pp. 77, 78; Alekseev, 1970, pp. 230–2; Ul'yanov, 1970, p. 167), the average being around 66 per cent (Klibanov, 1970, p. 73).

A characterisation of believers as predominantly old and female is, on the whole, borne out by reports from Western visitors of Orthodox church services (e.g. the report of an Austrian Catholic delegation in *Forum*, 1967, p. 351; Kiselev, 1967, p. 84; Struve, 1967, pp. 184, 185). Some observers, however, have been struck by the increase in the number of young church attenders in recent years, especially on major Church holidays (Ardabaev and Plotkina, 1970, p. 57; Petropavlovsky, 1973, p. 19). Only one Soviet sociologist emphasises the presence of young people among believers in the early sixties (Yankova, 1963, p. 77). According to one Soviet author, between 2 and 6 per cent of Orthodox believers are said to be young people under 25 years of age (Galitskaya, 1969, p. 393). Personal impressions gained from visiting Orthodox churches in 1973 in the towns of Moscow and Orel (RSFSR) confirmed the general view that services are predominantly attended by elderly women. But it was also found that Sunday services of some Moscow churches attracted a noticeable minority of men and young people under 40 years of age.

Statistics on educational and occupational status bring out the fact that Orthodox believers are concentrated in the lower social strata. Around 70 per cent of them are only semi-literate and a mere 1·2 per cent have had secondary education. In most regions, around half of Orthodox believers are not in employment at all (mainly pensioners and housewives), while the majority of the employed are clustered in low skill and low pay occupations (see Andrianov *et al.*, 1966, p. 143; Yablokov, 1967, p. 31; Pivovarov, 1968, pp. 147, 154; Gaidurova, 1969, p. 17; Eryshev, 1969, p. A40; Sapronenko, 1969, p. 4; Prokoshchina and Lensu, 1969, pp. 40*f.;* Ul'yanov, 1970, p. 185; Gagarin, 1971, p. 78). There are data to show that within a community Orthodox believers are of significantly lower occupational status than non-believers (Alekseev, 1970, pp. 239, 240, Table 5).

A comparison with data on social characteristics of Baptists (Chapter 7) makes it clear that the latter are, in general, somewhat better educated than Orthodox and recruit more of their working members from among the urban working class rather than the peasantry. This difference becomes even more marked when we compare the social characteristics of activists – members of the *dvadtsatka* or church council and choir singers – of both religious organisations. Research in Alma-Ata region of Kazakhstan revealed that only 14·4 per cent of Orthodox *dvadtsatka* members had more than primary education whereas there were 33 per cent among Baptist church council members. Similarly, of Baptist choir singers 68 per cent were under 40 years of age and 46 per cent had had middle education, while the respective figures for Orthodox were only 13 and 22·8 per cent (Chernyak, 1965, p. 42; 1967, p. 215).

These Soviet data on the social position of both rank-and-file and activist believers give the impression that members of the technical and cultural intelligentsia are almost completely absent among Orthodox believers. Only one Soviet author mentions students among church members (Yankova, 1963, p. 77). Gagarin (1971, p. 78) explicitly states that the rural intelligentsia is almost 100 per cent atheist, and Lebedev (1970, p. 156) found not a single believer among either the scientific-cultural or the technical-economic urban intelligentsia. Alekseev (1970, p. 239), however, acknowledges that 9·9 per cent of those concerned with 'management' of the collective farms studied were believers, and Arutyunyan (1970, p. 157) found that 3·4 per cent of the intelligentsia in his sample believed in God.

Some Western as well as Russian observers, however, claim that there has been a great religious revival and that, in the sixties and seventies, many members of the intelligentsia have turned to Orthodoxy (see the protest letter to the WCC by Odessa believers printed in Bourdeaux, 1969, pp. 160, 161; Petropavlovsky, 1973, p. 19; Lawrence, 1973, pp. 22–6). It is difficult to assess whether their claim or that of Soviet sociologists is nearer the truth. It is often said that Orthodox believers of higher social status do not profess their faith openly, or feel no allegiance to the Church as an institution. Being aware of the social consequences of making their belief public and intelligent enough to deceive interviewers, they could easily slip through the nets of sociologists and other observers. Struve (1967, pp. 214*f.*) calls them *Midnight Christians* or *Nicodemuses* and gives several interesting descriptions of the lives of some who 'were found out'. Evidence from various other sources tells us that members of the intelligentsia are **more involved** in the ROC than sociological and other official accounts reveal. We know, for example, that various protesters against state interference in the affairs of the Orthodox Church are both Orthodox believers and members of the intelligentsia (e.g. Levitin, Talantov, Solzhenitsyn), and that there are a number of painters who include religious symbols in their work (Glezer, 1976). Accounts of the circles of Orthodox intellectuals having gathered in the late sixties and early seventies for the discussion of religio-philosophical questions can be taken as evidence of the fact that, at the very least, islands of Orthodox intellectuals exist among contemporary Orthodox (Dubrov, 1974, pp. 8*f.*, *Dein Reich Komme*, 5, 1976, p. 11). Also the now defunct Berdyaev Circle, a group of political dissidents inspired strongly by allegiance to Orthodoxy, consisted to an overwhelming extent of members of the intelligentsia. Their membership of around sixty men was composed almost exclusively of members of the cultural and technical intelligentsia (for details see Osipov, 1972, pp. 153–4).

In personal contacts with Soviet intellectuals the present author received some confirmation of a recent upsurge of interest in the ROC which was, however, often decried as a superficial fashion. Some concrete, indirect evidence of a renewed interest in religion among the younger intelligentsia is given by the founding in 1966 of a voluntary Society for the Preservation of Historical and Cultural Monuments (mainly churches) after years of neglect and, more importantly, by a series of articles in the literary journal *Molodaya Gvardiya* (Young Guard) (e.g. the September issues of 1968 and 1969). The authors of these articles resurrect heroes and saints of the Orthodox Church and demand that they should again become a part of Russian general culture and history rather than being confined to the obscurity of church history. The expression of national pride about Orthodox saints and heroes is, of course, political heresy, and the courage needed to forge such a link between religious figures and patriotism is indicative of the authors' strong feeling on this subject. The founding of the Society for the Preservation of Historical and Cultural Monuments was less controversial but inspired by a similar concern to save the religious heritage and make it once again an integral part of Russian general culture. It is difficult to know whether this interest in the religious past is indicative of any religious feelings or whether it is merely founded on intellectual curiosity and aesthetic feelings. At the least, however, this interest and concern can be interpreted as a recognition of a close link between Russian culture and history and the Orthodox Church. Such an attitude does accord the ROC 'church' status in a sociological sense.

While the above-cited examples of involvement in the Orthodox Church by members of the intelligentsia suggest that there is a gap in the accounts of believers' social composition put forward in the Soviet sociological literature, we should not read too much into them either. The evidence does not permit us to determine how significant and widespread the hold of Orthodox religion on some sections of the Soviet elite really is, nor what the nature of any religious sentiments is. Generalisations in this area are therefore untenable. If, as seems likely, the largest part of the intelligentsia are non-believers, it is noteworthy that such estrangement from the Church on the part of the intelligentsia is not unique to the communist Soviet Union but was quite marked in pre-revolutionary Tsarist Russia (see Zernov, 1963, Chs I and II).

I have argued above that membership of the ROC, however defined, is no longer inclusive but still substantial, especially in the rural areas of the Russian heartland. The social structure of membership no longer mirrors that of the population, but is heavily biased towards the lower social and culturally backward strata. This bias is much less pronounced if only nominal membership (based on baptism) is considered, and there are some indications that mere spiritual allegiance to Orthodoxy, which rarely manifests itself socially, is given by members from both the most underprivileged and the most privileged strata. Before turning to examine the character of the religiosity of these various groups of members, a brief description of the church administration, the training institutes, and the social background and status of contemporary Orthodox religious functionaries is of interest.

### ORGANISATIONAL STRUCTURE AND RELIGIOUS FUNCTIONARIES

Church affairs are decided and administered by the strong and central power of the Holy Synod with the Patriarch at its head. The Holy Synod consists of eight members: three Metropolitans, the persons in charge of the administration of the patriarchate and foreign affairs, and three Archbishops serving in rotation (Appendix to R. Stupperich (ed.), 1967, p. 282). The Concilium (Russ. *Pomestny Sobor*), canonically the supreme administrative power, is not in practice very influential. Since the Revolution only three Councils have been in session, in 1918, 1945 and 1971. Each Council elected a new Patriarch and passed some new legislation. The most important postwar legislation, the new statutes of 1961 (see page 33), were passed by the Bishops' Synod. This Synod is convoked at irregular intervals (with government permission) to make important decisions.

The ROC is organised in seventy-six dioceses (*ZhMP*, 12, 1971, p. 6). The number of open churches has not been stated by the Church in recent years but is believed to be in the region of 10,000 (see discussion of this by Bourdeaux, 1970). In addition to the churches and the five religious training institutes (see details below), the Church has also between six and ten monasteries and ten to fifteen convents (Sapiets, 1976, p. 28).

According to Patriarch Pimen in 1976 there were thirteen Metropolitans, twenty-seven Archbishops, and thirty-five bishops (interview with Novosti, *Soviet News*, 13 April 1976, p. 150). Although the social status and spiritual influence of bishops among believers is said to be high and their financial situation very good, their positions are, in comparison with their counterparts in Western churches, very weak. The insecure position of the ROC in Soviet society is reflected in the insecurity of its highest functionaries. While up to 1940 they were sadly decimated by physical destruction in prisons and labour camps (for details see Struve, 1967, pp. 393*f*.), since the war they have been put under pressure by the constant threat of premature retirement or involuntary translation. These policies have had a twofold negative effect. Firstly, the decimation of their number, coupled with the non-existent (up to 1944) or insufficient training of new spiritual leaders, has necessitated the continuous replenishment of their number from among poorly qualified and not always worthy parish priests. Secondly, their enforced geographical mobility and the restrictions on their basic freedoms have prevented bishops from forming local power bases on the strength of which they could challenge the officials of state or church. All this has turned the hierarchy into an extremely fragmented and powerless body. In recent years, however, some positive effect of these policies has become discernible. The hierarchy has been cleared of any 'dead wood' and room has been made for the ablest young graduates of the theological training institutions. These men, having grown up during Soviet time, are both committed and more flexible, being unhampered by the weight of memories of the Church's stormiest periods. The data presented in Table 1 will give us some impression of the social composition of the hierarchy.

The data give us a fairly clear picture of the social complexion of the RO hierarchy, except regarding their social origins where the 'unknown' category is too large. Such a gap is quite common in Soviet data on social origins and is usually interpreted as camouflaging a high social position of members' fathers. The data presented in Section 2 demonstrate that the majority of bishops were born during Soviet time. Between 1956 and 1963, twenty-one new bishops, aged between 31 and 50, entered the episcopate. The average age in 1962 of consecrated bishops was only 41, and four bishops were under 32 (Struve, 1967, p. 141). From these younger bishops were recruited some of the men who occupy the top posts in the central administration. Among them, in 1970, were the head of the patriarchate's foreign affairs section and his deputy, the exarch of the Ukraine, the head of the patriarchal administration, the head of the patriarchate's editorial section, and the rector of the Moscow Theological Academy (Kurochkin, 1971, p. 110). The information on training (Section 3) tells us that a large proportion received their training relatively recently in the Church's own teaching institutions. The data on training and qualifications confirm my earlier point that bishops are not all sufficiently trained and have, in general, low academic qualifications.

At present the Church has a theological academy and seminary both near Moscow (Zagorsk) and in Leningrad and a seminary in Odessa. In 1973–4 the three seminaries had 422 resident undergraduate students, and the two academies had 147 undergraduate students and 27 postgraduate students (Oppenheim, 1974, pp. 5–8). The syllabus at these institutes is very traditional and limited, focusing mainly on Church history, theology, liturgics, the Bible and homiletics. Besides Latin and Greek, Hebrew (only in the academies), Church-Slavonic and a modern language, and the history, constitution and laws of the Soviet Union are studied. There is no training in Christian-Marxist dialogue (Oppenheim, 1974).

Theological training, coming after only ten years in a Soviet general school, is crammed into four years. Moreover, on their arrival students have only the most basic religious knowledge. Only since 1963 has postgraduate education become available to a few. In 1974 there were twenty-seven postgraduate students at the Moscow Academy, and twenty-five places for postgraduate study at the Leningrad Academy (Oppenheim, 1974, pp. 5, 7). In 1973 only three 'Master' and two 'Doktor' degrees were awarded. This lack of formal education is unlikely to be compensated for by informal qualifications as access to topical theological literature was extremely restricted during Stalin's time and is only slightly better today for the ordinary student.

In the library of the Moscow Academy and Seminary about 50 per cent of the books are pre-revolutionary, and in the Leningrad Academy they amount to 75 per cent (Oppenheim, 1974, pp. 5 and 7). Among post-revolutionary books held there in the early sixties none were by eminent Orthodox scholars of the emigration, such as Berdyaev, for example.

All the limitations of theological training, however, have to be viewed in the context of the Church's difficult position in a militantly atheist society. Faced

Table 1   *Social Composition of the RO Hierarchy in the Sixties (in absolute numbers)\**

| | |
|---|---|
| 1. *Social origin (i.e. occupation of father)* | |
| Priest or church servant | 16 |
| Peasant or collective farmer | 11 |
| Academic | 5 |
| Worker | 3 |
| White-collar worker | 6 |
| No information | 33 |
| | |
| 2. *Entry into clergy* | |
| Before the Revolution | 19 |
| In western territories before Second World War | 14 |
| Abroad | 8 |
| In the USSR between the Revolution and Second World War | 11 |
| In the USSR since Second World War | 20 |
| Unknown | 2 |
| | |
| 3. *Age* (average age 57 years) | |
| 30–39 years | 13 |
| 40–49 years | 8 |
| 50–59 years | 20 |
| 60–69 years | 13 |
| Over 70 years | 17 |
| Unknown | 3 |
| | |
| 4. *Training* | |
| Theological Academy | 33 |
| (Of these, as external students 12) | |
| Theological seminary | 13 |
| Abroad | 10 |
| Unknown | 18 |
| | |
| 5. *Academic qualifications* | |
| 'Candidat' of theology | 28 |
| 'Magister' of theology | 4 |
| 'Doktor' of theology in USSR | 1 |
| 'Doktor' of theology abroad | 1 |
| Degrees in other subjects in other institutions of higher education | 25 |

\* The data were collected by Patock, 1966, p. 66.

with an alarming shortage of parish priests the Church has chosen to concentrate on turning out as large a number as possible of adequately trained parish priests rather than a small theological elite.

The social composition and status of the lower clergy – the parish priests – have been shaped by similar factors to those of the bishops. Decimation of their numbers during the late twenties and the thirties and the insufficient training facilities have necessitated the retention of aged priests and the ordination of many poorly educated and badly trained men. The loss of religious functionaries through death is recovered only to a quarter or third by new graduates from the theological teaching institutes, although the intake of students into the theological institutes was increasing slightly in the seventies (Oppenheim, 1974, pp. 6–7). Many have both inadequate general and theological education, having been recruited from among psalm readers. Of the sixteen priests in Kazakhstan's Alma-Ata region, for example, three had complete or incomplete general higher education, four general middle education, and nine only primary or incomplete middle education. As regards theological training, one priest graduated from the theological academy, four from the seminary, one attended a school for psalmists, and ten had received no formal theological training whatsoever (Chernyak, 1965, p. 50). Many are, however, trying to acquire better qualifications by studying theology in correspondence courses. In the 1973–4 academic year 600 students, who were mainly practising priests, were enrolled for this course (Oppenheim, 1974, p. 5).

The intellectual inadequacy of priests does not remain unnoticed by their parishioners who, in general, have a low regard for their priests. They denigrate both their intellectual and moral qualities. (See, for example, Chernyak, 1965, pp. 46, 50*ff.*; Nosova, 1970, p. 347). One survey in a Belorussian village established that not a single believer mentioned the priest when asked whom he held in greatest esteem in the village, and less than 15 per cent of respondents considered turning to the priest for advice (Safronov, 1967, pp. 67, 69). These survey responses, however, have to be considered against the background of the fact that the ratio of believers to priests is very high in the contemporary Church, and that many believers simply do not have any personal contact with their priest. Lack of reverence for their spiritual leaders was also, of course, a prominent characteristic of Orthodox before 1917. But since the Revolution, this irreverence must have intensified as the cultural level of the general population has steadily risen, while that of the priest has often fallen relative to his potential parishioners. Whereas before the Revolution moral disapprobation was generally directed against the priest's begging and scrounging, necessitated by his low pay, today disapproval is expressed about the priest's high standard of living, facilitated by a higher than average income (see Nosova, 1970, p. 347).

But just as among bishops, the impact of resumed theological training has made itself felt in the parishes during the last two decades. A new generation of younger, energetic, imaginative and committed priests is spreading its influence in the country, especially in the larger towns (*Prichiny . . .*, 1965, p. 93; Krasnikov, 1968, p. 146). Such priests have tried, in recent years, to enliven the services by increasing and improving their sermons as well as developing more contact with individual believers (Chernyak, 1965, p. 55; Krasnikov (ed.), 1966, p. 146; Mukhin, 1969, pp. 20, 21). One author estimates that a third of all practising priests and theologians have received either middle or higher theological education since the Second World War (Kurochkin, 1971, p. 109). Some writers discern a polarisation into older, educationally and culturally backward, theologically conservative, politically careful or hostile priests on the one side, and younger priests who are better educated, politically more integrated, theologically liberal and more active in their parish on the other (e.g. *Prichiny . . .*, 1965, pp. 189–90). A study of priests in the Vorenezh region of the RSFSR describes each group as amounting to 25 per cent of all the priests, and the large remainder is said to be ideologically opportunistic and religiously weakly or not at all committed (Teplyakov, 1972, p. 151).

In general, the priest no longer knows or keeps in contact with his parishioners as his flock is usually too large and fluid. The more energetic and concerned priests are well acquainted with a small nucleus of committed and activist believers who keep them informed about developments in the area and among various groups of parishioners (Krasnikov, 1968, p. 147; Teplyakov, 1972, p. 152). Some of the older, more conservative and fanatical priests are also said to travel to outlying churchless areas to minister to believers' needs and to perform rites in their own or in believers' private dwellings (Teplyakov, 1972, p. 152). Thus among both believers and religious functionaries in the contemporary OC we find a majority of elderly and, generally, culturally backward and theologically conservative people, but among both a minority of younger, better educated and more dynamic people have acted as a leaven in recent years. This development is very pronounced and well documented as far as religious functionaries are concerned, but less tangible and poorly substantiated concerning believers. In the following chapter we shall turn to investigate the extent to which the social complexion of clergy and laymen in the OC have shaped the character of religiosity of contemporary believers.

Chapter 3

# The Russian Orthodox Church II

DIMENSIONS OF RELIGIOUS COMMITMENT AMONG
CONTEMPORARY RUSSIAN ORTHODOX
The following detailed account of the nature of Orthodox religiosity and the analysis of changes in this area are offered for three reasons: first, to fill the complete gap in the sociological literature concerning the religiosity of believers in communist societies; secondly, to show how a militantly atheist state can influence individual religiosity; and, thirdly, to prove that members of a 'church'-type organisation are, to an overwhelming extent, characterised by a weakly developed religious commitment. Glock and Stark's (1965, 1968) theoretical framework, broadly defined, provides the basic categories for this exercise.

*The Ideological and Intellectual Dimensions*
The ideological dimension refers to the fact that a religious person will be aware of and hold true certain beliefs about a transcendental force and the relations between this force and man and his world. The intellectual dimension suggests that individuals have some information about the basic tenets of faith, the scriptures, ritual and other religious traditions. Although Glock and Stark found that the relationship between the intellectual and other dimensions was weak, in Orthodox religiosity the relation between the intellectual and ideological dimension is perceived as being so close that the two dimensions are most usefully discussed in conjunction. Dogmatic positions forming the content of belief must first be known before they can be adopted, and dormant beliefs may be reactivated by a fresh and stimulating presentation of knowledge. Glock and Stark arrived at their conclusion because, unlike the student of Orthodox Christians, they could assume the most basic intellectual foundations of belief as given and were concerned with the more peripheral knowledge of Christian dogma and scriptures which is dispensable to belief.

Like most Western sociologists, Soviet sociologists agree that belief in a transcendental power is a central feature of Christian religious commitment providing a framework for all the other dimensions. They count as believers all those who have no doubts that a personal God exists, but they do not usually stipulate the holding of further beliefs (e.g. in life beyond death) as a qualification for inclusion.

While the contemporary Christian in the West is generally more likely to maintain the 'belief' rather than the 'activity' dimension of his religiosity, this is not the case for the Russian Orthodox. The cultic side of Orthodoxy has always been very developed and has, in relation to dogma, become even more prominent in post-revolutionary times in both services and theological literature. There is an overwhelming unanimity in the sociological literature about the fact that this development is even more distinct in individual religiosity where concern with rites and religious traditions is much more marked than preoccupation with tenets of faith. This fact is well illustrated by the higher number who participate in certain rites of passage (see pp. 60*f.*) than of those who profess a belief in God (see p. 46).

An examination of the nature of religious belief, according to Glock and Stark (1965, p. 24), can focus on three problem areas; the content of belief for the individual, the saliency of belief and the functions of belief. Soviet sociologists have mainly focused on the first aspect inquiring into *what* Orthodox believe, often assuming quite illegitimately that the quantity and degree of complexity of beliefs adhered to are necessarily indicators of the saliency with which they are held. In the emerging picture of the nature of Orthodox religious beliefs three characteristics are striking: there is a great discrepancy between the tenets of faith propagated by the Church and those held by individual believers; the religiosity of many believers contains a mixture of Christian and pagan magical beliefs; an extremely narrow and eclectic range of beliefs is professed, often only the bare minimum of a belief in a transcendent God.

The level of knowledge about tenets of Orthodox faith is very low in the Soviet Union. Only 20–30 per cent of believers are said to understand questions of dogma to a greater or lesser degree (Kurochkin, 1971, p. 98). This is confirmed by other authors who say that, with rare exceptions, Orthodox believers have little interest in the intricacies of dogma, a weak notion of the dogmatic meaning of ritual and of the content of religious literature and do not know the teaching of the Church nor understand the sermons (Yankova, 1963, p. 78; Andrianov *et al.*, 1966, pp. 198, 208; Kapustin, 1969, p. 90; Nosova, 1970, p. 354; Gagarin, 1970, p. 83). Although the level of knowledge has never been very high among Orthodox believers many studies point to a distinct deterioration over time as the impact of pre-revolutionary church school education wears thinner (Yankova, 1963, p. 81; Basilov, 1967, p. 158; Kapustin, 1969, pp. 90, 91).

Compared both with the level of religious knowledge among American Christians (see Glock and Stark, 1968, pp. 141*f.*) and, more importantly, with that of sectarians in the Soviet Union, the level of knowledge of Christian dogma and scripture is extremely low. As was pointed out above, dissemination of religious knowledge and reinforcement of faith were made difficult after 1918 by the complete social isolation of the Church (i.e. no access to educational institutions and means of communication) and, from the thirties onwards, by the lack of churches and religious functionaries in some areas of the Soviet Union. Besides, the low theological standards of some priests often result in sermons with little or incorrect information content (Kapustin, 1969, p. 91). A more sympathetic Western commentator describes sermons as 'unambitious and largely devotional in tone' (Petropavlovsky, 1973, p. 18). Even the well-staffed urban churches do not seem to give high priority to the dissemination of religious *ideas*, although sermons are reported as having increased in both quantity and quality in recent times in the towns as well as in the villages (Chernyak, 1965, p. 55; Mukhin, 1969, p. 20).

Consequently many believers have received little or no religious instruction and have had to form their beliefs without the aid of the Church, instructed and inspired by relatives and neighbours. In addition, the disappearance of the traditional parish and with it of a religious community has also had its effects on the nature of religious knowledge and belief. Whereas a communal religious group contributes to the maintenance of religious values and norms, a merely associational religious group is unable to exert such influence (see White, 1970, pp. 18*f*.). If there is no religious collective at all, as is the case in many now churchless areas of the Soviet Union, the resulting lack of reinforcement of belief in communal worship is likely to lead to a complete surrender of belief in time. Thus one study found that the proportion of believers in the population was 13–18 per cent lower in churchless areas than in those with a functioning church (Ul'yanov, 1971, p. 222).

It comes therefore as no surprise that the content of individual beliefs has somewhat departed from officially prescribed tenets of faith. One author describes the divergence as colossal, differences being both in content and form, as well as in degree of sophistication (Pashkov, 1969, p. 152). When asked to explain why they believed that there was a God, collective farmers in one survey put forward a number of primitive 'proofs', and hardly any theological arguments or references to the Bible were mentioned (Alekseev, 1967, p. 149).

Given the only limited influence of the Church in matters of belief and the low educational level of most believers it is not surprising to find that magical and folk beliefs are still quite popular in the countryside and exist side by side with religious ideas in the consciousness of believers. Although superstition is now less widespread than in pre-revolutionary times, certain magical beliefs have survived tenaciously. Thus, in the Orel survey, nearly as many collective farmers ascribed a prophetic function to dreams (40·5 per cent) as professed belief in God (41·5 per cent). A somewhat lower percentage of respondents believed in 'the evil eye' (35·4 per cent) and the efficacy of 'wise men or women' (23·3 per cent) (Alekseev, 1970, p. 235). A study of rural Orthodox in Stavropol region of the RSFSR established that as many as 21·2 per cent of believers were influenced by some superstitious notions (Sapronenko, 1969, p. 7). Other authors stress the prevalence among Orthodox believers of beliefs in miracles and healings and point to the existence of a variety of flourishing 'professions', such as clairvoyants, soothsayers and healers (Chernyak, 1965, pp. 49, 50; Kiselev, 1967, p. 191; Basilov, 1967, p. 161). The belief in witchcraft and unclean powers is seen as being in a rapid decline (Basilov, 1967, p. 162; Nosova, 1970, p. 354). The level of superstition was found to be significantly higher in areas where there was no working church (Tazhurizina, 1969).

A third and last prominent feature of the ideological dimension of contemporary Orthodox believers is the fact that they do not adhere to any complex and coherent belief system but profess only a few amorphous and eclectic elements of Orthodox faith (for general statements see Mandrygin and Makarov, 1966, p. 229; Kapustin, 1969, p. 90; Pashkov, 1969, p. 166). Although Orthodox theology emphasises *warranting, purposive* and *implementing* beliefs (see Glock and Stark, 1965, pp. 24–5), individual Orthodox sustain mainly the first kind, either not caring about or rejecting the others. Many survey respondents acknowledged only the bare minimum belief in a personal God. While beliefs about other Orthodox tenets of faith were generally probed, questions about Jesus Christ were surprisingly never raised.

Non-adherence to further Orthodox beliefs could be the result of lack of know-ledge about them or of their conscious rejection due to increased secularisation of general thinking. The evidence on this is inconclusive. Collective farmers studied in the Orel region of the RSFSR, for example, knew that the ROC postulates beliefs in hell, paradise and in the notion of an after-life, but four-fifths of all those who believed in God doubted the truth of these purposive beliefs (Alekseev, 1970, p. 235). The belief in life beyond death was doubted or rejected by 36·8 per cent and 65·6 per cent respectively of believers in two other surveyed villages (Yablokov, 1969, p. 140). Another author, too, stresses the fact that eschatological ideas were quite alien to most believers but points to both unfamiliarity and disagreement with such notions (Basilov, 1967, pp. 159, 160). Among Baptists, on the other hand, such doubt is infrequent.

Doubt or disbelief about an after life is also prominent, though somewhat less so, among people in Britain (see figures quoted by Wilson, 1976, pp. 14, 15). In Glock and Stark's (1968, p. 37) national survey of beliefs among American (nominal or actual) Christians in general, 50 per cent of Protestants and 52 per cent of Catholics were not absolutely sure about the existence of a life after death. Considering that their sample included sectarians and members of fundamentalist denominations, Russian Orthodox and American Christians seem to be fairly similar in their division into groups with this-worldly and other-worldly orienta-tions. Purposive beliefs about the existence and nature of God are rarely allied to implementing beliefs specifying the conduct of man toward God and toward his fellow men. Few Orthodox, for example, could spell out how they would express their love for God, and hardly any knew or followed the Ten Commandments (Andrianov *et al.*, 1966, p. 195).

Comparing the content of belief among Orthodox with that adhered to by American Christians as described by Glock and Stark (1968), one realises that the processes described above have, indeed, gone far. Although among American Christians divergence from official dogma and surrender of, or doubt about, many vital Christian beliefs is also apparent, religious orthodoxy seems to be compara-tively strong in most American denominations.

The special nature of belief among the majority of Orthodox, being character-ised by lack of complexity, of internal coherence and of correspondence with official Church doctrine, leads Soviet sociologists to assume that saliency of belief or degree of conviction among them is very low. The above features alone, how-ever, do not justify such an assumption. They would have to be interpreted together with characteristic traits of the other dimensions which also reflect saliency. It is generally implied in the Soviet sociological literature that belief has weakened during (an unspecified) recent time but little systematic evidence is put forward to support this claim. One inquiry, concentrating on changes in the nature of Orthodox religiosity, provides evidence which suggests that the belief dimension has not weakened very strongly. When respondents were asked whether they had noticed a weakening in the strength of their own or their friends' and relations' belief in God during the preceding decade only 14 per cent and 15 per cent respectively answered in the affirmative (Ul'yanov, 1970, p. 175, Table 36).

All three features of the 'belief' dimension of Orthodox individual religiosity –

lack of complexity, of internal coherence and of correspondence with official doctrine – are very congruent both with the lack of influence of the Church in matters of belief and with the socio-demographic complexion of believers, described above as predominantly rural, elderly and poorly educated. One sociologist notes a distinct relation between level of literacy and type of religious involvement. The lower the degree of literacy the more likely was a lack of interest in dogma and preoccupation with ritual (Kukushkin, 1970, p. 19). Unfortunately there are few studies of the nature of religious belief among urban believers. One investigator of both rural and urban believers in one region states that religious commitment is deeper among urban believers. In support of this conclusion he cites such facts as a higher proportion of believers who are influenced in their moral outlook by their religious views as well as the more active and vigorous congregational life in towns (Teplyakov, 1972, p. 85). This applies only if there is a church in the town. If Orthodox believers migrate from the countryside to a churchless town their religiosity soon weakens and eventually disappears (Saprykin, 1970, p. 222). The beliefs held by believers of more privileged socio-economic status in general are also nowhere discussed. The information we possess about individual intellectual dissidents and about circles and associations in the Orthodox tradition suggests that the intellectual and ideological dimensions of their religiosity are well developed, but one cannot draw any general conclusions from the evidence provided by such a small and selective sample.

*The 'Practice' Dimension*
Religious practice includes all the acts believers perform to give expression to their religious feelings and thoughts. Their aim is to demonstrate publicly or renew and deepen privately the relation to the transcendent power defined in their beliefs. The 'practice' dimension is thus closely related to the 'belief' and the 'knowledge' dimensions. If the acts are not related to the object of belief they are void of content and thus of spiritual significance. If the religious person believes in a transcendent power but does not know the dogmatic significance of the religious acts he performs, they are not necessarily spiritually meaningless as they may evoke religious emotions which connect the individual with God in a more diffuse way. Thus any study of the nature of religious practice must consider the meaning of those practices to the individual as well as the way in which different sub-dimensions are connected with the core dimension. While American sociologists, according to Glock and Stark (1965, p. 28), have neglected to inquire into the 'meaning' question, Soviet sociologists have shown particular interest in this aspect, because the expected results, as will be shown below, would help them to deflate claims as to widespread religious involvement among contemporary Russians. Some clear patterns of practice for different groups of Orthodox emerge from the research of Soviet sociologists. It is widely concluded by them that wide-ranging and frequent religious practice can be taken as an indicator of religious involvement, and vice versa.

In the religiosity of contemporary Orthodox the 'practice' element overshadows in importance all others, and practice is mainly of a public nature, i.e. ritual or cultic practice. Ritual practices can be divided into those religious acts which are closely connected to everyday life, to the family, the community and to social custom on the one side, and into those which have a more narrowly religious significance, i.e. having only a reference to dogma and which are enacted within the confines of the church building. It is the first group of ritual practices, comprising participation in rites of passage and church holidays, which have been most vigorously preserved by Orthodox. The second group of practices, consisting of attendance at worship in general and of participation in confession and communion in particular, have been abandoned to varying degrees by a large proportion of those who call themselves Orthodox.

Rites of passage, especially baptismal and funeral rites, are those religious practices through which a very large proportion of contemporary Russians are still connected with Orthodoxy. While figures for baptisms and weddings can be considered as being reliable (their registration with the local political authorities is required) those for funerals are probably underestimated. A large percentage of funerals are conducted 'by correspondence', and it is not clear whether these have always been taken account of in the figures below. Besides, of all the rites, religious funerals are most often conducted by Orthodox laymen if the services of a priest are difficult to obtain (e.g. Anokhina and Shmeleva, 1966, p. 123; Basilov, 1967, pp. 153, 154) and thus do not enter official statistics at all. Despite some variation, the trends in the performance of rites of passage are clear. During the sixties, the highest participation has been in funeral and baptismal rites, the average for the various regions being around 50 per cent of all those eligible (Yankova, 1963, p. 80; *Stroitel'stvo kommunizma . . .*, 1966, p. 221; Shevchenko, 1966, p. 33; Nosova, 1969, p. 18). Wedding rites, in contrast, have been more rarely requested. In different regions between 1 and 15 per cent of all those who got married received nuptial rites (Yankova, 1963, p. 80; Shevchenko, 1966, p. 32; Mukhin, 1969, p. 6; Nosova, 1969, p. 18). Moreover, participation in baptismal and funeral rites has remained fairly stable or declined only slowly. In contrast, there has been a steady decline of church weddings during the sixties (Chernyak, 1965, p. 33; Nosova, 1970, p. 350; Alekseev, 1970, p. 244; Gagarin, 1971, p. 90; Vasil'evskaya, 1972, p. 395), and extinction of this rite in the Orthodox Church is becoming a serious possibility.

These statistics reveal in several ways developments in the performance of rites of passage similar to those which have occurred in the Church of England. In the latter, too, participation in rites of passage is incomparably higher than in other church rituals and, although declining, their level is still very high. As in the ROC, participation in funeral rites is steadily high, and in marriage rites it is lowest and declining. But in contrast to the situation in the ROC, decline in the popularity of marriage rites has not been nearly as drastic in the Church of England, and the rite is nowhere near extinction. (For statistics on rites of passage in the Church of England, see Pickering, 1974, pp. 63*f*.).

Funeral and baptismal rites in the Orthodox Church have persisted incomparably more strongly than wedding rites for three reasons, apart from purely religious considerations. No decision by the persons being the centre of the rite is required, and relations making the choices for them are more inclined to opt 'just in case' for religious ceremonies for their dependents than they would for themselves. Escape from social pressure against a religious ceremony can be much more easily achieved than in the case of weddings. Baptisms are not held in the main church building, and infants are often brought by elderly relatives, while in the case of funerals the option of obtaining a blessing 'by correspondence' has in many cases reduced the public nature of the religious gesture. Lastly, no satisfying secular substitute rites are generally available for religious funerals. One reason for the preponderance of church funerals over baptisms lies, of course, in the fact that the object of the rite is an old person and thus very likely to have been a believer. In one survey, for example, around 85 per cent of women and about 40 per cent of men over 60 years of age were believers compared to around only 15 per cent believers in the 25–29 age-group, i.e. the group from which potential applicants for children's baptisms would come. (Figures from Alekseev, 1970, pp. 230, 231, parts of Diagrams 1 and 2.)

For couples to be married, however, the conditions are exactly the reverse. *Both* partners are likely to be subject to pressure against a church wedding from their superiors and comrades at work and in the *Komsomol* (Communist League), a church ceremony cannot be held anonymously, and aesthetically satisfying substitute rituals are enacted in the wedding palaces. It was established in the Vologda region of the RSFSR, for example, that requests for the performance of marriage rites declined fourfold in the six years since the introduction of wedding palaces in this area (*Pravda*, 18 April 1968, p. 2). None of these reasons would be really compelling in dissuading participants or their authorising relations from arranging a religious rite at these critical points in their lives if a strong religious need for their performance existed. Thus we need to examine to what extent participation in rites of passage is religiously motivated.

The discrepancy in the numbers of those declaring themselves Orthodox believers and those participating in rites of passage has induced Soviet sociologists to look closely at the motivations for such participation. Significantly, this has only been done in relation to baptism. It must be tacitly assumed that non-religious motivations are not very prominent in the case of funeral rites. Before we turn to consider what significance the rite of baptism has for contemporary Orthodox, we shall first examine some of the implications of the types of motivation utilised in the studies consulted.

The 'tradition' category seems to be a very loose one in some surveys subsuming such various influences on decision making as the force of *national* custom, of *family* custom, of public opinion (especially in villages), of popular superstition about the magical effect of baptism (see Aptekman's type 4), or the felt need to mark an important event in life in an emotionally satisfying and elevating way (see Aptekman's type 5). Kapustin (1969, p. 96), for example, who states that 60 per cent of all parents having their children baptised do this out of tradition, then continues by saying that 'a definite percentage of baptisms happens as a result of the fact that parents simply do not know another mechanism of observing such an important event in their life as the birth of a child'. Such parents do not seek baptism for reasons of tradition but out of a need for ritual. Tradition then directs them to the Orthodox Church as the institution to stage it. It might be argued that such a need for ritual is a religious motivation. This argument, however, loses its persuasiveness when it is considered that recently introduced rival secular rites – a name-giving ceremony or a 'New-born Child' festival – are also popular among the same parents, or even oust the religious rite. Thus the Gorky survey established that 57 per cent of parents baptising their children also went through the secular ceremony (Zelenkov, 1968, p. 96), while research in the Komi ASSR found that the introduction of the name-giving ceremony was followed by a 4·5-fold decrease in the number of baptisms over a six-year period (*Stroitel'tstvo* . . ., 1966, p. 226).

The fact that many parents have their children baptised out of reverence for, or fear of, older relatives suggests that although they themselves are no longer convinced Orthodox believers, they are still open to arguments about the importance of religion. In a rigorously secular society the arguments of a minority of religious persons would not carry such weight. However, frequently the pressure exerted by older members of the family does not simply consist of moral influence but of threats of negative sanctions in the case of non-compliance with the baptism request. As grandmothers are widely entrusted with the care of young children, because mothers are generally employed and state nurseries are not in sufficient supply, elderly religious relatives are in a strong position to get compliance (see, for example, Olshanski, 1967, p. 58). In a minority of cases the explanation of a child's baptism by reference to pressure from older relatives may be an excuse which allows socially more vulnerable young parents to shift the responsibility for the religious act. Other research, though, has borne out the religious influence of older persons on the rest of the family. A study of the relation between family structure and extent of religiosity found that families were much more likely to be religious if grandparents lived in the family household (Vasil'evskaya, 1972, p. 386).

Table 2  *Types of Motivation for Baptism of Children*

| | *Percentage of children baptised in different areas reported by these authors* | | | | |
|---|---|---|---|---|---|
| *Types of Motivation* | *Gagarin, 1971, pp. 88, 89\** | *Kapustin, 1966, p. 96* | *Zelenkov,\*\* 1968, p. 96* | *Olshanskii, 1965, p. 492* | *Aptekman, 1965, pp. 85ff.* |
| Out of religious conviction on the part of either or both parents | 13·7 | | 13·5 | 4·0 | 8·0 |
| Out of consideration for, or under the influence of, older family members | 28·7 | | 87·0 | | 33·0 |
| Out of tradition | 32·5 | 60·0 | 23·0 | | 36·0 |
| For the health and happiness of the child | | | | | 12·7 |
| For emotional impact | | | | | 10·3 |

\* The author does not account for the remaining 23·1 per cent.
\*\* Parents must have had more than one choice. The 13·5 per cent are described as being believers and waverers and the motive of religious conviction has been adduced by the present author.

Despite these reservations about the studies presented in Table 2, the general trends in motivations underlying this religious act are too clear to be ignored: only a small minority of parents are moved to the act of baptism by religious considerations, the number being smaller in the towns (columns four and five) than in the villages. A large percentage of baptising parents are themselves not believers but requested baptism for a variety of extraneous reasons. Some of these reasons, it is true, showed that their break with religion has been neither complete nor resolute, but as the vital 'belief' dimension was missing in their 'religiosity', the act of baptism had no longer a truly religious meaning for them. It is also interesting to note that, although many of the parents had rejected religious beliefs, they still clung to magical beliefs.

The finding of the above studies that many of those upholding religious rites are not believers is also borne out by other inquiries. One survey established that as many as one-third of all non-believers in one village still thought it necessary that children should be baptised (*Izvestiya*, 12 November 1971, p. 3), while an investigation into family attitudes to religion established that 37·4 per cent of families no longer convinced in their belief in God nevertheless baptised their children (Vasil'evskaya, 1972, p. 392, part of table).

Very similar findings have been reported for the relation between religious belief and the observation of religious holidays. The Orthodox Church has a great number of holidays divided into the general cyclical ones, closely associated with Christian dogma, and the more localised holidays connected with different saints (*prestol'nye prazdniki*). It is those in the former group which are widely and generally maintained, while the latter seem to flourish only in some areas, mainly in the old Russian heartland of Orthodoxy and are becoming forgotten in the more recently settled areas of the Soviet Union (see, for example, Basilov, 1967, p. 156, on Altai region). Of the holidays of the Christian cycle, Easter is the most universally observed holiday. Students of the nature of religiosity are unanimous about the fact that the celebration of Christian holidays is the most widely observed of all religious practices surpassing even rites of passage, and consequently, the most widely upheld aspect of religiosity in general. These acts of religious observance are not only maintained by the highest percentage of declared believers but also by the highest proportion of waverers and non-believers.

Like rites of passage, religious holidays are kept much more alive in the country than in the towns (Alekseev, 1970, p. 244). While believers amounted to around 30 per cent in rural Kazan region, holidays were still observed by about 40 per cent (Arutyunyan, 1970, p. 157). In the Yaroslavl town/RSFSR survey 71 per cent and 37 per cent respectively of families wavering or being indifferent in their beliefs nevertheless celebrated religious feastdays (Vasil'evskaya, 1972, p. 392, Table 22). A study of a collective farm in Novgorod region of the RSFSR notes that religious festivals were celebrated in almost every home, including those of party members (*Sovetskaya Rossiya*, 6 January 1972, p. 3). Participation in Easter and Christmas festivities in a Belorussia village has been described as 'being on a mass scale' (Mandrygin, 1966, p. 225). A count of church attenders during one day of the Easter festivities in the three Orthodox churches of the town Voronezh (RSFSR) established that around 30,000 people attended the service each time during the late sixties and early seventies (Teplyakov, 1972, p. 167). Seen in relation to the town's population of 660,000 in 1970 this is a relatively high level of attendance. The same author does note a slow but steady decline over the years. Even higher was the number of those visiting the graveyard on Easter Sunday, being 150,000 in 1968 and 90,000 in 1971 (Teplyakov, 1972). The present author, on a recent stay in Russia at the time of a church holiday, was struck by the wide awareness among people of this holiday. Many times people with no obvious attachment to religion spontaneously approached me with the question 'Did you know that it is "*Pokrov*" Sunday [14 October] today?'

It is noteworthy that, although the rate of participation in religious festivities has remained very high, there has been a decrease since the Revolution and that not all believers take part any more (Basilov, 1967, p. 156). The nature of the observance of these holidays naturally has also changed in comparison with pre-revolutionary days. Then, according to Anokhina and Shmeleva (1966, p. 123), church holidays were connected with church visiting, participation in cross walks and communal prayers. At home the lamps in front of the icons were lit, and prayers were said. Work on such days was considered sinful. Some of the developments noted above have been the result of a change in the nature of Orthodox religiosity, while others were necessitated by the state attitudes towards religion. Thus the public nature and community aspect of these holidays has been suppressed, with activity outside church walls being legally proscribed and absenteeism from work morally deplored. Abandonment of work on church holidays is, however, still widespread and not impossible to arrange for those with strong feelings on the subject.

While Saints' Days have become mainly occasions for visiting relatives and of jollities in the villages, ignoring any religious aspect (Anokhina and Shmeleva, 1966, p. 124), the holidays of the Christian cycle are still connected with devotional practices in home and church, in the towns as well as in the villages. The extent of devotional practice associated with them has, however, greatly declined and been abandoned altogether by many participants. The latter only preserve the folk customs connected with them in family celebrations (Alekseev, 1970, p. 247) and regard them as occasions where they can meet and communicate with friends and relatives. Some stop work on these days and put on holiday clothes. The collective farm private enterprise markets, for example, are always closed on such holidays, but most Orthodox no longer consider work on Church holidays sinful (Anokhina and Shmeleva, 1966, p. 124; Safronov, 1967, p. 70). Some of those aware of the religious nature of a holiday will engage in private devotional practice, but most only go to church.

Although Orthodox churches are immensely overcrowded on major holidays, not all those who are believers attend, while many of those attending have only the most minimal knowledge of the general significance of the feastday in question and of the content of the ritual associated with it (Chernyak, 1965, p. 48; *Stroitel'stvo* . . ., 1966, p. 226; Gagarin, 1971, p. 93). In the churchless areas, knowledge about the exact date of movable holidays is insecure, and many a time they have been celebrated on the wrong days or even twice when the errors became known (Basilov, 1967, p. 156). Yet, taking the country as a whole, the observance of holidays is less secularised than in many Western Protestant countries. Many more Orthodox have the urge to express their religiosity on church holidays by church attendance. This is all the more remarkable when one considers that for such attendance they have to give up a day's wage and sometimes have to travel up to 100 kilometres to the nearest church (as in the Komi ASSR, for example) besides risking social censure from atheist comrades and superiors.

Another form of ritual closely connected with family and community are the agricultural cults which occupied an important place in pre-revolutionary, predominantly agrarian Russia. Cults in this group have strongly declined since the introduction of collective ownership and of more sophisticated methods of cultivation and livestock rearing from the late twenties onwards. But even these cults are by no means extinct in some areas (Krasnikov, 1968, pp. 95, 96; Nosova,

1970, p. 354), although, significantly, they are mainly practised in connection with the private holding of collective farmers. Thus 25·7 per cent of believers in the Stavropol region of the RSFSR, for example, knew and applied various agricultural rituals in the cultivation of their own plot and livestock (Sapronenko, 1969, p. 7).

I have argued that ritual which is connected closely with the individual life-cycle, with family and community life, is still strongly adhered to both by Orthodox who consider themselves believers as well as by many of those who reject, are indifferent to, or doubtful about Orthodox dogma but still feel themselves part of the Orthodox tradition. We may now turn to examine the pattern of adherence to ritual and general sacred practice which lack both this close reference to everyday life and the habitual element. For this I shall consider quantitative and qualitative evidence on church attendance and participation in confession and communion in particular.

While an interpretation of figures on church attendance is fraught with numerous difficulties, we are spared one problem facing those interpreting church attendance figures in Western societies. Church attendance in Soviet society is not a mark of respectability and is unlikely to be maintained for that reason. Although some attenders may be pressed by more pious relatives or friends rather than by their own conscience into attending church, believers are not conforming to the expectations of a general public. On the contrary they are often defying public opinion when they attend church. Thus Soviet church attendance statistics present, if anything, an understatement rather than an overstatement of religious commitment. Also church attendance is made more difficult by the physical distance between church and believers in some areas. Some collective farmers in Orel region studied by Alekseev, for example, had to travel between 30 and 40 kilometres to the nearest churches (1967, p. 138). One study considering this factor established that 48 per cent of the population visit the church if there is one near, and only 27 per cent visit it if travelling is involved (Ul'yanov, 1971, p. 222). The figures on church attendance (in Table 3) will therefore have to be interpreted with these latter facts in mind. Unfortunately, sociologists collecting data on church attendance rarely mention the distance to the nearest church.

The data in Table 3, together with some qualitative information (Chernyak, 1965, p. 26; Safronov, 1967, p. 70; Ul'yanov, 1970, p. 173), tell us that, if a church is not too far away, the majority of Orthodox believers go to church some time during the year though only a minority go regularly. The fact that many Orthodox only feel compelled to visit the church on holidays is underlined by the fact that some churches are only open on such days. In Voronezh region in the RSFSR, for example, only thirty-four out of fifty-five churches are open all the time (Teplyakov, 1967, p. 150). Although we have no strictly comparable figures for Western churches a rough comparison with those for the Anglican Church during the late sixties (see Pickering, 1974, p. 69) shows that church attendance here is not all that much higher than in areas of the Soviet Union where a sufficient number of churches is available.

It is generally maintained by Soviet scholars that the number of church attenders has fallen, but this claim is rarely backed up by any figures. Even when concrete evidence is given, as for example, in Ul'yanov's survey (1970, p. 175), one must view these figures sceptically as the decrease may be due to the closure of churches in the surveyed area. During the anti-religious campaign

c

Table 3   *Attendance of Orthodox Churches in Selected Areas (in % of total no. of believers)*

| Area | Source | Regularly* | Church holidays | Rarely* | Never | Distance to nearest church |
|---|---|---|---|---|---|---|
| Rovno region/ Ukr. SSR | Andrianov et al., 1966, p. 200 | 19·3 | 57·1 | 12·5 | 11·1 | — |
| Yaroslav region/ RSFSR | Kukushkin, 1970, p. 13 | 28·7 | 23·7 | 28·7 | 18·9 | — |
| Orel region/ RSFSR | Gaidurova, 1969, p. 31 | | 14·0 | 33·0 | 53·0 | 25 km |
| Orel region/ RSFSR | Alekseev, 1967, p. 149 | | 57·0 | | 43·0 | 30–40 km |
| Orel region/ RSFSR | Pashkov, 1969, p. 153 | | 5·0††† | 43·0 | 48·0 | in district town |
| Penza town/ RSFSR | Lebedev, 1970, p. 147** | | 71·0 | | 29·0 | in the town |
| Penza region/ RSFSR | Ul'yanov, 1970, p. 173 | 3·0 | 24·0† | 36·0 | 14·0 | no church near |
| Yaroslav town/ RSFSR | Vasil'evskaya, 1972, p. 392 | | 42·6†† | | 57·4†† | in the town |
| Stavropol region/ RSFSR | Chuguev, quoted by Ul'yanov, 1971, p. 224 | 12·0 | 52·5 | 69·3*** | 14·3 | — |

* Regularly – every Sunday or more; rarely – once or twice per year.
** Calculated from figures given in this source. Waverers type I are included here.
*** Includes 30 per cent going four or five times per year.
† Includes also those going once a month.
†† The unit is the family, rather than the individual.
††† Go more than twice a year.

of the early sixties, the number of Orthodox churches was reduced by about half.

The social composition of attenders varies according to the occasion. Ordinary services are visited predominantly by elderly and old women who are even more strongly represented than among believers in general (Chernyak, 1965, p. 26; *Stroitel'stvo* . . ., 1966, p. 229; Kiselev, 1967, p. 84; Yablokov, 1969, p. 62; Kukushkin, 1970, p. 14). Prolonged observation of church attenders in three churches of one Moscow district established that women amounted to between 72·46 per cent and 90·69 per cent of worshippers and that 96 per cent were old or middle aged (Yablokov, 1967, p. 29). On religious holidays more men and some young people can be seen among worshippers (see, for example, Ardabaev, 1970, p. 51). Some studies (e.g. Vasil'evskaya, 1972, p. 392) establish that many waverers and even unbelievers also attend church, though probably not regularly.

Evidence from investigations into motivations of church-goers and from descriptions of their deportment during worship is ambiguous. One study found that the great majority went to satisfy strictly religious requirements (e.g. to receive the Eucharist or listen to the sermon) or tangentially religious ones, such as to put candles by icons or listen to the singing (Ul'yanov, 1971, p. 223). Another survey of emotions experienced during the service established that a majority of attenders (62 per cent) were deriving a variety of aesthetic and psychological satisfactions from it, suggesting more than a superficial involvement in the service. The remaining 38 per cent, however, went for various extraneous reasons such as search for social contact, family influence or habit (Andrianov *et al.*, 1966, pp. 200–5). Personal observation of believers during services has conveyed the impression that most of them are not only sincerely interested and involved in them but also very devout. The following description of a service in an Orthodox church conveys well the atmosphere during worship:

'The people pray together as a community and individually as persons. Every face is spiritually withdrawn, lips are gently murmuring: a human person is gently speaking to the personal God. And then, during the litanies, the doxologies, and the more important moments of the canon of the Eucharist, all make the sign of the Cross and bow deeply. This creates a rhythm of adoration. But this rhythm is no hindrance to a wide freedom of personal behaviour. It does not prevent the worshipper from feeling at home in God's house. He takes his candles to it, he venerates its icons.' (Struve, 1967, p. 193)

Even an atheist propagandist, after having observed believers during a service on the holiday of the Virgin, is moved to the following comment:

'I looked into the faces of the people and I saw that some of them sincerely believed every word of their spiritual pastor . . . In the eyes of many I saw tears . . . someone inaudibly murmured the words of a prayer asking the help of the Mother of God in urgent matters. However it was, one could feel that the festive service moved their hearts.' (Korotkova, 1974, p. 3)

Other observers, however, question the sincerity of many believers and claim that they go through the outward signs of devotion, reciting prayers absent-mindedly and mechanically, bowing and crossing themselves at the expected moments. Many priests are said to complain about the lack of reverence of contemporary believers (Chernyak, 1965, p. 26; Andrianov *et al.*, 1966, p. 204). Some indirect support for the point that religious involvement during church services is shallow is given by the fact that participation in those rites which symbolise deep religious commitment – confession and communion – have suffered a decline since the Revolution. While believers used to take part in these rituals three times a year, even keen believers do it now only irregularly. Middle-aged and younger believers observe these rites only very rarely or not at all (Andrianov *et al.*, 1966, pp. 205, 206; Anokhina and Shmeleva, 1966, p. 116). Only 19·8 per cent of one sample of believers reported to perform all the rites (Andrianov *et al.*, 1966). This discrepantly low participation (compared with that in rites of passage) in the Church's most central ritual practices is not only typical of the Russian Orthodox Church, but, according to Pickering (1974, p. 69), seems to be the characteristic pattern in most churches which are either legally established or are considered national churches. The example of the Church of England, the French and the Belgian Catholic Churches are mentioned.

The argument that religious commitment is shallow also receives support from the evidence on the more personal aspects of religious practice – acts of religious devotion. Here we need to consider private prayer, fasting and reading of the Scriptures. As prayer in Orthodox religion is closely connected with icons we have to examine at the same time the changing relationship of believers to their icons. The traditional relation of believers to their icons is well expressed in the following description of their functions in the pre-revolutionary peasant household:

'In the past the icon symbolised man's connection to God, it somehow concretised it and constantly reminded the believer of his religious obligations. Besides this the particularly reverent relation to icons is also explained by the fact that many were inherited reminders of fathers and forefathers, about important events in their lives, about the blessings of parents, about 'the day of the angel'. In every-day life as well as on special occasions icons played a great part in the life of pre-revolutionary peasants. They prayed in front of them, they blessed by them those entering marriage, the army or simply leaving home. With their help they hoped to shorten a fire or a drought, to make a new house holy. They called them as witnesses in family conflict, or at the conclusion of a transaction.' (Anokhina and Shmeleva, 1966, p. 117)

Another function not mentioned in the above description is that the 'beautiful corner', with its many icons and lamp, served to enhance the appearance of the peasant hut, usually being the only aesthetically pleasing object there.

Today icons are still widely kept, especially in the countryside, but there has been a strong change of emphasis in the individual's relation to them. A study of Orthodox in Ryazan region of the RSFSR reports icons in nearly every rural dwelling, some having iconostases with several tens of icons (Yankova, 1963, p. 81). In some other rural areas icons were reported in around 90 per cent of dwellings, while in urban areas they were found in between 14 and 63 per cent of households (Sapronenko, 1969, p. 7; Alekseev, 1970, p. 244; Nosova, 1970, p. 348; Lebedev, 1970, p. 147; Vasil'evskaya, 1972, p. 392). Even communists and atheists often had icons in their houses (*Sovetskaya Rossiya*, 6 November 1972, p. 3; Lebedev, 1970, p. 147). In areas without long Orthodox traditions icons were not quite so prevalent (Chernyak, 1965, p. 117).

In the overwhelming majority of houses icons are now merely a traditional decoration or, like photographs, a reminder of departed relatives from whom the icons were inherited. This last relation is underlined by the fact that icons are rarely new but have been handed down from generation to generation (Nosova, 1969, p. 17; Gagarin, 1971, p. 94). The subject matter of the biblical or local religious scene depicted on the icon is often not known by their owners. There is no indication in the literature that icons are still called upon as witnesses at important family or business events, but stories about miracle-working icons are still reported.

Only in between 15 and 30 per cent of homes are icons now the focus of devotional practice (Safronov, 1967, p. 70; Sapronenko, 1969, p. 7; Lebedev, 1970, p. 147) but in one rural region (Penza/RSFSR) as many as 51 per cent of those believers who had icons still expressed their devotion in front of them (Ul'yanov, 1971, p. 222). In general then, there seems to be no reliable connection between the possession of icons and religious belief, although at least one respected Soviet sociologist has taken display of icons as an index of religiosity (see Arutyunyan, 1966, p. 59).

Speaking of prayer in general, only a minority is reported as praying regularly at home (Basilov, 1967, p. 155). According to one survey, 20·4 per cent of believers prayed regularly at home or in church, 53·1 per cent prayed rarely, mainly in church, and 26·5 per cent of believers never prayed at all (Andrianov *et al.*, 1966, pp. 196, 198). Contrasted with the frequency with which prayers are said by American Catholics and most Protestants (Glock and Stark, 1968, p. 112, Table 39) as well as English people in general (Martin, 1967, p. 55), Orthodox believers pray little.

The same Soviet authors also collected some interesting information on the content of prayers. Out of a sample of 143 believers, 45·5 per cent prayed only for worldly benefits such as good health or a good harvest, 7 per cent asked to be forgiven their sins and to have their souls saved, and 47·6 per cent prayed both for worldly and other-worldly favours, but predominantly for the former (Andrianov *et al.*, 1966, p. 196). Such content of prayer is in marked contrast to that reported by American Christians who are much less inclined to ask for worldly favours (Glock and Stark, 1968, pp. 115, 116). It seems, though, that the Soviet survey did not probe all the possible responses, as prayers of thanks, for example, are not even mentioned.

Fasting, another form of personal religious practice prescribed by the Orthodox Church, has declined even more drastically. Neither the proscription of eating certain foods nor that of worldly amusement during certain times of the year are now taken much heed of. A small percentage of the older believers undertake token observances of fast, especially during the Great Fast, but hardly anyone does it systematically (Anokhina and Shmeleva, 1966, p. 116; Andrianov *et al.*, 1966, p. 206; Basilov, 1967, p. 155; Nosova, 1969, p. 19). Even in a rural area with a relatively high level of religiosity over 60 per cent of believers no longer observed fasts (Ul'yanov, 1971, p. 226).

Private reading of the Bible has never had a major emphasis in Orthodoxy and is practised even less today. Only a few contemporary Orthodox own and read religious literature of any kind. This is partly due to the generally low level of literacy among believers and partly to the underdevelopment of the ideological and intellectual dimensions of Orthodox religiosity. It would seem that the latter is the more important reason, because sectarians, who have similar educational handicaps, nevertheless manage to maintain a high level of personal Bible study.

## The Experiential Dimension

The experiential dimension implies some form of direct communication with a transcendental force and expresses itself in feelings, perceptions and sensations of such contact. There is little direct discussion of this dimension of personal religiosity in the Soviet sociological literature, the only exception being the study by Andrianov *et al.* It is difficult to know whether this omission is due to the fact that atheist observers find it impossible to perceive this form of religious involvement, or whether it is weakly developed in the religiosity of contemporary mainstream Orthodox.

It is necessary to distinguish between different types of religious experiences. The kind of experience associated with a radical expression of feeling, e.g. talking in tongues, is completely alien to Orthodox. A second form of experience expressing itself in mysticism and withdrawal from the rest of the believers in the past has been a notable characteristic of Orthodoxy, although not condoned by the Church. Perhaps the still vital remnants of various semi-Christian and magical cults today may be seen as giving room to such mystical religious experience of contact with supernatural forces unmediated by religious functionaries. These practices are reported in many regions of the RSFSR and sometimes involve large numbers of believers (see, for example, Yankova, 1963, p. 78; *Prichiny* . . ., 1965, p. 92; Kiselev, 1967, p. 91; Nosova, 1969, p. 92). Thus Orthodox believers still set aside many places as holy and travel there in the hope of establishing a closer communion with God. On the other hand, many of these cults are not truly experiential as they revolve around an intermediate person – a saint or wise man or object (such as a holy stone, tree or spring) – who or which are needed to establish contact with the transcendent force. Also communication is not desired for its own sake but for the tangible benefits it would bring to the pilgrim. Some are purely magical in character. A more truly mystical trend within Orthodoxy has been represented by a small group of 'holy' men or women withdrawing from society into solitude or a life of religious wandering in the hope of finding their way to God more easily this way. This form of religious experience is rarely found among mainstream Orthodox today but is more common among some groups of Old Believers and other smaller schismatic Orthodox groups. But all such expressions of religiosity are difficult to sustain in a society the laws of which proscribe a spontaneous public expression of religiosity outside the confines of the church.

A third form of religious experience consists simply of more subtle and less demonstrative religious feelings and perceptions. It is this third form of religious experience which characterises the religiosity of one section of contemporary Orthodox. The general impression is that the majority of those attending church (68 per cent) experience religious emotions, not the more extreme ones of fear or exaltation but the more gentle ones of peace of soul, joy, elation, inner liberation (Andrianov *et al.*, 1966, p. 204). Such feelings are general and diffuse, rather than specific and clearly focused on a divine presence. The Orthodox church service with its strong impact on all the senses rather than the intellect is ideally suited to evoke such emotions among attending believers. This impact of the service has been well described in the words of a Russian Orthodox poet:

'It is an immense lyrical and dramatic poem shot through with biblical images, expressed in the language of Plato, and it provides people with an anticipation of the coming Kingdom, a vision of the transfiguration, like that which the apostles experienced on Thabor, in which it is good to stay and put up one's tent. The Orthodox liturgy, with its hymns of venerable antiquity, profound thought and perfect style, with its icons and wall paintings . . . *is heaven brought down to earth.*' (S. Bulgakov, quoted in Struve, 1967, p. 192)

The experiential dimension of religiosity among Orthodox, consisting of rather diffuse feelings, thus seems to have little overlap with the intellectual and ideological dimension but a close relation with, or even dependence on, ritual practice. Rather than being the result of seeking, religious experience is evoked by a sensitising environment. The lack of experience of other emotions, e.g. of fear, however, may be due to the special make-up of their intellectual and ideological dimensions. Compared with the complex repertoire of religious experiences of American Christians elicited by the more subtle and varied questions of Glock and Stark (1968, pp. 125*f.*) the religious experiences of Orthodox seem unnaturally narrow, and one suspects that a whole variety of experiences remained untapped.

## The 'Consequential' Dimension

The consequential dimension is concerned with the effects of the first four aspects on the daily life of a religious person. Glock and Stark (1965, p. 35) envisage two rather different kinds of consequences, suggesting inquiry into what the individual receives (the rewards) and what he gives (responsibility) as a result of his religiosity. Here we shall investigate only the second aspect of the consequential dimension, which comprises essentially secular ethical beliefs and conduct. The first aspect, being in essence about the functions of religiosity, will be discussed separately below.

This dimension of religiosity is, in theory, of primary concern to Soviet sociologists as the hostile rejection of religion in communist ideology is based precisely on the condemnation of the impact of religion on social consciousness. While they have done much research into this aspect in connection with studies of sectarian religiosity, this problem is given surprisingly little systematic attention when the religious commitment of Orthodox is analysed. The consequences of religiosity for Orthodox, especially for the younger and middle-aged ones, are generally deemed to be not very great and thus not problematic. It is suggested that the underdevelopment of this dimension is due to the relative unimportance of the intellectual and ideological dimensions in the configuration of Orthodox religious commitment.

Orthodox religiosity, it is generally said in the Soviet literature, is highly compartmentalised. For the majority of Orthodox their religion is a thing apart from the rest of their social life, and little interplay between the social and religious sphere takes place (see, for example, Mandrygin, 1966, p. 229). The following description of a typical day in the life of a typical Orthodox believer illustrates very well this compartmentalisation of religious activity: 'On the Day of the Cosmonauts, believer S. [57 years old] watched the cosmonauts on television, then attended a church service, and after that took part in a "Name-Giving" ceremony [civil functional equivalent to the rite of baptism] in the palace of culture' (Andrianov *et al.*, 1966, p. 187).

Although lack of interpenetration between religious modes of thought and activity and secular pursuits is common to most 'churchly' religions, it is more amplified in contemporary Orthodoxy, because the 'belief' and 'knowledge' dimensions have regressed so strongly in the religious consciousness of individuals. The surrender of many doctrinal notions, such as the ideas of resurrection, last judgement and hell, means that believers are no longer restrained by fear of these eschatological visions in their secular conduct. Some researchers as well as priests are struck by the fact that the Orthodox emphasis on sin and with it the Ten Commandments have become meaningless to many believers who find their content irrelevant to their everyday lives (Andrianov *et al.*, 1966, p. 197). Orthodox thus differ significantly from members of American denominations who, if their denomination emphasises original sin, retain a relatively high degree of belief in this notion (Glock and Stark, 1968, p. 40).

The fact that Orthodox are not much influenced by their religion in their personal conduct is also due to another factor, namely, the loss of a parish religious community. Ethical behaviour is strongly dependent on the religious associational ties the individual has. Any individual, according to White (1970, p. 20), 'will adhere to religious norms to the extent that he is in a position to receive sanctions from other members of the religious groups'. These primary religious groups, we have argued earlier, are rarely to be found within a church congregation today. Moreover, religious individuals are, on the whole, much more exposed to sanctions from non-religious groups proscribing the diffusion of religious norms.

When dealing with the subject of social and political values and conduct of Orthodox, sociologists generally find that Orthodox do not differ from other citizens of the same social background (e.g. Zlobin, 1963, p. 111). They are said to accept communist social and political norms and to seek full integration into socialist society. One sociologist characterises the consequential aspect of Orthodox religiosity in the following way: 'For the majority of those who still remain religious, the chief principles in their life and activity have become loyalty to the socialist Motherland, support for the politics of the Communist Party, conscientious work creating spiritual and material benefits for the whole of society' (Ul'yanov, 1970, p. 166). Most sociologists paying any attention to the consequential dimension of religiosity merely generalise that Orthodox believers are socially more passive than non-believers. Most of these few studies are misleading, as they do not control for such vital factors as age and social position (see, for example, Ul'yanov, 1970, pp. 184, 185). There is, however, one excellent empirical study which establishes quite conclusively that Orthodox believers, regardless of age, occupation and education, are consistently less involved in voluntary (though officially organised) social activity in the socio-political and cultural-educational sectors and in the spheres of production and the local community (Pechnikov, 1968, pp. 62f.). Not surprisingly, the lowest participation by Orthodox believers was in the socio-political sector, and the highest was in fields with a social welfare aspect to them. The validity of these findings is slightly impaired by the fact that the deliberate exclusion of believers from participation in some areas of social activity, especially in the political sector, has not been taken into consideration.

The fact that a very low percentage of believing respondents connected their lack of social involvement in any direct way with their religiosity does not lead Pechnikov to conclude that there is no such direct link. He only notes that the consequential aspect is not strongly developed among Orthodox because official Orthodox ideology no longer strives to influence social conduct in a way damaging to socialist society. Indirect links between religiosity and social conduct, he argues, persist nevertheless because the whole ideological trend of religion – its negative influence on initiative and independent action, on the acquisition of scientific knowledge, on a development of interest in the social – works against the formation of social consciousness and initiative.

What then are the distinguishing characteristics of Russian Orthodox religiosity? Glock and Stark show little concern for the question of *centrality* of different dimensions or sub-dimensions within religiosity. Our discussion of individual religiosity in the Orthodox tradition has brought out that *centrality* is an important issue in trying to describe types of religiosity. Of all the dimensions, *practice* is by far the most prominent in the religious make-up of individuals influencing the whole nature of that religiosity. *Belief* is severely reduced, and the other dimensions all appear marginal in the constitution of Orthodox religious commitment. Religious practice, for contemporary Orthodox, is predominantly ritual rather than devotional practice, and among the various cultic and sacred practices some occupy a far more important place in the lives of Russian Orthodox than others. While rituals connected with the family and rural community have shown a remarkable stability at a time of much social upheaval, those presupposing a more personal commitment and a deeper appreciation of dogma have declined rapidly. It is said in the Soviet literature that ritual is increasingly being emptied of religious content and converted into traditional social custom. Loss of intellectual or even precise ideological content does not, however, necessarily mean that ritual is devoid of *any* content. Even though the dogmatic significance of many rituals is neither known nor believed in any coherent way, these rituals may evoke various emotions in their performers which relate them in a diffuse way to a power beyond themselves.

While similar developments have taken place in the religiosity of members of Western churches and are, to a large extent, a 'church' characteristic, the imbalance between the *belief* and *practice* dimensions is more accentuated in the Orthodox case, due to the specific conditions imposed on the church in a communist society. The low level of literacy among the older generation, especially in rural areas, is also likely to be a contributing factor to the marked incomprehension of, and indifference to, the intellectual and ideological dimensions of Orthodox religion.

The imbalance between the different dimensions of Orthodox religiosity raises some theoretical questions. Which dimensions are more crucial than others to the essence of Christian religiosity, and which indices are the most representative of a particular dimension? Does the loss of certain crucial dimensions in the individual's relation to Orthodoxy mean that this relation can no longer be called a religious one? There is general agreement among Western and Soviet sociologists on the fact that the dimensions of religiosity are, to a large extent, interdependent and that *belief* is the pivotal one without which none of the other dimensions would make sense. Soviet sociologists are quite explicit in their view that a relation to the Orthodox Church, entailing rejection of all its tenets of faith, is not a religious one. They take their position to its logical conclusion by stating that performance of those aspects of practice more exclusively connected with *belief*, e.g. the taking of communion or praying, are more indicative of religiosity than observance of those closely integrated into the individual life-cycle and family life, e.g. rites of passage or church holidays. In other words, they say that practice is more truly religious the greater is belief content, and that belief content is more likely to be lost if practice has a strong secular reference as well.

While this is not too problematic as a theoretical statement, it becomes difficult in practice to distinguish between religious acts or experiences that are based on some more or less coherent beliefs and those devoid of such content. In the case of practising Orthodox the emotional element is usually much more dominant in their consciousness than the ideological, and the belief content may be so minimal and diffuse that it cannot easily be articulated. This may then give sociological investigators the impression that it is non-existent. I am not saying that all those Orthodox carrying out some religious practice are unrecognised believers but merely that one cannot be too definite in classifying borderline cases in one way or another. While it is not difficult to distinguish a convinced believer from an atheist, it is very difficult to establish in one interview whether a person is a believer or a waverer.

Another problem, of which Soviet social scientists are well aware, is that although observance of religious practice may not be inspired by belief at one point in time, the fact of some connection with a religious milieu may facilitate the acquisition of belief at a later point in time, usually at the end of a person's life-cycle or at a time of crisis. Thus, although an Orthodox attending occasional church services without giving any spiritual significance to his activity is not manifestly religious, he may be latently religious. Therefore data on such ritual practices as participation in rites of passage have to be interpreted carefully and not be too easily dismissed as uninformative by sociologists of religion.

Bearing all these cautionary remarks in mind and allowing for some misinterpretation and non-recognition of facts by Soviet sociologists, it can nevertheless be said without hesitation that measured on any index of *regular* commitment the majority of Orthodox are not very deeply religious. Only a small minority of all those nominally Orthodox are deeply convinced believers, knowing and following all the prescriptions of the Church as well as expressing their religiosity in more private, spontaneous devotion. Among these, according to Chernyak (1965, p. 37), there is a very small minority of believers who – similar to sectarians – are active proselytisers, condemn non-believers and are completely uninfluenced by their socialist environment. A sympathetic and informed Western commentator goes even further and says that only the clergy and their families now fully live up to Orthodox precepts (Kiselev, 1967, p. 87).

The majority of Orthodox practise their religion more episodically, and their religious acts are guided by only minimal and vague notions about the object of their worship. They are motivated by habit rather than by inner necessity, and their secular thinking and conduct rarely reflect their religiosity. The majority of Orthodox are thus traditional Christians who believe and/or practise because their fathers and forefathers did so for centuries (see, for example, Alekseev, 1970, pp. 228, 229; Chernyak, 1965, pp. 37–40). A comparative investigation into motives for religiosity among Orthodox and Baptists brings out that over 62 per cent of Orthodox as against only 23 per cent of Baptists referred to tradition in their answers (Duluman *et al.*, 1970, p. 72, part of table). One author, who attempts to classify self-identified Orthodox according to the depth of their commitment, describes 9·7 per cent as convinced believers, 43·9 per cent as traditional believers and 46·4 per cent as waverers (Mukhin, 1969, p. 10).

In conclusion, let us consider how the religiosity of Orthodox believers compares with the religiosity of church members in Western societies. As far as the incomplete and quantitatively often imprecise information on the nature of religiosity among Russian Orthodox allows us to judge, the separate dimensions seem to be more closely inter-related than they are among both Protestants and Catholics in Glock and Stark's American sample. Low score on one index of *regular* religious commitment is usually accompanied by a low score on all the others, and vice versa, and only *episodic* ritual practice is difficult to relate to other indices of other dimensions.

If we compare Orthodox religiosity to the religiosity of members of other national or established churches, we find a striking similarity in general patterns and trends. Relatively low scores along almost all indices of religiosity, except participation in rites of passage, is not only typical of members of the Orthodox Church but of members of national churches in general. The difference between the religious commitment of Orthodox and members of Western churches is a difference of degree. Religious commitment of Orthodox, measured on most indices of religiosity, is lower than among members of churches in Western societies. Religious commitment of Orthodox in its present configuration is shaped by the interaction of influences emanating from the characteristics of both a 'church'-type organisation and a militantly atheist society. The Soviet stance to religion has thus served to accelerate a process of decline characteristic of the religiosity of members of most national churches in contemporary industrial society. A 'church'-type organisation, unlike the sectarian type, is in general peculiarly unsuited to counteract the corroding impact on religiosity of an atheist society. The fact that the Russian Orthodox Church has, on some aspects of practice, abandoned its 'churchly' stance and accepted innovations more consistent with a 'sectarian' stance (e.g. execution of religious duties by laymen) has halted the decline of religiosity to some extent. The comparative approach adopted in this book has so far led me to emphasise the decline of religiosity. It is now necessary to correct the balance somewhat and to place the Orthodox Church and its believers in the particular historical context of their existence since the Revolution. Given this focus, it is not so much the decline in religiosity but its steadfast maintenance which becomes remarkable. In the following some explanations for this will be explored.

## SOME EXPLANATIONS FOR THE PERSISTENCE OF ORTHODOX RELIGION

Given the fact that the religiosity of the majority of Orthodox is of a comparatively shallow kind, how can one explain the remarkable persistence of this religiosity in the face of great adversity? Besides the general dislocating influences on religiosity of an industrial culture experienced by capitalist and socialist societies alike, believers in the Soviet Union have had to reckon with great ideological pressure against them and with practical difficulties in expressing their faith in any form. Therefore the researcher is compelled to look for some powerful social forces that counteract these negative influences and help to keep religion alive. I therefore presumed that Orthodox religion and/or the ROC make it easier for adherents to deal with the manifold social tensions created by rapid social and political change and help them adjust to their social environments. But an examination of relevant data revealed no one clear integrative function of Orthodoxy. Instead I discovered that various types of social and psychological satisfactions were derived from their religiosity by different groups of believers. The evidence to substantiate these connections is only scanty, and my attempt to explain the persistence of Orthodox religiosity in this way can only be tentative and impressionistic. Before discussing these explanations I shall argue that many accepted sociological explanations for adherence to a religious world view do not hold in the case of Russian Orthodox.

Although Orthodox religiosity is most prevalent among the economically and socially least-privileged strata of the population there is no evidence to suggest that Orthodox believers are absolutely or relatively deprived in this respect. Absolute deprivation was ruled out by several studies (e.g. Mandrygin and

Makarov, 1966; Alekseev, 1967) which revealed that believers were more prevalent in collective farms which were economically stronger than others in the
same area. Relative economic or social deprivation compared with other individuals or groups is unlikely to be generated in a socially relatively homogeneous
milieu such as a Soviet collective farm where the majority of Russian Orthodox
are found. Political deprivation, in the form of resentment against socialism and
the social transformations effected by it, must also be ruled out as a causal factor.
Political discontent or protest, as we showed above, is rarely expressed by
respondents. Both religious functionaries and believers try, in general, to adjust
their religious beliefs and practices to the demands of the political authorities
and their ideology and strive to be fully integrated into socialist society. Search
for moral authority is also unlikely to be at the root of Orthodox religiosity.
Concern with moral precepts, with a secular ethic, we said earlier, is of minimal
importance in Orthodox religiosity, although there was some evidence that
changes have been occurring in this respect in the recent past. In any case the
Orthodox Church, unlike the sects, is unable to exert positive influence on the
economic, social or moral situation of its members. It does not try to inculcate
values which would raise members economically or socially. Its lack of emphasis
on religious and ethical ideas, as opposed to religious practice, coupled with the
inability to create a moral community to enforce standards of behaviour, does
not put the Church into a strong position to provide members with compen-
sations of a moral type. The small degree of lay involvement in church and
parish work does not permit members to acquire power and prestige within the
religious organisation, while outside the church organisation, in contrast to the
situation in the West, social ostracism instead of social prestige can be gained
from church membership.

Church membership, unlike sect affiliation, is also unlikely to secure inclusion
into a stable and supportive community, except perhaps for the small nucleus
of activist believers whose lives revolve around the church. Membership of a
given church is too large and fluctuating to evolve into a community, the priest
is too overburdened to become an organiser and arbiter of such a primary group,
and a tradition of extra-church informal religious and social activities has never
developed.

We may gain more plausible explanations of the persistence of Orthodox religiosity when we consider what cultural and/or psychological rewards are gained
by Orthodox Christians. Orthodoxy and the Orthodox Church, we emphasised
earlier, have been very closely connected with Russian history and general culture.
The close alliance between church and state up to the Revolution has meant a
strong interpenetration of church and secular culture at various levels, manifesting
itself in a variety of forms. Among the more obvious ones are the influence of
icon art on visual art in general, the fusing of religion with patriotism and nationalism, or the interweaving of religious rituals with folk customs and everyday
practices. The attempt to sever abruptly these manifold connections and the
failure, in most cases, to provide satisfying alternatives threatened to put large
sections of the population into a cultural vacuum. This threat was most acutely
felt in the countryside where relatively stable and isolated communities had
cherished the Orthodox cultural tradition for centuries, had few alternatives, and
were, and still are, much less touched by attempts to establish an alternative
socialist culture with its own forms of art, patriotism, ritual and holidays.

In these circumstances a surrender of Orthodoxy would have led to depriva-tion, and wide sections of the rural population and a much smaller proportion of the urban population have either never made this break with the Orthodox cultural and patriotic tradition or have rediscovered it for themselves. Orthodoxy and/or the Orthodox Church have therefore continued up to the present day to provide to members and adherents a variety of satisfactions of a broadly cultural kind besides, or sometimes instead of, narrowly religious rewards. The nature of the satisfactions gained differs with the social complexion of the group involved. The evidence for this relation is of a varied kind.

First, it has been shown by Soviet sociologists that Orthodoxy survived best in areas where it had established before the Revolution a strong cultural influ-ence (e.g. through an important monastery, or a centre of icon painting) (Alek-seev, 1967; Anokhina and Shmeleva, 1966, p. 126), and that it failed to establish itself strongly in areas where no such cultural tradition had been set up or re-created by a relatively homogeneous group of immigrants (see Basilov, 1967, p. 153). Sectarianism, on the other hand, did not depend on such long cultural attachments and established itself just in those areas where Orthodoxy did not take root.

Secondly, a more specific relation between Orthodoxy and Russian nationalism is also discernible. In a multi-national setting even non-believing Russians will often call themselves Orthodox to clearly mark off their national identity from that of Soviet citizens of non-Russian origin. This same close bond between Orthodox religion and Russian nationality was also forged by the short-lived, politically oppositional Berdyaev Circle (see pp. 37, 49) which wanted to carry this connection to the extreme by founding a new political order on the Church. Baptism in the Orthodox Church, it was argued above, is regarded by many as a national custom. Rather than symbolising a strictly religious commitment, bap-tism is often approached as an act of affirming a national tradition.

Thirdly, in recent times Orthodoxy has been rediscovered by some young Soviet intellectuals who receive satisfaction from immersing themselves in Russia's church-artistic and patriotic-religious history and want to share these satis-factions with their fellow Russians (see p. 49). In a similar way, the recently formed Society for the Preservation of Cultural Monuments was also founded by young intellectuals who realised the important contribution of the Orthodox Church to national culture and were anxious to preserve this cultural heritage. On a more individual level, this interest in and attraction to Orthodox art in the forms of its icons has recently had a resurgence among members of the Soviet intelligentsia, while the aesthetic and social customary value of icons has never been disregarded in the rural homes.

Fourthly and lastly, the Church's numerous religious holidays and the accom-panying ritual have become closely interwoven with everyday life, with family and community tradition in the more settled rural communities. They have re-mained cherished social customs where religious beliefs have long been sur-rendered. These holidays are frequently the only diversions and occasions of heightened significance which break up and structure the monotonous calendric cycle and enrich the frequently deprived rural life.

This attachment to Orthodoxy as a general cultural complex rather than just a religious belief system is widespread among members and loose adherents of the Church. This attachment has been disturbing enough to the authorities to initiate the publication of an instruction manual for atheist fieldworkers which tries to refute a connection between Orthodoxy and Russian culture (Zots, 1974). It is characteristic of members of all social strata, although different aspects of this general cultural complex are selected by different social strata with varying degrees of consciousness. It is most prevalent among the settled rural population although it has recently begun to make an impact on urban intellectual groups. In all cases it is, however, a turning to the Russian past for satisfactions which the Soviet present does not or cannot provide. This propensity to seek rewards of a widely cultural kind in the contact with Russian Orthodoxy seems to be associated with definite kinds of religious commitment. It is a traditionalist religiosity characterised by episodic ritual practice, by neglect of devotional acts, and by lack of interest in the ideological, intellectual and experiential dimensions. In the case of the more conscious identification with Orthodox culture by urban professional groups religious commitment is of a different kind. Here the intellectual dimension is, of course, paramount, and it is impossible to say if and how far the other dimensions are developed.

Let us now turn to consider what psychological rewards are gained from being associated with the Orthodox Church. All religions, it is generally recognised, provide for a variety of psychological needs and therefore may have therapeutic value. The degree to which any religious organisation is able to provide different kinds of psychological rewards depends very much on the nature of its belief system and the resulting ritual activities. The Orthodox Church, I feel, is especially well equipped to provide certain types of psychological satisfactions. Placing relatively little emphasis on dogma and imposing on members few prescriptions about conduct, the Church is not liable to create anxiety in its members. Its emphasis on liturgy and the special nature of its service, allied to the great sensuous appeal of its churches, evoke a distinct group of psychological responses in those attending worship. The services are not, as in some Protestant churches, designed to evoke intellectual involvement and excitement, nor, as in some sectarian groups, do they seek to excite participants emotionally into feelings of ecstasy. The steady gentle and melodious flow of words and music against a background of colourful visual splendour induces in those present the more quiet and steady emotions, besides aesthetic gratification (see, for example, Glagolev, 1969). Worshippers experience feelings of joy, peace of mind, liberation, elation, or relish the visual impact of the church interior or the chanting of the priests, the choir singing, or both. When they leave the church building they feel emotionally refreshed or psychologically rewarded. Psychological rewards are thus mainly gained by those who are actual rather than nominal church members and can only be achieved by church attendance and immersion into the pattern of services. This type of reward is thus closely associated with another type of religious commitment characterising what Soviet sociologists generally call the 'convinced believers'. These are, where possible, regular attenders who participate also in such rituals as confession and communion and express their devotion in front of the icons. They know vaguely and accept the belief content of rituals and of the service in general, are given to gentle forms of religious experience but are largely unaware of the complexity and exact nature of Orthodox faith. Although these two basic types of Orthodox have been presented as deriving distinctly separate rewards from their religious involvement, we do not intend to say that these rewards are mutually exclusive.

The rewards of both types of believers flow predominantly from their involvement in religious practice of the more public nature. It is the great dilemma of the Orthodox Church that the dispensation of both cultural and, even more, psychological rewards by the Church depends heavily on its physical rather than its spiritual or intellectual presence which, as the 1959–64 period of extensive church closures demonstrated, is more easily destroyed. It has been brought out above that the loss of a church is often followed by loss of belief among its former parishioners.

If a church is still in easy reach, however, attachment to the Orthodox Church through ritual and, resulting therefrom, emotional involvement gives members more stable ties than if their attachment had been predominantly ideological. They are more stable because they are the result of habitual activity which is not so likely to be questioned by the individuals themselves. Thus the striking changes in the social and intellectual climate of Soviet society since the Revolution are not seen as posing a challenge to religious affiliation because the latter is not perceived as commitment to a world-view. Consequently ritual involvement is much harder to attack and to discredit by conscious militant atheist education as appeal to the intellect is not very effective. For a long time the Marxist philosophical framework, which attacks religion on ideological grounds, blinded Soviet social scientists to the powerful influence of ritual. In recent years, however, awareness of this has developed and the attack on religion has shifted on to the ritual plane. The conscious and deliberate creation of civic rituals and festivities by the political authorities is largely motivated by anti-religious zeal. Whether this new challenge to Orthodox religion and the Church will be effective in the long run remains to be seen.

Chapter 4

# Orthodox Sects of the Soviet Period

Besides the most thriving and persistent sects of Western origin – the Baptists, Pentecostalists, Adventists, Mennonites and Jehovah's Witnesses – and the declining sects of Orthodox origins and pre-revolutionary genesis – the Molokans, Dukhobors, Khlysts, and Skoptsy – there are also those many small sects which have split off from the Orthodox Church during the period of Soviet power. They have remained close to Orthodox teachings and have protested chiefly against the conciliatory political stance of the Church towards the Soviet regime. During the troubled years of the first four decades of Soviet rule there sprang up a host of small sects, sometimes transitory and localised, sometimes more persistent and nationwide. Among the better-known ones are the Fedorovtsy, Cherdashniki, the True Orthodox Church, and the True Orthodox Christians. (For the names of and details about the many smaller, less well known sects, consult Fedorenko, 1965, pp. 205f.). Included in this group of 'Soviet' sects are also a few small sects which arose in the politically turbulent years before the Revolution with a reactionary defence of monarchism. These flourished in the post-revolutionary decade and later either merged with the new ascending Orthodox sects or have continued independently up to the present day. Among these are the Ioannity and the Innokenty.

These sects are relatively unimportant in terms of the size of their following and the scope of their social influence. They are nevertheless sociologically extremely interesting because they are the only religious organisations which actually *arose* in hostile response to the new political and social order and continue to sustain themselves by this militantly hostile attitude to Soviet society up to the present day. Study of them will acquaint us with the case of a sectarian group which radicalises its response to the world when state pressure on the sect is intensified. An additional point of interest is the fact that these sects constitute a divergent and particularly intriguing example of what Bryan Wilson (1970, p. 38) has termed the 'revolutionist' type of sect. They are also characterised by a well-developed 'thaumaturgical' element in their response to the world.

'Revolutionist' sects demand of their members faith in God's promise of the overthrow of this evil world and obedience to his commands about preparation for this event. They believe they will be eligible for salvation in the new world order which Christ will establish at his second coming. Unlike many other

Christian religious collectivities, 'revolutionist' sects make the doctrine of second advent and millennium the central point of their teaching. Rather than changing men themselves or just some aspects of this world they posit the innate evilness of this world and will settle for nothing less than its complete overturn. Although the Orthodox sects of the Soviet period fully conform to the above general definition of the 'revolutionist' type they depart considerably from the more detailed definition given by Wilson (1970, p. 42). While Wilson's type applies to 'revolutionist' sects in the Western world of the twentieth century and appears to be chiefly an abstraction from the characteristics of the main contemporary 'revolutionist' sects – the Seventh Day Adventists and Jehovah's Witnesses – Orthodox sects of the Soviet period are more akin to the pre-modern 'revolutionist' type of sect or millennial movement specified by Troeltsch (1931) and, more recently, by Cohn (1972). All these sects are distinguished by strong eschatological and mystical tendencies as well as by an ascetic life-style for their members.

The Ioannity had their origin in the 1880s when the Orthodox priest John (Russ. *Ioann*) of Kronstadt gathered a following. (The following account is based on Mitrokhin, 1961; Federenko, 1965; Belov, 1969; Duluman, Lobovik and Tancher, 1970, pp. 115–17). They formed a religious organisation after the 1905 Revolution and went underground after the October Revolution. In some areas they merged with other anti-Soviet sects of the Orthodox tradition, while in others they remained independent and can still be found today. Already before the Revolution the sect was extremely anti-socialist and gave in fact active support to the reactionary monarchist Black Hundreds movement renowned for its pogroms against Jews and anti-monarchist groups. After the Revolution the sect's full hostility was aimed against the new regime, and hopes about a return to monarchism were nourished by its members. It gained many recruits from formerly Orthodox prosperous peasants, dispossessed by the regime. Its religious teachings were basically Orthodox but were injected with a big dose of mysticism. John of Kronstadt is believed to have been Christ incarnate, other leaders are held to be Archangels, or members of the Tsarist family. 'Holy Men' who practise faith healings are highly revered in the sects. They live in small, conspiratorial groups, practising extreme asceticism and sometimes monasticism. Due to the illegal and secret existence of the sect since the Revolution, reliable estimates of the size of its membership are non-existent, but at the present time their following is believed to be very small. Nothing systematic is known about the social complexion of the sect's present membership.

The Innokenty, founded in 1908 by Hieromonk Innokent, are almost identical to the Ioannity in their monarchist, anti-Soviet tendencies, their mysticism, and their historical development. Their distinguishing feature is the adoption, after the Revolution, of a sacrificial rite, during which members were tortured in special 'chambers of death' in a sacrificial manner (Belov, 1969, p. 18). This practice led to the prosecution of leading members during the 1950s. According to Belov, the sect did not survive this loss of leadership. The Innokenty, indeed, are no longer mentioned in the sociological literature concerning contemporary sects but whether this is because of their complete demise or because of lack of information on a membership driven more deeply underground (as has been common in other Soviet religious organisations) must remain an unsettled question.

Sects of the Orthodox tradition arising after the Revolution were formed mainly after the Orthodox Church's declaration of loyalty to the Soviet regime was given in 1927 by Sergei, the Patriarch's *locum tenens*. Large groups of monastic elements, priests and parishioners considered this accommodation to the new regime a surrender of holy Orthodox principles or, at the least, of Orthodox independence. The sects arising at this time thus became a collecting basin for all sorts of dissatisfied elements who saw their entry into these sects as an opportunity to vent their hostility to the new social order and the regime and their dissatisfaction with a church which, in their eyes, had failed to do its religious and social duty by surrendering to the Soviet regime. From that time date the numerous pro-monarchist little sects like the Buevtsy, Fedorovtsy, Cherdashniki, Imyaslavtsy and, at the end of the twenties, the larger sect of the True Orthodox Church. The latter recruited heavily from the above-mentioned smaller sects (Mitrokhin, 1961, pp. 148f.). In the late forties, the True Orthodox Church became superseded by the very similar sect of the True Orthodox Christians. All the earlier sects spread and increased their following during the social upheaval of the collectivisation period, and some of them again later, during and after the Second World War.

Of the smaller sects we hear today only about the Fedorovtsy, named after the sect's founder and leader Fedor Rybalkin. In the early sixties the sect was still distinguished by apocalypticism and extreme asceticism. Members are said to have been fanatically anti-Soviet, refusing to hold personal documents issued by the Soviet authorities, such as passports, and to participate in any sector of socialist society (Aleksandrovich, Kandaurov and Nemirovskii, 1961, p. 65). Small illegal groups of the sect have been reported in some parts of the Soviet Union, though details are lacking.

The True Orthodox Church was founded in the late twenties by the Metropolitan Petrovykh in Leningrad and, feeding on the membership of the smaller Orthodox sects as well as recruiting new members, it quickly grew in size and spread into other parts of the Soviet Union (Mitrokhin, 1961, p. 149). Although the sect was supposedly 'dismantled' as counter-revolutionary in 1931 (Fedorenko, 1965, p. 211) it continued in strength to the end of the forties, when it became gradually displaced by the True Orthodox Christians, and finally disintegrated in the early fifties although isolated groups can still be encountered (see Mitrokhin, 1961, p. 147; Aleksandrovich, Kandaurov and Nemirovskii, 1961, p. 63). The religious and political ideology of the sect resembled that of its smaller forerunners. As its name indicates, the sect saw itself as the preserver of 'true' Orthodoxy which, in the eyes of its members, had been perverted by the present Church hierarchy. Consequently it idolised the pre-revolutionary Church. It recruited heavily from among Orthodox clergy and the large number of monks and nuns displaced by the closure of many monastic institutions (Mitrokhin, 1961, p. 155). At the beginning of the forties, a new sect – the True Orthodox Christians – gained ascendancy and gradually began to replace the True Orthodox Church. As the sect of the True Orthodox Christians is still in existence today and seems to be viable both in its numerical following and social composition, despite much persecution by the political authorities, a closer examination of its development, religious and social teachings, and its numerical strength and social composition in recent years is in order.

## TRUE ORTHODOX CHRISTIANS

According to a specialist on this sect (Nikol'skaya, 1961), the sect experienced the height of its development in the early postwar years. It flourished particularly in places where new Orthodox priests replaced old anti-Soviet priests who had been arrested (Nikol'skaya, 1961, p. 166). In the forties, the sect attracted large numbers of young people, and in the early fifties the sect spread from its central Russian homeland to places all over the Soviet Union (Klibanov, 1969, p. 173). The number of members during that period was no smaller than that of the Initsiativniks (see Chapter 7) in the 1960s. It began its decline in the late forties, and in the early fifties it lost nearly half of its adherents. At that time the alleged murder and terrorisation of some kolkhozniks and political administrators by some sect leaders led to a wave of arrests of their members (Klibanov, 1969, pp. 172, 173). In 1956–7 one wing of the sect, subsequently known as *Molchal'niki* (Silent Ones), radicalised its whole outlook and pushed separation from Soviet society to its limits. After her study of the sect in 1959, Nikol'skaya concluded that very few True Orthodox Christians were left in the Soviet Union (Nikol'skaya, 1961, pp. 171*ff*.). But the author did not take into consideration that a nationwide campaign against the sect had just been staged. It did not occur to her that many members of the sect might have gone completely underground. This assumption is implicitly borne out by Klibanov (1972, p. 55) who, after a second visit to the Tambov region, admits quite frankly that the research team underestimated the strength of the sect in 1959, due to its clandestine character. Today the sect still persists in many parts of the Soviet Union (see details below).

True Orthodox Christians see themselves as guardians of the 'true' Orthodox heritage and cultivate nostalgia for the pre-revolutionary Church. Hostility to the contemporary Orthodox Church is strong. This hostility is not founded, as in many Western 'revolutionist' sects, on dissatisfaction with the Church's ability to satisfy religious needs. The Church is rejected solely for its political role, for its accommodative stance to Soviet power. True Orthodox Christians have thus radically changed Orthodox social and political teaching. But they retained the main religious teachings and practices of the Orthodox Church (especially those emphasised before the Revolution) and merely gave them a change of emphasis. However, their sectarianism entailed the departure in significant ways from 'church'-type organisation and the omission of some ritual practices. True Orthodox Christians have no professional priests but religious leaders evolve from within their midst and are called 'elder brothers in spirit'. These sectarians believe that they can establish direct contact with Christ and that the mediatory services of a priest are unnecessary. Services are held in great secrecy in different private homes or in remote natural places, and prayer meetings take place daily. Neophytes are carefully scrutinised over a period of time and need reliable introductions before they are admitted to meetings. The sect's organisation in general is very loose, and groups are, as far as we know, small and localised. A national leader figure is not mentioned in the literature although some co-ordination at regional level exists. True Orthodox Christians have surrendered most sacraments, retaining only baptism, confession, and communion in altered form. Both eschatological and mystical elements are strong in the sect's teaching and also greatly influence its practice. True Orthodox Christians are said to know their religious teaching much better than Orthodox and Old Believers and also practise it more faithfully and regularly (Gagarin, 1971, p. 144). They contain a much higher proportion of what Soviet sociologists call 'fanatical' and 'convinced' believers than the former (Dem'yanov, 1974, p. 116). During the late sixties and early seventies, however, the number of fanatical and deeply committed members has begun to decrease even on this radical wing of Orthodoxy (Gagarin, 1971, p. 144; Dem'yanov, 1974, pp. 114f.).

As among Old Believer Priestless, the eschatological and apocalyptical visions of the Orthodox Church have been magnified and have been moved to the centre of their teaching. More importantly, anti-christological notions have lost their general character and have been clearly related to a specific historic period, the Soviet era. They believe in, and are continually aware of, the presence of Anti-Christ in Soviet society. The latter is for them the expression of Anti-Christ. Social, technological or cultural-educational progress is taken as direct evidence of the fact that Anti-Christ is at work. This spirit, for them, is so imminent and pervasive that they live in constant expectation of apocalypse and Christ's second coming. Curiously, the literature about the sect does not deal with the question of the exact timing of the apocalypse. We do not know therefore whether members have been waiting in vain for this event and what problems this may have caused. Although beliefs about the nature of the expected millennium are never made explicit either, we can deduce from the general social views of members what they are hoping for. Unlike some other 'revolutionist' sects they are not looking back to a society of primitive communism as practised by the early Christians but True Orthodox Christians are advocating the return to a more immediate past, longing for the restoration of a monarchist, primitive agrarian, private property society, 'uncontaminated' by education and social and technical progress.

True Orthodox Christians are filled with such certainty about the approaching end that they are moved to warn their fellow men about its imminence. For this purpose they have devised an ingenious means of spreading their message which effectively circumvents the restrictive and vigilant Soviet authorities and reaches a large cross-section of society. This device is the religious chain letter which both warns the recipient of the approaching end and threatens him with terrible retribution if he fails to copy out and pass on the letter to a specified number of people. (The whole text of such a letter is printed in *Nauka i religiya*, 12, 1966, p. 8.)

Besides warning others of the coming end, True Orthodox Christians spend much of their time and energy in warding off Anti-Christ and protecting themselves against his influence. They isolate themselves from the rest of society, sometimes going as far as cutting off water and electricity supplies to prevent spiritual pollution. This separation from the rest of society has been carried to its extreme conclusion by one wing of the sect, the Mol'chal'niki. In 1956–7, at a time when the sect had been decimated by widespread arrests, one group radicalised its whole outlook and completely closed itself off from all non-Mol'chal'niki. They withdrew into their houses, bricked up windows, barred doors, and only went outside in cases of extreme necessity. In addition, they use the cross, which they have endowed with magical power, to keep Anti-Christ at bay. Their houses and stables are marked with crosses for spiritual protection.

If they have to leave them they continually cross themselves, touching all parts of their body. When approached by outsiders Mol'chal'niki will cross their ears, their eyes, and their mouth to signify that they have not heard or seen anything and will never talk (Nikol'skaya, 1961, p. 186). They perceive everywhere a struggle between holy and unclean forces. Holiness for them is embodied in various objects of nature, while unclean forces dwell in all worldly men and practices.

Thus True Orthodox Christians, unlike Western 'revolutionist' sects, do not base their eschatological visions on a theory of historic development nor do they think in cosmic terms. For them the arrival of Anti-Christ and apocalypse are firmly connected with a specific period and country – with the contemporary Soviet Union. Signs for Anti-Christ's arrival are not so much given in scriptural prophecies but by the appearance of social phenomena closely connected with the new political order. Bible study has never been well established among the largely illiterate Orthodox lay folk, and at the present time Bibles are a rare commodity.

Such adamant hatred of the regime was bound to attract counter-measures from the political authorities, and the sect has experienced several efforts to destroy it through the arrest of leading members. Such measures only served to strengthen the sectarians in their convictions and resolve. They have led, as the birth of the Mol'chal'niki wing has shown, to the sect's more extreme rejection of the world around them.

The Orthodox Church as an institution, embodying a spiritual tradition, is not rejected, and the pre-revolutionary and Tikhonite Church is even idolised. The Church is condemned for its compliance with the policies of the political regime and only from the period of its official declaration of loyalty to the state in 1927 onwards. Thus the 'revolutionist' response of True Orthodox Christians contains a distinct political protest about a well-defined political act – the establishment of socialism in Russia and the Church's acquiescence in it. It is fair to add, though, that for many members the decisive alienating experience was not the establishment of socialism in itself (epitomised, for these peasants, by collectivisation), but the ruthless way it was introduced and the catastrophic consequences it had for many middle and all rich peasants.

In contemporary Western 'revolutionist' sects disillusionment is much more diffuse and rarely has clear political implications. This is demonstrated by a recent study of Jehovah's Witnesses in Britain (Beckford, 1975). 'Revolutionist' aspirations of pre-modern sects, on the other hand, such as those of the Taborites and, later, of the Anabaptists of Münster, had political overtones as distinct and concrete as those of the Soviet True Orthodox Christians. Among these late medieval sectarians apocalyptical and eschatological tendencies were inspired by feelings of love for the fellow oppressed and by the hope to return to the primitive communism of early Christians. Among True Orthodox Christians, however, the hatred of a relatively egalitarian political regime and the longing for a return to a strongly hierarchical class society are the driving forces. Nor are members predominantly from the bottom levels of society but a majority are dispossessed, formerly well-to-do peasants. Thus the content of their eschatology is clearly related to the nature of the society they live in and to their own social positions, and is again evidence of the strong political element in their religious response.

The fact that the sect has been able to sustain members' commitments over more than two decades, unlike the majority of pre-modern 'revolutionist' sects or millennial movements, is probably due to the fact that attention is mainly focused on the events prior to apocalypse, on the gradually extending rule of Anti-Christ in Soviet society. As this rule can, in theory, be extended *ad infinitum*, a serious testing of members' beliefs probably has not occurred.

Some of their practices and beliefs can be seen as a 'thaumaturgical' response in the way Wilson defined it (1970, pp. 167*f.*). Although this response does not form the doctrinal core of the sect it constitutes a fairly central and substantial component which comes a close second to the 'revolutionist' response. True Orthodox Christians differ from contemporary Western 'revolutionist' sects in the ways they try to avoid spiritual contamination by Anti-Christ and to ensure their salvation by magical practices. As they dwell chiefly on developments preliminary to the eschatological events, i.e. the extension of Anti-Christ's rule in Soviet society, their efforts are mainly directed at keeping Anti-Christ at bay. For this purpose they have developed a network of superstitions and magical practices. They try to warn others of the impending doom in a highly emotional way. Their practices remind the sociologist much more of medieval sectarians than of contemporary Western 'revolutionist' sects. The efforts of contemporary Adventists, for example, to give their religion some scientific footing would be completely alien to True Orthodox Christians, as would be the endeavour of modern Jehovah's Witnesses to gain converts by rational argument and persuasion.

The second distinctive feature of True Orthodox Christians, their infusion of dogma and ritual with an archaic mysticism, is also reminiscent of religious groups in less-developed societies rather than of contemporary Western sects. These mystical tendencies, it must be noted, have long been an integral part of Russian Orthodoxy although they were often condemned by the official Church. Today these traits are only weakly preserved in some informal Orthodox groupings but are a strong and vital ingredient in the religion of True Orthodox Christians. They believe that the Holy Ghost dwells in inanimate objects and places of nature where True Orthodox Christians are worshipping, as well as entering select men. They revere both 'holy' men and places in nature, ascribing supernatural powers to them and developing cults around them. Such 'Men of God', dressed in special black clothes, take up religious wandering. They try to stimulate and uphold the faith in the places they visit as well as keeping up ties between separate local groups. Areas around certain stones, lakes or springs are counted as holy places. Their water is believed to have healing power and serves to cleanse believers after unavoidable contact with 'unclean' powers. A large number of such places are listed for the regions of Tambov and Lipetsk alone (Klibanov, 1969, pp. 157, 172; Nikol'skaya, 1961, p. 180). The 'religious scene' at one such holy spring, which attracted self-styled 'Men of God' who claim to heal, chase out devils and generally to perform miracles, and where large crowds of True Orthodox Christians as well as some Orthodox gathered, is brought to life by the following interesting description by a Soviet sociologist.

'Such [a Man of God] was, for example, the dumb Filya Korolev. He was attended by two "lay sisters" who had spread among the backward [*temny*] True Orthodox Christians the legend about his Tsarist origin . . . and his sagacity. Several women, convinced about his "holiness", had harnessed themselves to his cart in place of the horses and took this rogue from spring to spring. Filya, by gestures, gave "advice" and made "forecasts" which were then explained by the lay sisters. In return he received money and treats from believers . . . Many rogues at springs made themselves out to be "exorcists", "healers" and "prophets". Under the influence of superstition sick women and children bathed in the spring hoping to get healed or stood motionless for hours expecting the appearance of "God's face" on the surface of the water. Here hysterical women were also shrieking, and new arrivals were praying aloud. All this taken together created a mood of extreme religious exaltation, in the atmosphere of which the leaders of the True Orthodox Christians also did their preaching . . .' (Nikol'skaya, 1961, p. 182)

True Orthodox Christians have also overemphasised and expanded the ascetic elements in Orthodoxy which are now greatly relaxed or even totally abandoned in the Orthodox Church. The sectarians were partly moved to strengthen asceticism because their anti-christological beliefs forbade them to make use of many provisions and conveniences provided by Soviet society rather than because they saw any primary virtue in particular acts of renunciation. Thus besides living very spartanly because of self-imposed rules of fasting, their anti-christological beliefs do not permit them to avail themselves of such diverse provisions as employment in the (almost exclusively) socialist sector of society, state welfare services, factory-made clothes, and even piped water and electricity. From 1955 onwards, their self-imposed asceticism even included celibacy. Some of the above restrictions and deprivations, however, have not been endured consistently by all members. The celibacy edict eventually led to protests and transgression on the part of the younger members of the sect and caused serious internal conflict. In the seventies, according to Klibanov (1972, p. 55), some sect members in Tambov region have even begun to disregard the interdiction of work in the socialised sector of the economy, but according to Dem'yanov (1974, p. 110), True Orthodox Christians still do not enter collective farms. Further relaxation of hostility towards the state and its institutions in the seventies is evident in the facts that contrary to sect teachings, children of True Orthodox Christians have not been kept away from school after the primary stage and that very few members have refused to be interviewed by a Soviet sociologist studying the sect in four central regions of the RSFSR (Dem'yanov, 1974, pp. 112, 113).

All these religious responses are, of course, closely bound up with distinct political and social orientations among True Orthodox Christians, some of which have been already indicated in the preceding passages. The Soviet political regime and socialist society are rejected wholesale and wholeheartedly, and members of the sect go to great lengths not to be involved in any institution or socio-political activity officially organised or sponsored. Thus they refuse to hold official documents, to do national service, to receive pensions, to join youth or political organisations, to keep their children at school beyond the primary stage, to vote and, most importantly, to work in the socialised sector of the economy. Members maintain themselves either by working as small, independent artisans or tinkers, by selling produce from their garden plots, by speculating with goods in short supply, by painting and restoring icons and making crosses, or they do not work at all and are supported by relatives and fellow believers (Gagarin, 1970, p. 376 and 1971, p. 159; Nikol'skaya, 1961, p. 170; Aleksandrovich, Kandaurov and Nemirovskii, 1961, p. 64). Many have given up work completely in the expectation of the imminence of Christ's second coming, and in the seventies 40 per cent of those of working age were still not in employment (Dem'yanov, 1974, p. 121). True Orthodox Christians naturally keep themselves apart from other people around them and counter efforts to involve them in some kind of discussion with the stereotyped answer 'As God wills it' (Nikol'skaya, 1961, p. 186). This complete alienation from the society they live in is well illustrated by a newspaper article reporting the cross-examination of one young sectarian by an official of a district military enlistment office:

'Entering the room, he [the True Orthodox Christian] fervently . . . crossed himself.
"Your name is Bobrovskii?" –
"God knows," answers the fellow, again energetically crossing himself.
"You are a reservist?" –
"I am a Christian."
"You are a citizen of the Soviet Union?" –
"No, I am a godly person."
"If you believe in God, please, believe. But you must submit all the same to the laws of Soviet power." –
"I submit to God's laws." '

*(Komsomol'skaya Pravda,* 15 April 1959)

This strong and active hostility to the political regime, the institutions and practices of socialist society and to their fellow citizens is also a more extreme assertion of the principle of sectarian exclusivity (see Wilson, 1970, p. 29) than is found among members of 'revolutionist' sects in the Western world. Although the latter also strive to keep themselves apart and live in a sectarian world of their own, they only sever the ties of general social intercourse with non-members rather than attempting to break off *all* relations with the outside world. This basic difference on the part of Soviet 'revolutionist' sectarians can again be attributed to the clear political motivations underlying their religious response.

The question about the reasons for such deep alienation is best answered by an examination of the sect's past and present social composition. In the early years of its existence, the sect recruited predominantly from formerly rich and middle peasants embittered by collectivisation and, presumably, its attendant violations of justice and humanity (Nikol'skaya, 1961, p. 163; Gagarin, 1970, p. 377) as well as from people shocked by the ruthless handling of the Orthodox Church during the late twenties and the thirties (Nikol'skaya, 1961, p. 166). The strong apocalyptical leanings of the sect are aptly interpreted by Nikol'skaya (p. 184) as the tendency 'of the liquidated *kulak* [rich peasant] class to perceive its own historical end as the end of the world, as apocalypse'. Today the sect still attracts the few remaining individual peasants (market gardeners) as well as various people 'offended by the Soviet government who see in membership of the True Orthodox Christians a channel for the expression of their dissatisfaction' (Gagarin, 1970, p. 377). Inevitably, the sect has also taken in what Gagarin calls 'loafer elements'.

The fact that members have been largely attracted to the sect to express their dissatisfaction with and protest about some aspect of past or present Soviet social reality also comes out in other social characteristics of True Orthodox Christians.

Unlike many other religious organisations in the Soviet Union, during the sixties the sect attracted a high proportion of middle aged (30–50-year-olds) and a significant number of young people as well as more men than is usual (around 30 per cent). During the seventies, however, the age/sect composition of the sect in the central regions of the RSFSR has deteriorated. The sect no longer attracts young people. This occurred partly because the present generation does not nurse the same amount of grievances against the state as previous generations, and partly because the sect's prescription of celibacy during the forties and fifties reduced the number of young people in the community. Those under 50 years of age formed only 30 per cent of the membership in the central regions of the RSFSR (Dem'yanov, 1974, p. 108, Table 1). The proportion of men had sunk to 19 per cent (ibid., p. 111). These sectarians are not, like most Orthodox, mainly elderly women who seek various psychological gratifications or continue religious observance for the sake of tradition or out of habit. On the contrary, they are people in the prime of their lives who put a lot at risk (often including their liberty) to profess their 'revolutionist' beliefs. These must, therefore, be based on strong and pervasive disillusionment with their social environment. In general, members are poorly educated rural people (Nikol'skaya, 1961; Gagarin, 1970, p. 380) who do not know how to express their dissatisfaction in a more sophisticated and effective form. Only 4·5 per cent of members in a recent survey had more than primary education (Dem'yanov, 1974, p. 110, Table 2).

Let us now turn to consider the numerical strength and general vitality of the sect during the last decade. Nikol'skaya, in her 1961 article, implied that the sect was in decline. Neglect to study the sect on the part of Soviet atheists and social scientists as well as on that of Western religious circles gives the impression that during the last decade the sect has been insignificant. But this impression is false and is probably only due to the facts that the sect is clandestine and does not have any ties with other religious organisations or Western sympathisers. The few data we possess, however, show that the sect is not insignificant in numerical terms nor lacking in vitality, even if some decline has taken place during the last decade (see Klibanov, 1972; Dem'yanov, 1974). A study of the sect in the early seventies in four central regions of the RSFSR established that there were around 1,500 members in these areas (Dem'yanov, 1974, p. 106). Earlier local studies found that in Voronezh region in 1965 the sect had 350 members (Teplyakov, 1967, p. 156). In Tamov region in 1971, it was the second biggest sect (after the Baptists) when over 400 members were identified in seven districts of that region (Klibanov, 1972, p. 55). In the Komi ASSR its membership remained relatively stable during the 1958–64 period, in contrast to that of other sects there (Gagarin, 1970, p. 379).

We have no other quantitative information about membership in the sect, but we know from various accounts that the sect has existed in many parts of the Soviet Union between 1959 and 1971. Thus in 1959 and the early sixties the sect was represented in the Sumy and Lugansk regions of the Ukraine, in the regions of Altai, of Tambov, Lipetsk, Ryazan, Voronezh, Kirov and Saratov in the RSFSR, as well as in the Mordvinian ASSR, the Chuvash ASSR, the Kazakh towns of Alma-Ata and Chimkent, and in various villages and settlements (*Nauka i religiya*, 1960, p. 53; Nikol'skaya, 1961, p. 162; Aleksandrovich, 1961, p. 63; *Central Asian Review*, 1963, p. 353). The *émigré* Metropolitan Filaret, basing himself on Soviet press accounts, adds to the above areas also the Ukrainian regions of Ternopol and the Krym, some Siberian and Far Eastern towns, as well as the Uzbek republic, as places where True Orthodox Christians have been active during the 1960s (*Publik*, 30 October 1970). Gagarin gives us information on the sect's presence in the Komi ASSR where it flourished through the sixties in several towns, settlements and villages (Gagarin, 1970, p. 367). Mol'chal'niki have been reported only in the Tambov region (RSFSR) where they had tens of members in 1959 and where thirty were still in existence in the early seventies (Nikol'skaya, 1961, p. 173; Dem'yanov, 1974, p. 107).

Although we have only sketchy information about the sect's social composition we can say with reasonable certainty that the sect in the near future will remain viable in terms of its age structure and is not likely to become as sedate and inert as some of the old Russian sects of the Orthodox tradition in which elderly people predominate. Irrespective of its following in numerical terms, the sect's organisational existence is strengthened by the fact of its clandestine character, and its religious and political fanaticism provides a match for the efforts of Soviet authorities to extinguish this politically disloyal religious group. On the other hand, its conscious cultivation of the more mystic and reactionary features of the Orthodox Church is unlikely to gain the sect a wide social appeal. Its following is most likely to remain restricted to the poorly educated groups in Soviet society which are drastically declining.

The study of the True Orthodox Christians has clearly brought out that an ostensibly religious organisation may become the vehicle to express political protest, and that there are still small but persistent groups opposed to a socialist society whose members cannot give vent to their political hostility in any other form. The fact that True Orthodox Christians are strongly politically motivated has had a determining influence on their religious and social teachings, on their ritual practice, as well as on their organisational form. The predominantly reactionary political world-view underlying their religious response has turned them into a 'revolutionist' sect of a kind which is no longer found in Western society. The form of its religious response is more reminiscent of earlier, less-developed societies. The content of its apocalyptical and eschatological notions, however, being inspired by the sentiments of political reaction, differs from that of both the pre-modern and contemporary 'revolutionist' sects. The presence of a marked thaumaturgical response, usually only associated with less-developed societies, is also inconsistent with what we know about Western 'revolutionist' sects.

Chapter 5

# The Old Russian Sects

Sects proliferated in Russia long before the Revolution when they found fertile soil among the politically and economically oppressed mass of the peasants. The most widespread and best known were the Khlysts, Skoptsy, Molokans and Dukhobors and their various branches. Although these sects are essentially a social phenomenon of feudal Russia and had started to decline before the Revolution, their continued existence today makes it advisable to analyse why these sects have lingered on, how they relate to the new social order and how they have changed under its impact. The relative unimportance of these sects (in terms of both membership and social influence) in the present time and the paucity of data about them (excepting only the Molokans) necessitate a very short and sketchy outline of their characteristics, historical development, social complexion and religious orientations today. Only the Molokan sect will be analysed in

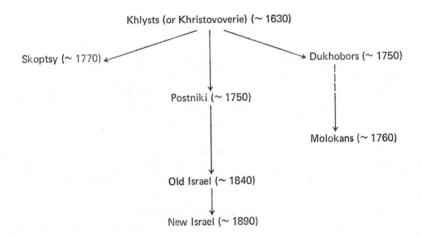

greater length and detail, and much of what is said about the latter is representative of the other Old Russian sects.

Although each of the above sects is distinct from the others in terms of its religious message they are also closely related to each other in several ways. All four are part of the same tradition of protest against religious and social domination by the Orthodox Church and the feudal social order and have, indeed, evolved one out of the other through the centuries of their existence. Figure 1 illustrates how they are related and when each sect evolved. Of these sects, the Khlysts are the oldest, the first written record of their existence dating back to the 1630s. Over a century later, around 1750, both the Skoptsy and the Dukhobor sect evolved out of the Khlysts. Not long afterwards one of the Dukhobor leaders formed the Molokan sect. The Khlysts survived the formation of these new sects. Although undergoing internal schisms (into Postniki and the New and Old Israel) and changes in dogma through the centuries, the Khlysts have preserved their essence up to the present time. Before the Revolution, of the four sects the Dukhobors were the smallest, the Molokans the largest and the other two fell somewhere in between. Today they are all radically reduced in number, but the Molokans are still the largest, the Dukhobors have taken the second place, and the sects of the Khristovoverie and the Skoptsy are near to extinction.

All these sects were persecuted by the Church and the state until 1905, some more persistently and ferociously than others. On the eve of the Revolution, according to Bonch-Bruevich (1959, p. 175), the membership of all the sects numbered 6 million. Since the Revolution, all have drastically declined and ceased to proselytise.

## THE KHLYSTS

The Khlysts interpret the Bible prophecy of Christ's second coming spiritually, believing that he returns in the soul of each one of them already during their life-time. Their services prepare members spiritually for the reception of the divine spirit which is achieved by a form of ecstatic singing and dancing, called *Radenie* (Engl. zeal, fervour). Talking in tongues and interpretation of these prophetic utterances are common during such meetings. Ascesis in preparation for the *Radenie* consists of abstention from various foodstuffs, intoxicants and sexual relations, and of exposure to all sorts of sufferings. In some communities members who 'mortified their flesh' to an extreme extent were considered spiritually more worthy and were venerated as leaders in whom the spirit of Christ was particularly strong. The sect's name 'Khlysty' is supposed to have derived from the two facts that they venerate some leaders as Christs (Russ. *Khristy*) and that, in some local groups, lashing themselves with twigs (Russ. *khlestat'*) before the *Radenie* was customary. Khlysts called themselves, and were widely known as, 'Men of God' (Russ. *Lyudy Bozhie*). In the contemporary Soviet sociological literature Khlysts and their later forms and branches of Postniki and Old and New Israel are generally subsumed under the collective name Khristovoverie after their common characteristic of believing their leaders to be Christs.

As might be expected, such an old, widely disseminated and loosely organised sect was not spared internal divisions. Around 1750, under its new leader Kopylov, the sect experienced some changes in dogma and secular ethic and became known under the name Postniki (Fasters) due to the extension and tightening-up of fast regulations. Although the *Radenie* and the reception of the Holy Ghost still formed the centre of their faith, sect leaders now became regarded as personifications of Christ rather than just being filled with his spirit as it was the case with earlier leaders. This new claim by leaders left no room for the spiritual gratification of rank-and-file members. The perpetuation of democratic traditions now fell to the Dukhobors who evolved roughly around this time. A century later, the Postniki, in their turn, experienced internal schism when, in 1840, a branch called Israel or later Old Israel, broke away. Followers considered themselves the chosen people of Israel destined to introduce 'God's kingdom' on earth. Asceticism was slightly relaxed. The movement was well organised and quickly spread out, having around 25,000 followers in the 1880s. Shortly after its leader's death in 1885, however, the sect began to fall apart and a new branch, calling itself New Israel and led by a new Christ, largely replaced it. The New Israel sect further extended and strengthened organisation, regarding the whole of Russia as 'the heavenly kingdom' and setting up a virtual hierarchy to rule it as well as curtailing the more spontaneous mysticism of rank-and-file members. The New Israel sect departed so considerably from the main teaching of the Khlysts that it is usually regarded as a separate sect in the literature. Besides the 'spiritual diversion' of the *Radenie* the New Israel also introduced dramatisations of Christian mythology on a grand scale, with actors believing themselves to be the persons they portrayed. Thus we read about a dramatisation of the ascent to Mount Zion as late as 1907. The sect was greatly weakened when around 10 per cent of its members emigrated to Uruguay in 1911–12. Unlike the other old Russian sects, the Khristovoverie maintained outward ties with the Orthodox Church, visiting some services, preserving some of its practices and cultic objects. This was partly done as a tactical manœuvre designed to conceal sectarianism from the persecutors and partly because the sect had been unable to make a complete break.

Sects of the Khristovoverie had a large proportion of very rich members, large peasants and merchants. While Khlysts believed in an other-worldly kingdom to come and thus never voiced political protest actively, New Israelites believed that God's kingdom must be built here in this world. New Israelites, at the eve of the Revolution, became very accommodating to the secular power of the Tsar. After the Revolution there was initially some revolutionary enthusiasm among New Israelites but most turned into opponents of the regime during the collectivisation period. At that time the regime withdrew its approval for communitarian enterprises of the sect, and sect members received the same treatment as *kulaks*.

Today Khlysts, unlike Dukhobors and Molokans, still keep themselves apart from Soviet society, refusing even employment in the socialised economy. For example in Tambov region of the RSFSR, in 1959 all Postniki maintained themselves by private enterprise market gardening and set themselves more obstinately apart from their socialist environment than members of most other sects (Malakhova, 1961, p. 110). Khlyst families made a very good income and this financial success would be regarded by them as a proof of the truth of their faith and way of life (Klibanov, 1969, p. 57).

Before the First World War, there were about 20,000 New Israelites, 15,000 Old Israelites and 3,000 Postniki in Russia (Klibanov, 1965, pp. 83–4). But already before the Revolution the sects of the Khristovoverie had been losing members, being ousted by the Dukhobors and Molokans (Klibanov, 1965, p. 68). Today, there are only a few isolated groups of Postniki and Israelites left, the latter counting their followers only in tens (Malakhova, 1970, p. 30). Small groups of Khlysts are said to exist in the regions of Tambov, Kuibyshev, Orenburg and Rostov, as well as in the northern Caucasus, Transcaucasia and the Ukraine (Puchkov, 1975). I have come across only one report of a group of New Israelites and this group had declined drastically. The 408 New Israelites present in

Voronezh region in 1928 had been reduced to 36 by 1965 (Teplyakov, 1967, pp. 155, 156). How far this process of decline is the result of a loss of attraction and how far it is due to the forcible suppression of this relatively small sect in the 1920s and 1930s is difficult to know. Probably both factors have been important, although sects with great religious vitality could not have been as decimated as the Khristovoverie are today. Unfortunately there is no mention in the Soviet literature of New Israel groups in the Don and Caucasus areas where their following is said to have been most numerous at the beginning of the twentieth century. It would have been interesting to see whether the Caucasian groups, like those of the Molokans, had more fully survived than those in central Russia.

The few data available about contemporary Khlysts show that, although the sect is near to extinction, the rate of decline has been slow in comparison to that of other old Russian sects. For example, the 500 Postniki who lived in 1915 in the area of today's Tambov region of the RSFSR had been reduced to just over 200 by 1959 (Malakhova, 1961, p. 107). They thus survived much better than the Molokans in the same area who suffered a sixteenfold decline (i.e. from 8,000 to 500) in the same period. But as the age structure of the communities in Rasskazov town and the Zherdevsk district of this region show, total extinction is not far off (Malakhova, 1970, p. 32; Klibanov, 1972, p. 54). Their relatively slow rate of decline is undoubtedly due to their persistent refusal to accommodate themselves to the regime they reject and to their success in keeping themselves apart from the socialist sector of their society. But their persistence until today is best regarded as a lingering on in spite of extremely unfavourable conditions for their survival rather than as the result of any religious vitality or attraction they still possess. The asceticism, forming a central tenet of their teaching, has proved too difficult to maintain in present-day society. In contrast to the Molokan and Dukhobor sects, their organisational existence is also not prolonged by quasi-ethnic identification of members with the group, as the Khristovoverie never cultivated the extreme exclusivity of the other two sects.

## THE SKOPTSY

The sect of the Skoptsy (Engl. Castrators) evolved out of the Khlysts around 1770. While retaining many of the latter's religious practices, teachings and customs, the Skoptsy changed them in some crucial aspects. They developed the asceticism of the Khlysts to its logical conclusion by preventing sexual activity by compulsory castration with a hot iron. This 'baptism with fire', as they called it, became the centre of their teaching. Although they retained the *Radenie* of the Khlysts, it lost its sacramental character for them and only 'baptism with fire' could free a man from sin and ensure his salvation. This castration was demanded of converts to the sect and imposed on any children Skoptsy had had before castration. Women were not made infertile but many cut out their breasts. The founder and most notable leader of the sect, Selivanov, a serf from Orel province (now RSFSR), was regarded as both Christ himself (rather than just being filled with his spirit) and Tsar Peter III, the assassinated husband of Catherine the Great. Skoptsy carried the veneration of their 'Christ' much further than other sects of the Khristovoverie. They worshipped his picture, the amulets he distributed and various relics such as fingernails and hair-clippings. Despite the great sacrifice the sect demanded from converts it expanded rapidly after some initial difficulties. Skoptsy attracted interest in all sections of society, and their generally very rich members (as the result of ascetic living) were respected and trusted creditors. New recruits were often made from among poor peasants by the promise to them of the same material prosperity, and initial financial support was usually given (Bonch-Bruevich, 1959, p. 285). After Selivanov's death, his followers came to believe that he would soon reappear among them to inaugurate the millennium. At the eve of the Revolution the sect is believed to have had about 100,000 members and to have been extraordinarily active (Conybeare, 1962, p. 367).

After the Revolution the sect rapidly declined. Fedorenko (1965, p. 121) gives the figure of 2,000 members for the year 1929 which suggests a radical reduction of their number during the first year of collectivisation, the generally wealthy members probably having received the treatment of *kulaks*. Big trials of Skoptsy in Leningrad and other places from 1929 onwards showed that the sect was still much alive (Malakhova, 1970, pp. 44*ff.*). After these trials Skoptsy were driven even more into the religious underground from where they conducted anti-communist propaganda (ibid.). Not surprisingly, documentation of this process of decline and any data on surviving groups are almost completely lacking in the literature. It is only said that the sect is almost extinct and that only isolated groups of individuals are still spread over the RSFSR. Klibanov (1972, p. 55) mentions the existence of a few dozen Skoptsy scattered all over Tambov region. According to information given to the present author personally, there is still a community of around a hundred members in Orel region (RSFSR), the cradle of this sect. Although castration has long been abandoned among them, sexual abstinence is still the norm. The sect has managed to perpetuate itself by raising orphans of the Second World War and, at present, by adopting the children of relatives.

THE DUKHOBORS

While the Skoptsy took up one aspect of the Khlysts' teaching – their asceticism – and developed it to its logical conclusion, the Dukhobors developed their teaching in another direction. Their name *'Dukhobortsy'*, meaning Spirit Wrestlers, was ascribed to them by an Orthodox bishop who proclaimed that this radical sect fought against the Spirit. The sectarians took over this name but interpreted it to mean that the Spirit fought in them. Like the Khlysts, the Dukhobors believe that God's spirit enters and dwells in those living righteously; Christ for them is reborn in every believer. They do not, however, adhere to the *Radenie* of the Khlysts. While Khlysts prove themselves worthy of the reception of the Holy Spirit by asceticism, Dukhobors prepare themselves by leading a morally exemplary life. Salvation, for them, will only be gained by good works in this life. Although the teaching that the Holy Spirit enters every sect member alike had already given a great democratic impulse to the Khlyst communities, the Dukhobors developed the social teaching flowing from the doctrine more logically and consistently. Their notion of the brotherhood of all men led them to espouse a radical pacifism and to practise mutual assistance. They embraced the ideal of equality of all men and attempted to apply it to the economic and social spheres as well as the sexual. Contrary to pre-revolutionary peasant culture, women were regarded as equals and were given full voting rights (Bonch-Bruevich, 1959, p. 291). They regard Christ as the only leader and have in the past rejected the rule of worldly authority, including sometimes that of the Tsar.

They have tried to organise their lives in accordance with these moral principles, emulating the existence of early Christian communities. Although more consistent in the pursuit of these moral ideals than all the other old Russian sects and often coming close to their application in practice, they also periodically violated them in a serious manner. Like the Khlysts, they believed that their leaders were at a higher spiritual level than ordinary members and venerated them as God-men or Virgins. Their deep veneration of their leaders and unconditional acceptance of the latter's autocratic rule of the community stood in both sects in glaring conflict with their espousal of democracy and the rejection of worldly leaders. Among the Dukhobors, the autocratic tendency was particularly strongly developed as the common territorial base of the sect lent itself well to the combination of spiritual and worldly rule in a theocracy. At various times during their long development, however, Dukhobors actively rejected the rule of the Russian Tsar, refusing to comply with orders that stood in contradiction to their teaching. The Dukhobors approached more closely the ideal of economic equality than any other sect on Russian soil when, at some periods of their long history, they established communism of production and consumption. At other times, however, economic differences and exploitation were as great in Dukhobor villages as elsewhere in Russia, although neighbourly help always flowed more generously among them than outside their communities. A special communal monetary fund was set up expressly to help brethren in need.

The Dukhobors were also more radical than the Khlysts in their abandonment of the rites, sacraments and cultic object of the Orthodox Church and in their severance of all ties with the latter. They reject all rites and external attributes of worship, and their meetings are held in utter simplicity and devoted only to singing, preaching and prayer. The Church has always been regarded with extreme hostility. Although Dukhobor teaching is based on the Bible and some of their psalms are taken from it, they even reject the Bible as 'a collection of dead words' and substitute for it their own 'Living Book', i.e. an orally transmitted collection of psalms, verses and songs enshrined in the memory and hearts of the faithful. It is this latter aspect of their religion which differentiates the Dukhobors from the otherwise very similar Molokan sect. During their long history, punctuated by different leadership, Dukhobor teaching remained fluid and was changed a lot. Above we have merely given the broad outlines of their dogma and secular ethic and have not had space to relate the many minor subtleties of their teaching nor the frequent changes in emphasis through the centuries. Conybeare, basing himself on a nineteenth-century observer, describes the Dukhobors in the following way:

'Their superior morale marked them out among the surrounding population as ears of corn among tares. They were equally distinguished by their comfortable circumstances – this being due to the aid they rendered to each other in misfortune. In their teaching and conduct brotherly love was inculcated above all other virtues, and charity and sociability characterized their mutual relations.' (Conybeare, 1962, p. 285)

The Dukhobors have had a long and eventful history and only very broad outlines can be given here of those events which have decisively shaped their present state. Their development is usefully divided into five distinct periods (see Porakishvili, 1970). (For a more detailed discussion of the teachings and history of the Dukhobor sect consult the excellent study by Woodcock and Avakumovich, 1968.) During the first formative period around the 1790s, followers were gathered locally among the peasants around Ekatarinoslav (now Dneprpetrovsk in the south-eastern Ukraine) and a little later in Tambov province (now RSFSR).

In the second period, under their leader Kapustin, dogma was decisively shaped, and a mass following was recruited from all over Russia. The radicalism and success of the sect drew upon it the anger of the Orthodox Church and the government, and persecution began. In 1802, however, the sect was given permission to settle its members in a compact community at the then uncolonised periphery of the empire, on the fertile soil of Melitopol district on the river Molochnaya or Milky Waters. Dukhobors from all over Russia migrated to the new home of the sect, and only small groups of Dukhobors remained outside the tightly organised and efficiently run sectarian theocracy. These were mainly Siberian and Far Eastern communities.

During the third period, in the Milky Waters community, Dukhobors attempted to put their teachings into practice, establishing communism of production and consumption. This experiment was largely successful and lasted for almost thirty years when social differentiation set in again.

The fourth period in their development was initiated by their forcible resettlement in 1841 in the unfertile and climatically inhospitable area high up in the Caucasus mountains at the Turkish border, now in the Tbilisi region of Georgia. Here the attempt at communitarian living was repeated, worked for a while, but eventually gave way again to economic differentiation. Internal strife about succession after the death of the childless leader Lukeriya Kalmykova led to schism, dividing the sect roughly along the lines of existing economic differentiation. The poorer majority of around 11,000 members formed what became known as the Large Party with Petr Verigin as its leader, while the richer elements of the community (around 2,000 members) formed the Small Party, led by Gubanov. The latter succeeded, with government support, in establishing themselves as the 'true' representatives of Dukhoborism and appropriated the considerable communal Dukhobor monetary fund. The members of the Large Party, having suffered injustice and persecution, became increasingly radical in both their economic organisation and their political responses to the Tsarist autocracy. Later, the Large Party split again giving rise to the Middle or Vorobev Party (named after its leader). When persecution of Dukhobors, especially of the Large Party, became increasingly intolerable at the end of the nineteenth century, Dukhobors decided to emigrate. After a short, disastrous attempt by a few thousand Dukhobors to settle in Cyprus, over 7,000 of them (mainly members of the Large Party) emigrated to Canada between 1898 and 1900. In 1909, according to Russian official sources, there were about 15,000 Dukhobors left in the whole of the Russian Empire, of which 13,000 were in the Caucasus (Woodcock and Avakumovic, 1968, p. 273).

The fifth period, for the Russian Dukhobors, was marked by calm and passivity after the departure of their more radical brethren, and the superior moral tone and conduct of the community became conspicuously lowered (see Bonch-

D

Bruevich's 1922 account of his visit to the sect at that time). The Canadian community, however, continued its social experiments and political confrontations. The 1917 October Revolution was greeted with initial joy and enthusiasm by most Dukhobors at home and abroad who hoped for greater tolerance and understanding from the new regime. By now the Russian Dukhobors had increased their number to almost 20,000 (Woodcock and Avakumovic, 1968, p. 277). The sixth and last period of Dukhobor history, the Soviet era, is of particular interest to us and must be reviewed in more detail. Unfortunately, documentation of events is only sketchy and almost non-existent for the 1937–59 period.

As the Bolsheviks did not succeed in establishing control in the Caucasian homeland of the Dukhobors until after the Civil War, the Dukhobor communities continued undisturbed well into the twenties. When the new regime penetrated into the Caucasus they proceeded very cautiously and tactfully against the Dukhobors. Lenin himself recommended a slower and more careful transfer to socialism in the Caucasus (Porakishvili, 1970, p. 113), and the local officials treated Dukhobors very generously in the early post-revolutionary years (ibid.). Although Dukhobors were sympathetic to the new regime they never contemplated giving up their theocracy in favour of the new social order which was being created in the Soviet Union. They rejected the introduction of socialist political and educational organisations into their communities and strongly opposed any state interference in their internal affairs. Thus a *Komsomol* (Young Communist) organisation had to stay underground until 1925 and remained very uninfluential until 1928 (ibid., pp. 117, 118). The attempt by the authorities in 1924 to take into public ownership the Dukhobor central monetary fund was met with such strong resistance that they had to give up their endeavour. Dukhobors also managed to keep the civil administration of their district and villages in their own hands, manning the local soviets completely with their own members (ibid., pp. 113, 118). Collectivisation was naturally also resisted, and by 1930 merely six poor farm households had been made into a collective farm. Only in 1937 did the majority of Dukhobors enter collective farms (ibid., p. 123). Dukhobor leaders clearly recognised the incompatibility of their religion with Soviet ideology and explained their unwillingness to join collective farms like this:

'As we, after the example of the Canadian Dukhobor-Communards, live in communal form [Russ. *obshchina-kommuna*] it means that we already have a collective farm, but we cannot enter into the collective farm suggested to us because we are religious people and love to work with thoughts about God and a prayer on our lips.' (Quoted by Malakhova, 1970, p. 75, from an undisclosed source)

Dissemination of atheist propaganda remained equally ineffectual. Propagandists were ill equipped to debate with the knowledgeable and committed Dukhobors. Their pre-revolutionary record of opposition to the autocracy, the suffering endured because of this, and the sympathy they had enjoyed from some Bolsheviks made atheist propaganda among them a politically delicate matter. Up to 1927 local authorities had not even dared to go among Dukhobors with atheist propaganda (Porakishvili, 1970, p. 130). Only after 1937, when collectivisation and the introduction of general education (in 1930) were accomplished, did

atheist propaganda make some headway. In this concerted and consistent resistance to sovietisation Dukhobors were more persistent and successful than their
Molokan neighbours (ibid., pp. 133–5). Unlike the Molokans, Dukhobors also
do not seem to have defected in large numbers to rival ascending religious sects
like the Baptists, although some defections occurred.

In the early 1930s the Soviet authorities realised that mere persuasion had not
succeeded in making Dukhobors surrender a single aspect of their separate sectarian existence (Druzhinin, 1930, p. 14). From 1930 onwards force was applied,
and large-scale imprisonment and exile of the more wealthy and influential
leaders broke the Dukhobor resistance and secured their entry into collective
farms (Porakishvili, 1970, p. 123). In the Caucasian village of Gorelovka alone
eighty families were sent into exile during that time (Woodcock and Avakumovic,
1968, p. 296). From then onwards the decline of Dukhobor exclusivity and
religious vitality was strong, although some losses in sectarian zeal and radicalism
were noted long before the Revolution. The Dukhobors outside the chief
Caucasian communities (consisting of eight villages) in Rostov region and the
Far East fared much less well and could not resist penetration by the non-
Dukhobor communists after 1929. Of the ten Dukhobor villages on the Amur,
for example, five disappeared completely between 1926 and 1932, and their total
population declined from 2,311 to 207 during that period (Putintsev, 1935,
p. 405, quoted by Woodcock and Avakumovic, 1968, p. 296). We have no
information on the development of Soviet Dukhobors for the period from the
late thirties to the late fifties.

At the time of writing, Dukhobors in Transcaucasia still exist as distinct and
compact communities. The picture emerging from the few scanty reports about
them suggest that they are now primarily a cultural-ethnic group with a distinct
material and spiritual culture, having a strongly developed sense of identity and
history. But their religious ideology and practice have become weakened to a
degree which makes it impossible to describe them any longer as a religious sect
in the sociological sense of the term. While in the first two decades after the
Revolution the Dukhobors jealously guarded their own traditions against sovietisation, today the impact of Soviet society on their way of life and religion has
been stronger than on most other sectarian communities. Evasion of collectivisation and avoidance of participation in Soviet social and political organisations is
never reported about them. Education, formerly thought unnecessary by them, is
now fully accepted and a relatively high percentage of young Dukhobors have full
middle (ten years) and even higher education (Malakhova, 1970, p. 76; Porakishvili, 1970, p. 127). Many are employed in government institutions. In 1966 twelve
Dukhobors received governmental decorations for special services at work
(Malakhova, 1970, p. 76). Religious belief is now only professed by an estimated
third of the Dukhobor population (ibid.), mainly by the middle-aged and old
semi-literate and illiterate among them (Porakishvili, 1970, p. 140, Table 6). The
Dukhobor secular ethic, their concern for equality, brotherhood and peace, has
become detached from its religious framework and has survived well to the
present day (Klibanov, 1969, p. 93). These values, which are consonant with
those of communist ideology, did not have to be surrendered in the contest
between Dukhobor religion and Soviet political ideology. Religious practice has
been more weakly preserved than belief. A Sunday service, attended by a Soviet
sociologist in 1968 in Gorelovka, the old centre of the sect, attracted thirty

people, twenty-five of them being women between 45 and 70 years of age (Klibanov, 1973, p. 57). Adherence to religious rites of passage, however, has been more persistent. Baptismal and funeral rites are still accepted by about half of all Dukhobors, even by many unbelievers (ibid., p. 58). It is interesting to note that the members of the Small Party – the religiously and socially *less* radical party at the time of schism – now take much greater pains to preserve the old Dukhobor rituals and traditions than do the followers of the Large Party who now emphasise the secular-ethical ideals more strongly (Fedorenko, 1965, p. 127). Unfortunately no comparative information is available about the smaller Dukhobor concentrations in Rostov region (RSFSR), Azerbaidzhan, Orenburg region (RSFSR), the Ukraine and in the Far East. It would have been interesting to see whether religious decline has gone even further in these geographically less insulated communities, as was the case for Molokans (see below).

The relatively wide-reaching secularisation of this once extremely radical sect has been due to two factors. The fact that the sect consisted of large compact communities maintaining themselves by agriculture made it impossible for its members to go into the anonymity and safety of the religious underground, despite their strong determination during the early Soviet period to resist soviet-isation. Once the Soviet authorities had broken down that initial resistance and had found ways and means to undermine Dukhobor religion, sovietisation was facilitated, as in the case of the Molokan sect, by the existing similarities between the Christian socialism of the Dukhobors and the political ideals and goals of the Soviet regime. It is likely that the Dukhobors would have resisted sovietisation more militantly and would have asserted their sectarianism more resolutely if the radical wing of the sect – the Large Party – had not been so decimated by emigra-tion to Canada. The sectarian militancy the *émigré* Dukhobors displayed in confrontations with the Canadian political authorities (see Woodcock and Avakumovic, 1968) has shown that the sectarian spirit was still strong in them and was not easily broken by government interference and changes in the wider society.

More insight about the factors both undermining and still sustaining the Old Russian sects can be gained from our study of the Molokan sect for which more adequate sociological data are available.

### THE MOLOKANS

The Molokan sect, one of the strongest and most influential in pre-revolutionary Russia, is today moving towards extinction. This process, however, has not gone equally far in different geographical areas of the Soviet Union. Here an attempt will be made to assess and explain the extent of both the sect's general decline and the differential rate in different communities.

*Religious and social responses in historical perspective*
The Molokan sect evolved out of the Dukhobor sect in the second half of the eighteenth century. The name Molokans or 'Milk-drinkers' had been given to the sect as a nickname by the Orthodox by 1765 because its members were said to have drunk milk during fast-time. The Molokans themselves deny this tale about the origin of their name and generally prefer to call themselves Spiritual Christians (Russ. *Dukhovnye Khristiane*). They grew up in opposition to the highly

ritualistic, liturgy-oriented and strictly hierarchical Orthodox Church and the feudal social order associated with the Church. They were essentially a rural and peasant sect, although, unlike the very similar Dukhobors, a significant proportion of their members were also merchants, industrialists and townsmen (Russ. *mesh-chane*). They first appeared in the heartland of the Old Russian sects, the provinces of Tambov and Voronezh, but quickly spread into the southern provinces and Volga areas. The centres of the sect developed into strong, relatively wealthy and enlightened communities. Religious persecution in the 1840s drove large numbers of them out of these provinces to the periphery of the empire into the Caucasus and to the Far East. They were keen and active proselytisers.

On the eve of the Russian Revolution, although already declining, they were still the largest and most widely spread Russian sect. One of their pre-revolutionary leaders estimated their number to be over a million in 1913 (N. F. Kudinov, *Dukhovnye Khristiane: Molokane*, p. 4, quoted in Klibanov, 1965, p. 181). This figure is also given by the well-known Bolshevik historian, Bonch-Bruevich, but A. Klibanov (1965), the most notable contemporary Soviet historian of sectarianism, regards this claim as far too high.

Internal dissent resulted in numerous schisms splitting the sect into a great number of branches. Some of the better-known ones are the Constant Molokans, the Priguny or Leapers, the Communist Molokans, the Molokans of the Don branch and, the most recent schismatic group, the Maksimisty. The Communist and Don Molokans were already disintegrating before the Revolution and are not mentioned in accounts of the contemporary sect.

Constant Molokans still adhere to the teaching of Simon Uklein, the sect's founder, and they form the largest part of the contemporary sect. The Leapers owe their name to the fact that they work themselves into religious ecstasy during which they start leaping about. Like Pentecostalists, they place great emphasis on the Holy Ghost who descends on the chosen. Leapers are still numerous today. Maksimisty, named after the founder and charismatic leader of the Leapers, Maksim Rudometkin, split off from the branch of the Leapers during the late 1920s.

The Molokans completely abandoned the Orthodox concern with liturgy and renounced nearly all ritual. Their belief that faith must prove itself by good deeds led them to renounce sacraments and icons as useless for the achievement of salvation. They hold meetings devoted solely to prayer, singing and sermons on moral and spiritual themes. They have rejected a hierarchical organisation and do not have any priests or churches. Their groups are led and generally administered by elders who evolve out of their midst. Any member of the community can address the congregation and put forward his interpretation of the Bible. This democratic sentiment flows from their idea that God's spirit enters every man equally. Their teaching is based on the Bible though, unlike the Western sects on Soviet soil, they do not take its content literally but allegorically. Their conception of God is the most distinguishing feature of their faith, shaping not only the other tenets of their dogma but also their whole outlook on man and society. They view God highly abstractly, as a supreme spiritual force, as the highest form of reason which can reside in any person. They believe in a trinitarian God but Christ does not appear to hold a very prominent place in their teaching.

The Molokan sect stands apart from most of the other sects in Soviet society by its different response to the world. While the sects of Western origin are, in Wilson's terms, either 'conversionist' (the Baptists and Pentecostalists) or 'revolutionist' (the Adventists and Jehovah's Witnesses) and the sects of Soviet origin mainly 'introversionist' or 'revolutionist', the Molokans can be said to belong to the 'utopian' type. Wilson stipulates the following characteristics for the 'utopian' type of sect: belief in the possibility of salvation in society; the re-making of existing social relations by *human* efforts working out God-given principles; and the withdrawal from society into spatially segregated communities to work out the social organisation for salvation (Wilson, 1970, p. 47). Molokans rejected the exploitative social relations of the feudal order and obeyed the Tsar only out of necessity, not from reverence. They believed that Molokans did not need worldly government and could best organise their communities themselves. In general, the Molokans do not express their hope for salvation in eschatological terms, but have a this-worldly orientation. Their belief that man can establish God's kingdom here on earth and their vision of the social conditions which would constitute such a kingdom, although based on the Bible, have strong political overtones. In fact, it is emphasised in the Soviet literature that Molokan groups are often more strongly united by their distinctive secular ethic than by narrowly religious orientations. But it is their conception of God which committed them to the socio-political values of equality, brotherhood, pacifism, the use and development of human reason, and self-perfection through work. They hold that because the supreme spiritual force resides in every man, then all men must be equally capable of good. Thus all are deemed worthy to live and it is sinful to kill.

Before Soviet policy made it impossible, Molokans formed their spatially segregated, though not isolated, communities in which they attempted to live according to their beliefs. These principles were rigorously applied only during the short-lived experiment in communal living of the Communist Molokans. The Dukhobors were much more serious in their quest for social equality. In most communities during the long history of the Molokan sect, social equality remained just a cherished ideal from which their practice departed considerably. Social differentiation in Molokan villages was marked, and the richer Molokans used their wealth to secure religious influence. Nevertheless, when exploitation of economic and religious privilege by sect leaders became pronounced, the ideal of equality was invoked and attempts to restore the balance were made. Often conflict would break out over the violation of the equality principle, especially when the mood in the wider society supported it, such as at the time of the 1905 Revolution. (See the rebellious words cited by Klibanov, 1965, p. 174, from a 1906 Molokan journal.) Other socio-political values were more successfully realised, especially the 'brotherhood' principle. No Molokan ever had to face economic ruin, for help from fellow believers to those in material distress was always forthcoming.

Their communities, although sometimes insulated from the rest of society (in the Caucasus, for example) were never isolated from it. They did not set themselves apart from the rest of society as other sects usually described as 'utopian'. Although the Molokans naturally considered their type of social organisation superior to that of their feudal social environment, the drive to impose their social principles on the rest of society does not appear to have been highly developed. In these two respects they do thus depart somewhat from Wilson's 'utopian' type and resemble more the 'reformist' type. But unlike sects of that type they have not agitated for piecemeal reform but have envisaged a basic transformation of society according to Christian principles.

The Molokan sect also has another significant attribute to which Wilson has not given great emphasis in his description of the 'utopian' type. It is most congruent with this type as it emphasises its political leanings (i.e. reliance on human power in the reorganisation of social conditions). Molokans have great faith in human reason. They do not believe that man is powerless by himself and has to put his fate entirely into God's hands, but exalt the human power of reason. They are convinced that man can perfect himself morally and intellectually and shape his own environment. This conviction has turned Molokans into strong advocates of education and scientific and technological progress. This characteristic manifested itself in pre-revolutionary times in the founding of such Molokan ventures as the Society of Educated Molokans and Kudinov's Progressive Movement around the time of the 1905 Revolution. The former sought to bring science and Molokan religion into harmony by disregarding the authority of the Bible in all matters conflicting with science. Among Kudinov's many progressive objectives was the raising of the educational level of all Molokans at a time when education was still the privilege of a few (for details, see Klibanov, 1965, pp. 175–7).

Such a short summary of a long and involved period of Molokan history is bound to be somewhat oversimplified. Changing social circumstances, schisms of some sections of the sect and embourgeoisement of others meant frequent deviations from dogma and secular ethic which cannot adequately be covered here. The above outline of the Molokans' belief system is thus best seen as that adhered to with varying degrees of fervour by the mainstream of the sect.

With the assumption of Soviet power in 1917 and the subsequent radical restructuring of society, Molokans were forced to readjust their response to the world. The Bolsheviks, although opposed in principle to all religious currents, were very sympathetic towards the rationalist religious sects at the time of the Revolution. Some even admired the way that they ran their communities and hoped that they would stimulate a general socialist transformation of the countryside. This sympathy on the part of some and toleration on the part of others continued for a number of years after the Revolution. In the euphoria and chaos of the immediate post-revolutionary period a number of new Molokan communes developed, and the sect in general flourished. This period of friendly-to-tolerant coexistence finished in the late twenties (Klibanov, 1965, p. 250) when the closing of Molokan communes began. What had caused this change in state–sect relations?

Even Soviet writers acknowledge that from the beginning the Molokan sect had had a very positive attitude towards the Soviet state and the socio-political transformation it had effected. Molokans did not regard socialism as a rival to their own belief but saw a great compatibility between the two. They hailed the new social order as an expression of the Molokan values of equality, brotherhood and intellectual progress. Leaders urged their followers to support the new regime with all their strength; communities gave generously of their funds and proceeds and bestowed on their communes high-sounding socialist names. The only friction between the political and the religious forces was the Molokan refusal to take up arms against the regime's enemies. But this friction was not

serious enough to jeopardise relations to the extent to which they deteriorated after 1926. The reason for the change has to be sought in the political
leadership's new policy for the transformation of the countryside (Wesson,
1963, p. 76).

By the end of the twenties the Soviet government had come to the conclusion
that the only effective path of agricultural development lay in the setting-up of
collective and state farms. Communes, they decided, were not very efficient
economically, nor did they create the brand of socialist consciousness the political
leaders favoured. Sectarian communes, however economically successful individually, were now discouraged, and Molokans were urged to join collective farms.
It becomes obvious from the sources that compulsion was used in certain cases
to dissolve sectarian communes (Kozlova, 1966, p. 306; Klibanov, 1965, p. 250).
It remains unclear whether compulsion was a consistent policy in all areas, or
whether some communes just died a natural death in the economic competition
with collective farms.

One source (Tul'tseva, 1969, p. 207) intimates that the destruction of sectarian communes did not occur mainly for economic reasons but seemed to be
directed against the ideological threat a consolidated Molokan community posed.
Tul'tseva mentions a Molokan application to transform their commune into an
exclusively Molokan collective farm. This was refused and communards were
forced to merge with non-religious peasants into a collective farm. Although
many Molokans complied with the collectivisation order, others did for the first
time develop hostility towards the Soviet regime and put up stiff resistance. They
would rather leave the land and work in the towns than join collective farms
(Bograd, 1961, p. 116; Kozlova, 1966, p. 306). One group in Armenia, for
example, adopted a particularly intransigent attitude towards the Soviet regime.
It split off from the main body of the sect over this issue and formed a new
schismatic group – the Maksimisty.

But whether compulsory or voluntary, this driving of Molokans into collective
farms dealt a grave blow to the sect (see the detailed account by Iskrinskii (1932)
about the effect of collectivisation on Molokan and other sectarian groups in the
northern Caucasus). It is impossible to determine to what extent the ensuing
decrease in membership was due to geographical dislocation, with its attendant
disruption of religious communities, and to what extent it was due to religious
disillusionment caused by increased contact with the alternative world-views
offered by both the new Western sects and the Communist Party. Many writers
point out that the revolutionary fervour and the class conflict in the wider society
at the time of both the Revolution and collectivisation deeply affected the social
climate in Molokan communities. The poorer strata in the community became
aware of their inferior economic status, and class conflict disturbed communities
everywhere. New branches were formed, or many left the sect entirely during
this time, especially the younger sectarians (see, for example, Bograd, 1961, p. 115;
Tul'tseva, 1969, pp. 202, 205). It has to be pointed out, however, that defecting
Molokans did not all become unbelievers but, as many authors show, turned in
large numbers to the Baptist sect which was coming into prominence after the
Revolution (Morozov, 1931). In Ryazan region (RSFSR), for example, whole
Molokan villages went over to the Baptists (Zlobin, 1963, p. 96).

Many adherents were lost during this time although the process of decline had
already begun before collectivisation. Statistics collected by Soviet social scientists

show conclusively that the originally large Molokan communities in the central Russian areas and in the Far East declined drastically during the Soviet period, both in the early post-revolutionary years and during postwar time (Aleksandrovich, Kandaurov and Nemirovskii, 1961, p. 59; Malakhova, 1961, pp. 80, 100; Bograd, 1961, p. 59; Sosnina, 1962, p. 14; Tul'tseva, 1969, p. 204; Klibanov, 1972, p. 54). Although we have no comparable pre- and post-collectivisation figures for the Armenian and Georgian communities, it becomes clear from the sources that the loss in numbers in these areas was not nearly as severe as in the central Russian regions. The communities in Georgia's northern Caucasus still had about ten thousand members at the end of the twenties (Klibanov, 1965, p. 240), and a Georgian comunity studied by Zolotova in 1962 had lost hardly any members during the preceding twenty-five years, but had even had a revival after the centenary celebrations in 1953 (Zolotova, 1962, pp. 151, 158). The Armenian communities studied by Kozlova in 1963/4, although alleged to have been losing members, were all still viable in numbers.

There is no evidence to suggest that the continuing decrease in numbers since the period of collectivisation is due to any policy of persecution by the political authorities. Due to the greater degree of compatibility of communist ideology with the Molokan secular ethic than with other sectarian world-views, there have been few areas of friction and consequently there has been little need to interfere in the internal life of religious communities. The 1970 register of civil rights prisoners, listing members from nearly every religious group, does not mention one Molokan. Why then, have they nevertheless continued to decline? An examination of the more detailed data on socio-demographic characteristics and socio-political responses of Molokan communities in the early sixties will provide us with an answer to this question.

*Socio-demographic distribution and social composition*
Information about contemporary Molokan groups is uneven. While there are detailed studies about some central Russian and two Caucasian centres and more scanty data about other Caucasian groups and the Far Eastern community, there is none at all on the remaining communities. After giving a short general overview of Molokanism in the Soviet Union today we shall focus on the central Russian communities and the Caucasian groups in Tbilisi (Georgia) and in an Armenian village. One author estimates that the number of Molokans in the Soviet Union today is about 13,000 (Malakhova, 1968, p. 13). Only Constant Molokans, Leapers and Maksimisty are mentioned in the literature, but the existence of small groups of other branches in some areas must not be excluded. Constant Molokans still seem to be the largest branch, and Maksimisty only a very small group. Maksimisty have not only taken over the name of the legendary Leaper leader Rudometkin but also most of his early teaching (the Leapers themselves have abandoned it). They differ considerably from other Molokans, extolling suffering and emphasising eschatological ideas (Zolotova, 1962, p. 154). Constant Molokan communities are registered with the Soviet authorities, while Leapers and Maksimisty are illegal. The practice of leaping about during moments of religious ecstasy is regarded as a risk to health, while the Maksimisty are held to be politically hostile.

Besides the groups that form the main subject of this paper, there are large groups in the republic of Azerbaidzhan, the autonomous northern Osetian republic and smaller ones in the Ukraine, the Orenburg region, Turkmenistan, the Far East, Siberia and Moldavia. In Azerbaidzhan the biggest community in 1960 was in its capital, Baku. Its prayer meetings are said to have attracted between 200 and 300 Molokans. Besides this registered community there were also unregistered groups of Leapers and Maksimisty in Baku as well as many smaller groups of all branches outside the capital (Gladkov and Korytin, 1961, pp. 33–40). In the northern Osetian ASSR there was a large community in Ordzhonikidze (Zolotova, 1962, p. 157). In Turkmenistan's capital, Ashkhabad, around fifty people attended prayer meetings in the early sixties, the overwhelming majority being female and old. A similar picture is drawn about the town Mary (Chiperis, 1964, pp. 75–7). One Molokan is quoted as summing up the fate of Molokanism in Turkmenistan in the following words: 'Our fathers and forefathers were Molokans and so are we. We have very little left, we are living out our last days. When we die, Molokanism also dies' (ibid., p. 79). Outside the Caucasus, the community in Blagoveshchensk already mentioned also consisted mainly of old and female members in 1960 (Sosnina, 1962, p. 15). We have no information about any other communities.

The four studies (three sociological, one ethnographic) of Molokan (probably Constant Molokans) communities in Tambov and Voronezh regions (RSFSR) all show a similar picture of decline: small communities of predominantly elderly and female members with little renewal from within and none at all from outside the community's families. Thus in 1959 in the whole of Tambov region there were left only 330 Molokans spread over five rural districts and two towns (Malakhova, 1961, p. 99). In the Rasskasov town congregation, for example, 80 per cent of members were elderly or old (ibid., p. 100), and in the Michurinsk town community of twenty-eight members 86 per cent were over 50 years old and only two members were under 40. All were hereditary Molokans (Bograd, 1961, p. 117). When the Tambov region study was repeated in 1971 decline had advanced even further. By then 90 per cent of Molokans in this area were over 60 years of age, the nucleus of the sect being formed by the over-70 year olds (Klibanov, 1972, p. 54). In Voronezh region only two of the ten pre-revolutionary communities were left during the 1960s. Those studied in 1966 had both only around thirty members each (Tul'tseva, 1969, pp. 209, 210). In both groups the majority of members were old and mainly retired. The rural group had not even any longer a preacher and had received no new recruits during the last twenty years (ibid., p. 210). Thus in terms of both structure and dynamics of membership the Molokan sect in its traditional homeland differs strongly from the newer sects of Western origin in this area. These all have a higher percentage of younger members and are more successful in recruiting new members both from within and outside the sectarian community. They have consequently been able to keep membership figures much more stable than Molokans in the RSFSR. Molokans of this area also differ from other sectarians in two other respects. A much higher percentage of their working members are employed in industrial production (Malakhova, 1961, p. 102) and, although having a low formal educational attainment, members (especially male ones) have both an impressive informal education and high educational aspirations for their children. In none of the numerous studies of the Western sects in Russia have such wide cultural attainment and high educational aspirations ever been attributed to members. On the contrary, the lack of them is generally bemoaned.

The two very thorough and detailed studies of the Molokan sect in Georgia and Armenia reveal stronger and more stable Molokan communities, although some socio-demographic trends are similar. Thus in Georgia there are still over 3,300 registered 'Constant' Molokans and about 500 Leapers, the illegal Molokan branch. In Tbilisi (Georgia's capital) alone there were in 1961 five congregations with 1,742 members between them (Zolotova, 1962, pp. 156, 157). In Armenia there were still communities in seven villages (ibid.). In the Armenian village studied by Kozlova there were in 1964 a community of Leapers with 269 members, a 110-strong group of Constant Molokans, and a group of 55 Maksimisty (Kozlova, 1966, p. 307). Unlike the central Russian communities the Caucasian ones have managed to keep membership at a fairly stable level by renewing themselves from members' children (Zolotova, 1962, p. 157). But they, too, have not attracted any outsiders into the community (Kozlova, 1966, p. 361). As the average age of their members was lower than that of central Russian Molokans extinction is not an immediate threat.

Renewal from within, however, is gradually becoming less reliable. Although Molokans have close extended families and live in tight-knit communities the religious influence of the older generation over the younger one has been waning. Marriage out of the community was becoming accepted in some of the Armenian groups (Kozlova, 1966, p. 310), and the relatively high educational achievement encouraged in Molokan children often estranges them from the traditional way of life of the religious community (Kozlova, 1966, p. 316). This process was very noticeable in the Tbilisi communities where over 70 per cent of members were over 50 years of age and those under 30 came to only 3·2 per cent (Zolotova, 1962, p. 156). In the Armenian communities the age structure was still much healthier with the middle aged (between 30 and 50 years) and the young (up to 30 years) still predominating in numbers (Kozlova, 1966, p. 308). But the process was not uniform in the three Armenian communities studied. Kozlova's interesting comparison of Molokans of three different schismatic groups – Constant Molokans, Leapers and Maksimisty – shows that the group of Constant Molokans had much less vitality than the other two and was similar in age structure to its Georgian counterpart. The Maksimisty, with 41·9 per cent of their members under 30 years of age, were the most thriving group while the Leapers fell halfway between the other two (ibid.). Kozlova's data on the occupational position of Molokans reveal that there is a very high percentage of collective farmers in the communities of the Constant Molokans and Leapers but none among the Maksimisty (ibid.). Unfortunately Zolotova does not provide us with any data on occupation, but the largely urban character of her sample makes it unlikely that many are collective farmers.

On their own all these socio-demographic data give us little explanation of either the general decline of Molokanism or the differential rates of decline in various geographical areas. The tempting hypothesis that central Russian and Georgian communities have declined more than the Armenian ones because of their urban and non-agricultural character does not hold when confronted with the case of the Maksimisty. In this most thriving community there is not a single collective farmer and 52·7 per cent of members work in industrial production in the town of Dilizhan (Kozlova, 1966, p. 308). To gain a feasible explanation we have to interpret these data in conjunction with information on socio-political responses of Molokans to their Soviet environment.

*Religious and social orientations of contemporary Molokans*

Molokan religious dogma, with its this-worldly orientation and its image of man as capable of moral and intellectual self-improvement, has resulted in a distinctive and influential secular ethic. The very similarity of their ethical postulates to some of the tenets of the Soviet communist moral code has made it much easier for Molokans than for adherents to other religious beliefs to welcome the basic objective of a socialist society; the harnessing of man's powers to the creation of a society where equality, brotherhood and material and intellectual progress reign. How does all this manifest itself? Unlike many other sectarians, Molokans do not strive to withdraw from worldly affairs but are concerned to involve themselves actively in them. Despite their low level of formal education Molokan men avidly read literary and political classics as well as newspapers, and take a keen interest in national and international politics and in the progress of science and technology (Kozlova, 1966, p. 311; Tul'tseva, 1969, p. 216). Elders include information about current affairs in their sermons (Kozlova, 1966; Bograd, 1961, p. 139). Parents try to give their children middle or higher education (Kozlova, 1966, p. 316). In interviews many Molokans stressed the great similarity between communist and Molokan ideals and credited the Soviet state with having realised many objectives of Molokan religion (Bograd, 1961, p. 118; Malakhova, 1961, p. 103). The achievements of Soviet society are praised in sermons, and communist holidays are keenly observed. Molokan respect of Soviet power also manifests itself in observance of laws on religion. They do not proselytise outside their communities (Zolotova, 1962, p. 157) and usually do not deny the state the right to their children's moral education by keeping them away from youth organisations (ibid.) as many other sectarians do. Molokans have a positive work attitude and work for the good of society (Tul'tseva, 1969, p. 216). They are tolerant towards non-Molokans and practise neighbourly help by giving material support to people both inside and outside their own communities (ibid., p. 217; Kozlova, 1966, pp. 317, 318).

All these attitudes and modes of behaviour are ascribed to Molokans both in the central Russian regions and the Caucasian republics, but they do not characterise all the branches of Molokanism to the same extent. As Kozlova shows, this characterisation applies most strongly to the Constant Molokans. Of them she says that 'they try with all their might to adjust their religion to contemporary Soviet life' and that their children are just like any other Soviet children being represented among the town's Party and scientific workers, teachers and engineers (Kozlova, 1966, pp. 315, 316). All this applies with less force to the Priguny and not at all to the small and recent schismatic group of Maksimisty. The Maksimisty try to keep themselves completely apart from the political, social and cultural life of their Soviet environment. They have a much less favourable attitude to their worldly masters and concentrate all their energy on the internal life of their religious community. Here strict discipline is demanded from members and their children (Kozlova, 1966, p. 316).

These patterns of socio-political responses are accompanied in each community by definite patterns of religious vitality. The Constant Molokans – the group most adjusted and attuned to Soviet life – are facing an organisational decline reflected in the age structure, can rely only on a weak religious commitment and discipline in the community, and have become very flexible in the interpretation of their religious dogma. The Maksimisty, however – the group most hostile to Soviet values and practices – have remained most vital organisationally (41·9 per cent of their members are under 30 years of age), can call on a committed and disciplined congregation, and they take a completely orthodox stand on matters of Molokan dogma. The Leapers – the branch taking a middle position between Constant Molokans and Maksimisty in their secular life – occupy also a halfway position as far as their religious life is concerned.

This definite pattern of an inverse relationship between positive socio-political involvement and religious vitality does offer us a clue to the understanding of the general decline of Molokanism in the Soviet Union. It is the very progressiveness of the Molokan secular ethic, the very similarity between it and some postulates of the communist ethic, which have led to the failure of its religious ideology. By propagating the idea that the Soviet powers are putting into practice Molokan religious principles, Molokanism has made itself superfluous. Molokanism in general no longer presents an alternative to people who have rejected the dominant ideology. This is why Molokanism flourished in Tsarist times when it provided the perfect alternative to both the dominant religious and secular ideologies, but now fails to attract any new members from outside its own communities. Those looking for an alternative world-view will now turn to the sects of Western origin (see Chapter 8). Even as far as internal recruitment of new members is concerned the sect's social and cultural progressiveness have had negative repercussions. By granting their children the opportunity for middle and higher education and by exercising leniency with regard to their extra-community activities in political youth organisations, they have lost many of them as community members.

Yet the sect has retained a large number of its old members and gained, with varying success, some new members from among their children. It has been able to do this because it still offers one thing to its members that cannot so easily be found in the wider society: community and a sense of brotherhood manifesting themselves in mutual material and moral support. A quotation from a Molokan elder sums up this community spirit very well: 'Whether it is night or day, whether I am sleeping or awake, if some joy or misfortune happens [in the community], they call me, and I go to read to them [Bible words fitting the occasion]' (Kozlova, 1966, p. 318). Kozlova points out that this certainty of receiving brotherly help and sympathy keeps members in the community even when their faith has gone (ibid.).

But as pointed out above, adaptation to the reality of Soviet life has gone equally far among the groups in the central Russian regions as among the groups in the Caucasian republics, excepting only the Maksimisty. How then is one to explain the differential rate of decline in the two geographical areas? An explanation must be sought in the type of community the groups in different parts of the Soviet Union were able to preserve. Molokans in pre- and early postrevolutionary years lived in compact, spatially segregated communities all over Russia. While none of them isolated themselves from the wider society, some were much more insulated from it than others and thus withstood the impact of sovietisation much better. The Caucasian Molokans were situated in mountain-surrounded republics the territory of which had been taken into the Russian Empire relatively late in its history. The groups in the heartland of Russia were not protected against disruption by barriers of an ethnic or geographical kind as those in the Caucasus must have been. Molokan communities in the Caucasus have been surrounded by ethnic groups of a different culture and language and, through years of isolation and intermarriage, became known as a separate ethnic group. Molokans in the RSFSR, however, have found it much harder to keep their identity when merged into collective farms with other non-Molokan Russians. This is confirmed by Porakishvili who points out that Dukhobor and Molokan communities in Georgia in the 1920s kept themselves completely apart from the surrounding Armenians and would not accept in their midst any propagandist from among them (1971, p. 113). The central Russian Molokans were more exposed not only to communist ideology but also to the beliefs of other sects, notably those of the Baptists. Also the various decrees concerning collectivisation were implemented more quickly and more effectively in the Molokan communities near the political centre than in those on the political periphery. Lenin's advice to effect the transfer to socialism more cautiously in the Caucasus seems to have been heeded. Authorities in these areas did not enforce the laws on religion for a long time and did not even like to propagate atheist ideas among the Spiritual Christians there. In a 1927 Georgian Party document the following complaint appears: 'Up to now the local administration has looked upon the sectarians [Dukhobors and Molokans] as a special kind of people and have not dared to go among them to conduct anti-religious propaganda' (quoted in Porakishvili, 1970, p. 130). Thus it seems likely that the communities in Georgia and Armenia managed to consolidate themselves again in the time between the initial disruption caused by the Revolution and the full impact of Soviet economic and social policies in the mid-thirties.

To sum up, the Molokan sect in Soviet Russia has experienced a general decline because it no longer provides an alternative to that offered by the communist socio-political environment both on the ideological plane and on the level of community organisation. Molokans have not only ceased to protest against the political and social order but have also surrendered their claim to a distinctive philosophy of life. Molokans have declared most of the tenets of their religion to be coterminous with the socio-political and moral values in the dominant communist ideology. The sect has ceased to remain a haven for all those in search of an alternative belief system. In support of this conclusion is the fact that the most successful religious organisations (in terms of retaining old and attracting new, especially younger members) in the Soviet Union today are those which have not fully adjusted to Soviet reality or have even come out in opposition to some of its features. It is to these sects that people in search of an alternative ethic now turn.

Sects of the 'utopian' type are likely to develop in one of two ways. Either they break up quickly because life in a sectarian community of this type is too exacting. Or they turn to cultivate community for its own sake rather than as a model for the reorganisation of the wider society, and thus adopt an 'introversionist' response to the world. The Molokans, except for the small schismatic group of Maksimisty who have become as 'introversionist' as Soviet society would permit, have followed neither pattern. They are gradually disintegrating, not because they have surrendered their faith, but because utopia, in their estimation, has been realised by political means. Because socialist society, for many Molokans, has put into practice most principles of their faith, they have abandoned their protest stance and are largely continuing their 'sectarian' existence by the force of tradition.

That principle of the Molokan ethic which the sect has not fully surrendered – the provision of brotherhood and neighbourly love in a close-knit community – has become more and more difficult to implement. This is happening partly because Molokans themselves have never isolated themselves but have accepted social values, e.g. involvement in the wider society, high educational achievement, which tend to work against the establishment of a tight-knit traditional community. It is also due to the fact that the wider society does not tolerate communities based on other belief systems, even if they are as sympathetic to the dominant ideology as Molokan religion is. This loss of community has been much slower for the more remote and better-insulated groups in the Caucasian republics. But with time even these groups will have to give up their distinctive identities and become fully assimilated by their Soviet surroundings. The Molokan sect is therefore likely to continue its slide towards extinction.

# Chapter 6

# Old Believers

'Old Believers' is the collective name for a large group of extremely divergent religious organisations which developed out of a religious current dating from the middle of the seventeenth century. Although Old Believers are the second biggest contemporary Russian religious group and have played an important part in the development of pre-revolutionary Russian society, they have been studied relatively little both inside and outside the Soviet Union. In the West, studies of contemporary Old Belief amount to only a few extremely sketchy and limited descriptions covering the period up to about 1963 (Kolarz, 1962, ch. 4; the postscript to Hauptmann's book (1963); Struve, 1967, ch. 10). In the Soviet Union Old Believers are not only relatively poorly researched but are also rarely the focus of militantly atheist concern. Their neglect by Western scholars must be due to a variety of factors: to a paucity of Soviet primary sources as well as to an almost complete lack of *samizdat* literature on them, to the absence of contact between Old Believer organisations and Western churches, and to the confusing complexity of this religious movement, due to its great internal differentiation. Soviet scholars and atheist activists, in addition, probably feel less urgency to focus their attention on Old Believers because in general they consist of inward-looking, highly privatised religious groups which, with a few notable exceptions, appear to pose little challenge to the official ideology and provide little scope for the zeal of atheist fieldworkers. Here we shall examine, as far as the data permit, details of their recent development, of their organisational set-up and social composition and, most important, of their religious and socio-political orientations. This will show whether the relatively relaxed Soviet stance towards Old Believers is based on a correct estimation of the relation between Old Belief and Soviet society.

## HISTORICAL DEVELOPMENT AND PRESENT TRENDS

Old Believers originated in 1666 when several minor changes in the performance of ritual actions and service books initiated by Patriarch Nikon precipitated a major division in the Russian Orthodox Church. Those opposing these changes became known as Old Believers and, led by Protopop Avvakum, went into schism. The opposition to Nikon's changes was not so much founded on the conviction of the immutable sacredness of each small detail of ritual but was directed against the general spirit in which these changes were initiated. These changes were motivated by the Patriarch's desire to bring Russian Orthodox ritual practice into line with the Greek pattern and amounted in the eyes of many believers to a voluntary surrender of Russian religious independence from Constantinople. More important, these changes were imposed in a very autocratic manner at a time when the lower clergy felt that the upper clergy was encroaching on their rights and generally oppressing them. Old Believers, by opposing Nikon's changes, thus asserted patriotic and democratic values against the increasing autocracy of the Church hierarchy. The following quotation from an early Old Believer leader will illustrate the democratic impulses of the Dissenters:

'We recognize a single head, the Lord Jesus Christ, and as directors of the Church we recognize such bishops as will govern it not as autocrats, but in accordance with the rules of the holy councils; not applying the holy canons merely at their good pleasure, but in accordance with conciliary councils; not applying the holy canons merely at their good pleasure, but in accordance with conciliary deliberations concerning them . . .' (Hegumen Parthenius, *The Spiritual Word*, pp. 27–44, quoted by Conybeare, 1962, p. 150)

Differences over aspects of dogma were not involved.

The more independent-minded and oppositional elements among the Russian peasantry saw the new religious movement as a unique opportunity to express their protest not only against the Church but also against the autocratic rule of the Tsar who backed the Patriarch and, at the same time, to achieve a degree of internal democracy. The new schismatic movement (Russ. *raskol*) soon gained a large following and became a serious challenger to the established church. Religious differentiation went hand in hand with greater social differentiation. Many peasant Old Believers became prosperous merchants and small- and large-scale industrialists. Thus Old Believers posed a challenge to both the religious and the social establishment and were declared illegal and, at times, harshly persecuted. Respite from persecution was gained only a few times during several centuries, particularly under Catherine the Great. The constant persecution and resulting isolation drove Old Believers into increasing religious fanaticism. Old Belief became associated with extreme asceticism, other-worldliness, isolationism and religious sacrifice, in some cases going as far as collective suicide by the burning alive of the whole community. Only after the 1905 tolerance edict did they gain legal status although many of their members had, by then, already gained wealth and prestige in their worldly affairs.

Not long after schism from the Orthodox Church, in the 1690s, Old Believers were rent by internal disputes and divided again. The two resulting basic currents were the Popovtsy and the Bespopovtsy, i.e. those having priests (popular Russ. *pop*) and the Priestless. Not long afterwards, these, in turn, split into numerous branches, especially the Priestless. While before the Revolution there were more than thirty different branches of Old Believers, today there are no more than ten left (Katunsky, 1972, p. 46).

Old Believers in general are legally recognised in the contemporary Soviet Union, although many of the smaller groups do not conform to the Soviet law demanding registration of religious organisations with the local political authority. Only the extreme group of True Orthodox Christian Wanderers (see below) are considered political enemies and are therefore illegal.

Although there are tremendous differences between the different Old Believer branches, which sociologically span a wide spectrum from radical sect to conservative church, they possess some common distinguishing features. As the literal translation of their Russian name Staroobryadtsy – 'Old Ritualists' – indicates, they are united by extreme traditionalism in their relation to religious ritual, by a dedication to the preservation of Orthodox ritual in its pre-Nikonian form.

Like all religious organisations of Russian origin, Old Believers have declined since the Revolution. Although figures on both pre-revolutionary and present-day membership are extremely vague and impossible to verify, they do illustrate this decline clearly enough. Other qualitative information (see below) also supports such a conclusion. Pre-revolutionary statements of membership are not dependable because the 1897 state census underestimated the strength of the illegal religious rival to the established church, and nationwide research of the size of this far-flung religious current by sympathetic scholars was difficult without state support. Thus estimates of Old Believer membership at the eve of the Revolution vary between just over 2 million (this figure includes all other sects) in the 1897 census, 9 million (Putintsev, 1928, p. 5) and 20 million in 1922 (Bonch-Bruevich, 1959, pp. 174–5). This latter estimate is also supported by the well-informed American scholar Conybeare (1962, p. 248) whose work is based on research in Russia on the eve of the Revolution. Bespopovtsy, according to the last reliable detailed Russian statistics in 1880, far outnumbered Popovtsy (Uzov, quoted in Conybeare, 1962, p. 246).

By the 1960s, according to Soviet scholars, the numerical strength of Old Believers is supposed to have dwindled to only 1 million (Fedorenko, 1965, p. 102; Milovidov, 1966, p. 203). The estimates are not accompanied by a definition of membership. My guess is that, like Orthodox Church membership figures, they are based on church attendance. But, as will be shown below, church attendance alone is not a reliable indicator of religious commitment among Old Believers and would tend to underestimate it. Furthermore, the Soviet figures must even be an underestimate of church attendance as the Church of the Belokrinitsa convention alone, according to Western observers, is supposed to have had 1 million adherents in the early sixties (Hauptmann, 1966, p. 272; Struve, 1967, p. 220). Even if this latter figure is an overestimate, membership (based on attendance) of the Belokrinitsa Church together with those of the Beglopopovtsy and the most numerous Bespopovtsy must surely far exceed 1 million. The few available statistics for individual geographical areas do not permit a reliable estimate of overall membership. But the fact that such sparsely populated areas as the Komi ASSR and the Udmurt ASSR are inhabited by 2,300 and 1,000 Old Believers respectively (Gagarin, 1971, p. 98; Ivonin, 1973, p. 18) does tend to support an overall membership figure in excess of 1 million.

Even if the exact extent of an overall decline in membership cannot be ascertained, the fact of a drastic loss of adherents during Soviet time cannot be denied. Such a numerical decline is shown by many field studies of most Old Believer settlement areas (*Prichiny* . . ., 1963, p. 38; Milovidov, 1963, pp. 126, 127 for Ryazan region/RSFSR; Kogan, 1964, p. 40 for the Zabaikal area/Buryat ASSR; *Prichiny* . . ., 1965, p. 159 for the Belorussian centres; Gagarin, 1971, p. 99 for the Komi ASSR). Only the Latvian Old Believer communities have been relatively stable in recent years (Podmazov, 1970a and 1970b). Milovidov sees this decline of membership as having started already in the twenties, increased in tempo in the thirties, halted in the forties and fifties and resumed again in the sixties

(Milovidov, 1969, pp. 88, 89). A study of sects in Siberia locates the most drastic decline of Old Believers in the decade following the Revolution when Siberian Old Believers declined from 26,000 to 8,700 members. Many are said to have defected to the rapidly growing Protestant sects (Kostenko, 1967, p. 10). But the decline has not affected the different currents evenly and is least strong among Bespopovtsy (Simon, 1970, p. 118).

We now turn to a description of the separate branches and outline their recent development. As little is known in the West about Old Believers, the description of them will be a little longer than for other religious groups in order to help the reader gain a picture of this religious current before proceeding to the discussing of sociological issues. The latter will consist of an examination of their socio-political orientations, social composition and religious commitment.

*The Popovtsy*
The Popovtsy are divided into three branches: the Old Believer Church of the Belokrinitsa Hierarchy, the Old Believer Church of the Ancient Orthodox Christians or the *Beglopopovtsy*, and the *Edinovertsy*.

Of the Popovtsy, the Belokrinitsa Church has always been and still is by far the most important in terms of numerical strength and influence. In recent times, it has even extended its influence at the expense of the Beglopopovtsy (Katunsky, 1972, p. 58). It contains about half of *all* Old Believers today. As its name suggests, this current of Old Believers considers itself to be a church and has, indeed, most of the characteristics of a 'church'-type organisation. It was founded in 1846 in the Bosnian Belokrinitsa monastery by the adoption of its own archbishop (rather than of a runaway Orthodox priest). Today it is still headed by an archbishop under whom serve several bishops and around a hundred priests. It has no training institute for new priests, and most of the existing ones are old and poorly educated (Katunsky, 1972, p. 95). New priests are, as a rule, chosen from among believers familiar with church tradition and regulations. They are given a short course of instruction and are consecrated by the laying on of hands (Milovidov, 1966, p. 211). From the Orthodox Church it is set apart today mainly by its different tradition and its continued adherence to some small details of pre-Nikonian ritual and cultic objects, while cult in general, dogma and the structure of its hierarchy hardly differ. The Orthodox Church officially recognised the Belokrinitsa Church in 1971, and the latter is the only Old Believer organisation maintaining permanent relations with the Orthodox Church, the old spiritual enemy. In some areas, members have been seen visiting Orthodox churches and vice versa (Milovidov, 1966, p. 221). In fact, a reunion of the two at some future date is not inconceivable.

The spiritual centre of the Church is in Moscow (Rogozhskii cemetery) from where the five eparchies with their between 100 and 150 churches are administered (Milovidov, 1969, p. 95; Fedorenko, 1965, p. 104; Simon, 1970, p. 118). The Church has its adherents mainly among Russians in the European part of the Soviet Union – in the RSFSR (Moscow and Volga regions, Don, Kuban, north Caucasus and the south-western regions), the Ukraine (Vinnitsa, Odessa, Kirovograd and Chernigov regions), and in Moldavia, but has also a few congregations in other parts. The majority of Belokrinitsa Popovtsy are concentrated in and around Moscow and in the Gorky area where there are still compact Old Believer settlements (*Prichiny* . . ., 1963, p. 36; Milovidov, 1969, p. 95), but even a remote area like the Udmurt ASSR had as many as twenty churches in the early seventies (*Ivonin*, 1973, p. 18).

The Old Believer Church of Ancient Orthodox Christians or the Beglopopovtsy, as the two names indicate, also aspires to church status and had built its hierarchy originally from priests who had defected from the Orthodox Church. Only in 1923 did it establish its own hierarchy. The nick-name 'Beglopopovtsy' remained. This current commands only a small and diminishing membership concentrated in twenty parishes administered by an archbishop, two bishops and eighteen priests (Fedorenko, 1965, p. 104). Although this church differs little from the Belokrinitsa Church it is said to be stricter than the latter in maintaining prescriptions and taboos of Old Belief. It is still hostile to the Orthodox Church.

The spiritual centre of the Church is now in Novosybkov in the Bryansk region of the RSFSR. It was transferred there from Kuibyshev in 1963 because it had lost too much support in the Volga regions (Katunsky, 1972, p. 58). Areas of support are in the regions around Bryansk, Kursk, Leningrad, Moscow, Perm and Kuybyshev, as well as in the Udmurt ASSR, the Buryat ASSR and the Siberian regions of Chita and Krasnoyarsk (Milovidov, 1969, p. 96; Puchkov, 1975, p. 164). In and around Moscow it is supposed to have had 2,000 members in the early sixties (*Prichiny . . .*, 1963, p. 36).

The Edinovertsy allied themselves to the Orthodox Church at the beginning of the eighteenth century. They recognised the authority of the Orthodox hierarchy but preserved for their members the right to conduct services in accordance with pre-Nikonian ritual prescriptions. While during the first half of the eighteenth century large numbers of Old Believers accepted this compromise to escape increasing state and church pressure on their lives, today this branch has very few members left. Edinovertsy are found mainly in and around Moscow, and little else is known about them.

## The Bespopovtsy

The Bespopovtsy, lacking the constraint and guidance derived from a hierarchy, have split into many branches and small local groups which have developed in different directions. The main branches left today are the Pomortsy, the Fedoseevtsy, the Filipovtsy, the Stranniki and the True Orthodox Christian Wanderers. Although all continue to reject a hierarchy, some have evolved a stable organising centre. Their spiritual leaders, or tutors as they are called, are elected from among the community and receive the mercy of the Holy Ghost through the blessing by another such tutor. They have no liturgical-sacramental functions. Although many communities have churches they do not depend on them, but worship is mainly based on the family unit, the family head often acting as spiritual leader. In the Komi ASSR today, for example, the 2,300 Bespopovtsy have not a single church, and the number of qualified religious leaders is said to be diminishing (Gagarin, 1971, pp. 98–103).

While in the past there was a lot of antagonism between the different branches, now only the small groups on the extreme fringe maintain their intransigence towards other Priestless. The Pomortsy and Fedoseevtsy are said frequently to co-operate informally (Katunsky, 1972, p. 51). The most notable expression of this is the joint publication of an annual calendar by the Moscow Fedoseevtsy, the Moscow Pomortsy and the Riga Pomortsy.

No overall figures for any Bespopovtsy branch are available. It is said that Bespopovtsy have far more congregations than Popovtsy (Milovidov, 1969, p. 96). Among estimates of adherents in individual geographical areas are one for Moscow town and region of 4,000 (*Prichiny* . . ., 1963, p. 36), for the Komi ASSR in 1969 of 2,200–2,300 (Gagarin, 1971, p. 98), for the Udmurt ASSR of twenty congregations (Ivonin, 1973, p. 18) and for the Mogilev region of Belorussia of 1,000 members in 1963 (*Prichiny* . . ., 1965, p. 159). Bespopovtsy are widespread and can be found in the Baltic republics, Belorussia, the Ukraine, in the regions of Novgorod, Pskov, Arkhangel'sk, Kirov, Leningrad, Gorky, Sverdlov and Perm in the RSFSR, as well as in the Komi ASSR, the Buryat ASSR, the Karelian ASSR and the Tuvin Autonomous Region (Kol'tsov, 1964, p. 13).

The most numerous and influential branch are the Pomortsy (Milovidov, 1966, p. 221). They are strongest in Latvia and Lithuania, where they gained members from the Fedoseevtsy, and in Moscow. Significant concentrations have also been reported in Belorussia's Mogilev and Vitebsk regions and in Estonia (Kol'tsov, 1964, p. 22) as well as in western Siberia, the Urals, and in the regions of Kirov and Rostov (Puchkov, 1975, p. 164). Pomortsy have no formal central organisation but the Lithuanian Highest Old Believer Council in Vil'nyus makes efforts also to unite congregations outside Lithuania (Podmazov, 1970a, p. 9). The large Moscow and Riga congregations, however, do not submit to the Vil'nyus Highest Council. One author speaks of the Highest Council as being the organiser of three- to six-months' training courses for spiritual tutors (*Nastavniki*) but discloses no further details (Katunsky, 1972, p. 60). The Pomortsy are the most worldly and accommodative to political power among the Bespopovtsy. Even by the reign of Peter the Great they included a plea for the Tsar in their liturgy.

The Fedoseevtsy, under their leader Fedoseev, split off from the Pomortsy at the beginning of the eighteenth century over the latter's accommodative stance to the autocracy. Doctrinal or ritual differences played no role in the split. To this day, the less numerous Fedoseevtsy hardly differ from the Pomortsy on such issues but are said to be still less compromising than the latter, although they also acknowledge and co-operate with Soviet power. According to Soviet scholars, because of their greater conservatism and intransigence in matters of faith, they have lost many members to the Pomortsy. One author goes as far as to forecast a complete absorption of Fedoseevtsy by Pomortsy in the Baltic republics (Podmazov, 1970a, p. 9). Unlike the Pomortsy, the Fedoseevtsy have no formal co-ordinating organisation. They are internally divided over the old Bespopovtsy issue of whether there can be a marriage sacrament or not. Of the two chief congregations, the Moscow Preobrazhenskii congregation (based on the cemetery church of that name) rejects the marriage sacrament and is generally very conservative, while the Riga Grebenshchikov community acknowledges it. The Moscow Fedoseevtsy are the most influential group and are the informal leaders of most Russian communities, and their Riga brethren claim authority among Latvian Fedoseevtsy. Fedoseevtsy are also found in Belorussia, and in the regions around Pskov and Novgorod (Puchkov, 1975, p. 164).

The Filipovtsy are quite a small branch formed by the monk Filip in the eighteenth century. In pre-revolutionary times they were noted for their extremism, as their members often immolated themselves when persecutors drew near. Today very little is known about them. The Moscow group is also based on the Preobrazhenskii cemetery church. Groups also live in the regions of Arkhangel'sk and Orel and in the Karelian ASSR (Puchkov, 1975, p. 164). They are said to be more radical than the two bigger Bespopovtsy branches. They were notable for their absence at the 1969 Zagorsk peace conference at which all the Old Believer organisations discussed above were represented. Their isolationism is of a passive nature as they are not singled out in the Soviet literature for hostility to Soviet power like the Stranniki and True Orthodox Christian Wanderers.

There is disagreement among Soviet writers as to whether the Stranniki and True Orthodox Christian Wanderers are just two different names for one group (Milovidov, 1969, p. 97; Fedorenko, 1965, p. 106; Gagarin, 1973), or whether they are two distinctly different groups (Katunsky, 1972, p. 52; Trubnikova, 1964, p. 173). As far as the scanty information on the True Orthodox Christian Wanderers permits judgement, the present author believes them to be a separate group. But as they overlap in all but a few decisive characteristics with the Stranniki they can conveniently be covered in the same section.

Among Old Believers there has always been a radical wing, distinguished by their extreme isolationism, hostility to political power, and strong eschatological visions. Before the Revolution, the radical fringe groups were sometimes called Beguny (Engl. Fugitives), sometimes Stranniki (Wanderers). Stranniki divided into 'worldly' and 'true' Wanderers. While the 'true' Stranniki completely broke with the world and led an ascetic and devout wandering life, the 'worldly' group stayed in society providing sustenance, shelter and permanent organisation for their wandering brethren and vowing to become 'true' Wanderers at a later stage in their lives. Naturally only the 'true' Stranniki were a spiritual elite, keeping themselves 'clean' from the corrupting influence of the world in which Anti-Christ ruled. Some Stranniki perceived Anti-Christ in concrete terms, seeing the Tsars, especially Peter the Great, as impersonations of him. Others thought of Anti-Christ as a spiritual force, an unclean power, permeating all aspects of worldly society. In the years after the Revolution, they were only called Stranniki and were mainly of the 'worldly' kind. They maintained their traditional dogma, equating Anti-Christ now with Soviet power. In the 1920s, the 'true' Stranniki became prominent by gaining recruits from among those opposing the new political regime, especially during the collectivisation period. (The information on them below, and later in the chapter is taken from *Nauka i religiya*, 1963, nos. 1, 8, 11; 1964, 4; 1968, 9; Milovidov, 1966 and 1969; Katunsky, 1972, pp. 51–2, 64.) They have cut themselves off completely from the economic, social and cultural life of Soviet society. Their settlements are connected with the outside world only by narrow footpaths through the taiga. They maintain themselves by a combination of gathering and cottage industry and gardening. In the old communities of 'worldly' Stranniki, minorities withdrew into hermitage and became known as Mirootrechniki (Engl. World Renouncers).

In the postwar years groups with the same characteristics appeared under the name True Orthodox Christian Wanderers. The differences between the two branches of Old Belief, if the one available detailed description of a group of True Orthodox Christian Wanderers is, as its author implies, typical of the others (Trubnikova, 1964), are of the following kind. While the 'true' Stranniki cut themselves off from civilised society, both physically and spiritually, by withdrawing into the natural wilderness, the True Orthodox Christian Wanderers stayed in the inhabited world but withdrew from spiritual contact with it into artificially constructed hideouts. The physical isolation of the Stranniki turned them into a completely inward-looking, passively hostile sect, while the True Orthodox Christian Wanderers could break their isolation every now and then to recruit new members and to express their hostility to the political and social order *actively*. While the Stranniki are a classical example of an 'introversionist' sect (in Wilson's sense) the True Orthodox Christian Wanderers appear to be a mixture between an 'introversionist' religious sect and a conspiratorial political underground group. Both 'true' Stranniki and True Orthodox Christian Wanderers live in small communities. While Stranniki settlements may consist of family units, individual hermits, or be of a monastic kind, True Orthodox Christian Wanderers completely reject family life and, though having sexually mixed communities, uphold a monastic life-style. Some Stranniki communities have had no contact with the outside world whatsoever since they left in the twenties and have only recently been discovered by scientific expeditions. Gagarin (1971, p. 116) reports that Mirootrechniki in the Komi ASSR live as individual hermits in the wilderness in such primitive conditions that they are dying a slow death. Other Stranniki wander around preaching, living on what their listeners provide. Some groups of Wanderers are connected to the outside world by a go-between who takes upon himself the sin to keep inevitable contacts with the 'unclean' world. He takes to market the food grown or gathered by the Stranniki and buys with the proceeds such essential goods as salt, matches and simple craft tools (Katunsky, 1972, p. 96). The mediator between the religious group and the outside world is more important for the True Orthodox Christian Wanderers, who call such a person 'the benefactor'. As these radical sectarians attempt to withdraw from the world while staying physically in the world, often in big towns, they need a front man who officially owns and runs the house in which they are hiding and who earns some of the money on which the community lives. While ordinary members are not even allowed contact with relatives by letter, the sect leader travels freely to recruit new members and generally to maintain the clandestine organisation as well as distributing some of the religio-political literature produced in great quantities by those underground. Both Stranniki and True Orthodox Christian Wanderers are said to be small and unimportant branches of Old Belief, but it is doubtful whether the authorities are aware of the existence of all their groups, especially when they are as clandestine as the True Orthodox Christian Wanderers. About Stranniki we know that there are approximately 210 in the Komi ASSR ('true' and 'worldly' ones). True Orthodox Christian Wanderers, according to the account of the Alma-Ata group, can be found in many streets of that town and in other towns (Trubnikova, 1964, p. 164). The fact that this sect runs several underground training schools for new spiritual 'cadres' points to a wide dissemination of the group. Such schools are said to have existed in Yangi-Yul (Uzbekistan) and Tyulkubas (Kazakhstan), and 'to have sprung up like mushrooms' in many places during the late fifties/early sixties (Trubnikova, 1964, p. 169). The sect is also mentioned by several other authors (e.g. Katunsky, 1972, p. 52) who do not, however, reveal any further details about it.

This summary of the development of Old Believers during the Soviet period and of the general state of the currents and branches remaining at the present time has shown that they contain a wide spectrum of organisational traits but also have preserved many basic similarities. I have only briefly touched on the nature of socio-political orientations and religious commitment among the different groups and shall expand on this below. I shall also examine in some detail the social complexion of Old Believers. It will be shown how this is related to their organisational and general ideological tendencies.

## SOCIO-POLITICAL RESPONSES OF OLD BELIEVERS

In this section I shall analyse relations between the Soviet state and the various Old Believer organisations as well as the responses of individual believers towards the political regime and the social order. Unfortunately, these relations are not nearly as well documented as they are for other churches and the Western sects, chiefly because no *samizdat* literature is available on Old Believers.

Today Old Believer organisations fully recognise the Soviet state and are loyal supporters who endorse the general political and social policies of the regime. But this has not always been the case. The Bolsheviks' assumption of power had been met with general hostility and active opposition. Old Believers are supposed to have given large-scale moral and material support to the counter-revolutionary forces of General Kolchak (Milovidov, 1969, pp. 77f.). According to Soviet writers, by the end of 1922 they came to realise the futility of active opposition and recognised the Soviet regime. It does not become clear from the literature under what circumstances and in what spirit this loyalty was declared. The fact that the loyalty declaration was given at the same time as that by the Orthodox Church suggests that it probably was politically engineered rather than freely given. It seems to have been a communal effort by the Popovtsy, and the larger Bespopovtsy branches (Pomortsy and Fedoseevtsy). The fact that this declaration of loyalty was only an uneasy truce for many is well illustrated by the fact that individual Old Believers continued their resistance passively right into the thirties, standing aloof from the social organisations and institutions of the new Soviet order, such as schools, youth organisations, elections and, particularly, collective farms. This passive hostility to the new social order is well documented for the Bespopovtsy of the Komi ASSR (Gagarin, 1973, pp. 49ff.). The Highest Old Believer Council of the Baltic Pomortsy officially recognised Soviet power as God-given in 1949, that is, only four years after the incorporation of the Baltic States into the Soviet Union (Podmazov, 1970a, p. 11). The smaller Bespopovtsy branches continued to stay aloof and either perished organisation-ally or took up 'wandering' to escape involvement in the society created by the new regime. It was in the early twenties that the pre-revolutionary branch of the Beguny (Fugitives) was reactivated as the branch of the Stranniki or Wanderers who preferred life in the wilderness of the taiga to that in socialist society. Their rejection of Soviet society became symbolised by their destruction of all Soviet documents. The small Bespopovtsy branch of the Filipovtsy, although not as extreme and hostile in their rejection of the Soviet state, also opted for setting itself apart from the new social order. We have no information about what form of isolation is adopted by this branch.

This configuration of political orientations among different Old Believer branches has remained basically unchanged up to the present day. Popovtsy and the large Bespopovtsy branches are still regarded as organisations loyal to the state while Filipovtsy are regarded with suspicion and Stranniki are declared anti-Soviet and illegal. The only change since the war has been the emergence of the True Orthodox Christian Wanderers who are more actively and effectively anti-Soviet than the Stranniki. Both consider Soviet power as Anti-Christ and isolate themselves to avoid any contact with it.

Loyalty to Soviet power by the Popovtsy and larger Bespopovtsy organisations has manifested itself in a variety of ways. They not only refrain from words and actions which could be interpreted as hostile to the new social order but also express it in positive ways. Sermons have lost their politically hostile overtones and withdrawal from society and disowning of citizens' obligations are no longer urged. On the contrary, preachers often call believers to do selfless work for the good of the motherland and peace (*Stroitel'stvo* . . ., 1966, p. 111). Organisations issue declarations of support (e.g. the 1956 declaration of support for the resolutions of the 20th Party Congress by the Baltic Bespopovtsy) and mark Soviet holidays such as the anniversary of the Revolution and the First of May in the Old Believer calendar (the annual communal publication of Pomortsy and Fedoseevtsy). They stress the fact that they were a persecuted religious group in Tsarist times and not allied with the old social order. They also continually affirm their ardent patriotism and consider the education of believers 'in the spirit of love and devotion to the Motherland' one of their most important duties (Katunsky, 1972, p. 85). Organisations try to prove their loyalty by carrying out public duties like working in the Soviet peace movement (*Stroitel'stvo* . . ., 1966, p. 111) or voicing moral condemnation of imperialist aggression (Katunsky, 1972, p. 76). Most of the examples given in the literature seem to refer to the activities of the Baltic Pomortsy who must, therefore, be considered to be in the forefront of efforts for political accommodation.

The political disloyalty of the Stranniki today appears to be a frozen gesture and does not manifest itself in any spontaneous expressions of political hostility. The continuation of their isolation is more the maintenance of an old tradition than a gesture based on strong political sentiment. As most of them have had no contact with Soviet society since the early twenties they no longer know the enemy they are continuing to fight. The suggestion by one author (Gagarin, 1971, p. 116), that their intransigent stance no longer expresses a social protest, therefore carries conviction.

The True Orthodox Christian Wanderers, however, are a different case. Unlike the Stranniki they know the society and political order they are fighting, and their equation of Soviet power with Anti-Christ is based on strong sentiments which periodically find expression in anti-Soviet actions. The schools for young sectarians not only foster a nostalgia for Tsarist Russia and a hate of Soviet society but also acquaint students with practical details about the present social order so that they are better equipped to fight it. Thus the syllabus of the Yangi-Yul school contained lessons on Marxism and on the Communist Party (Trubnikova, 1964, p. 169). A search of the hideout of one group of True Orthodox Christian Wanderers produced much anti-Soviet material (ibid., p. 163).

The socio-political attitudes to Soviet power adopted by Old Believer organisations are also widely echoed by rank-and-file believers. Old Believers in general are said to fulfil their duties as citizens, including national service, and participate in socially useful work (Katunsky, 1972, p. 94). They do not only observe religious holidays but Soviet ones as well. Many Old Believers see communism and Soviet patriotism as being identical with the ideas of Christianity and, according to Milovidov (1966, p. 219), can truly be called Christian socialists. Most Old Believer organisations try to forget the not-so-cordial relations between them and the state during the early years of Soviet power. Only a few old people will not forget and foster these memories. These people, according to Katunsky (1972, p. 80), are small in number and of no account in the organisations.

The picture of socio-political responses to Soviet power and socialist society emerging from a study of Old Believers is very similar to that which emerged from the study of Orthodox and their Church. In each case, the overwhelming impression is one of loyalty to the state at the level of both organisation and individual, with a small, strongly disaffected minority of members having organised separately in oppositional radical fringe groups. There is an uncanny similarity between the political hostility of the sect of True Orthodox Christians and the Old Believer branches of Stranniki and, even more so, of True Orthodox Christian Wanderers.

While we have gained a reasonable picture of socio-political orientations adopted by the various Old Believer organisations and their members, we have no information on the response of the state to Old Believers. We do not know whether the regime favours Old Believers because of the leftist inclinations of some of their leading members before the Revolution (e.g. S. Morozov, a Moscow industrialist who gave financial support to the Bolsheviks) and because of their ardent Russian patriotism, or whether Old Believers have had to endure the same restrictions as the other major religious organisations. The fact that the Church of the Belokrinitsa Convention lost 200 out of 300 congregations and 100 out of 200 priests between 1958 and 1968 (Simon, 1970, p. 118) suggests that Old Believers suffered as badly as the other religious organisations during Khrushchev's anti-religious campaign.

## THE SOCIAL COMPOSITION OF OLD BELIEVERS

Soviet sociologists have published sufficient information on the social background of Old Believers to give us a reasonable picture although there are gaps and insufficient detail. The data provided do not suggest any significant differences in social characteristics between Bespopovtsy of the larger branches and Popovtsy, although the sample of Popovtsy communities is too small to permit a definite conclusion. As the overwhelming majority of Old Believers fall into these two groups it is justified to speak of the social composition of Old Believers in general, as most Soviet writers do. It is also true to say, as many Soviet writers do, that Old Believers do not differ much socially from the Orthodox. Like Orthodox, Old Believers are predominantly elderly and old, female and poorly educated (*Prichiny* . . ., 1963, p. 39; Milovidov, 1963, p. 128; Podmazov, 1967, pp. 69f.; Podmazov, 1970a, p. 67; Gagarin, 1971, pp. 100–2; Gagarin, 1973, pp. 62–3; Ivonin, 1973, p. 19), but the proportion of members over 50 years of age and of women is consistently a little lower among Old Believers, particularly among the Baltic Old Believers. This difference also comes out in the representation of the sexes on the church council: a far higher percentage of male Old Believers than Orthodox men are involved in church administration (*Prichiny* . . ., 1963, p. 196; Podmazov, 1970a, p. 12; Katunsky, 1972, p. 99). As among Orthodox, younger people (under 40 years of age) are said to be extremely rare in Old Believer congregations (Milovidov, 1963, p. 128; Basilov manuscript, p. 22, quoted by Milovidov, 1966, p. 210; Gagarin, 1971, p. 100; Ivonin, 1973, p. 19).

In one urban Latvian Bespopovtsy congregation, however, 33 per cent of members were under 45 years of age (Podmazov, 1970b, p. 67), and in a Siberian urban Popovtsy congregation a significant number of young people are reported to have attended services during 1966 (Katunsky, 1972, p. 99). (For greater detail on the social characteristics of Old Believers, see Lane, 1976, pp. 219–23.)

One suspects that most authors again equate membership with church attendance and are saying that there are few young people at church services or prayer meetings. If, as is generally stressed in the literature, Old Belief is now based on family life and Old Believer families are very patriarchal and strict (see *Nauka i religiya*, 2, 1973, p. 28; *Prichiny . . .*, 1963, p. 38) one may then expect many young people to be immersed in the Old Believer tradition. Two authors mention the fact that young Old Believers do not usually practise their religion but merely retain the belief dimension (Basilov manuscript, pp. 22–4, quoted in Milovidov, 1966, p. 210; Podmazov, 1970b, p. 68).

Among Stranniki and True Orthodox Christian Wanderers a different picture prevails. Unfortunately no systematic data have been collected on members of either branch but the qualitative information on their communities gives us some clues. The fact that the non-monastic Stranniki communities are based on family units and that members are totally insulated from the secularising effect of Soviet society must mean that the social composition of these groups roughly corresponds to that of society at large in terms of sex and age. All we can say about social characteristics of True Orthodox Christian Wanderers is what we know about members of the one group which has been studied. Of the eight people mentioned, all, except the regional leader who was middle-aged, were very young people. The group consisted of a young student from a technical college, a young woman with technical education, three schoolgirls, and two young skilled workers, one of them being the 'benefactor' (Trubnikova, 1964, pp. 161–2). Thus the group differs entirely from other Old Believer groups, but whether it is typical is difficult to know. The fact that the sect has organised several schools expressly to equip *young* people for proselytising work (ibid., p. 168) indicates that there must be a fair number of young people in the sect.

As regards the socio-geographical distribution of Old Believers over the Soviet Union, there are also similarities to that of Orthodox. Like the Orthodox Church, and unlike the sects of Western origin, Old Believers are still only to be found in their traditional settlement areas and have not managed to expand into the newly developed areas of the Soviet era nor even into the newly created industrial settlements in their homelands. Old Believers, it appears, are totally inactive or ineffective in proselytising and setting up new groups. Thus movement to a town without an Old Believer community has usually meant religious isolation and eventual loss of faith. In the Komi ASSR, for example, Old Believer communities have remained in their rural setting and individual migrants to the towns have abandoned their religion (Gagarin, 1971, pp. 97, 98). If, however, individual Old Believers move to towns with existing communities, they tend to join these on their arrival. Both in Latvia and the Ryazan region of the RSFSR, where a movement of Old Believers from the country to the town was indicated, the urban congregations were more thriving than the rural ones (Podmazov, 1970a, pp. 10–11; Milovidov, 1963, p. 128).

## THE NATURE OF RELIGIOUS COMMITMENT
## AMONG OLD BELIEVERS

As with Orthodox believers, we shall analyse the nature of Old Believer religiosity with the help of Glock and Stark's theoretical framework, appraising separately the various dimensions of their religious commitment (for theoretical and methodological considerations see the discussion on pp. 56*f*.). For lack of alternative sources, the analysis will be based entirely on Soviet empirical work in this area. Where possible, comparisons with the findings on the religiosity of members of other religious organisations in the Soviet Union will be made, mainly with the closely related Orthodox.

### The ideological and intellectual dimensions

Before the Revolution Old Believers were known for their relatively high level of literacy and their great zeal in both interpreting and producing religious texts. Although interest in ritual predominated, the Bible was avidly studied if only in search of texts justifying or exalting positions adopted on ritual practice, organisation and social ethos. The democratic structure of Old Believer organisations and the considerable lack of professionalisation meant that, unlike among Orthodox, rank-and-file believers were often very erudite in matters of dogma. In contrast, today both the ideological and the intellectual dimension of Old Believer religiosity are weakly developed. At present, Old Believers still underemphasise dogma in relation to ritual but the relationship between the two has become more imbalanced as dogma is now rarely evoked as the basis for ritual practice.

As among Orthodox, this manifests itself in a general lack of knowledge of, and of interest in, ideological notions in general, and in their main repository – the Bible – in particular. A large proportion of Old Believers have never seen, let alone read, the Bible (Kogan, 1964, p. 41; Milovidov, 1966, p. 211; Podmazov, 1967, p. 71; Katunsky, 1972, p. 87; Gagarin, 1973, p. 78). According to Milovidov (1966, p. 211) one finds people who are thoroughly familiar with details of Old Belief only in the larger urban congregations in the Baltic and south-western areas of the Soviet Union, or among the extreme fringe groups. A general lack of intellectual involvement comes out in believers' attitudes towards religious books. While before the Revolution books and manuscripts of all sorts were produced in great quantity and reverently passed down from generation to generation, today Old Believers own very few of these old books and will quite willingly sell those they have to interested antiquarians and ethnologists. For example, in one district of the Komi ASSR, whose Old Believers were formerly considered the ideological leaders of the wider area, 16·7 per cent of believers still owned such books, while in a less prominent community of that area only 10 per cent possessed them. Only the World Renouncers still maintain and cherish small libraries in their hermitages (Gagarin, 1973, pp. 77, 78). Although intellectual and ideological religious involvement has thus suffered a great decline among Old Believers, they are still said to be greater than among Orthodox. This manifests itself in the fact that a higher percentage of Old Believers still study and know questions of their faith and pass their religion on to their children by instructing them (Gagarin, 1973, p. 80).

Individual beliefs correspond more to the official religious belief system than is common among Orthodox, and they are less vague and uncertain. Old Believers are more likely to adhere to literal interpretations of the Bible and primitively concrete ideological notions. As in the case of the Orthodox, maintenance of belief has an emotional rather than intellectual basis. They are not given to pondering over and discussing their beliefs and, unlike the evangelical sectarians, are usually unable to explain and defend them in encounters with atheists (Podmazov, 1967, p. 71).

Some ideological notions are, however, preserved with tenacity. Eschatological notions still stir some sections in Old Belief, especially the older generation in the communities of the smaller Bespopovtsy branches. Consequently, for many of these Old Believers the notions of an after-life in heaven or hell still possess relevance. Only among the younger believers is religious belief becoming more narrowly focused and more neutralised, consisting only of a belief in God (Milovidov, 1966, p. 212). Implementing beliefs, specifying the conduct of man towards God and his fellow men, are not very prominent in the religiosity of Old Believers (Katunsky, 1972, p. 89). It is generally implied in the Soviet sociological literature that saliency of belief is stronger among Old Believers than among Orthodox (Gagarin, 1971, p. 113; Milovidov, 1969, p. 95), although Old Believers, like Orthodox, are said to be predominantly traditionalist rather than deeply convinced believers (Gagarin, 1971, p. 111 and 1973, p. 79).

These features of the ideological and intellectual dimensions of Old Belief are very congruent both with the social composition of believers and with the structure of their religious organisations. The preponderance of elderly and poorly educated members as well as of elderly, formally untrained religious functionaries and leaders explains the rigid adherence to the old unsophisticated ideological notions and the relative indifference to intellectual involvement in issues of religious ideology. The communal rather than associational nature of Old Believer communities and the emphasis on the family as the basic unit for religious involvement has facilitated the better maintenance of religious values and norms than is possible in the predominantly associational religious groups formed by Orthodox believers. The lack of dependence on professional spiritual leaders and fixed houses of worship among the Bespopovtsy has rendered them flexible and less vulnerable to the impact of anti-religious campaigns and has, therefore, safeguarded greater continuity in the spreading of religious ideas than has been possible in the 'church'-type organisations. Both communalism and lack of professionalism are, of course, more typical of Bespopovtsy and one would, therefore, expect greater steadfastness and erudition in matters of belief among them. Unfortunately, the available data are insufficient to make a detailed comparison on this aspect between Popovtsy and Bespopovtsy. Empirical data are mainly on the various Bespopovtsy branches. Below I shall examine, as far as the data permit, how the ideological and intellectual dimensions of religiosity differ in the various Bespopovtsy branches.

As said before, belief has both more width and more depth among Bespopovtsy than Popovtsy. We possess no detailed information on the content and nature of belief among Popovtsy but it is generally said that the nature of their religiosity differs hardly from that of Orthodox. Among Bespopovtsy there is a distinct continuum in these two respects from the large Pomortsy branch upward to the small branches of Stranniki and True Orthodox Christian Wanderers (Gagarin, 1971, p. 118). Among the latter, the old eschatological notions have been maintained with almost undiminished force, and interpretations of dogma have, in general, not departed from the fundamentals of Old Belief. Among the literature found in the secret retreat of the Alma-Ata True Orthodox Christian Wanderers, for example, manuscripts on dogmatic questions abounded. A long composition, called 'The Universe', held articles on various topics and the notion of Anti-Christ figured largely in most of them (Trubnikova, 1964, p. 163). In one of the Siberian Stranniki retreats, too, eschatological ideas were not only believed but also had great influence over members' lives. For instance, when one of the women hermits was asked why she lived this withdrawn and extremely ascetic life she answered unhesitatingly 'to earn, in this short life, eternal life' (Shamaro, 1968, p. 20). This expectation of death and preoccupation with after-life was found to be widespread not only among the older members of this community but also among the young there (ibid., p. 21). Expectation of the approaching end of this world was based on the realisation that 'true' Christians, like them, were dying out and that unbelief was spreading.

In other Bespopovtsy branches doubt and indifference about eschatological and anti-christological notions had gone far among the large urban congregations, especially among the Baltic Pomortsy, while in the smaller, more remote communities belief in these notions was still relatively strong (Milovidov, 1963, p. 132; *Prichiny . . .*, 1965, pp. 159–60; Podmazov, 1970a, pp. 15–16, 1970b, p. 57, 1970c, p. 98; Gagarin, 1973, p. 71). The fact that anti-christological notions have lost much influence among Old Believers is underlined by the observation that, in contrast to earlier periods, few people now have any thoughts about the date on which these events are to take place. Except for a few leaders, eschato-logical happenings have become far-off vague and abstract possibilities (Gagarin, 1973, pp. 76, 77).

In contrast, ideological notions concerning the creation of the world and images of God held by Latvian Pomortsy still coincided with fundamental positions. Thus 98·5 per cent of one sample believed in the biblical version of man's creation, and only 10 per cent of another sample held an abstract image of God (Podmazov, 1970c, p. 57), although some urban leaders and more educated members are now turning to more sophisticated interpretations and images (ibid.). Both positions are much more fundamentalist than those held by Soviet believers of other faiths. In the Komi ASSR, for example, 48 per cent of Old Believers, as compared with 24 per cent of Orthodox, held to the biblical description of man's creation (Gagarin, 1971, p. 113).

*The practice dimension*
The ritual or practice dimension is strongly developed among Old Believers, presumably because they became preoccupied with the issues which led to their schism from the Orthodox Church in 1666. One outward indication of the pre-dominance of ritual over dogma in the consciousness of believers is the fact that contemporary Old Believers rarely have a Bible but often possess books specify-ing procedure during services. Among the 154 books owned by one group of Bespopovtsy in the Komi ASSR, for example, all but seven were almost exclusively devoted to ritual issues (Gagarin, 1971, pp. 77, 78). Not only is ritual more prominent in theory but Old Believers are also said to be stricter and more zealous in its performance than are Orthodox (Milovidov, 1963, p. 136; *Prichiny . . .*, 1965, p. 209). This applies especially to Bespopovtsy. One writer found members so engrossed in the ritual aspect of their religion that he describes

the majority of Old Believers 'as perceiving of their life in the form of an endless ritual' (Katunsky, 1972, p. 88). At the same time, however, Old Believers are also said to be becoming negligent in the execution of their ritual obligations (Milo-vidov, 1966, p. 211). Here reference is probably made to the large component of weakly committed and wavering believers who form the majority, but do not set the tone, of many communities.

Although quantitative data on rites of passage are rare we have enough quali-tative data to gain a reasonable picture of present-day trends in this area. As among Orthodox, the performance of rites of passage is said to be the most persistent part of religious practice and of religious commitment in general (Podmazov, 1970a, p. 17). While one writer (Gagarin, 1971, p. 102) notes a general decline in the performance of rites of passage (over an unspecified period), others point to a strong decline only in requests for the celebration of wedding rites and to little or no decrease in baptismal or funeral rituals (see *Prichiny* . . ., 1965, p. 159; Podmazov, 1967, p. 72; Katunsky, 1972, p. 98). The fact that the celebration of the wedding rite has become a rare incident in contemporary Old Believer communities all over the Soviet Union and in all branches is attested to by several authors (I'lina, 1960, p. 121; Lebedeva, 1962, p. 35; *Prichiny* . . ., 1965, p. 159; Katunsky, 1972, p. 98), although in many cases civil registration of mar-riage is not sought either.

Baptismal and funeral rites, on the other hand, are still widely performed, the second being more persistent than the first. In Bespopovtsy communities there is a deeply rooted belief that non-baptised children are spiritually unclean and that neglect to baptise them is tantamount to a voluntary surrender of the children to Anti-Christ (Gagarin, 1973, p. 92). Even in mixed marriages children of the union were said to be baptised in the Old Believer faith at the beginning of the sixties (Lebedeva, 1962, p. 36). In one village in Zabaikal area in 1960, every child living and born in the village was found to be baptised (Kogan, 1964, p. 42).

Systematically collected figures on rites of passage are given only for the Bespopovtsy communities in the Komi ASSR. Speaking about children born after 1960, Gagarin's figures suggest that 68 per cent of all families associated with Old Belief had one or more of their children baptised. Among believing Old Believers this proportion rose to 81·1 per cent, and as many as 44·3 per cent of non-believing families baptised their children during that period (Gagarin, 1973, p. 95). In another village of that area nearly all children were said to be baptised, including those of many Party members and Komsomols (ibid.). Of all families who lost one of their members between 1960 and 1969, 51·7 per cent gave them a funeral in the Old Believer tradition, and 77·6 per cent arranged remembrance ceremonies (Russ. *pominki*) for them (Gagarin, 1973, pp. 98, 100). The remem-brance ceremonies extended over several weeks and much time and money was spent on them. Not surprisingly, the number of families acting out of religious conviction was much bigger than in the case of baptism (ibid., p. 98).

In many Bespopovtsy communities the mode of solemnising these two impor-tant events in the individual's life-cycle has changed. A spiritual leader is no longer invited to perform these acts but a family member or an old woman steps in (I'lina, 1960, p. 121; Kogan, 1964, p. 42). This movement towards greater lay involvement in performance of rites is not surprising in a religious current where lay involvement is high anyway and where lay leaders are becoming rare or are increasingly losing authority among believers (Milovidov, 1966, p. 211; Gagarin, 1973, pp. 86*ff.*). It is also indicative of truly 'religious' motivations for these acts rather than of a yielding to pressure from religious leaders or to a desire for a 'beautiful occasion'.

Additional information about motivations for baptism was collected among Bespopovtsy in the Komi ASSR. The bulk of parents (51·8 per cent) are said to have had their children baptised out of tradition or in conformity with public opinion, while only 6·8 per cent are said to be motivated by religious conviction. But, as pointed out above (see p. 61), the 'tradition' category of motivation is an extremely vague and unsatisfactory one and does not tell us clearly what motivated baptising parents. If, as seems likely, the author subsumed under the category the belief traditional in this area that an unbaptised child is at the mercy of Anti-Christ, then this motivation is clearly founded on religious beliefs. More information would be needed to draw definite conclusions on both the rate of persistence of these rites and the motivations behind their performance and to make comparisons with the Orthodox pattern in this area.

Religious holidays, especially Easter, Christmas and Whitsun, are said to be widely observed in Old Believer communities though there are considerable variations in the mode of observance (Kogan, 1964, p. 41). While in some communities they are only occasions for jollities and rest (I'lina, 1960, p. 121) in others they are marked by ritual and devotional practice. In Latvian rural communities, for example, everyone observed holidays, and in urban communities only 5 per cent ignored them. Of the other 95 per cent, 42·9 per cent observed them at home in some specified way, and 52·1 per cent – a high percentage – visited the chapel on those occasions (Podmazov, 1970a, p. 17). In other geographical areas, too, far more people attended services on holidays than on ordinary days (Milovidov, 1963, p. 128; *Prichiny* . . ., 1965, p. 208). Between 1965 and 1966 attendance at church on the major holidays in the Novosibirsk Popovtsy congregation rose for three of the four holidays mentioned (Katunsky, 1972, p. 98). Believers from churchless areas journey to a place with an open church on such holidays (Milovidov, 1963, p. 128).

Ritual connected with the individual life-cycle and family and community life is, with the exception of the marriage rite, still vigorously upheld by Old Believers of most branches. Unfortunately the data do not enable one to analyse the social characteristics and motivations of those taking part in these rituals so that it is difficult to make deductions about the degree of religious involvement associated with them. This uncertainty about the existence of religious motivations is less strong when we turn to ritual practice connected with communal worship, i.e. church attendance in general and the taking of confession and communion in particular.

Regular church attendance among most branches of Old Believers, as among Orthodox, is quite low. One does not, of course, always know whether respondents had easy access to a chapel or prayer house. From one author we learn that churches of the Belokrinitsa hierarchy are well attended in the towns of Moscow, Gorky, Vinnitsa and Kaluga, but poorly in most other places. Out of the 2,000 parishioners in Astrakhan (RSFSR), for example, only 40 to 50 are regular attenders and up to 150 Popovtsy attend on major holidays (Kol'tsov, 1964, p. 29). The overwhelming majority (180) of a group of 228 Pomortsy in the Udmurt ASSR never went to prayer meetings and less than 5 per cent attended regularly (Ivonin, 1973, p. 20). Among Latvian Bespopovtsy the situation was somewhat better, with 20·8 per cent in rural areas and 33·1 per cent in urban areas never attending services at all (Podmazov, 1970b, p. 17). Belorussian sociologists have noted poor and falling attendance (*Prichiny* . . ., 1965, p. 159). Church attendance in the compact Old Believer settlements (Popovtsy and Bespopovtsy) in the Volga regions around Gorky has also been reported to be at a low level, and those present at such services often had arguments about the correct procedure (Basilov manuscript, pp. 11–13, quoted in Milovidov, 1966, p. 210). A survey in the Komi ASSR of 790 Bespopovtsy established that 1·1 per cent went to church regularly, 24·6 per cent on major holidays, 10·2 per cent rarely, and 64·1 per cent never attended (ibid., p. 87). This particularly low rate of attendance must be largely due to the lack of churches in the neighbourhood. Chapels of Pomortsy in villages of Ryazan region were only attended by about fifteen elderly believers (Milovidov, 1963, p. 131). A Popovtsy village church in Ryazan region (RSFSR) had only twenty to twenty-five regular parishioners in 1961. Popovtsy churches in big urban centres attract larger congregations as they recruit from the surrounding villages. Even so the services of the Ryazan church of the Belokrinitsa hierarchy were only attended by 50 to 60 believers on ordinary days and by 100 to 120 on holidays in the early sixties. Church income here, too, was not high and said to be falling (Milovidov, 1963, pp. 128–9). The Novosibirsk church of the Belokrinitsa Popovtsy showed a healthier picture. Although the number of services held in 1966 fell slightly from 108 to 88 in 1965, attendance seems to have kept stable and high, and income from church collections and fees for the performance of rites was high and rising (Katunsky, 1972, pp. 97–8).

In many Old Believer settlements during the sixties and early seventies communal worship was either non-existent or services were held only on major holidays. In the Komi Old Believer villages, groups of between fifteen and twenty people met in private houses on church holidays, and some villages had abandoned communal worship altogether (Gagarin, 1973, pp. 83*f*.).

Among the Stranniki and True Orthodox Christian Wanderers there is no strict division between public and private worship and the hours devoted to worship in general are high among both. Thus, among the Siberian Stranniki discovered in the taiga in 1965, the peasant log hut was both a homestead and a church and every hermit both a priest and a worshipper. On ordinary days these sectarians would spend up to ten out of twenty-four hours on prayer services and on holidays, even more (Shamaro, 1968, p. 17). The members of the Alma-Ata group of True Orthodox Christian Wanderers spent virtually all their time on religious matters leaving even the housework mainly to their 'benefactor' (Trubnikova, 1964, p. 170).

In general, believers attending church are members of the older generation. For example, out of seventy-one believers under 35 years of age in Daugavpils (Latvia), only five attended services regularly and a further nine went on holidays (Podmazov, 1970c, p. 68).

The few data we have on participation in the sacraments of confession and communion do not give us a complete picture, but a low level of commitment in these matters is generally indicated (e.g. Gagarin, 1973, p. 91) and can be inferred from the low level of church attendance. In Daugavpils, however, as many as nearly two-thirds had been taking confession at varying intervals conforming with church prescription. A similar pattern is perceived for the rural areas (Podmazov, 1970c, p. 107).

In general then, ritual practice in chapel or church is almost consistently low among adherents of the various branches in different parts of the Soviet Union. In large urban centres attendance is higher because a small number of churches cater for a large number of believers. Only the radical fringe groups form an exception. Let us now turn to investigate whether devotional practice or the more personal forms of piety in the various branches also correspond to this picture.

Regarding these personal forms of piety, most writers discuss only fasting and a few mention praying and keeping icons. Old Believers have always considered fast a necessary means for the attainment of salvation, and fast has been understood widely as a time 'during which the soul renews itself, is raised or even prepared for its heavenly domicile' (Podmazov, 1970, p. 106). It thus means a lot more than the mere abstinence from food and refers to a total spiritual state. Prayer is an integral part of fasting. Prayer among Old Believers is carried out according to set rules and occupies a great deal of their time. Those who pray regularly spend up to five out of every twenty-four hours in prayer (Gagarin, 1973, pp. 124, 125). The World Renouncers prayed up to eight hours per day.

The study of Pomortsy in the Udmurt ASSR reports a low level of devotion but, significantly, it was higher than that of church attendance. While only 10 members attended chapel regularly, 34 prayed frequently; 180 never attended church but those never offering private prayer numbered only 130 (Ivonin, 1973, p. 20). The Pomortsy in Ryazan region are said not to remember the words of Old Believer prayers but were observing the rules of fast, though mainly the female members (Milovidov, 1963, p. 131). In an Old Believer village of the Zabaikal area with 500 farmsteads a mere 10 people observed fast conscientiously and another 45 during token periods (Kogan, 1964, p. 45). In contrast the level of private devotion was quite high among Bespopovtsy in the Komi ASSR where, in 1969, 32·1 per cent prayed regularly, 45·3 per cent irregularly and only 22·6 per cent never prayed at all. A mere 8 per cent did not remember any of the traditional Old Believer prayers (Gagarin, 1973, p. 89). Fast among the latter was also fairly widely observed, with 65·6 per cent keeping all or some of the fasting rules. Those who fasted consistently submitted themselves to considerable rigour, going without meat and milk for long periods (Gagarin, 1973, pp. 90, 125). In Latvia, 15 per cent and about 22 per cent observed all fasts in urban and rural areas respectively, 24·6 per cent and 21·7 per cent observed token fasts (mainly the first and last week of the Great Fast) and 60·3 per cent and 56·3 per cent did not observe them at all (Podmazov, 1970b, pp. 106, 107). Only among the True Orthodox Christian Wanderers in the Alma-Ata group was fast consistently observed, or probably carried even further than Old Believer faith prescribes. Members lived extremely ascetically, eating fast-type food regularly or often going without any food at all. Extra fasting was also imposed as punishment for transgressions (Trubnikova, 1964, pp. 167, 168, 173). Information about Old Believers' attitude to icons is rarely offered in the literature, and it is not even clear whether all branches venerate icons. One study of the 'Family' Old Believers in two villages of the Zabaikal area showed that nearly all houses had icons and eight-ended crosses (I'lina, 1960, p. 114; Kogan, 1964, p. 41).

Religious devotion, although not at a high level among Old Believers, is still kept up well and is certainly more widespread than ritual practice dependent on church or chapel. In general, it seems to be more frequent and more intense than among Orthodox, especially in the communities on the geographical periphery of the Soviet Union. The level of religious devotion is usually taken as a particularly good indicator of the depth of religious commitment. We can therefore conclude that the lower level of public worship among Old Believers is not entirely due to religious indifference but must be partly influenced by extraneous factors, such as the shortage of places of worship and of religious functionaries.

The religious practice of Old Believers is most clearly distinguished from that of adherents of other Christian faiths by the inclusion of 'avoidance' ritual. The great courage, spiritual steadfastness and close community Old Believers developed during centuries of fierce persecution by state and church fostered in them a sense of being a spiritual elite which must set itself apart from the world where Anti-Christ rules. To safeguard their exclusivity and to avoid any contamination from contact with the world which would prejudice their chances of salvation they established avoidance ritual. This permeates the everyday life of believers and regulates their relation with heretics and their world. Avoidance ritual flows from the complex of anti-christological beliefs prominent in Old Believer ideology, especially in that of Bespopovsty. According to these notions, all those who have not adopted Old Belief live in a world ruled by the spirit of Anti-Christ. The rule of Anti-Christ began, of course, with the Nikonian reforms in 1666. Not only people are considered spiritually unclean but, by association, all material goods, practices and institutions adopted since the rule of Anti-Christ are also thought to be polluted in this way. Like adherents of many primitive religions, Old Believers therefore have traditionally distinguished between people and a lifestyle which are spiritually pure and those which are unclean, and they have developed a whole system of interdictions or taboos of contact between the two to avoid ritual pollution. In the following, we shall examine what Old Believer avoidance ritual traditionally consists of and to what extent such ritual is upheld today.

Traditional Old Believer avoidance ritual may be separated into those practices regulating contact with heretics themselves and those taboos forbidding contact with various aspects of the material and intellectual culture. Avoidance of contact with heretics and their world has been developed to varying degrees in different branches. At one extreme the really 'pure' Old Believers in the small branches have avoided all contact whatsoever with the outside world, while members of other branches have only regulated the degree and manner of that contact. Marriage out of the community therefore has been taboo in all branches. Medical care by heretics has also been rejected. When social contact could not be avoided, Old Believer practices have been aimed at minimising physical contact, such as upholding a strict separation of eating and drinking utensils. Visitors from outside their community have been given 'the worldly dish', and on visits to heretics Old Believers have brought their own spoon and cup. Post-Nikonian introductions to Russian material and intellectual culture, which are rejected as spiritually polluted, are various foodstuffs and provisions (such as tea, sugar, potatoes, sweets, matches, soap), technological inventions (e.g. electricity, piped water and modern transport), social customs (e.g. smoking, shaving and modern clothing) and even new expressions or words. All such avoidance practices are extremely difficult to maintain in any advanced industrial society characterised by high density and turnover of population as well as by a high rate of innovation in all fields. Their maintenance is made even harder in an industrial society with a socialist ethos where collective endeavour is being continually counterposed to aspiration for exclusivity. Seen in this societal context, Old Believer avoidance practices, although rapidly declining, have been remarkably persistent.

Complete separation from 'the world', as we have shown above, was still current in the sixties among some Stranniki and True Orthodox Christian Wanderers. In some Stranniki communities in the Siberian taiga and northern Urals separation from the world is said to be enforced occasionally by devious means. If it is noted that a member is weakening in his religious commitment other members will dare him to prove himself by some illegal exploit which is then later used for preventing his departure into the world (Katunsky, 1972, p. 64).

In recent years there has been left little of the hostility to outsiders that Old Believers were once known for, but they have still been keeping themselves aloof from the surrounding population (Gagarin, 1973, p. 135). Religious endogamy has remained the norm among Old Believers from which departures have caused severe conflict between the generations. But in recent years this norm has been increasingly disregarded by the younger generation of some branches.

In general, one can say that avoidance ritual and taboos have been most weakly preserved or have been completely abandoned among the larger branches, in the less remote communities, or in areas settled by a mixture of the various branches. Thus these rituals are now almost extinct in the mixed communities of the Zabaikal area (Lebedeva, 1962, p. 20), among the Pomortsy of Latvia (Podmazov, 1970c, p. 109), the Volga communities around Gorky (Milovidov, 1966, p. 220) and among the various branches in Ryazan region (Milovidov, 1963, p. 130). Practices which were considered terrible sins not so long ago, such as eating potatoes and sugar or smoking, shaving and listening to the radio or using the medical service, have become widely accepted in these communities, often even by their leaders (Milovidov, 1966, p. 212). Avoidance rituals and various taboos were still being preserved by a relatively large section of believers in the smaller branches, especially in the Siberian areas, or in areas where compact groups of one Bespopovtsy branch form a village or figure prominently in the population. Thus some Pomortsy in compact communities of Ryazan region still kept 'worldly' eating utensils, and in a village exclusively settled by Pomortsy the middle-aged and elderly men neither smoked nor shaved (Milovidov, 1963, p. 131). In the Baltic, where these practices had died out in the large and influential Pomortsy branch, they have been continued on a small scale among some groups of the smaller and more radical branch of the Fedoseevtsy (Podmazov, 1970c, p. 109) as well as among Estonian Fedoseevtsy (Kol'tsov, 1964, p. 24). In the Udmurt ASSR some Bespopovtsy still abstained from the use of electricity, piped water and modern transport (Ivonin, 1973, p. 21). In two settlements of the Tuvin ASSR, too, the more committed believers still declined the use of electricity, and children were not given sweets or toys (*Nauka i religiya*, 2, 1973, pp. 28–30).

An especially good picture of adherence to these avoidance rituals is given for the compact Bespopovtsy communities in the Komi ASSR (Gagarin, 1973). Although here, too, many believers have given up these practices, a very sizeable minority continued to observe some or all of them. Among those who came to ignore these practices various sentiments about their breach of faith prevailed. Many felt very guilty about their lapses and made all sorts of excuses for them, while another group of believers thought that their forefathers were very wrong in adopting these ritual practices in the first place (Gagarin, 1973, pp. 81–2). Gagarin enlightens us, too, on the circumstances which led to the abandonment of one taboo, that on the eating of potatoes. It seems that Old Believers every-where came to accept potatoes through the force of circumstances, during the famine of the 1920s, rather than through religious indifference. The keeping of a 'worldly' dish for visiting non-Old Believers was still fairly widely adhered to in the Komi ASSR. In one area, as many as 61 per cent kept up this ritual, and among the World Renouncers and the 'true' (rather than worldly) Stranniki all observed it conscientiously. A large proportion of the men observed the taboos on smoking and shaving, and many of the women still wore the traditional Old Believer clothes. Various foodstuffs were also avoided by a minority of believers. In one area, for example, 11·7 per cent of believers did not drink tea. Acceptance of technological innovation, modern entertainment and educational events has also been much slower among Old Believers than among Orthodox of the Komi ASSR although the social characteristics of the two are very similar. Thus, while 40·1 per cent of Orthodox went to the cinema, only 26·8 per cent of Old Believers permitted themselves such pleasure. Non-acceptance of these advances on the part of Old Believers very often has been justified explicitly in religious terms. The considerable persistence of all these avoidance practices and taboos, Gagarin argues, is only partly based on strong anti-christological beliefs and partly on the idea that adherence to these practices helps to preserve self-identi-fication as Old Believers and the maintenance of that old exclusivity Old Believers still cherish (Gagarin, 1973, pp. 119, 135–7).

*The experiential dimension*
Unfortunately, there is not a single systematic study of the experiential dimen-sion of Old Believer religiosity although incidental snippets of information sug-gest that it has been well developed and has taken quite varied forms. Thus, in the past, forms of experience have ranged from the mysticism of religious hermits to the mass hysteria of whole communities burning themselves alive. During the sixties and early seventies religious wandering, hermitage and pilgrim-age, in order to obtain better communication with God, were still relatively common among some branches of Old Believers and distinguished the nature of their religiosity most clearly from that of adherents of other Christian faiths in the Soviet Union. Lack of information precludes any deeper study of this dimension of religious commitment.

*The consequential dimension*
Under this heading I shall again only consider the 'responsibility' aspect, the question of how Old Believers differ in their social–moral responses to their world from non-Old Believers (see discussion of this point on p. 71). Again, this dimension of religiosity is very inadequately researched in the contemporary Soviet Union, but the *ad hoc* information gained suggests that the consequential dimension is, in general, more strongly developed among them than among Orthodox. In an inquiry in the Komi ASSR, for example, as many as 71·4 per cent of respondents thought that their religion influenced their life and was very

useful to them (Gagarin, 1973, p. 108). For Old Believers their religion is not as strongly compartmentalised as for Orthodox because, as we have shown above, eschatological beliefs still affect the social conduct of some sections of believers to a significant extent. In contrast to the situation among members of the sects of Western origin, belief in eschatology has little influence on moral beliefs and conduct and consequently has not had the effect of raising moral standards among them (Gagarin, 1973, p. 127). Instead, their particular ideological focus has induced them to keep themselves socially aloof to cultivate exclusivity and even isolationism. This has influenced many of their responses to Soviet social institutions. There still is a widespread reluctance among Old Believer parents to let their children stay the full term (ten years) at school, or to let them join youth organisations. Children are said to oppose parents on these points, and many Old Believer children now receive as much education as other children. Thus in a Tuvin ASSR community about half of the Old Believer children stayed on at school during 1968–71 (*Nauka i religiya*, 2, 1973, p. 32). In the Komi ASSR it has been impossible for many years to even start a group of Young Pioneers in some Old Believer settlements (Gagarin, 1973, pp. 131, 132). Adults show little interest in reading non-religious books or even papers or in attending any function outside their community. On all these aspects there is a significant difference between Orthodox and Old Believers (ibid., p. 119). Old Believers (excepting the True Orthodox Christian Wanderers and the hermit Stranniki), however, differ little from non-believers in their involvement in the work and political community. Unlike members of some other sects, Old Believers do now work in collective or state farms. In general they also strive to be full members of the political community, being as loyal citizens as non-believers. In some ways they probably even feel themselves to be superior citizens because they see themselves as true patriots, as preservers of the true Russian heritage.

*Conclusion*

Religious commitment of Old Believers does not only cover a wide range of variability from members of urban Popovtsy at the one end to hermit Stranniki at the other but is also variable within each community. We have brought out the great differences in religious commitment between members of the different branches, and between branches in different socio-geographical locations. The commitment of Popovtsy at the one extreme is said to be almost the same as that of Orthodox believers, while the religiosity of true Stranniki and True Orthodox Christian Wanderers is highly developed on all dimensions and their responses to the world are classical examples of extreme sectarianism hardly ever found now in the Western world. In between these two poles we must locate the large Bespopovtsy branch of the Pomortsy which can be likened to a denomination in Latvia and to a sectarian religious group with some denominational tendencies in the RSFSR – as in the Ryazan region groups. The Latvian Bespopovtsy have mainly maintained the ritual dimension of religious commitment and have abandoned aspects of Bespopovtsy faith which hindered adaptation to the Soviet political and social order. They have, however, maintained their hostile attitude towards the Orthodox Church. The Ryazan Pomortsy, in contrast, although politically loyal, have not accommodated themselves to Soviet society to the same extent as their Latvian brethren in other ways.

The available data also show great differentiation in religiosity within Bespopovtsy communities. As in Orthodox parishes, there is a large group of believers, who have now very weak links with the religious collective and whose religious commitment is weakly maintained along most dimensions of religiosity. Then there is a small group of religious activists grouped around the lay leaders for whom the religious community and Old Belief still form the centre of their lives. Both among Orthodox and Old Believers the bulk of members are traditionalist believers who adhere to their faith because their forefathers have done so for generations before them. Although they still profess a belief in God they are blind rather than conscious believers and do not reflect or even know much about the object of their faith. They practise their religion only very episodically, being mainly connected to the religious collective by the observation of some rites of passage, holidays and, for some, very occasional church visits. The nucleus of convinced and conscious believers among both Orthodox and Old Believers shows a deep commitment in both belief and practice. They are active within the religious community and try to organise their lives in accordance with their religious beliefs. Old Believers, in addition, because they faithfully observe avoidance ritual and taboos, maintain a religious exclusivity and have a stronger elite conception. Old Believer activists also have a better religious knowledge than Orthodox of the same type (for descriptions of different types of Old Believers see *Prichiny* . . ., 1965, pp. 207, 208; Katunsky, 1972, pp. 94–5; Gagarin, 1973, pp. 103–5).

An important difference between Orthodox and Old Believer parishes is the size and influence of these groups within the community. The size of the highly committed group, although small in both religious organisations, seems to be bigger among Old Believers, and this active nucleus appears to be more influential among the latter. These differences must be attributed to the facts that Bespopovtsy enjoy a high degree of lay participation in religious affairs and a communal rather than associational organisation, as well as having a stronger sense of mission. It is probably the existence of these differences in the nature and size of the active nucleus which give observers of both religious organisations the impression that Old Believers are more deeply committed than Orthodox, even though the rank-and-file members of both religious organisations are almost identical in the degree of shallowness of their commitment. The highly committed group among Old Believers seems to be similar in nature to the equivalent among Western sects, both sharing an evenly strong development of all dimensions of religiosity as well as a tendency to isolate themselves in many respects from the wider society, although the highly committed members form a larger proportion of the total membership in Western sects.

Let us now turn to the question of what sustains Old Believer religiosity in a society so unlike the social order that called this religious current into existence. What are the factors which keep their religion not only relevant in the changed circumstances but also worth perpetuating in the face of strong disapproval from the wider society to do so? As in the case of Orthodox believers, there are a variety of reward patterns binding Old Believers to their religion and no one pattern clearly predominates, nor do the few available data permit any definite judgements as to the relative importance of these patterns.

The predominantly ritual-oriented character of Old Belief and the great beauty and sensuous impact of its services evoke in participants a variety of gratifying emotions, such as feelings of peace, joy, calm, consolation, or aesthetic pleasure.

But experience of these emotions depends very much on the provision of regular public worship, performed in churches by trained religious functionaries. Such provision is now mainly provided in Popovtsy congregations, while Bespopovtsy outside the Baltic republics are increasingly being deprived of this elevating environment and of men experienced at conducting worship in the appropriate way.

Broadly cultural satisfactions, however, are derived by Popovtsy and Bespopovtsy alike. Old Believers, as we said earlier, started their religious life as defenders of the *Russian* spiritual heritage against the imposition of the Greek tradition and, ever since, their religious life has been devoted to preserving this heritage. Not only in their religious life but in all their everyday pursuits they have tried to uphold old Russian habits and customs as, for example, certain styles of dress and general appearance. The centuries of persecution by the authorities heightened in them the awareness and pride about their special mission. This sense of having deep roots in the Russian past, of being patriotic defenders of a national heritage, is still experienced by Old Believers today and fills them with pride and satisfaction. Closely related to this sense of mission is the strong feeling of group identity, of being a member of a community different and apart from the rest of society. Unlike the communities of the evangelical sects, their communities are welded together not only by a common faith and a network of moral and financial support, but by a common spatial base, centuries of intermarriage and the experience of a common heroic past. In this respect they are very similar to the Old Russian sects of Molokans and Dukhobors. This very pronounced sense of mission and identity must be particularly valuable in a society where both industrial and political culture are not conducive to the formation of communities of this type. It explains the adherence to the religious group of the majority of members earlier termed 'traditionalist' who stay in the religious community even though their religious belief is gone.

While it is quite plausible that religion in the Soviet Union has maintained itself in the individual and private sphere, it comes as a surprise that whole communities can in some respects withstand the pressure from Soviet power to conform to a Soviet socialist norm. In a society which is intensely suspicious of, and hostile to, groups trying to separate themselves in some respect from the socialist collective, the survival of Old Believer communal identity and exclusivity is truly remarkable. As in Tsarist times, their success in this respect must be attributed partly to the nature of the Soviet Union as a geographical, rather than a sociopolitical unit. Even the Soviet regime cannot extend its control equally effectively over the wide and climatically and topologically varied expanse of land which constitutes the Soviet Union. Consequently, Old Believer communities on the climatically less hospitable geographical periphery, such as those in the Komi ASSR, have maintained their religious life and group identity much better than those in urban-industrial areas of European Russia.

Although Old Belief was originally associated with political protest, with defending the democratic value of rank-and-file participation against autocratic rule, today it no longer provides members with political compensation. The exception to this is the branch of the True Orthodox Christian Wanderers, among whom religious attachment affords the opportunity to express political hostility. Membership of this extreme Old Believer branch affords one of the few opportunities in contemporary Soviet society to express a total rejection of its social and political order.

Now that we have gained a general picture of socio-political orientations, social composition and the nature of religious commitment of Old Believers, we can answer the question posed earlier as to whether the relatively relaxed Soviet stance towards Old Believers is based on a realistic appreciation of their persistence and influence in Soviet society. There is no straightforward answer. On the one hand, Old Believers (especially Bespopovtsy) constitute more formidable ideological opponents than Orthodox, because their religiosity is stronger along several dimensions, including the most important consequential dimension. They are also more persistent opponents because religion is transmitted more effectively in a communal type of organisation. In these two ways Bespopovtsy are thus similar to the Western sects which are militantly opposed by Soviet atheists. On the other hand, however, unlike these sectarians, Old Believers do not proselytise nor do they make such a strong impact on their own young as the former. Neither do they attract attention by the sheer weight of their number as do Orthodox. On the contrary, they are an inward- and backward-looking religious current, and they are localised in compact groups rather than dispersed among the population. Unlike the extreme sectarians, they are politically loyal (except the extreme fringe) although, unlike the sects of Western origin, they espouse a *Russian* nationalism irreconcilable with official Soviet internationalism. To sum up, Old Believers, particularly Bespopovtsy, have some of the qualities making them potential ideological adversaries of some weight, but other peculiar features neutralise and render harmless these oppositional qualities.

# Chapter 7

# Baptists

Sociologists of religion engaged in the study of sects usually accept the following generalisations about their origins and development. Sects arise as protest movements against an established church and/or the social conditions in the wider society. It is not always easy for a sect to maintain its protest, particularly when it recruits a second generation of adherents. A process of accommodation may then commence. If the adjustment to society is extensive, or if the sect adopts increasing formality in its arrangements, it may become similar to a denomination (Martin, 1962; Wilson, 1966). Wilson has pointed out that the extent of a sect's eventual conformism to dominant social patterns depends on the type of sect at issue. He emphasises that 'sects of the "conversionist" type are most likely to fulfil the conditions which transform sects into denominations and are least likely to enjoy the circumstances preventing this process' (Wilson, 1959, p. 14). When this movement towards the denominational position does occur, the sect often becomes divided between those favouring and those opposing the process of accommodation. Tension arises between members with 'sect'-like and members with 'church'-like orientations, and the balance between these tendencies determines the sect's development. Usually such conflict can be discussed and compromise may be reached, but sometimes it leads to schism. The group with sectarian orientations breaks away and tries to re-create the spirit of protest which again sets it apart from the rest of society. Such intra-sect conflict or even schism may take place for various reasons.

In the case of 'conversionist' sects, conflict may ensue between old and new members because excessive recruitment of new members may entail an influx of weakly committed members who do not share the protest sentiments of the older members and thus make it impossible to maintain the sectarian spirit. This apparently purely religious conflict is usually, however, the expression of an underlying social conflict (Wilson, 1959, p. 211). One group of members has not kept pace with the social advancement and subsequent enhancement of intra-sect power of another section and expresses its protest against this inequality in religious terms. Research in the West has shown that members of religious organisations expressing strong sectarian orientations are likely to be the economically and/or socially underprivileged sections of the organisation (see Dynes, 1955; Demerath, 1965). Such social division in the organisation may be latent for a long time and may lead to schism only if it is exploited by leaders engaged in a power struggle at the top of the organisation.

All these theses about conflict between sectarian and denominational tendencies in religious organisations and about the social characteristics of the protagonists have been derived from studies of the development of religious organisations in Western capitalist society. In this chapter an examination of both an established 'conversionist' sect and its schismatic group will show that these generalisations do not hold in the social context of Soviet society. The Union of Evangelical Christian Baptists and its recent schismatic group, the Initsiativniks, will be discussed.* A short description and analysis of the postwar development of the sect and its schismatic group will be followed by an analysis and comparison of the social characteristics of their respective members. After exploring some explanations for the socio-religious responses of both Baptists and Initsiativniks the most feasible will be elaborated in greater detail. Besides contrasting my conclusions with those of sociologists of religion in Western society I shall also show that the stock explanation by Soviet sociologists for the persistence of religion in their society is inadequate in the case of the Initsiativniks. The data will disprove the thesis that religion persists because a certain section of the population is not yet integrated into the socialist 'working collective' (i.e. into the large sector of highly mechanised industrial enterprises which forms the backbone of the Soviet economy and provides the socio-cultural environment for the new socialist man).

Groups of both Baptists and Evangelical Christians were first formed in Russia in the second half of the nineteenth century. These sects arose in protest against Western religious and social establishments and they were easily transplanted on to Russian soil. Despite persecution they grew steadily in the unsettled social and political conditions of the period between the emancipation of the serfs in 1861 and the 1917 Revolution. But their real expansion took place only after the October Revolution. The extensive social and political upheavals of revolution, civil war, collectivisation and, finally, the Second World War, provided fertile ground for sects in general and the Baptists in particular. While they had only about 100,000 members before the First World War, their number had risen to 500,000 by 1927 (Mitrokhin, 1966, p. 74). During the intense anti-religious campaign of the thirties numbers declined drastically by about half but rose again when persecution subsided in the war and postwar years. Following efforts at *rapprochement* between the sects for a very long time, in 1944 Evangelical Christians and Baptists united at both local and national level into one organisation. The union in 1944, although convenient to the Soviet authorities, seems to have been a result of the genuine wishes of leaders and members of both sects who recognised their great affinities in dogma and ritual. Although there are occasional references in the sociological literature to power struggles on the basis of pre-1944 sect affiliation, there is little convincing evidence in either Soviet or Baptist writing to support this claim. The admission of 18,000 Mennonite Brethren into the Union in 1963 seems to have gone equally smoothly though the Mennonites have endeavoured to keep themselves separate at local level. The addition of 25,000 Pentecostalists to the Union in 1945 (*Bratskii Vestnik*, 1, 1960, p. 87) has proved more problematic. The significant differences in both dogma and ritual between the two sects, especially the Pentecostalist practice of glossolalia, have caused much conflict in the Union at both local and national level.

* The Union of Evangelical Christian Baptists represents a merger of most Soviet Evangelical Christians and Baptists, over half the Pentecostalists and most of the Mennonite Brethren. For convenience I shall refer to this Union hereafter as the Baptist sect. The Initsiativniks are also called the Council of Churches of Evangelical Christian Baptists.

After 1944 the central co-ordinating body of the Union – the All-Union Council of Evangelical Christian Baptists (hereafter AUCECB) – was able to re-start the publication of a journal, to hold congresses, to send representatives abroad and, since 1968, to arrange a correspondence course for training new presbyters.

## SECT MEMBERSHIP

The present-day strength of the Baptist movement is difficult to assess because several conflicting estimates of membership of the AUCECB have been given in recent years. Only isolated membership figures for individual congregations are available, and thus aggregate figures of total membership cannot be checked. (The list of congregations in Appendix A below gives some indication of the distribution and strength of the sect.) More seriously, we have no figures on the size of the illegally existing groups. Although a figure of 545,000 full members had been given to the World Council of Churches in 1962 by the AUCECB itself (*World Christian Handbook*, 1962, p. 221), at the 1966 Moscow congress of the Union the much lower figure of 250,000 members was mentioned (*Bratskii Vestnik*, 6, 1966, p. 17). According to the *Baptist Times* (28 January 1971), during the sixties the sect had surpassed the 1927 figure and is said to have had 550,000 baptised members and a constituency of about 3 million. At the 1974 congress of the Union the figure of 535,000 was mentioned (Sawatsky, 1975, p. 12). In addition, there exist a very large number of unregistered congregations. A Baptist presbyter of an unregistered congregation, who emigrated to Germany, said that in the seventies almost half of all Baptist congregations were unregistered. He claimed that, except in the large cities, the illegal congregations are invariably much larger than the legal ones. His last congregation in Sigulda in Latvia, for example, had 300 baptised members while the local registered group had attracted only 30 people (*Religion in Communist Lands*, 1, 1974, pp. 24–5). An appeal by Frunze (Kirgizia) Initsiativniks in 1974 said that as many as two-thirds of all Evangelical Christian Baptists are not registered (*Religion in Communist Dominated Areas*, 1 and 2, 1974, p. 10). These claims are borne out by detailed local studies. The study of Baptists in the Voronezh region of the RSFSR mentions 20 unregistered congregations and 103 unregistered smaller groups as against only 8 registered congregations (Teplyakov, 1972, p. 156). A study of sects in Azerbaidzhan reveals that all rural and two of the four urban congregations were not registered (Gladkov and Korytin, 1961, p. 44). These unregistered Baptists often are Pure or Free Baptists, Baptists of the Old Faith, Initsiativniks or similar schismatics and also ordinary Evangelical Christian Baptists. In total the large number of illegally existing Baptists and the some 550,000 officially recognised Baptists make this sect the largest on Soviet soil and the third largest Baptist group in the world.

Although losses in membership in several regions in the last fifteen years have been reported by Soviet sociologists (e.g. Mandrygin and Makarov, 1966, p. 234; Klibanov, 1969, pp. 60–72; Gagarin, 1971, p. 128; Klibanov, 1972, p. 52; Tabakaru, 1973, p. 4) gains or stability of numbers were acknowledged for others (e.g. Bograd, 1961, p. 125; Gegeshidze, 1964, pp. 23–5; Mandrygin, 1965a, p. 4; *Stroitel'stvo . . .*, 1966, p. 72; *Dein Reich Komme*, 1, 1975, p. 5; *Religion in Communist Dominated Areas*, 4, 5, 6, p. 63). A very thorough study of Baptists in a typical region of the RSFSR states a relatively small decline from their highest level of membership of 3,609 in 1957 to 2,378 in 1970 (Teplyakov, 1972, p. 156). According to the leading Soviet specialist on Baptists, L. Mitrokhin, Baptists have been holding their numbers steady on a national level during the preceding decade (Mitrokhin, 1974, p. 90). Baptists themselves report a small increase in total membership. At the 1970 congress of the AUCECB an increase in membership of 13,000 since 1967 was reported (*Bratskii Vestnik*, 2, 1970, p. 24), and at the 1974 congress an increase of 12,000 during the preceding five years was claimed (Sawatsky, 1975, p. 5).

'SECT'-LIKE AND 'DENOMINATIONAL' TENDENCIES

Viewed in sociological terms, the Baptists are a religious organisation which has persisted for several generations, converting a large number of followers, institutionalising and centralising its organisation to a significant extent, initiating some professionalisation of religious functionaries, and even taking far-reaching steps in ecumenicalism. It seems that such an organisation can hardly be called a sect any longer and has, like its Western counterparts, assumed a distinctly denominational character. But a closer examination will reveal that appearances are deceptive and that in most of their responses the Soviet Baptists are still distinctly sectarian.

Though the 'conversionist' Baptists are very active proselytisers, they have never had great revivalist campaigns. Except during the 1920s and the 1945–50 period, they have grown very steadily. This is partly due to the restrictive conditions of their militantly atheist environment and partly to a conscious policy on their own part. They strictly uphold the principles of admission by test of merit and expulsion of the unworthy. Soviet sociologists point out that the period of probation before baptism is taken very seriously. During the probationary year candidates receive instruction from the presbyter and other senior members, and prior to acceptance the applicant has to appear before the church council. There are always more applicants for baptism than are accepted. In Moldavia, for example, no more than 40 per cent of applicants were successful in the sixties (*Religion in Communist Dominated Areas*, 4, 5, 6, p. 64) and, in addition, the local groups were regularly purged of those considered unworthy (ibid.). In Voronezh region between 1950 and 1964, 531 people were baptised while 312 members were expelled (Klibanov, 1969, p. 77). In one Belorussian village studied, forty-two people were expelled between 1953 and 1963 for such offences as drunkenness, theft from neighbours, malicious gossiping and religious passivity (Mandrygin and Makarov, 1966, p. 236). The attempt by the Soviet authorities to isolate socially religious organisations and to prevent their organisational renewal has not had the effect of making Baptists lower their standards but, on the contrary, has made them adhere to the merit principle more firmly than their counterparts in countries tolerant of religion.

Such a rigorous policy has ensured the preservation of deep commitment to religious practice and of thorough knowledge of doctrinal positions, as well as of moral fervour and Christian charity. These are singled out as distinguishing characteristics of Baptists by nearly every writer in the field. Eighty-eight per cent of Baptists in eastern Belorussia and 85 per cent in Donetsk region, for example, visited the prayer house regularly at least once a week (Prokoshchina and Lensu, 1969, p. 202; Mashenko, 1971, p. 13). In a Komi ASSR survey 80 per cent were found to be attending prayer meetings regularly, and 81·3 per cent prayed habitually at home (Gagarin, 1971, p. 128). Baptists know their teaching very well, and the majority own and regularly read their own Bible (which is a rare commodity in the Soviet Union) (see Zlobin, 1963, p. 110; Mitrokhin, 1966, p. 95; Nikonov, 1969, p. 117; Gagarin, 1971, p. 128). Those who are not literate enough to read the Bible on their own get many opportunities to acquaint themselves with its content during services. During services between four and six sermons are delivered, and about 60 per cent of these are on Biblical themes (Yarugin, 1971, p. 150).

Though Baptists have considerably institutionalised and centralised their organisation, this has not had the effect of threatening the autonomy of local congregations in many matters, except during events between 1960 and 1963. Local congregations not only select their own presbyters and preachers and determine the scope and character of their religious activity but also elect the central leaders through delegates. The central organisation has the following functions: advising on spiritual issues, maintaining unity in the Union, keeping communities in touch by the circulation of a journal and maintaining a middle hierarchy of regional senior presbyters. The latter invest local presbyters, advise congregations in their regions and arbitrate between conflicting factions. The central apparatus is maintained solely by voluntary local contributions. But centralisation has had an unintended side-effect. Besides jeopardising local autonomy somewhat in matters of organisation, it also threatens the maintenance of exclusivity. The existence of a central organisation has given the Soviet authorities an instrument by which, through threats and concessions, they can undermine the exclusivity of members. As this process of socio-political accommodation to Soviet power by Baptist leaders is a vital factor in the recent development of the sect it will be discussed more extensively at the end of this section.

An agency for the training of religious functionaries was created in 1968, but the effect of this attempt to professionalise local leadership has so far been insignificant. As these courses have only very recently been instituted after a break of forty years and offer just 100 places at a time, the overwhelming majority of presbyters are still laymen who combine their religious duties with employment in a secular occupation. Three hundred presbyters are said to fulfil their duties on a full-time basis while about 30,000 presbyters, deacons and preachers execute them in their spare time (Simon, 1970, p. 129). The great emphasis on lay preachers (large communities may have up to twenty) and the Baptist principle of the priesthood of every believer are sufficient to counteract attempts at professionalisation and preserve the sectarian characteristic of lay involvement.

Although ecumenicalism is usually considered a sure sign of an organisation's denominational character, this, again, applies only partly in the case of the Soviet Baptists. While the merger of the very similar Baptists and Evangelical Christians required little surrender of doctrinal or ritual positions by either party, the not entirely voluntary entry of Pentecostalists into the Union affected mainly the latter who, as a minority in the Union, had to make the major concessions. At local level, the Pentecostalist influence has, if anything, served to strengthen rather than weaken sectarian orientations (Fedorenko, 1965, p. 183). Nevertheless, the acceptance of all these mergers does show again that Baptist leaders, in an effort to preserve the external strength of their organisation, are willing to make compromises with Soviet power which weaken internal sectarian vitality.

A further effect of this 'administered' ecumenicalism is the attenuation of elite status in the self-conception of Baptists. Although in the parishes the collective of believers is still continually counterposed to 'those outside', to other collectives (Mitrokhin, 1966, p. 218), many believers have become more tolerant of people outside their sect. They concede that members of other sects have the same chances to be saved and sometimes even admit them to their services if they do not have a prayer house of their own. In a Belorussian survey 32·9 per cent of respondents advocated and exercised complete tolerance towards other sectarians, 60·4 per cent were intolerant in their attitudes towards members of other sects but did not carry these attitudes over into their behaviour while 6·7 per cent – of which nearly 70 per cent were Initsiativniks – insisted on their elite status in theory and practice. A minority of Baptists conceded the chance of salvation to members of the Orthodox Church and even to atheists. Yet even the latter did not completely surrender a claim to elite status for Baptists, arguing that membership of their sect guaranteed a superior hope for the attainment of moral conduct and salvation (Prokoshchina and Lensu, 1969, pp. 218–20). Ecumenicalism at international level, such as joining the World Council of Churches (wcc), is also still opposed by many local congregations who cannot reconcile their eschatological vision of being the chosen with membership in an inter-church organisation. Their hostility towards the wcc is vividly expressed in their naming it the 'Babylonic Whore' (*Bratskii Vestnik*, 3, 1969, pp. 67f.).

Concerning the sectarian principle of exclusivity, denominational tendencies have been asserting themselves strongly at the level of central leadership, while the principle is still widely adhered to at local level. Exclusivity demands that members put allegiance to the sect before that to any secular organisation or ideology. Whereas for church members, religion is compartmentalised, for sectarians religious values inform all their attitudes and guide their life activities. Social experiences are interpreted in religious terms and those likely to interfere with sect allegiance are avoided. As pointed out earlier, the creation of a central Baptist organisation has provided the Soviet authorities with an instrument by which they can, through threats and concessions, undermine members' primary allegiance to the sect and channel it towards socialist organisations. They have stipulated to the Council the responses of sect members to many aspects of their socialist environment and instructed them to filter them down to local level. By responding to threats and concessions Baptist leaders are not only accommodating *themselves* to secular power but are also influencing members at local level towards acceptance of communist socio-political values to the detriment of allegiance to Baptist principles. They have, in fact, begun to change in subtle ways the Baptist secular ethic. Through their journal *Bratskii Vestnik* and at congresses Baptist leaders have extolled the achievements of the Soviet government, demanded respect for all men in power and urged believers to become more socially involved (see, for example, the six-page leader in *Bratskii Vestnik*, 5, 1967, pp. 4ff.). They also advise members to make full use of Soviet educational and cultural provisions (Chiperis, 1964, p. 80).

These admonitions have been partly successful in so far as many Baptists put respect for secular power and laws before loyalty to Baptist dogmatic principles. A Baku presbyter, for example, refused to baptise a young couple and a teacher because their acceptance into the congregation might attract the attention and disapproval of the authorities to it since official ideology holds young, well-educated people to be immune to religion (Gladkov and Korytin, 1961, p. 44). The Belorussian survey established that the majority of respondents had abandoned the Baptist position on war. Only 33 per cent of respondents still opposed war and no more than 4 per cent rejected military service (Prokoshchina and Lensu, 1969, pp. 198, 199). Also many parents have rejected the Baptist principle that the family is a domestic church and that children must be brought up in the spirit of Baptism. They leave the decision to their children and are even proud if they decide to join the Communist Party (ibid., p. 49; Manuilova, 1970, p. 205). In Moldavia, for example, it was said to be rare for Baptist parents to forbid their children to enter the Young Pioneers or Komsomols, to take part in extra-curricular school activities or to read fictional literature (Tabakaru, 1973, p. 10). Yet Baptists are still much more zealous in imparting religious education to their children than are Orthodox. In a Ukrainian sample about half of the respondents gave their children a religious education as against only 16 per cent among Orthodox (Duluman, Lubovik and Tancher, 1970, p. 94).

This effort by the leadership to adapt Baptist teaching to the demands of their political masters has made little impact on some aspects of the Baptist world-view, and many local groups seem to be completely untouched by it. Thus Baptists are still known for viewing life in strongly religious terms, and withdrawal from social involvement and disavowal of a common cause with communism are still widely preached and practised at local level. An Ashkhabad presbyter, for example, condemned any kind of war including one to defend the Soviet Union and advised his congregation not to take part in the building of communism (Chiperis, 1964, p. 78). Another study revealed that Baptists, as a rule, avoided all social and cultural functions held in the school club or collective farm office (Mandrygin and Makarov, 1966, p. 236). Although Baptists are known for their good performance at work and for the fact that many have brought honour to their brigades by securing medals and decorations, Baptists do not perceive their work in communist terms. As many as 78 per cent in the Belorussian sample saw their work primarily as a means to gain salvation (Prokoshchina and Lensu, 1969, p. 97). Also happiness in life is viewed largely in religious terms. A comparative survey of Baptist and Orthodox believers found that 62·22 per cent of Baptists as against only 6·25 per cent of Orthodox defined happiness in such terms. Baptists do not as a rule have a social life outside the Baptist community: 92 per cent in one sample stated that they communicated with their neighbours only out of necessity (ibid., pp. 109, 110). Girls would rather stay single than choose a non-Baptist marriage partner (*Conference Report* . . ., 1969, p. 4; Prokoshchina and Lensu, 1969, p. 109).

It is interesting to note that Baptist leaders, who make compromises with the Soviet authorities on matters of dogma and secular ethic, refuse in strong terms to tolerate the influence of modernising Western theologians like Harnack, Hartmann and Bultmann. The AUC has resolved that 'not a milligram of this modern poison' must enter the theological training programme for presbyters (*Bratskii Vestnik*, 6, 1966, p. 17; 3, 1969, p. 63).

Baptists in the Soviet Union are thus a comparatively large, third-generation 'conversionist' sect which has made compromises about sectarian principles, and 'sectarian' tendencies are still stronger in it than 'denominational' orientations. At various times during the fifties 'sectarian' elements tried to assert themselves against those with 'denominational' leanings. Such attempts were those of the 'Pure Baptists', the 'Perfectionists' and the 'Free Church', which tried to re-establish fundamental Baptist positions. They led to schisms during the fifties in various communities such as Voronezh (Aleksandrovich, Kandaurov and Nemirovskii, 1961, p. 65), Baku (Gladkov and Korytin, 1961, p. 43), and Kazakh-stan (Sulatskov, 1966), but never became national movements. This preservation and periodical resurgence of radical sectarianism is very much due to the fact that the Baptists have existed in a socialist and militant atheist social environ-ment. Measures adopted by the state to weaken the sect have, in the long run, strengthened its religious vitality. Thus the severe restriction on training profes-sional religious functionaries has helped to preserve the priesthood of all believers, keeping lay members informed and involved. The lack of facilities for national organisation has kept local congregations active and independent. The intolerant state attitude towards and persecution of sect members has forced Baptists to re-examine and reaffirm their commitment to their belief, all the time preventing the formation of the more assured and relaxed religious stance characteristic of members of denominations. The need to defend their faith in confrontations with militant atheists has given them a firmer grasp and deeper knowledge of Baptist doctrine. Discrimination in educational and occupational fields against professed believers has worked in the direction of only attracting the more committed believers into the sect.

German and English Baptist delegations visiting the Soviet Union are always struck by the deep piety of Soviet Baptists and admit somewhat shamefacedly that religious commitment among their own followers appears shallow in com-parison with that of their Soviet brethren. One recent German visitor likens the atmosphere and tone in Baptist congregations to a revivalist spirit and renders an interesting account of two Caucasian congregations.

'The presbyter starts the service with the greeting: "Christ has risen" and all jump to their feet and answer: "He truly has risen". This is repeated twice. We shall not easily forget this spontaneous Easter joy . . . Songs are started up loudly, with strength and vitality. Only every tenth person has a hymn book, the rest sing by heart. How different it sounds when the songs come from the heart.'

'When the communal prayer [German *Gebetsgemeinschaft*] begins, a young girl is the first to pray. She confesses her sins and begs Jesus Christ to accept her life. She prays with tears flowing, loudly and with intense emotion. When her prayer does not stop the preacher begins a hymn, and all join in . . . The girl's loud calling out in prayer is enveloped by quiet singing which is meant as comfort and as an answer about Jesus Christ's salvation. Without understanding the words we are moved ourselves and understand what is taking place. Other young people, boys and girls, join her in prayer. The parents have tears streaming down their cheeks. This evening five young people choose Christ.' (S. Kerstan, quoted in *Dein Reich Komme*, September 1974, pp. 8, 9)

But the state's policy on religion has not only consisted of restrictive and punitive measures. Some concessions have been made to Baptist leaders which, generally speaking, have given the sect a more secure organisational base and have enhanced the power and prestige of sect leaders. The acceptance of these concessions, probably made by Baptist leaders in the sincere hope of strengthening their organisation, have put the sect on the road to a denominational position and thus, ultimately, weakened its religious vitality. This has occurred not only because acceptance has automatically involved the sect in a more accommodative attitude towards the state, but because these concessions by the state have had to be bought in the end with even greater concessions on the part of the Baptists.

## THE SCHISM IN 1961 AND THE EMERGENCE OF THE INITSIATIVNIKS

In 1960, new 'Union Statutes' and a 'Letter of Instructions' for senior presbyters were adopted by the AUCECB, and their content was filtered down to all member congregations. The full text of the 'Letter of Instructions' has never been published but various extracts and summaries have been given in the Initsiativnik journal *Bratskii Listok*, 2–3, 1965, and in the sociological literature (e.g. Klibanov and Mitrokhin, 1966, p. 86; Mitrokhin, 1966, pp. 80*f*.). The 'New Statutes' have been reprinted by the Initsiativnik leaders. (For the full text see Bourdeaux, 1968, pp. 190*f*.). These new regulations demanded in essence the surrender of vital sectarian principles and can only have been imposed on the AUCECB by the Council for the Affairs of Religious Cults. They stipulated the abandonment of the practices of admitting children to services or organising them in any form of Sunday school activity, and of preaching and proselytising by ordinary congregation members. They demanded that the number of baptisms of people between 18 and 30 years of age be restricted to the absolute minimum and that the probation period be increased to three years (Yashin, 1969, p. 18). They made general provision for the further strengthening of the central Union Council at the expense of local autonomy and negated any responsibility or concern for the many unregistered Baptist congregations. Most Baptist leaders as well as rank-and-file members either did not recognise the threat to their sectarian principles which compliance with these stipulations involved or they valued a superficial peace in state–sect relations more highly than the religious vitality of their organisation. But a minority of local leaders and members were not prepared to accept these conditions of state appeasement and put allegiance to their organisation in first place.

Thus the 1960 'Letter of Instructions' and 'Statutes' sharpened the latent conflict between 'sectarian' and 'denominational' elements in the Baptist sect and eventually led to schism. In 1961 an opposition group of local leaders and activists formed to protest against compliance with the new regulations and called for a congress to discuss their abolition. In 1962 leaders of the new movement met and formed an Organisation Committee (OC) with a five-man presidium elected to organise a congress. When repeated demands for the calling of a congress were ignored by the AUC the final break occurred between the two opposing factions. The OC, which by then had attracted a mass following, established itself as the true church and excommunicated AUC leaders and a number of senior presbyters (Simon, 1969, pp. 503–4). In 1965 the already deep rift between official and schismatic Baptists was formalised when the OC transformed itself into the Council of Churches of Evangelical Christian Baptists (CCECB). This new schismatic group is variously called the Council of Churches, the Initsiativniks, the

Action Group or the Reform Baptists. There are a lot of conflicting estimates as to the number of members, and it is difficult to gauge which are correct. Mitrokhin's (1966, p. 81) estimate of 20,000–30,000 in 1965 must therefore be taken only as a rough guide. Since 1966 numbers have fluctuated a lot. Although no up-to-date estimate of membership is available we know that their following is still large.

The leaders of the new movement worked out amendments to the 1960 Statutes and made public their view of the Baptists' position in Soviet society. (See *Bratskii Listok*, 1961, reprinted in full in Bourdeaux, 1968, pp. 190*f*.). The basic differences between Initsiativniks and legal Baptists are well brought out by contrasting their respective programmes. The first section of the Initsiativniks' programme, 'The Word of God is the only fully sufficient and absolutely authoritative guidance for the church' (*Vestnik Spaseniya*, 1964, 2, 6, p. 2), is paralleled by a much tamer first principle among the legal Baptists: 'The Holy Bible [Old and New Testament] forms the basic teaching of Evangelical Christian Baptists' (*Bratskii Vestnik*, 1966, 1, pp. 44–5). While sections 3 to 6 of the Initsiativnik programme are found in almost identical form in the Baptist programme, sections 2 and 7 of the Initsiativnik programme are significantly omitted in the more moderate Baptist programme. Section 2, stipulating that 'the preaching of the gospel as the witnessing for Christ is the main task and basic mission of the church' asserts the duty and right to proselytise widely. Section 7, positing the 'general priesthood of believers' (*Vestnik Spaseniya*, 1964, 2, 6) emphasises the need for every ordinary member to preach and proselytise. They are thus a direct challenge to state regulations. Though these principles have been traditionally a basic Baptist teaching, the official Baptists surrendered them in order to avoid such a challenge.

Thus Initsiativniks reasserted the 'sectarian' principle of exclusivity and demanded complete independence from the state to achieve this. In contrast to Baptists, they hold themselves and their children much more apart from the influence of Soviet socialism. Examples of their attempts to gain spiritual separateness range from non-participation in communist youth organisations to refusal to carry arms for the Soviet Union (e.g. *Travel Report . . .*, 1970). They also stress the autonomy of local congregations from the AUC and defend the rights of unregistered congregations.

Although it is generally stated in the sociological literature that the Initsiativniks did not change the sect's dogmatic positions but merely tried to reaffirm old ones for the initiation of a spiritual rebirth, one study speaks of a basic change in dogma, a shift from a passive position where men put all hope on God to one where believers *act* independently in accordance with a knowledge of God's will (Gal'perin, 1970, p. 9). Such a teaching accords very well with the Initsiativnik movement's exceptionally high degree of religious activism. They have agitated widely in both word and deed for their demands, publishing their own journal, writing petitions and protest letters to government organs and even demonstrating in Moscow. In the Altai area, for example, more than sixty different declarations and applications were sent to the authorities in 1965 alone (Andreev, 1973, p. 15). They established a secret printing press which had printed over 100,000 New Testaments and hymn books when it was discovered by the political authorities in 1974. (*Newsletter of the Missionary Society 'Licht im Osten'*, September 1974). Besides the reassertion of the principle of sectarian exclusivity and the greater activism in 'the war for God', Initsiativniks are also said to be more prone to emphasise eschatology than are Baptists (Gal'perin, 1970, p. 11).

The Soviet government has recognised the threat that such a radical schismatic group has posed and has reacted quickly. It has tried to dissolve the Initsiativniks by a policy combining both leniency and force. On the one hand, the AUCECB were allowed to revoke in 1963 and 1965 most of the controversial regulations in order to encourage the schismatics to return. But, on the other hand, the schismatics were declared illegal and members were harassed, fined and arrested on a mass scale. There have been many moves at reconciliation by the AUCECB and one-fifth of the original number of Initsiativniks were said to have returned to it by 1966 (Klibanov, 1969, pp. 177, 178). But the schism has not healed, and Initsiativniks are still strong and active in the 1970s. At the 1974 Congress of the AUCECB it was admitted that as many new members had been gained by the Initsiativniks as had left them to return to the AUCECB (Congress proceedings reported by Sawatsky, 1975, p. 14. See also the report of a Baptist presbyter, who emigrated to Germany, about the strength of the Initsiativnik movement in the seventies in *Religion in Communist Lands*, Vol. 2, 1, 1974).

Thus in 1961 the tension between 'sect'-like and 'denominational' tendencies erupted into serious conflict. Conflict was not merely between the 'sect'-like and 'denominational' elements, but the state interfered as a third party and hardened conflict. By its goading the moderate and threatening the radical elements in the Baptist movement, compromise was made impossible and schism inevitable. The upholding of sectarian principles became possible by separation only.

On the face of it the reasons for schism seem to have been differences about the principles of Baptist association. But, as Wilson points out (1966, p. 193), such an explanation must not be accepted too lightly as schismatics often justify the break by doctrinal argument when, in reality, the difference between groups is often of a social nature. Both Dynes and Demerath also stress that social differences usually form the base for differences on matters of dogma. One way to establish the real motives for action as against those professed by the actors themselves is to determine the socio-economic characteristics of actors and to try to deduce real motives from any emerging patterns. In the following section the socio-demographic characteristics of both official and schismatic Baptists will be outlined. We shall then be in a position to examine both whether the theses of Western sociologists concerning the social base of religious conflict are borne out by the Soviet data and whether Soviet sociologists have generalised unduly when they describe the typical religious believer and the causes for his religiosity.

## THE SOCIO-DEMOGRAPHIC DISTRIBUTION AND SOCIAL COMPOSITION OF BAPTISTS

Baptists, at their early peak in 1927, were particularly strong in the Western areas of the Soviet Union. Their social composition was almost identical to that of the population as a whole (Klibanov, 1969, p. 73). Since then the Baptist sect has changed significantly in a number of ways. In the sixties and early seventies they were spread over all the Soviet Union. They were more widely spread than Orthodox believers and other sects. Unlike Orthodox believers, they were relatively weakly represented in the northern, central and Volga regions of the RSFSR and strongly in some of its border regions (Rostov, Krasnodar and

Stavropol regions, the Urals and Siberia), in some central Asian republics (especially Kazakhstan, Kirgizia and Uzbekistan), in some Caucasian areas, and especially in the western republics, i.e. the Ukraine, Belorussia, Moldavia and the Baltics (except Lithuania). According to one study, during the early sixties 50 per cent of Baptists were in the Ukraine, 30 per cent in the RSFSR and 7 per cent in Belorussia (*Stroitel'stvo . . .*, 1966, p. 71). This estimate may be roughly accurate, although it neglects the considerable strength of Baptists in some of the central Asian republics and in Siberia. It is notable that the numerically really strong congregations (i.e. with at least 1,000 members) are all, excepting only Moscow and Leningrad, outside or at the fringes of the RSFSR. They are in Kiev, Kharkov, Rostov, Tbilisi, Tashkent, Novosibirsk, Omsk, Tallin, Riga, Alma-Ata, Karaganda, Frunze and Dzhambul (*Bratskii Vestnik*, 1966, 6, p. 17). It is interesting that Baptists are weak in those republics which have a strong national church of their own, Armenia and Lithuania, as well as in predominantly Moslem areas.

Baptists are no longer a predominantly rural sect. It seems that they have an equally large or even slightly larger urban membership (see, for example, Mandrygin, 1965a, p. 4). Rural congregations are generally weak and declining while urban ones are strong and have been growing (Aleksandrovich, Kandaurov and Nemirovskii, 1961, p. 64; Zlobin, 1963, p. 100; Mandrygin, 1965b, p. 23; Prokoshchina and Lensu, 1969, p. 40; Klibanov, 1972, p. 52). In Minsk region, for example, the number of urban believers has steadily grown, and in the late sixties they were 47 per cent of all Baptists in the region (Prokoshchina and Lensu, 1969, p. 40). In some areas Baptism has been an exclusively or almost exclusively urban phenomenon. In Turkmenistan, for example, there are said to be no rural congregations (Chiperis, 1964, p. 75) nor were there any in Sverdlovsk region (Kolosnitsyn, 1969, p. 133), while in the Komi ASSR rural Baptists amounted to only 5 per cent of all Baptists (Gagarin, 1970, p. 365). All over the Soviet Union the large and flourishing congregations are in towns or workers' settlements of an urban type (Aleksandrovich, Kandaurov and Nemirovskii, 1961, p. 64; Zlobin, 1963, p. 106; Filimonov, 1974, p. 25). A list of Baptist congregations in the Appendix brings out that hardly any large industrial town is without its Baptist community. Several writers point out that Baptists are often newcomers to town life and tend to live on the outskirts of the cities where they try to preserve a rural environment, having their own houses with large kitchen gardens (Mandrygin, 1965a, p. 9; Chernyak, 1967, p. 214; Prokoshchina and Lensu, 1969, p. 40; Gaidurova, 1969, p. 26; Kolosnitsyn, 1969, p. 134; Serdobol'skaya, 1971, p. 13). This strongly urban character of the Baptist sect distinguishes it from other Soviet religious organisations, especially from the Orthodox Church which still has its stronghold in the countryside.

While Baptists have thus spread their influence in terms of their geographical and urban/rural distribution, they have lost it in most other social areas during the Soviet period. Since their heyday in the early 1920s they have aged considerably (Klibanov, 1969, pp. 65, 66) and have become a sect of predominantly female, elderly people of fairly low educational and occupational status or, more often, without employment (i.e. pensioners and housewives). Various surveys conducted during the 1960s and early 1970s show that more than three-quarters of Baptists are female and poorly educated, just under half are over 60 years of age and over half are not in employment. The data also show that this process has not progressed equally far in all geographical areas. Baptism has lost most social influence in areas where it is relatively weakly represented anyway – in the heartland of the RSFSR, in Tambov and Voronezh regions. The sect's social complexion is organisationally more viable in such areas as Kazakhstan, Kirgizia, Belorussia, Ukraine, Moldavia, western Siberia and the Komi ASSR. In Moldavia, for example, as many as 82 per cent of Baptists were in employment in 1973 (Gazhos, 1975, p. 34). The greater vitality of the sect in these areas is also reflected in the lesser and slower numerical decline of Baptism in such areas (e.g. Bryanov, 1965, p. 10; Chernyak, 1965, pp. 69, 70) and the greater activism of members (Andreev, 1973, p. 6). While such an age/sex structure puts Baptists at a slight disadvantage compared to the smaller sects of Western origin, it compares favourably with that of Orthodox believers (see the comparative social statistics on Western sects in the Ukraine in Eryshev, 1969, pp. A41f.).

Although Baptists have deteriorated absolutely in terms of age and sex and relatively in educational characteristics, they have not completely lost influence among the more advantaged social strata. They still attract a significant minority of young, relatively well-educated and qualified people. Believers under 30 years of age amount to 10 per cent or more in several areas (e.g. Leningrad, Lipetsk region, Kazakhstan, Komi ASSR, Turkmenistan and some Moldavian towns). One study of believers among youths gives the proportion of Baptists under 25 years of age as between 6 and 15 per cent (Galitskaya, 1969, p. 393). Those under 40 years of age come to an average of 18 per cent of the total but in some areas to more than a quarter. Klibanov (1970, p. 73) puts the number of those between 20 and 40 years of age in Baptist congregations at 19·6 per cent. Moreover, in some regions the proportion of young members has been increasing over the last decade. In Moldavia, for example, around 30 per cent of all newly baptised members have been under 30 years of age in recent years (Tabakaru, 1973, p. 6). It must also be borne in mind that in many congregations the younger members left in 1961 to join the Initsiativniks and that, up to then, the age structure was much less skewed. In Novosibirsk, for example, up to 1961, 15–18 per cent of members were youths, while after the schism their proportion fell to 0·4 per cent (Kostenko, 1967, p. 38).

As far as education is concerned, over 10 per cent have incomplete (seven to eight years') or complete (ten years') middle schooling. In recent years the average length of study has probably risen too. The Kuybyshev congregation, for example, is described as having several members with higher education in its midst (Mandrygin, 1965b, p. 14). A study of Siberian sectarians also reports the emergence in recent years in some congregations of highly literate preachers with professional qualifications and speaks of their success in recruiting workers, pupils and students (Kostenko, 1967, p. 36).

Around 23 per cent of all surveyed Baptists during the period under consideration were members of the working class, i.e. the majority of *working* Baptists were members of the urban working class. Moreover, in some areas (e.g. Moldavia) the percentage of those working in industrial production has been increasing over the last decade (Tabakaru, 1973, p. 8; Gazhos, 1975, p. 33). When we get more detailed figures, like those for Baptists of Alma-Ata town, it is revealed that quite high percentages are skilled white-collar workers. Thus 55 per cent of all white-collar and 66 per cent of all manual worker Baptists were skilled in the Alma-Ata sample (Chernyak, 1967, p. 213). The impression that Baptism has considerable support among the working class is well illustrated by the following remark by a Russian Orthodox to a traveller to the USSR: 'God has raised up the Baptists in this age, so that the Gospel may be heard at the work bench and in places where no Orthodox priest could go' (Lawrence, 1973, p. 23). Orthodox believers, in contrast, scored very much lower along all these social dimensions. Young, relatively well-educated workers were a very rare phenomenon in most Orthodox congregations. There was also, during that period, a small minority among Baptists of members of the intelligentsia. These are said to be in technical and applied scientific occupations and hardly ever in the 'liberal' professions (Gazhos, 1975, p. 34). Baptist believers in urban areas are said to be similar to rural ones in terms of age and sex, but, as might be expected, have higher educational and occupational qualifications (Tabakaru, 1968, p. 7).

Kolarz's (1962, p. 306) assertion that Baptists are representative of the Soviet people both socially and ethnically is, as our data have demonstrated, misleading and oversimplified. While the Baptist movement contains more diverse social and national groups than other Soviet religious organisations, it certainly does not contain them in representative proportions. It over-represents the non-working population, has more workers than collective farmers and under-represents the highly qualified manual and non-manual workers. Ethnically it is overweighted with the Slavic nationalities (Russians, Ukrainians, White Russians) as well as containing a big German component. It has not had significant influence among the Asian Moslem population and the tribal minorities, nor has it made an impact among Armenians and Georgians. The 943 strong (in 1964) congregation of Dzhambul (Kazakh SSR), for example, consisted of 455 Russians, 239 Ukrainians, 225 Germans, 14 Belorussians, and only 10 people of other nationalities. There was hardly a native of Dzhambul in the congregation (Mandrygin, 1965a, p. 7). Similarly, the congregation in Baku (Azerbaidzhan) was 80 per cent Russian (Gladkov and Korytin, 1961, p. 45).

## THE SOCIO-DEMOGRAPHIC DISTRIBUTION AND SOCIAL COMPOSITION OF THE INITSIATIVNIK SECT

Information from Soviet sociologists on Initsiativniks is more scanty. To obtain additional information on the schismatics I had to extract data in a cumbersome roundabout way. I systematically collected and analysed the personal statistics of 826 Initsiativniks who have been tried by, or come into some sort of conflict with, the political authorities between 1961 and 1972. The data have been collected mainly by consulting numerous lists of prisoners, and other documents compiled and sent to the West by the 'Council of Baptist Prisoners' Relatives' and by Civil Rights Groups. (These documents are collected by, and, available at, the Centre for the Study of Religion in Communist Lands in Keston, Kent; they have often been confirmed and supplemented by Soviet press reports and can be considered reliable.) The Initsiativniks represented in this sample are mainly (91·3 per cent) rank-and-file members and come from all corners of the Soviet Union. The only bias in the sample may be that the data reflect the differential anti-religious zeal of local Soviet authorities. The long time-span of collection of eleven years should compensate for such geographical bias to a large extent. Although one might expect urban authorities to be more militant in anti-religious measures, this bias ought to be evened out by the fact that believers in rural small-scale communities must be much more noticeable than in the anonymous urban environment. The data from our own survey provide us with almost full (99 per cent) information on the geographical, urban–rural and sex distribution of Initsiativniks, with partial (68 per cent) information on their age distribution, and with very incomplete data on their occupation, education and nationality. Most of the data on social background have been taken from records of court proceedings and newspaper reports.

When we turn our attention to the social composition of the Initsiativniks we get some striking differences in the socio-demographic composition of membership from that of Baptists. The distribution of Initsiativniks between large geographical-administrative units is presented in Table 4. This brings out the fact that the western republics – Moldavia, Belorussia and the Ukraine – had a higher concentration of Initsiativniks than the RSFSR. In Moldavia in 1967 there were said to be 400 Initsiativniks in twenty different population centres (*Kommunist Moldavii*, 1967, p. 70). Within the RSFSR Initsiativniks were very unevenly distributed. Nearly half of those in my sample were in Siberia and the southern border regions. They were weak in the Caucasian republics, being completely absent in Armenia. In central Asia, except Turkmenistan, they were well represented, especially in Kazakhstan where the ratio was 4·9 per million. They were weak or non-existent in republics or autonomous regions where there are few Russians or Ukrainians, such as Turkmenistan, Bashkir ASSR, Karbadino-Balkar ASSR, Mordvinian ASSR and Checheno-Ingush ASSR. Lastly, their weak representation is notable in the two Lutheran Baltic republics where Baptists are relatively

Table 4    *Geographical Distribution of Initsiativniks*

| Geographical-political unit | Total pop. in '000s* | Total no. of Initsiativniks | No. of Initsiativniks per m. of pop. |
|---|---|---|---|
| RSFSR | 126,561 | 407 | 3·2 |
| Altai region only | 2,766 | 49 | 16·0 |
| Krasnodar and Stavropol regions only | 6,362 | 70 | 10·9 |
| Caucasian republics (Georgia and Azerbaidzhan) | 9,208 | 22 | 2·4 |
| Central Asian republics (Kaz. SSR, Kirg. SSR, Uz. SSR, Tad. SSR) | 27,941 | 120 | 4·2 |
| Kazakhstan only | 12,129 | 59 | 4·9 |
| Rostov region only | 3,730 | 34 | 8·5 |
| Kursk region only | 1,496 | 23 | 16·0 |
| Moldavia | 3,368 | 20 | 6·1 |
| Belorussia | 8,684 | 70 | 8·2 |
| Western Belorussia | 2,337 | 28 | 11·2 |
| Eastern Belorussia | 6,347 | 42 | 6·4 |
| Ukraine | 45,516 | 117 | 3·9 |
| Western Ukraine | 7,536 | 9 | 1·2 |
| Eastern Ukraine | 37,980 | 168 | 4·4 |

* *Narodnoe Khozyaistvo SSSR v 1965 g*, pp. 9, 10, 14–18, 20.

strong. For Belorussia and the Ukraine we analysed separately data for Initsiativniks from the western parts of these republics which were acquired by the Soviet Union only during the Second World War. This was done to test the claim generally advanced in the Soviet literature that the sects are much stronger in these parts because of the population's greater social and political immaturity. While this claim receives support from the data for Belorussia, it is not borne out for the Ukraine where Initsiativniks were much stronger in the eastern regions. In general, the data show that the Initsiativniks are strong in areas of deportation and exile and in regions of recent rapid urban and industrial development. Some, like Siberia and central Asia are, of course, notable for both.

Table 5 very clearly brings out the fact that the Initsiativniks have a disproportionately high share of urban members in all areas. They predominate in large towns (over 100,000 inhabitants). List 2 in Appendix A shows that these are mainly industrial towns, many connected with heavy industry. The question arises whether Initsiativniks became what they are because of the pressures associated with rapid industrial and urban development, or whether, as some

Table 5  *Urban–Rural Distribution of Initsiativniks*

| Geog.-Admin. unit | Percentage of urban pop.* | Percentage of urban Initsiativniks | Percentage of Initsiativniks in large towns |
|---|---|---|---|
| RSFSR | 59·0 | 77·0 | 52·0 |
| Caucasian republics (Georgia and Azerbaidzhan) | 48·5 | 87·0 | 27·0 |
| Central Asian republics | 39·0 | 70·0 | 56·6 |
| Moldavia | 28·0 | 60·0 | 45·0 |
| Belorussia | 39·0 | 71·4 | 48·5 |
| Ukraine | 52·0 | 71·5 | 45·8 |

* *Narodnoe Khozyaistvo SSSR v 1965*, pp. 9, 10, 14–18, 20.

Soviet authors (e.g. Klibanov, 1969, p. 88) claim about Baptists in general, they were Baptists first and then migrated to large urban centres to join viable Baptist communities. These data by themselves do not suggest an answer but other data presented later in the chapter will be more suggestive.

Turning to sex distribution, my own data show that there is a great preponderance of male Initsiativniks in all areas, the average being as high as 94 per cent. The high number of men in the sample must be due to the fact that men are more often activists in the sect and therefore more liable to be arrested. While it thus does not demonstrate that men predominate among Initsiativniks it makes it highly unlikely that they are as weakly represented as among Baptists.

The age distribution of Initsiativniks (see Table 6), although showing minor deviations between geographical areas, does again exhibit clear trends. In every area the younger age groups (up to 40) predominate over the older ones, and in every area by far the largest number of Initsiativniks are in the 30–40 age group. The higher number of those in the over-60 age group than those in their forties and fifties in several areas may be explained by the relatively large number of religious leaders (seventy-two) among the convicted who customarily tend to be old in the Baptist sect.

Table 6   *Age Distribution of Initsiativniks as of 1965*

| Geographical area | Total no. of Inits | Age known N | Age known % | Up to 30 N | Up to 30 % | 31–40 N | 31–40 % | 41–50 N | 41–50 % | 51–60 N | 51–60 % | 60+ N | 60+ % |
|---|---|---|---|---|---|---|---|---|---|---|---|---|---|
| RSFSR (excluding the areas below) | 205 | 146 | 100 | 43 | 29·5 | 57 | 39·0 | 13 | 8·9 | 13 | 8·9 | 20 | 13·7 |
| Siberia, Altai and Far East | 102 | 51 | 100 | 11 | 21·5 | 19 | 37·2 | 8 | 15·6 | 9 | 17·6 | 4 | 7·8 |
| Autonomous republics and regions | 100 | 74 | 100 | 16 | 21·6 | 24 | 31·0 | 10 | 13·5 | 7 | 9·4 | 17 | 22·9 |
| Central Asian republics | 120 | 78 | 100 | 19 | 24·4 | 42 | 53·8 | 8 | 10·2 | 5 | 6·4 | 5 | 6·4 |
| Caucasian republics | 23 | 19 | 100 | 0 | 0·0 | 11 | 57·7 | 3 | 15·7 | 4 | 21·0 | 1 | 5·2 |
| Moldavia | 20 | 10 | 100 | 2 | 20·0 | 5 | 50·0 | 1 | 10·0 | 0 | 0·0 | 2 | 20·0 |
| Belorussia | 70 | 59 | 100 | 7 | 10·9 | 24 | 41·9 | 6 | 10·6 | 11 | 18·4 | 11 | 17·6 |
| Ukraine | 177 | 120 | 100 | 31 | 25·4 | 50 | 45·5 | 13 | 11·6 | 16 | 18·8 | 10 | 8·9 |
| Unclassified | 9 | 4 | 100 | 2 | — | 1 | — | 0 | — | 1 | — | 0 | — |
| | 826 | 561 | 100 | 131 | 23·3 | 233 | 41·5 | 62 | 11·0 | 66 | 11·7 | 70 | 12·4 |

Although data on occupational status are known for only 9 per cent of the sample and are insufficient to make reliable deductions, they do suggest broad trends which are supported by other information. The preponderance of workers over collective farmers fits in with the highly urban character of the Initsiativnik movement. The workers in my sample were not, as Soviet sociologists usually assert about Baptists, mainly unskilled and/or working in isolation from the 'production collective'. The majority worked as skilled and semi-skilled workers in industrial enterprises. Professionals in this sample and in other accounts were usually in occupations with a strong vocational component such as engineers, economists, agronomists or doctors, rather than being in the 'liberal' professions (see also Tabakaru, 1970, p. 5; Gagarin, 1971, p. 370).

Although the percentage of members with known education is again too small (4 per cent) to make certain inferences, one might note that those with a relatively high level of education are in an overwhelming majority. This does, of course, fit the picture of the typical Initsiativnik who is under 40 years old and urban.

Although nationality is not always in the personal statistics of believers one can deduce a certain amount from their surnames. These show that the vast majority of them are Slavic (Russian, White Russian or Ukrainian). In addition, one national minority, the Germans, are disproportionately highly represented among Initsiativniks in those areas to which they were deported. Thus in the central Asian republics 33 out of 36 members in rural areas were Germans, while in urban areas they amounted to 19 out of 84. In Siberia 35 out of a total of 102 Initsiativniks were of German origin.

Some of the data about Initsiativniks presented above are borne out by those collected by Soviet sociologists (see Klibanov, 1969, pp. 114–15; Gagarin, 1971, p. 124; Andreev, 1973, p. 15). The results of their surveys fully support my point that the younger age groups form the overwhelming majority of Initsiativniks. Klibanov and Mitrokhin (1967) state that the young (20–40 years of age) amounted to over 50 per cent in some congregations. This is also confirmed by Serdobolskaya's study of Leningrad Initsiativniks (1963, p. 117). Their exceptionally youthful character has even led to them being called 'Young Baptists'. Several studies also point out that the Initsiativniks continue to attract the younger age groups in large numbers into the sect. Most of these surveys confirm the fact that a far higher number than among Baptists are male and in employment. They provide little information on occupational status. Only the Tambov study mentions educational qualifications – over 80 per cent of respondents have had some sort of secondary education (Klibanov, 1972, p. 53). These results are in keeping with my own. In addition, our knowledge of the general fact that membership of the 20–40 age group is highly correlated in the Soviet Union with being relatively well educated (i.e. having incomplete or complete secondary education) and qualified can lead one to assume that Initsiativniks come predominantly from the section of Soviet society born and raised under socialism. They joined the sect at a time when socialism was well established in the Soviet Union.

Initsiativnik leaders also come from the younger, more educated urban strata. We know that their leaders – Prokoviev, Kryuchkov, Vins and Baturin – were in their prime years when they started or joined the movement and that Prokoviev was a graduate teacher (Kim, 1964, p. 4), Vins a graduate economist (Bourdeaux, 1971, p. 74) and Kryuchkov an electrician. We can deduce from their organisational work and writing that they are highly literate and astute men.

The above outline of the social composition of Baptists and Initsiativniks has brought out very clearly that the religious schism in the Baptist sect is also a division along social lines. Firstly, while both Baptists and Initsiativniks are particularly strong in areas away from the geographical centre of the RSFSR (except a few large central Russian towns), Initsiativniks appear to be more highly concentrated in large urban industrial centres on the geographical periphery in areas connected with both political dissent and economic development or growth (e.g. Kazakhstan, Siberia, the industrial areas of the western Ukraine, northern Caucasus and the Urals). Secondly, while the Baptists have retained predominantly female, elderly, poorly educated and poorly qualified members who are often removed from the economic and ideological centres of Soviet society, Initsiativniks have attracted a high proportion of younger, relatively well-educated and qualified people who are full members of the Soviet economic and social system. They are, in fact, from that section of Soviet society which Soviet Marxist ideology envisages as producing the 'new socialist man' and which is regarded as the backbone of Soviet society.

## EXPLANATIONS OF THE SCHISM

This summary of findings on the social characteristics of Baptists and Initsiativniks does not accord with the generalisations advanced by Western sociologists about actual or potential (those with 'sect'-like tendencies) schismatics, nor does it fit the most prevalent Soviet sociological explanation for the persistence of religion in socialist society. Our data show that the schismatics (who have strong 'sect'-like orientations) are certainly not the economically or socially underprivileged section of the Baptist sect but, on the contrary, have as a rule superior economic and social status.

It is more difficult to disprove conclusively the argument that the Initsiativniks split off from the main body of the sect because they were underprivileged in terms of intra-sect power but some weighty points can be raised against this view. The split is clearly not the result of a power struggle between national sect leaders on the All-Union Council but the schism is much deeper, cutting right across the sect involving both leaders and rank-and-file members. Among the Initsiativniks there is no leader of the charismatic type, but a democratic collective leadership. In the early years of the conflict the Initsiativnik leadership made no bid for power but tried for a long time to arrange discussions in a democratic manner by calling for a congress. That the schism was not merely the result of a power struggle for leadership is also supported by the fact that rank-and-file members have become deeply involved. In many places congregations have split into opposing factions. Secondly, the schism is also not caused by a revolt of rank-and-file members against religious leaders. Many of the Initsiativniks held local power positions prior to the schism. Thus over 6 per cent of my sample had been religious leaders of some sort. The study of the split in Ryazan congregation (RSFSR) also reveals that nearly all the schismatics had been leading activists, mainly young, well-educated preachers (Zlobin, 1963, p. 102).

It is often suggested in the Soviet literature that the Union of Evangelical Christian Baptists, being a collection of disparate elements, has been plagued from the beginning by periodic schisms, resulted from power struggles between the two main partners in the Union. The 1961 schism is said to be only the latest and most effective of such breakaway attempts (Klibanov, 1969, p. 113; Brazhnik, 1969, p. 6). Our evidence leads us to reject this claim. A close study of previous schismatic movements, such as the Pure Baptists or Free Baptists, shows that these were not so much struggles of Baptists against Evangelical Christians, but more attempts to preserve local autonomy against encroachment from the AUC. Initsiativniks, too, gained many members from congregations previously un-affiliated to the AUC, from congregations that nursed some sort of grievance against the central organisation or against the state (see Yashin, 1969, p. 19; Gal'perin, 1970, p. 8). While a power struggle between Baptists and Evangelical Christians may have widened the rift in some local splits, it is unlikely to have been the decisive element. The majority of the Initsiativniks are postwar joiners of the sect and must therefore have identified with it as it emerged from the 1944 Union rather than with either of the component sects. Although it is true that Baptists predominated among those initiators of the schism who had a clear allegiance to either of the component sects, Evangelical Christians and Pente-costalists also joined the Initsiativnik faction, and the programme of the move-ment was general rather than biased towards Baptist principles (Brazhnik, 1969, p. 6). Besides, Initsiativniks have been very successful in areas where hardly any Evangelical Christians are present, such as in western Siberia (Andreev, 1973, p. 13). Thus the explanations that religious division or schism is usually indicative of social conflict or power struggle within a religious organisation and that schismatics are the underprivileged section of membership do not hold in the case of the Soviet Baptist schism.

The other popular explanation that dissent or schism in 'conversionist' sects occurs when sectarian principles are endangered by a large influx of weakly committed members is also disproven by the facts. Firstly, the Baptist sect has had no great revivalist campaigns and, although not growing evenly from year to year, has expanded fairly steadily. The figures below on the number of bap-tisms in Moldavia illustrate this point.

*Number of Baptisms in Three Areas in Moldavia**

| Area | 1945–50 | 1951–5 | 1956–60 | 1961–5 |
|---|---|---|---|---|
| Region A | 169 | 61 | 102 | 73 |
| B | 20 | 8 | 11 | 36 |
| C | 37 | 43 | 17 | 20 |

\* *Religion in Communist Dominated Areas* 4, 5, 6, p. 66.

The biggest congregations in Moscow (5,000 members) and Leningrad (3,500 members) have each grown by over 100 new members a year (Russell, 1970). In all congregations together, about 5,000 believers are baptised each year (*Bratskii Vestnik*, 6, 1968, pp. 22f.). As pointed out earlier, admission to the sect is still strictly on merit. Secondly, the schismatics, who stand for preservation of Baptist principles, are predominantly (about two-thirds) postwar joiners and not long-standing members of the sect (Klibanov and Mitrokhin, 1967, p. 95; Klibanov, 1969, p. 114). Thus the Soviet Baptist schism presents us with the strange situation that, generally speaking, sectarian tradition and fundamental values are asserted by the younger against the older (in some cases, founder) generation.

The most prevalent explanation by *Soviet* sociologists for the persistence of religion in socialist society, while borne out by the facts about religious believers in general, fails completely in the case of the Initsiativniks. The explanation that religion persists among those strata in Soviet society whose positions in society do not yet conform in some or all respects to the norms of Soviet socialism does not fit the facts about Initsiativniks. As pointed out earlier, a high proportion of Initsiativniks come from the most advanced sector of Soviet society, from urban industrial centres, and have enjoyed all the social and cultural provisions as well as the political education of the socialist stage. But the end result of this socialisation process has not been a new socialist man but religious man. Although most Soviet sociologists simply ignore the Initsiativnik case when they generalise about religious believers, a few have considered it. They have stepped outside the usual theoretical framework and treated the phenomenon of the Initsiativniks separately in an *ad hoc* way. But the emerging explanations, which will be discussed below, remain too vague and unsystematic to be satisfactory.

Thus we are faced with a situation where the schism in Soviet Baptism and the social background of the schismatics do not fit into the general explanatory frameworks of either Western or Soviet sociologists of religion, and a new explanation is called for. In the following section I shall attempt to arrive at such an explanation by making a close examination of the responses of Baptists and Initsiativniks to their socialist social environment. One of the explanations offered by a Soviet sociologist (Klibanov, 1969, pp. 113–14) and taken up by another (Gagarin, 1971, p. 126), though insufficient by itself, will serve as a useful starting-point to this discussion.

Klibanov divides the Initsiativnik movement into two groups with different motivations for schism. The first group, for him, consists of religious moderates whose grievances are purely about matters internal to the sect. They are rank-and-file believers who are dissatisfied 'both with the moral complexion and aptitude for action of local leaders as well as with the form and style of central leadership on the AUCECB'. Into the second group Klibanov puts religious fanatics whose religious extremism is an expression of deep dissatisfaction with their socio-political environment. This second group contains a small proportion of older people 'who formed their world-views during the period of class struggle in the countryside . . . and who had experienced much and forgotten nothing' (Klibanov, 1969, p. 114). The larger proportion is formed by those who grew up in the war and immediate postwar period and did not receive much education in school or family. 'Finding themselves without experience and moral training in the hard living conditions of the postwar period they adopted a nihilistic relation to social actuality, scepticism and bitterness' (ibid., p. 114). Gagarin describes this latter group rather vaguely as people 'who were disillusioned about social ideals, about their inability to find a place in the struggle for lasting human interest' (Gagarin, 1971, p. 126).

Klibanov and Gagarin put their fingers on two important points. First, the schismatics are not all of the same kind but have different social orientations. Secondly, their religious radicalism is not a protest against some *particular* experience of social inequality (e.g. low occupational status) but is an expression of a more general and deeper disillusionment. Klibanov, however, does not probe deeply enough when he describes the more moderate Initsiativniks as merely dissatisfied with intra-sect politics. Discord about sect politics, as

Aleksandrovich, Kandaurov and Nemirovskii (1961, p. 65) quite rightly point out, is really disagreement about relations with the surrounding communist environment and thus of wider social significance. Let us now consider in more detail the two groupings within the Initsiativnik movement, their relative importance in it and the socio-political attitudes that underlie their religious rebellion.

Sectarianism in the Soviet Union in general and the schism in the Baptist movement in particular are better understood if regarded as a protest against the total domination of communist ideology, i.e. domination not only over social and political relations but also over personal morals and the ethics of interpersonal relations. Most believers now concede to the political authorities the right to determine material development as well as socio-political relations but they challenge their right and competence to influence moral standards. In other words, they are prepared to accept the economic, social and political policies embodied in communism but refuse to accept it as a general philosophy of life, i.e. a philosophy which gives guidance on the meaning and purpose of life and charts the spiritual development of man.

This stance towards the Soviet order characterises particularly aptly the orientations of the majority of Baptists. A Baptist preacher in Syktyvkar (Komi ASSR) expressed this very well when he told an interviewer: 'I am convinced that the communists will build the material and technical base of communism without us. But they will never solve the task of civilising man without us' (Gagarin, 1970, p. 369).

The threat of total domination by communist ideology became more acute again in the late fifties when Khrushchev's anti-religion campaign began. For Baptists, it reached a climax in 1960 when Baptist religious autonomy was severely restricted by the regulations issued in the New Statutes and the 'Instruction Letter' to senior presbyters described above. The more urban, younger and middle generations in the Baptist sect recognised the grave threat to their sectarian world contained in these new regulations. They realised that further centralisation of sect organisation would endanger their ideological autonomy, and that prohibition of proselytising and of instructing the young in religion would weaken the influence of their philosophy of life in the competition with that of communism. The new restrictive regulations not only led the Initsiativniks to religious radicalism but their protest was expressed in a militant political manner. Like non-religious dissenters, they asserted their rights in a well-organised manner through the political channels available to Soviet citizens – protest letters and demonstrations. This policy, worked out by the well-educated leaders, must in turn have had the effect of attracting more educated and politically aware believers into their movement.

When the protest movement of the Initsiativniks became established it inevitably attracted another, smaller group of Baptists who were more generally and more bitterly hostile to the communist system. They were not, as the majority of Initsiativniks, drawn to religion as a complementary but as an alternative world-view to communism and rejected the theories embodied in communism wholesale. They were, therefore, eager to join any opposition movement available. Though there is little information in the Soviet sociological literature on the background and motives of these elements within the Initsiativnik movement, a few inferences may be made. First, hostility is unlikely to have been nourished by nationalist disaffection. Baptist religion, having close Anglo-American and

German connections besides being of a multi-national composition, is a bad vehicle for the expression of nationalist sentiments, except perhaps for the Germans. Even in their case, however, other explanations are more persuasive. It is freely acknowledged by some Soviet writers that Germans were directed into religious organisations because of their terrible experiences during the war and early post-war period (see, for example, Belimov, 1972, p. 15). Secondly, the passage of time makes it unlikely that many Baptists are still inspired by the hate engendered during the class struggle in the Civil War.

A more likely source of hate and bitterness are memories of maltreatment, imprisonment and deportation during the Stalin period. This motive is mentioned most frequently when individual cases are discussed in the Soviet literature. It is often said that many Baptist leaders, especially of unregistered congregations, have a record of conviction for criminal, civil or political offences (Chernyak, 1965, p. 75; Gagarin, 1966, p. 30). But one has to interpret such statements most carefully as many religious leaders are known to have been arrested during the thirties on pretexts or for their religious conviction on questions such as military service. This latter proposition is also supported by the fact that there are high concentrations of Initsiativniks in former deportation areas, and by the pre-ponderance among Initsiativniks of an easily recognisable group of deportees – Germans. In Siberia, for example, children of deportees (*spets-pereselentsy*) are said to form the nuclei of Initsiativnik groups (Andreev, 1973, p. 13). This leaves open, of course, the question of what aspects of Soviet reality caused enough dis-illusionment to lead this group of people into conflict with Soviet power in the first place.

Lastly, we must not discount the possibility that a number of Initsiativniks are disillusioned with present-day socialist society, although it remains largely unclear what the grounds of their disaffection are. In the sociological literature only one narrow area of conflict is singled out – relations between Baptist groups and *some* local authorities which have violated the laws on religion. Initsiativnik groups are supposed to have flourished in areas where 'administrative persecution' has been rife (e.g. Brazhnik, 1969, p. 10) and in places where the local political authorities would not register congregations and thus maintained their illegal status (Mitrokhin, 1974, p. 89). It is not clear, however, whether registration has always been deliberately withheld, or whether congregations have sometimes preferred to remain unregistered. Yet there must have been feelings of more general disillusionment with Soviet society. A stance of rejection of the whole system comes out in remarks like 'Communism and Baptism can have no goals in common' (Survey respondents cited in Prokoshchina and Lensu, 1969, p. 187; Aleksandrovich, Kandaurov and Nemirovskii, 1961, p. 65). Speaking about Bap-tists in general, Yablokov (1965, p. 48) notes that a small number of them turned to religion because of general disillusionment with the conduct of their fellow citizens in the social and economic sphere. It is noteworthy that the vices these believers singled out – bureaucratism, bribery, speculation, toadyism and plunder-ing of social property – were all generated by the malfunctioning of the socialist social and economic system rather than by universal individual shortcomings as some Soviet explanations of their behaviour would have us believe.

It must be pointed out that the totally disillusioned and politically hostile group forms a minority within the Initsiativnik movement. Initsiativniks in general are not hostile to the Soviet system as a whole. The majority are either indifferent or favourably disposed towards the socio-economic transformation state and Party have effected. Furthermore, the more generally hostile attitude of the minority is not sanctioned by the Initsiativnik leadership. Initsiativnik leaders made it clear that, like the Baptists, they are loyal to the Soviet state, support its socio-economic goals and only oppose its interference in religious affairs (see, for example, their protestation of political loyalty in the appeal to Khrushchev of 13 August 1963, reprinted in Bourdeaux, 1968, p. 59). Unlike some of the more hostile sects, the illegal Pentecostalists and Jehovah's Witnesses, Initsiativniks have not gone into the religious underground but have tried to fight for their rights within the framework of Leninist thought on religion and the 1918 laws on religion (see the letter by Vins and Kryuchkov addressed to Brezhnev in 1965; full text in Bourdeaux, 1968, pp. 105*f*.). Such responses have been too systematic-ally thought out to be just a facade put up by leaders to safeguard their exist-ence.

Interviews with rank-and-file Baptists and Initsiativniks reported in the socio-logical literature bring out that, in contrast with some of the smaller sects, there is little *general* hostility towards the regime. (Unfortunately Soviet researchers rarely make clear what proportions of their sample are Baptists and what Init-siativniks, but tend to lump them together under the term 'Baptists'.) Respondents in the Belorussian sample, for instance, when questioned about their attitudes towards and conduct in socialist activities (such as trade union activity, socialist competition at work), divided into the following groups: only 7·7 per cent were hostile, 55·5 per cent were indifferent, 33·5 per cent were sympathetic but inactive, while 3·3 per cent were sympathetic and actively involved (Prokoshchina and Lensu, 1969, p. 157, Table 9). Many even welcomed the political ideas of com-munism and professed loyalty to those in power but were not very interested in the socio-political affairs of their country (ibid., p. 168). The overwhelming majority (91·2 per cent) claimed to observe Soviet holidays, such as the anni-versary of the Revolution (ibid., p. 170). In a western Siberian sample 65 per cent of the respondents thought that communist and Christian ideas were identical, but such opinions were often based on a very primitive definition of communism as a state of material sufficiency. When the communist philosophy of life was singled out for discussion, believers responded less positively (Andreev, 1973, p. 19).

Some of the Baptists hostile to the communist system have neither joined the Initsiativniks nor remained followers of the AUCECB. In 1961 many joined forces with the illegal branch of Pentecostalism which affords a better chance to express political dissent (Gladkov and Korytin, 1961, p. 43; Zlobin, 1963, p. 106; Serdobol'skaya, 1963, p. 121; Gagarin, 1966, p. 27; *Religion in Communist Dominated Areas* 4, 5, 6, p. 64).

The majority of Initsiativniks, as pointed out above, merely protested about the total ideological domination by communism implied by the imposition of the Instruction Letter and tried to reaffirm the autonomy of their own philosophy of life from that postulated by the state. This contention can be supported by data emerging from the various Soviet sociological studies of Baptists and Init-siativniks. Attitude studies among Baptists and Initsiativniks brought out that they were exceptionally preoccupied with questions of spiritual development in general and issues of private and public morals in particular. Two content analyses of sermons in the Baptist congregations of Volgograd region and of

Astrakhan (RSFSR) established that sermons were inseparably connected with the discussion of moral problems (Nikonov, 1969, p. 178; Yarugin, 1971, pp. 150f.). Thus in Yarugin's analysis the discussion of moral issues dominated between a quarter and a third of all sermons (ibid.). This is also confirmed by Mitrokhin's study of Baptist congregations (1966, p. 151). The following moral themes are brought up in these sermons: moral ideals, the influence of religion on the moral progress of humanity, love for one's neighbour, work attitudes, and interpersonal relations in the family and in society (Yarugin, 1971, p. 156). The following extract from a sermon is a good example of Baptist concern for morally exemplary living: 'Both at home and at work we have to spread a life-giving essence' (Chernyak, 1965, p. 89). New members are often attracted to Baptism by its moral teachings (*Religion in Communist Dominated Areas* 4, 5, 6, pp. 63ff.; Gagarin, 1970, p. 365; Ermakov, 1973, p. 165). They had been searching for a strong moral code and found that joining the sect had helped them to stop smoking and drinking (Zlobin, 1963, p. 103; Gagarin, 1971, p. 136). A Baptist doctor who has had occasion to treat many alcoholics suggested to an interviewer that the only way to bring an end to drunkenness was to spread the Baptist faith (Gagarin, 1970, p. 370). Often the sect attracts the wives of habitual drunkards who are drawn to the sect's image of 'clean living' (Chiperis, 1964, p. 78). But not only believers stress this moral integration function of the Baptist sect. It is also noted with some alarm in the general press that the claim to moral leadership by Baptism is convincing some groups of young people (*Uchitel'skaya Gazette*, 14 September 1971; *Komsomol'skaya Pravda*, 3 September 1971).

Concerned with morality at a higher level, some believers thought that 'all moral categories – duty, conscience, honour . . . etc. – lose their meaning without a belief in God' (*Prichiny . . .*, 1965, p. 203). Not surprisingly, many therefore point to the superior moral conduct of believers over non-believers (Prokoshchina and Lensu, 1969, p. 143). In one survey 30 per cent of Baptists as against only 9 per cent of Orthodox thought that moral conduct could not be achieved by non-believers (Yablokov, 1969b, p. 130), while in another as many as 54 per cent felt this way (Andreev, 1973, p. 21). Not surprisingly, therefore, Baptists list as one of the main deficiencies of Soviet society its inability to establish firm moral standards (Chernyak, 1969, p. 318; Prokoshchina and Lensu, 1969, pp. 83ff., 121, 189; *Religion in Communist Dominated Areas* 4, 5, 6, pp. 63ff.) Baptists in the Belorussian sample were noted for noticing only 'the shortcomings, evil and dirt' in Soviet society. A mere 6·3 per cent noticed any moral progress (Prokoshchina and Lensu, 1969, p. 121), while 81·5 per cent acknowledged material and technological progress (Ignatenko and Prokoshchina, 1971, p. 256). Ryazan Initsiativniks, too, in encounters with the young, 'underlined in all possible ways the shortcomings in "worldly life" to prove that genuine truth, the real meaning of life can only live in "communication with God" ' (Zlobin, 1963, p. 103). Among moral shortcomings prevalent in Soviet society, Baptists and Initsiativniks list irresponsible and unconscientious work attitudes, drunkenness, hooliganism and shaky sexual and familial morals. As many as 64 per cent in the Belorussian sample saw such moral shortcomings as obstacles in the way to reaching full communism (Prokoshchina and Lensu, 1969, p. 189).

Many Baptists express, in one way or another, the view that they resent most of all the claim by the Soviet authorities to have the right and competence to influence the moral training and spiritual development of the young generation.

They believe that Soviet schools cannot educate children but merely instruct them and that genuine education can only be given by religious organisations. This explains the great reluctance of many Baptists and Initsiativniks to let their children join youth organisations which claim to impart moral training. The activity of the Initsiativniks since the split has also shown that one of the areas of greatest concern to them is the moral instruction and spiritual development of the young. They are not prepared to leave these to the influence of communist agencies of socialisation. Press reports on Initsiativnik trials bring out that these sectarians took great personal risks to exert their influence in these areas. Despite grave deterrents they strove to set up and instruct groups of young people all over the Soviet Union. Lastly, the exceptionally harsh persecution of the Initsiativniks by the Soviet authorities shows that the latter have well understood the challenge to their ideology posed by the Initsiativniks' militant upholding of an alternative philosophy of life. Between 600 and 800 Initsiativniks have been imprisoned, many more fined and generally harassed since the split in 1961 up to 1974 (Council of Relatives of Imprisoned Baptists, *Bulletin* 11). The Initsiativniks are a dangerous movement in the eyes of the political authorities because their religion does not exhaust itself 'in the *knowledge* of God's word' but concentrates on '*its practical application* in life' (Gal'perin, 1970, p. 11). Zlobin, speaking about Ryazan Initsiativniks, sums up rather well this ideological challenge:

'The lesser political loyalty of sectarians (compared with Orthodox) in relation to our society and state (e.g. on the question of the possibility of building communism, in relation to the achievement of culture, etc.) is fully to be expected. If, for example, among Orthodox believers . . ., traditional and culture-oriented religiosity is more widespread, and they do not, on the whole, know the Bible, then the faith of sectarians, abstaining from most ritual, is to a much higher extent based on conviction, on the knowledge of religious dogma. And a more detailed knowledge, a more conscious adherence to a reactionary ideology hostile to communism, does essentially entail less political loyalty, a more open standing aside from society.' (Zlobin, 1963, p. 111)

## THE MORAL COMMUNITY

This strong moral component in Baptism not only expresses itself in believers' attitudes and actions but pervades the whole structure and image of the sect. Moral behaviour is not only advocated from the pulpit but structural supports are provided to help realise it in daily life. Baptist congregations have strong communities in which believers are tied to each other by close bonds of family, friendship and neighbourly support and surveillance. Thus, in various congregations all over the USSR, around 75 per cent of believers were connected to others in the congregation by ties of blood (Gegeshidze, 1964, p. 21; Kostenko, 1967, p. 36; Mashenko, 1971, p. 14; Manuilova, 1972, p. 16), and even in the capital, Moscow, between 30 and 40 per cent had relations among congregation members (Klibanov, 1969, p. 100). In addition, most members were also related to others by ties of friendship, meeting for Bible reading, sewing, etc., in each other's houses between services. Their communities resemble closely those total Calvinist communities in which moral behaviour is upheld by a combination of support and sanctions. 'The community is able fully to control and regulate the behaviour of believers in everyday life' (Mashenko, 1971, pp. 16, 17). The presbyter sees himself as much as a community leader (see sections 13 and 14 of the presbyter's handbook immediately below) as a spiritual counsellor. Help in matters of every-day life is provided to all in need on a regular basis, while friendship and sup-port is withdrawn if the behaviour of any member gives rise to criticism. Control by the community is made difficult, however, as far as the work environment is concerned. But even here surveillance is sometimes kept up as Baptists often try to work in the same enterprise (Gaidurova, 1969, p. 26; Mashenko, 1971, pp. 16, 18).

Particularly high standards of human quality are expected from religious func-tionaries. A high level of moral standards and human wisdom as well as the ability for strict but benign leadership are expected of all presbyters. Senior presbyters are subject to both regional and Union Council surveillance while other presbyters are watched over by their seniors and by the congregations. The quali-ties expected from a local presbyter are set out in the following extracts from a handbook for them:

(1) The first quality of a presbyter must be a fervent love for Christ . . .
(2) Your personal life must be pure and holy. You must strive for victory over every sin. Let your heart be the purest in the community.
(3) In all relationships be an example to your entire church.
(5) Improve yourself! Study the Bible – you must know it better than everyone in the community. Study spiritual literature. Ceaselessly raise your cultural level.
(7) Be faithful. Do not forsake the work of God due to the absence of earthly goods.
(8) Live modestly. Learn to be content with little.
(11) Fear pride and conceit! Do not lord it over the church, but be a servant to all.
(12) Love all your flock! Beware of having favourites! Love the disagreeable ones!
(13) Know all your flock! Know their number; have an exact membership list. Know each one individually! Know their spiritual condition, their gifts, their joys and trials, and their family life.
(14) Visit church members in their homes! Render personal love to the weak, the needy, the mournful and afflicted.
(19) Do not censure other churches!
(22) Be clean and tidy in your appearance! A clean body and clean clothing contribute to your authority.
(23) Be an example in fulfilling civic obligations and train your members to do likewise. Your church must fervently love its country and people.
(A. V. Karev, 'A Handbook for Presbyters', *Bratskii Vestnik*, 3, 1946, pp. 28, 29)

This image of morally exemplary spiritual leaders appeals especially to con-verts from Orthodoxy, where experience of corrupt and compromised behaviour by religious functionaries has not been infrequent (see, for example, the accounts of priests in Bourdeaux, 1969, pp. 187, 209). Furthermore, while Orthodox priests receive a high salary by Soviet standards, Baptist ministers render their dedicated service to the religious community free or for an extremely small remuneration.

The question arises why Baptists in general and Initsiativniks in particular reject the moral code embodied in communism and give the question of morals such a central place in their own world-view. For an answer we have to turn back to the social characteristics of Baptists and Initsiativniks analysed earlier in this chapter. Baptists, and even more so Initsiativniks, we found, are strong in urban areas. Initsiativniks especially tend to live in the larger urban centres in areas which have had a lot of industrial development or a high rate of growth in the postwar period. Several studies suggest that they are new to this urban industrial setting, living on the edges of towns where they try to re-create their recently lost rural environment. Some writers even mention the great difficulties experienced by these migrants when they first arrive in the towns (Mandrygin, 1965a, p. 9; Filimonov, 1974, p. 26). Many people do not only migrate from country to town, but at the same time to the completely new geographical environment of such development areas as Siberia or central Asia. That these migrants figure strongly in Baptist congregations is brought out by a study of Kazakhstan congregations. There the percentage of immigrants among new congregation members amounted to 60 per cent in 1959, 80 per cent in 1960, 75 per cent in 1961, 62 per cent in 1962, over 57 per cent in 1963 and to about 52 per cent in 1964 (Bryanov, 1965, p. 9). In the Soviet Union industrial development and social upheaval have not only been confined to urban areas. Industrial settlements are scattered all over the countryside, and even completely agricultural areas have experienced much upheaval as a result of the combined effect of collectivisation and technological progress. Thus it appears that both Baptists and Initsiativniks have among them a large number of men and women who have not long ago lost a stable social environment with traditionally fixed customs and regulations. The personal and social upheaval connected with the sudden immersion into urban and/or industrial life has undermined their previous way of life and has created great social insecurity and moral vulnerability. This anomic situation has been further aggravated by the fact that many of the host towns and settlements, having only recently sprung up or expanded, had not established a stable environment themselves. In this context the rigid and strong moral code of a religious organisation, which preserves moral values reminiscent of a more traditional society, offers them guidance and inspiration in their bewildering transition period. In addition, the allocation of new functions (e.g. visiting the sick in the congregation) and the provision of new social relations restore to the migrants a fresh sense of identity. The communist moral code, although also containing the slightly oldfashioned moral postulates of an earlier period, has failed to gain authority among these uprooted people.

We might conclude by saying that the Baptist movement in the Soviet Union is a social phenomenon which, despite repression by the political regime, has persisted and, at times, flourished in the postwar period. Generally speaking, Baptism is not a response to the socio-political programme of a socialist society but to the development programme of an industrial society. As in the United States at the turn of the century, the opening up of new frontiers and the colossal expansion of some established areas accompanied by large-scale industrialisation and urbanisation have created in Soviet society an anomic situation in which Baptism has found fertile ground. Its provision of a strong moral code, charity and close-knit community have helped many of those uprooted in these social upheavals to reorientate themselves in their new environment. As happened in the United States, this colossal expansion is coming to a halt, and the newly created urban-industrial environments are stabilising themselves. In these circumstances one would expect the Baptist sect to lose much of its sectarian moral fervour and continue its movement, already begun, towards a denominational position. But the anti-religious policy of the socialist regime, instead of weakening religious vitality of the sect, by its interference slowed down this movement towards a denominational position and, in 1961, partly reversed the trend by precipitating schism in the sect. In contrast with Western religious organisations, sectarian principles were asserted neither by the socially underprivileged section of membership nor predominantly by the older members, but were militantly upheld by the younger, more educated and aware members of the sect. Thus, while the flourishing of Baptism in general can be seen as a response to the development character of Soviet society, the schism in the sect and the birth of the Initsiativnik group occurred in response to the exclusive ideological nature of socialist society.

Chapter 8

# The Smaller Sects of Western Origin

## SEVENTH DAY ADVENTISTS

Seventh Day Adventists owe their name to the fact that they emphasise the second advent of Christ before the inauguration of the millennium and look forward to the overturn of this world. Although this tenet was central to their faith only during the early founding years in the USA the sect is still classified as belonging to the 'revolutionist' type. Present-day Adventists have become somewhat less concerned with a pre-millennial advent and have instead broadened their faith to include a variety of other tenets (e.g. keeping of the Sabbath on Saturday, health reform). Some doctrinal positions of Seventh Day Adventists tend to pull the sect in the direction of accommodation to some of the values of the wider society, while other tenets of faith may encourage opposition to ruling values. Which of these tendencies gains the upper hand at any one time depends to a large extent on the nature of their surrounding social environment. We shall therefore consider how the impact of Soviet society has affected the balance between the 'sect'-like and 'denominational' orientations of Adventists in the Soviet Union, and how the development of the sect has consequently taken a slightly different turn from that of its Western counterparts.

First, however, a short introduction into the history of Soviet Adventists and a description of their organisation and strength in the contemporary Soviet Union are in order. Adventism was introduced into Russia relatively early, in 1886. At its beginning the sect was mainly concentrated in the Ukraine, the Baltic provinces and in the Caucasus. It remained relatively small up to the Revolution, having claimed 6,720 members in 1916. After the Revolution, up to 1932, the sect doubled its membership, and between 1932 and 1945, like the other Soviet sects at the height of Stalinism, it went into decline and obscurity (*Blagovestnik*, 6, p. 31, quoted in *Stroitel'stvo . . .*, 1966, p. 82). After the war, the sect resumed its activity with renewed vigour and increased its numbers until the 1960s when its growth is supposed to have come to a halt (*Stroitel'stvo . . .*, 1966, p. 82). But this arrest of growth may have been a temporary phenomenon caused by the Khrushchev anti-religious campaign.

After the Revolution, Adventists were initially very hostile to the political regime but changed their attitude in 1924. A congress of the sect meeting in that year sent a declaration of loyalty and support to the new government, and the sect seems to have maintained this position ever since. Not even the administrative dissolution of the sect's organisational centre in 1961, because of alleged illegal activity,* nor the restriction on contacts with Western counterparts, seem to have affected the sect's stance to the political authorities. But as in most religious organisations in the Soviet Union, a vocal minority in the sect was vehemently opposed to accommodation to Soviet power and went into schism. This new splinter group, calling itself Reform Adventists or Adventists of the True Remnant, not only refused to support the new regime but also adhered much more strictly to Adventist positions on the keeping of Sabbath, refusal of military service and generally rejected the demands of socialist society. In 1929 they formed an underground centre. The government declared this small schismatic group illegal. But the Adventists of the True Remnant have maintained themselves up to the present day and do not seem to have abandoned their intransigent stance towards Soviet power. A second schismatic group, the Christians of the Seventh Day, who during the thirties urged a return to the spirit of Ellen White's days, are much less distinct from the parent body and appear to be very insignificant (Belov, 1968, p. 66).

In the sixties, the sect (excluding its schismatic groups) is said to have had 21,500 members according to a Soviet investigator (Belov, 1973, p. 62), while the 1967 handbook of Western Adventists gives their number as 40,000 organised in 834 churches (quoted by Wilson, 1970, p. 116). As usual, we have no means to verify either figure, nor do we possess any estimates of the strength of the illegal Adventist groups. Few figures on the size of local congregations have been released. We learn only that, in relation to the other sects of Western origin, Adventists are smaller (Klibanov, 1969, p. 95) but more stable in their membership. Few falls in membership have been reported in the various regions of their predominance (Lentin, 1966, p. 59; Belov, 1968, p. 220; Belov, 1973, p. 140; Klibanov, 1969, p. 98), and there are even some indications that the sect has developed a new vigour in the late 1960s (Tabakaru, 1970, pp. 6–7).

Groups of Seventh Day Adventists exist in the Ukraine, Belorussia, Moldavia, Latvia, Estonia, some regions of the RSFSR (especially in the south-west) and in some areas of the east and of central Asia (*Stroitel'stvo* . . ., 1966, p. 82). They are disproportionately strong in the western republics, 45 per cent being concentrated in the Ukraine, 20 per cent in Latvia and Estonia, 8 per cent in Moldavia, and only 17 per cent in the RSFSR, 7 per cent in central Asia and Kazakhstan and 3 per cent in other republics (Lentin, quoted by Klibanov, 1969, p. 98). The biggest contingent in proportion to the population is in the Baltic republics where they have been historically strong. Unlike the other Western sects, they are thus not strongly represented in the northern, far eastern and central Asian areas of the Soviet Union – the areas associated with deportation and labour camps. Reform Adventists, in contrast, have more support in central Asia and the Altai region of Siberia as well as having a following in the western Ukraine, Moldavia and the northern Caucasus (*Stroitel'stvo* . . ., 1966, p. 82).

### Religious and Social Orientations

Like Adventists in Western societies (see Schwartz, 1970), Soviet Adventists manage to combine contradictory orientations in their religious outlook. While

---

* Nowhere in the literature are the circumstances of the closing-down discussed, which arouses a strong suspicion that illegal procedure was used.

expecting the overthrow of the existing world and entertaining millennial hopes they nevertheless have a strong this-worldly orientation. Their 'revolutionist' tendencies have not filled them with disdain or indifference for life in the present world. On the contrary, they appear to be intent on making the best of life in this world and, unlike the Witnesses, seek neither constantly to denigrate their socialist environment nor to deny acceptance to their political rulers. In effect, their 'adventist' orientations appear to be no more dominant or central in their general outlook than they are among Pentecostalists (see section below), while they appear certainly much less dominant than among Jehovah's Witnesses. For example, when proselytising, Adventists will usually dwell on their concern for moral self-perfection rather than introducing adventist ideas (Belov, 1968, p. 135). Their response to Soviet society is more positive than that of Pentecostalists and Jehovah's Witnesses and similar to that held by large sections of registered Baptists. The adoption of a world-affirming response by sectarians is usually associated with a disregard for the principle of exclusive allegiance to the sect tenets of faith. The response of Soviet Adventists, however, is only partly due to a weakening of exclusivity and partly flows directly from the this-worldly orientations implied by some of their tenets of faith and prescriptions. A detailed examination of their attitudes to Soviet society and of their social conduct, coupled to an attempt to account for their genesis, will substantiate this point.

Adventism contains a variety of teachings which foster this-worldly and highly realistic orientations, such as a strong emphasis on the faithful execution of the Ten Commandments and the necessity to strive for moral perfection, a positive evaluation of science and technology, health reform and the recognition of state power as God-given. While a demand for faithfulness to the Ten Commandments may lead, as will be shown below, to conflict with the wider society, its more notable effect seems to be to direct the concern of Adventists towards their fellow men outside the sect and to integrate them into society in the process. In stark contrast to the 'revolutionist' Witnesses and more like the 'conversionist' Baptists, Adventists stress love for one's neighbour and are consequently always ready to dispense charity to those in need. Helping those in need outside the sect compels them to be 'of the world', and their involvement with the miseries of non-members necessarily integrates them into society. Thus Adventists, unlike many other sectarians, stress the need to work in production in order to get to know their fellow citizens (Belov, 1969, p. 211). Like the Baptists, they also are renowned for good work attitudes and performances (Belov, 1968, p. 153). Their preoccupation with moral propriety and their effort to execute all their worldly duties to the best of their ability are concerns also close to the heart of socialist ideologists, even if convictions spring from different spiritual foundations.

In contrast to most other Soviet sectarians, Adventists value science and technology and the achievements gained through them. They see science as a gift from God and perceive no conflict between it and religion but view them as complementary (Belov, 1968, pp. 168–71; Lentin, 1966b, p. 291). Preachers are familiar with popular scientific literature and present new advances as signs of God's great plan. Adventists praise modern technology for its usefulness in spreading their teachings (ibid., pp. 293, 296). They welcome the advance of knowledge in general and claim that they have never opposed the spread of education (Serdobol'skaya, 1962, p. 147). Although they obviously do not advance the materialist world-view propagated by Soviet ideologists their general attitudes to knowledge and its application puts them in tune with the more diffuse cultural climate in Soviet society characterised by a stronger faith in the beneficial influence of education and technological advance than is found in Western societies.

The health reform of the Seventh Day Adventists, positing the need for a clean and healthy body (as a temple for the spirit), is not only very congruent with general opinion in society but also directs the energies of Adventists into practical work which both gives them a favourable image in the eyes of their fellow men and integrates them into society. Adventists are not only known for advocating and practising clean living (no alcohol and no smoking), but they also succeed in channelling their members into the medical services or in recruiting from among medical personnel, mostly at the middle level but also at the top level among doctors (Lentin, 1966a, p. 11; Kostenko, 1967, p. 36; Belov, 1968, p. 124; Tabakaru, 1973, p. 7). In general, Adventists are said to try to project an image of themselves as progressive and humanitarian believers (Belov, 1968, p. 158).

The Adventist acknowledgement of state power as God-given is not a central tenet of faith but it has nevertheless decisively influenced their responses to the Soviet political rulers, to Soviet ideology and to Soviet society. The sect pledges loyalty and support to the Soviet government, and individual preachers refrain from teaching non-involvement in society's affairs. Those with more hostile feelings, it seems, have been syphoned off into the anti-Soviet schismatic groups of Reform Adventists. This lack of hostility to worldly power is in marked contrast to the theoretical position of Western Adventists. It does not become clear from the literature whether Adventists in the Soviet Union have always differed from Western Adventists in this respect or whether this constitutes a change of dogma in response to pressure from the Soviet state.

Many Adventist theologians and rank-and-file members stress the compatibility of communism and Adventist faith (Belov, 1973, pp. 163–4; *Prichiny* . . ., 1965, p. 149). Unlike some Baptist theoreticians, however, they do not advocate a fusion of communism and their religion nor do they put forward Christian socialist arguments (Lentin, 1966, p. 38), although the conviction of some Adventists that communism assures human happiness in *this* world (ibid., p. 65) goes a fair way towards such a position. Also their integration into society does not go beyond a certain point. While they advocate and practise involvement in the world of work they demand that members' spare time must revolve around the sect, and voluntary socio-political engagement (e.g. in neighbourhood courts, local administration, cultural work) is discouraged (Belov, 1968, p. 119).

All these responses to their society by Adventist believers, although propelling sect members towards integration into the wider society, are therefore *not* manifestations of a weakening allegiance to the sect's values and cannot be described as accommodative. As a number of the sect's values have from the beginning been congruent with those of the wider society a conflict of allegiances has not arisen about them. But a religious organisation, the teaching of which has many points of contact with the ideology of the wider society, is more likely to develop 'denominational' tendencies.

There are, however, other Adventist teachings which force members to decide whether allegiance to the sect takes preference over loyalty to the state and obedience to its laws. The reference here is to the Adventist emphasis on the fourth and sixth Commandments. The fulfilment of these Commandments, interpreted more concretely as refusal of military service and, more importantly, as keeping Sabbath on Saturday rather than Sunday, are considered necessary preparations for Christ's second advent. In contrast to the situation in Britain, in the Soviet Union Saturday has until recently not been a rest day in many occupations and is still a working day on collective farms. Neither are children free from school on that day. A demand for exemption from military service on grounds of conscience is considered an affront to the communist motherland. Consequently, conflict will arise from adherence to these tenets of faith, and the way Adventists deal with their conflicting allegiance is more likely to reveal whether the sectarian principle of exclusivity has been preserved or not. Their schismatic brethren, the Reform Adventists, have no doubt that Seventh Day Adventists have surrendered these principles, putting the law of the state before that of God (Belov, 1969, p. 67; Fedorenko, 1965, p. 193). The various bits of evidence presented in the scientific–atheist literature, however, deny such a complete surrender. In general it is said that believers are told to put God's word before the law of the state and that, if confronted with the choice, believers should not shrink from offending against Soviet law. There is little information on the question of conscientious objection to military service. It does not even become clear from the literature whether Adventists are given the option to do military service in non-combatant units and are thus able to avoid a crisis of conscience. There is some evidence to show that many Adventists endeavour to observe the Sabbath, even if sometimes in a compromise form. While many probably choose jobs which would allow them to have their rest day on Saturday, others remain absent from work on Saturdays (*Prichiny . . .*, 1965, p. 201; *Sovetskaya Moldavia*, 1967; Belov, 1968, p. 112). Children are said either to be kept away from school (Gazhos, 1975, p. 72) or, probably more often, are sent to school but are told not to do any work (*Prichiny . . .*, 1965, p. 203). Adventists are also said to be prepared to break the laws on religion and deliberately set out to attract young people into the sect by arranging cultural or leisure activities for them (Belov, 1968, p. 143). We are, however, given no systematic information to evaluate how general all these offences against the law are and can therefore conclude only tentatively that observance of the principle of exclusivity among some sections of Seventh Day Adventists asserts the 'sectarian' orientation against the setting in of 'denominational' leanings.

'Denominational' tendencies must also be held in check to some degree by the 'revolutionist' doctrine of Adventists, even if this doctrine is no longer dominant in their religious world-view and is rarely translated into concrete terms. The fact that a second coming and the overthrow of this world is still expected is pointed out by Klibanov who discerned a significant increase from 1950 onwards in the eschatological content of sermons as well as a more general preoccupation with the notions of Armageddon and a second coming (Klibanov, 1969, p. 130). The fact that these notions received different concrete content in the various geographical areas suggests that believers were not merely adhering to the letter of their original creed but were giving more spontaneous expression to their religious feelings. Another author, too, reports a preoccupation with the discovery of signs heralding the end of this world. The growth of atheism and anti-religious propaganda are said to be taken as such a sign (*Serdobol'skaya*, 1963, p. 151).

If the sect's tenets of faith and practices give members many points of contact with the wider society, and if the sect enjoins members to go into the world, the self-conception of the sect as an elite as well as its sense of self-identification may be weakened. It appears that Soviet Seventh Day Adventists, unlike Jehovah's Witnesses, do indeed make few claims for elite status. They are said to be tolerant of other sects as well as of non-believers. Their sense of self-identification, however, has remained strong even though the physical boundaries between them and the world are not very firmly drawn. They have managed to preserve their self-identity because they possess a number of distinctive tenets of faith and practices which set them apart both from other sects and from the rest of society. Besides the already-mentioned adventist doctrine and the keeping of Saturday as the Sabbath, the sect is also distinguished by demanding a tithe from members in the form of 10 per cent of their income.

The latter practice not only contributes to a clear and continuous demarcation of sect boundaries but also serves to ensure that only highly committed people become members. The Soviet Seventh Day Adventist sect seems to be a very stable and close-knit religious group in which members are recruited heavily from among neighbours and relations and in which hereditary membership is common: in Moscow 60 per cent of the Adventist congregation lived in the same neighbourhood, and 30–40 per cent were related to each other (Klibanov, 1969, pp. 99–100). New members were heavily recruited from members' children (ibid.; Belov, 1968, p. 136; Serdobol'skaya, 1963, p. 146). Not only do Adventists live in proximity to each other but they also try to work together. Thus, for example, in Alma-Ata region whole brigades in construction works consisted entirely of Adventists (*Central Asian Review*, 1963, p. 350).

Admission of new members both from outside the sect and from members' families is still strictly by test of merit. Only those who have been baptised after a period of probation are considered members with full rights. If an Adventist moves to another town and wants to be admitted to the local congregation he must submit a letter of recommendation from his previous presbyter (Belov, 1968, p. 186). Persistent violation of the sect's code of conduct leads to expulsion (ibid., p. 189).

Another important feature of Soviet Adventists which arrests the sect's movement towards a 'denominational' position is its organisation. While in the West Adventists have both a strong central organisation and a professional leadership, in the Soviet Union the sect has neither, and local self-government and a priesthood of all believers are the norm. These organisational features have not been consciously chosen by the sect and are, to some degree, circumvented by informal arrangements. These include the co-ordination of local groups by travelling senior sect members as well as some informal training arrangements. They are thus not an *indicator* of 'sect'-like orientations, but their imposition on Adventists by the state is bound to preserve 'sectarian' leanings much longer than would have been possible in a bureaucratised organisation with extensive professionalisation.

To sum up, Soviet Adventists, due to the nature of some of their beliefs and practices, have been less successful in curbing 'denominational' tendencies than have Pentecostalists, Initsiativniks and Jehovah's Witnesses. But, more than in the West, some of their tenets of faith and practices still conflict strongly with the ideology of their society and the demands made on its citizens. The ensuing conflict between sect and state has counteracted 'denominational' tendencies to a considerable extent. The balance of 'sectarian' and 'denominational' orientations attained by the Soviet Adventists likens them much more to the 'conversionist' Baptists than to the other 'revolutionist' sect – the Witnesses. Similarities between Adventists and Baptists are not only found in their responses to Soviet society but also in their previous religious affiliations as well as in the characteristics of their respective membership.

## Social Composition

Like Baptists, Adventists recruit new members mainly from among former Orthodox and from members of their own families, and they attract former Baptists (Belov, 1969, p. 141). In terms of social characteristics of members, they are considered identical to Baptists by one author (Lentin, 1969, quoted by Klibanov, 1969, p. 100), and the data collected in a number of local surveys bear out this claim with one or two exceptions. Like the official Baptists, Adventists attract a higher proportion of individuals with formal education (between 12 and 15 per cent have incomplete and complete secondary education), of women (around 83 per cent) and of older people (between 45 and 55 per cent are over 60 years old) than do the other sects of Western origin (for greater detail see Lane, 1976, pp. 326, 327). Data on Moldavia and the Ukraine, however, give a slightly different picture. There the proportion of men, of young people and of people with secondary education is considerably higher (Lentin, 1966, p. 10; Belov, 1968, pp. 205f.; Gazhos, 1975, pp. 50f.). Among those with better education women are said to predominate and are usually medical workers, such as nurses and orderlies (Lentin, 1966a, p. 11). Studies carried out in the late sixties and early seventies note a large increase in young recruits. Thus, in Moldavia, of all those taking baptism between 1969 and 1971 around 35 per cent were between the ages of 18 and 22, and in some villages young people amounted to 75 per cent of newly converted members (Tabakaru, 1973, p. 7). In Siberia, too, pupils and students have in recent years been drawn into the sect (Kostenko, 1967, p. 36). While Baptists have also experienced such a rejuvenation many of these new recruits have been syphoned off into the illegal branch of the Initsiativniks.

Unlike Baptists, Adventists are said to be more strongly represented in rural areas (Klibanov, 1969, p. 101), but this may simply be due to the fact that the latter predominate in the western republics which are less urbanised than the rest of the Soviet Union. In the industrial areas of the Urals, on the other hand, they were 100 per cent urban (Kolosnitsyn, 1969, p. 134). A more significant difference in the social profile of Adventists is that they have a slightly higher proportion of people with complete middle and higher education. This trend has become more obvious in the late sixties to early seventies. Such an improvement was noted in Moldavia (Tabakaru, 1973, p. 7; Gazhos, 1975, pp. 49f.) and Siberia (Kostenko, 1967, p. 36). This trend was particularly notable among presbyters, the majority of whom had secondary education and a few higher education (Kostenko, 1967, p. 36; Belov, 1968, p. 214; Tabakaru, 1973, p. 7) as compared with a very small percentage with such educational attainments among Baptist presbyters (ibid.).

This greater attraction of the Soviet Adventist sect to educated people is attributable to some of the sect's distinctive teachings and features of organisation. Adventists' positive stance to science, technology and learning in general makes their faith more congruent with the world-view of those who have received specialist or general advanced education, while their adoption of the 'health reform' appeals to medical personnel in particular. The more democratic organisation of local congregations and the more open channels for advancement to religious influence which the sect provides for capable individuals must also enhance its attraction to the better-educated believer. Capable women, in particular, have much better chances in the Adventist sect than among Baptists to fill positions of authority (Tabakaru, 1973, p. 5).

In conclusion, of all the Soviet sects of Western origin Adventists are characterised by the most incongruous mixture of 'sectarian' and 'denominational' orientations. While official Baptists are distinguished by 'denominational' leanings at the top of the sect's hierarchy and by 'sectarian' stances at grassroot level, Adventists maintain 'sect'-like and 'denominational' orientations side by side in an uneasy coexistence. Although Soviet Adventists share this feature with their brethren in the West (see Schwartz, 1970, pp. 79f.) it is based on quite a different relation to state and society. Some of the Adventist tenets of faith seem to be more congruous with the values of socialist society than with those in Western societies. Ethical rigorism, faith in science and technology and concern for a healthy body are more in keeping with the communist moral code and the pioneering spirit of Soviet society than they are with the moral outlook and climate of opinion of citizens in Western societies. At the same time Soviet Adventists are distinguished from their brethren in Western societies by the fact that some aspects of their religious faith are still strongly in tension with the ideology of the wider society. In contrast with the situation in western societies, a 'revolutionist' religious orientation, however attenuated, is still considered a challenge to the political ideology, and religious prescriptions implying only the slightest disloyalty to the demands of the socialist society lead to conflict. In addition, 'sectarian' tendencies are reinforced by the state's restrictive posture towards their organisation. Consequently, questions about primary allegiance, religious identity and boundaries, sectarian consciousness and procedures for admission are all still lively issues among Soviet Seventh Day Adventists even if a conflict between the demands of their religion and communist ideology is no longer always perceived by all. A clear and all-round perception of an unbridgeable gulf between the two ideologies can now only be found among Reform Adventists. Unlike Seventh Day Adventists, this illegal branch has preserved a distinct 'revolutionist' response to society and is now closer to Jehovah's Witnesses than to its legally recognised brethren.

## PENTECOSTALISTS

It is well known by sociologists of religion that Pentecostalism has been one of the most burgeoning religious movements of this century, not only having expanded rapidly in the changing urban conditions of the USA but also having spread to many parts of Europe and, more profusely, to the developing and urbanising centres of Latin American and African countries (see Hollenweger, 1972; Wilson, 1970, pp. 88f. and p. 197). It is less commonly known, however, that Pentecostalists are also a relatively large and thriving sect in the Soviet Union where they have grown in relative isolation from Western Pentecostal groups. Nevertheless, Pentecostalists in the Soviet Union have developed along similar lines, sharing with their Western and Third World brethren the heightened emotional atmosphere in services, features of organisation and of social composition of membership. On the other hand, they also display significant differences in religious and social orientations which are clearly shaped by their particular location in the socio-political environment of Soviet socialist society. A more detailed study of the sect's historical development, its organisational structure and members' religious and social orientations, as well as of their social characteristics, will establish these observations more clearly.

Pentecostalism of Western inspiration emerged in Russia only at the beginning of the twentieth century but long before that there existed a tradition of mystical enthusiastic sectarian religion stressing visitation by the Holy Ghost and the reception of gifts from the Spirit, particularly the gift of tongues or glossolalia. The ancient sect of the Khlysts and the Molokan branch of Priguny (see Chapter 5) immediately come to mind. The Russian Pentecostal movement proper began on the eve of the First World War, sparked off by the efforts of a missionary returning from the USA to Finland (then part of Russia). His first converts, the Russians N. I. Ivanov and N. P. Smorodin, spread the new teaching from Leningrad into the north-western areas of Russia, into the Ukraine and the Caucasus. The small sect formed out of this movement were called Smorodintsy, but are also known as Edinstvenniki or Evangelical Christians in the Apostolic Faith. Although this sect commanded quite a following in its early years, at the present time it holds only a small minority of Soviet Pentecostals. According to Fedorenko (1965, p. 178), their theological position is that of the 'Jesus Only' movement. The sect has maintained a distinct identity until today but little is known about its teachings, organisation and general development.

Pentecostalism in Russia gained a real impetus only in the early 1920s when Voronaev, a former Baptist, returned to Russia from the USA with the express purpose of establishing a Pentecostal movement there. He was inspired by the American Assemblies of God movement for which he considered himself a missionary. Thus, from the very beginning, Pentecostalism in the Soviet Union had no connections with the Russian Orthodox Church but was self-consciously sectarian, copying the already-established pattern of its American counterpart. The movement's founder, Voronaev, worked initially from within already-established sects – the Ukrainian Baptists and Evangelical Christians – and used them to gain a foothold after his return from emigration.

During the movement's first three years, 50 per cent of members were former Baptists or Evangelical Christians. In later years more new converts were attracted (Durasoff, 1969, pp. 72–3). Naturally Voronaev's intrusion into, and successful work in, these two sects drew upon him their leaders' intense anger. This rivalry between Pentecostalists and Evangelical Christian Baptists, as we shall later show, has continued up to the present day.

Voronaev gained most converts in the Ukraine but he also managed to expand into the Russian Federation, though with less success. In the more relaxed political climate of the first post-revolutionary decade Voronaev seems to have proceeded undisturbed in his vigorous missionary activity, helped by financial support from the American Assemblies of God and an unnamed Christian organisation. Only during these early formative years did Soviet Pentecostalism experience something akin to a Western revivalist campaign. In the Ukraine alone, Voronaev claimed around 17,000 members in 1928 (*Evangelist*, 1, 1928, p. 1, quoted by Durasoff, 1969, p. 73). The first All-Union Congress of Pentecostalists, meeting in 1927, expressed its loyalty for and support of the Soviet regime and admonished members to participate in military service (Fedorenko, 1965, p. 180). After 1928, the growth of the sect was slow and, more importantly, took part mainly clandestinely. In 1930 Voronaev was arrested, and from that date onwards little is heard about Soviet Pentecostals until they re-emerged in 1945.

In addition to these two major branches of Pentecostalism several smaller movements arose, such as the Zionists (mainly in the Ukraine), the Perfectionists, the Shaker Pentecostalists and the Sabbatarian Pentecostals. Thus, as in the West, Pentecostalism was from the beginning characterised by great internal variation and lack of central organisation, although Voronaev was a very dynamic leader.

In 1945, around 25,000 Voronaevtsy (64 per cent of their total) entered into union with the Evangelical Christian Baptists (*Bratskii Vestnik*, 1, 1960, p. 87). One scholarly publication claims, however, that as many as 60 per cent stayed outside the Union (*Stroitel'stvo . . .*, 1966, p. 91). As the Pentecostalists had to give an undertaking to curtail severely the practice of their central and most distinctive rituals it has to be assumed that this union was not one of love but of convenience. It enabled Pentecostalists to achieve that legal recognition which secured them a modicum of organisational security. Those groups not entering the Union could not register with the authorities and, therefore, rendered themselves illegal. (In recent years, however, some registrations of non-affiliated Pentecostal groups have been reported by foreign visitors; *Minority Rights Report*, 1970, p. 34.) The discussion between leading Pentecostalists and Evangelical Christian Baptists about the conditions of merger is said to have taken place in a peaceful and fraternal atmosphere but the resulting document shows that the union was achieved at one-sided sacrifice by the Pentecostalists. The following extracts from the document clearly illustrate this point:

(8) Considering the word of apostle Paul about the fruitlessness of unknown tongues in the absence of an interpreter, both sides agree to abstain from unknown tongues in general meetings (i.e. joint services).

(9) In conjunction with the operation of the Holy Spirit in the services, recognising that there may be manifestations leading to the destruction of the decency and the decorum of the service (I Cor. 14:40) both sides agreed to provide an educational programme against this type of manifestation, recalling that God is not a God of confusion, but of peace (I Cor. 14:33).

(10) In view of the fact that the Evangelical Christians and the Baptists do not practise footwashing the present Agreement recommends that the Christians of the Evangelical Faith conduct educational work designed to achieve a common understanding with the Evangelical Christians and Baptists on this question, aiming towards unity, and uniformity of public worship . . . etc. (*Bratskii Vestnik*, 4, 1957, p. 36)

Nine years later, Pentecostal members of the Union were even forbidden to communicate their experiences of glossolalia in *individual* encounters with members of the other sects in the Union (*Bratskii Vestnik*, 1, 1955, p. 5).

The fact that just over half (64 per cent) of only the Voronaevtsy could agree to a merger on these conditions demonstrates the unpopularity of this union.

Further evidence of the incompatibility of this merger with Pentecostal religious orientations is the steady stream of Pentecostal defectors from this constraining partnership (Aleksandrovich, Kandaurov and Nemirovskii, 1961, p. 131; Grazhdan, 1965, p. 27; *Stroitel'stvo* . . ., 1966, p. 91; Moskalenko, 1966, p. 83). In one Ukrainian region, for example, 38 per cent of those who had joined the Union left it again between 1945 and 1949 (Fedorenko, 1965, p. 183). In some localities bitter rivalry and hostility is reported between a separate Pentecostal group and a congregation of Evangelical Christian Baptists, and defections from Baptists to Pentecostalists are common (e.g. Gladkov and Korytin, 1961, p. 43; Serdobol'skaya, 1963, p. 121; Zlobin, 1963, p. 106; Gegeshidze, 1964, p. 23; Fedorenko, 1965, p. 183; Gagarin, 1966, p. 27). It has also been acknowledged on the pages of the Union's journal *Bratskii Vestnik* that the doctrinal notion of Baptism in the Holy Spirit is causing great difficulties in the Union (see, for example, *Bratskii Vestnik*, 2, 1949, pp. 6–8 and 3, 1962, p. 11).

This politically induced and widely unpopular merger has had a significant influence on the Pentecostal movement in the Soviet Union. It will be shown below how it served to radicalise or, at least, arrest any 'denominational' tendencies in both the religious and socio-political responses of the Pentecostalist groups which stayed outside the Union or left it in disillusionment in subsequent years.

*Socio-Demographic Distribution and Organisation*
In the sixties, Pentecostalists were said to be the second biggest sect on Soviet soil (Klibanov, 1969, p. 95). Membership figures for *all* the Pentecostal groups are not available for recent decades. In addition to the estimated 40,000 Voronaevtsy there must be several thousand Pentecostalists in the minor branches, but little is known about them. We also have no reliable information on present trends in membership.

Like most other sects, the Christians of the Evangelical Faith have managed to expand into several areas of the Soviet Union. Besides being strong in their initial base, the Ukraine (over half of the membership is supposed to be concentrated here, according to Klibanov, 1969, p. 76), in Belorussia and Moldavia, they have gained firm footholds in central Asia and Kazakhstan, and in Transcaucasia. They also have groups in the RSFSR but their presence here is generally weak. One publication estimated that 25 per cent of all Pentecostalists were in the RSFSR in the early sixties (*Stroitel'stvo* . . ., 1966, p. 92). Smorodin Pentecostalists are said to predominate in the Baltic republics, in Kirov, Leningrad, Novgorod, Perm (all RSFSR) and in the Udmurt ASSR (Kol'tsov, 1965, p. 6). In general, Pentecostalists have been slightly less successful than the Baptists in spreading their influence *all over* the Soviet Union, and congregations are usually much smaller.

As among Pentecostalists in the West,* organisation of the Soviet movement is extremely weak but in a different way. While Western Pentecostalist organisations have generally an exceedingly formal and tight organisation at the national level and a more loose and amorphous one in the local congregation, Soviet

---

* Pentecostalism in the West is, of course, extremely varied, and no generalisations about the whole movement can be made. The following comparison of Soviet with Western Pentecostalism refers only to the independent (i.e. outside other churches) large, second-generation (or more) organisations such as the Assemblies of God, the Church of God, the Elim Foursquare Gospel Association, etc.

independent Pentecostalism is decentralised, and strong and tight-knit local groups enjoy a large degree of autonomy. Although one section of the Soviet Pentecostal movement is formally affiliated to the All-Union Council of Evangelical Christian Baptists this central body seems to have had little effect on organisation. While Baptists have built a stable hierarchy, influencing local groups through regular visits, regional conferences, national congresses and a journal, and have established a training course as well as strong organisational links with Western Baptists, the Pentecostalists seem to have none of these of their own. On the pages of *Bratskii Vestnik*, the mouthpiece of the Union, little can be found of particular relevance to the Pentecostalists. Independent Pentecostalists do not even have their own meeting places but assemble in small groups in private houses (Chernov, 1960, p. 17). The general impression conveyed in the sociological literature is that the congregational pattern of organisation rules supreme and that there is little communication on a national level.

Bryan Wilson (1970, p. 75) has ably demonstrated that the absence of enduring organisational cohesion at local level in the West has been a consequence primarily of the peculiar Pentecostal teaching and, secondarily, of the social composition of the membership attracted by the sect's style. In the Soviet Union the organisational pattern of Pentecostalists is, in addition, shaped by another factor. This is the determination of the political authorities to limit the effectiveness of Pentecostalists by depriving them of amenities to consolidate and extend their influence among the Soviet population. Pentecostalists are clearly, and quite correctly, rated as more anti-Soviet than the official Baptists, as the following descriptions of them illustrate:

'In many Pentecostal congregations individuals come forward as "prophets" and leaders who are hostilely inclined to the Soviet system; therefore, in these congregations there are sometimes harmful political sermons.' (*Osnovnye voprosy nauchnogo ateizma*, 1966, p. 137)
'Pentecostalism is the most poisonous kind of religious superstition. It is deeply reactionary and anti-human, it cripples man physically and morally.' (Chiperis, 1964, p. 79)

Their inclusion into the Union mainly enables the political authorities to gain information of, and control over, the volume and distribution of the sect's membership and activity. The social composition of the Pentecostal movement detailed below has so far prevented the development of any protest movement, such as that of the Initsiativniks among Baptists, against these restrictions. But the emergence of Pentecostalist *samizdat* documents since 1974 (see *Religion in Communist Lands*, Vol. 1, 6, and Vol. 3, 1–3) protesting about harassment by the political authorities should lead us to expect such a movement in the future. Wide sections of the Pentecostal movement even favour their amorphous existence because it is less conspicuous to the atheists.

This lack of central organisation, however, does not mean that local groups are loosely organised. On the contrary, they are very hierarchical, and the presbyter is extremely powerful. Strict admission procedure is characteristic, and surveillance of members is extensive (Moskalenko, 1966, pp. 155*f*.). Thus Soviet Pentecostal groups differ significantly in this respect from English Pentecostalists (see Wilson, 1967, pp. 148*f*.) who were said to find it difficult to adjust from the revival atmosphere to a stable congregational life. This posed considerable problems for their minister. The Soviet Pentecostal movement, in contrast, recruited only slowly and selectively during the last decade and has bound its members strongly to the local group by fostering a sense of belonging to an ideological enclave in a hostile society. Despite their similarity in social background with early Western Pentecostalists, Soviet believers have been welded into firmly established local groups due to the pressures from the wider society.

*Social Composition*

Pentecostalism in the United States, Europe and the Third World gained its *original* recruits from a distinct social milieu which has been surprisingly uniform across societies. It has attracted predominantly recent immigrants, either from other countries or from the countryside to the towns. Besides being both poorer and culturally more backward than the bulk of their host population they are generally believed to be under various forms of psychological stress as a consequence of their sudden immersion into a new and alien environment and their poorly developed skills for coping with these changes. At the present time, however, members of the large Pentecostal groups in the USA and Britain are no longer from the bottom levels of their respective societies but are predominantly respectable working class or lower middle class (see Schwartz, 1970, p. 44; Hollenweger, 1972, p. 59). The more disadvantaged groups now flock to the new smaller and marginal groups such as 'The Latter Rain' movement.

Data on Soviet Pentecostalists are not good as far as their life histories are concerned though there is much information indicating that Soviet Pentecostalists are similar in their social characteristics to the first generation members of Western Pentecostal sects and differ on significant aspects from members of other Russian sects. Pentecostalism in Kazakhstan, for example, is said to have become established in the middle twenties at the time when large numbers of immigrants from the Western areas arrived (Grazhdan, 1965, pp. 20–1). The same can be said about Pentecostalism in the Komi ASSR. In Georgia, too, Pentecostalism only arose with the arrival of evacuees during the Second World War (Gegeshidze, 1964, p. 8). Among urban Pentecostalists in Sverdlovsk region there were only 3·9 per cent born in a town (Kolosnitsyn, 1969, p. 134). The strength of Pentecostalism in the western republics is harder to explain. These are not immigration areas although rural–urban migration took place on a large scale. In general, we know that Pentecostalists in most areas are predominantly urban at the present time (Grazhdan, 1965, p. 30; Chiperis, 1964, p. 75; Kolosnitsyn, 1969, p. 134). Although Pentecostalists, like other Soviet religious organisations, are said to attract predominantly elderly people, congregations with a relatively high percentage of young people (up to 35 per cent) have been reported (Gegeshidze, 1964, p. 10; Grazhdan, 1965, p. 65).

Much evidence then points to the fact that Soviet Pentecostalism also recruits heavily from recent migrants but it is difficult to determine in the Soviet context whether they were first migrants and then became Pentecostalists, or whether they became migrants because of their Pentecostal affiliation. It is said to be a characteristic feature of Pentecostalists in the Soviet Union that many families and especially leaders stay no longer than two or three years in one place (Yakovlev, 1961, p. 24; Kol'tsov, 1965, p. 11). Such a high rate of geographical mobility is partly motivated by a wish to avoid becoming known to local militant atheist organisations and occurs partly in response to religious prophecies about impending doom in one geographical area and the likely occurrence of great joy in another (Yakovlev, 1961, p. 24).

Soviet Pentecostalists are similar to Western first-generation members in other social characteristics. We possess quite conclusive information that Pentecostalists come predominantly from the lowest educational and consequently social groups. Baptists, who also have among themselves a large number of recent migrants, in contrast do not recruit so heavily from the lowest social groups but take in a wider range of the educational spectrum while Initsiativniks were found to attract a relatively large number of well-educated members. A large majority of Pentecostalists are said to be semi- or illiterate (between 75 and 95 per cent), although there are striking exceptions (see Kol'tsov, 1965, p. 8, on the group in the Georgian town Gori; *Sovetskaya Belorossiya*, 23 April 1974, p. 4). In some Kazakhstan congregations this poorly educated group consisted of over 90 per cent of the members (Grazhdan, 1965, pp. 67, 68). Even in Moldavia, where the educational level of the general population is higher than in central Asia, 75 per cent of members were found to be semi- or illiterate. Among those Kazakhstan sectarians in employment, unskilled labourers and poorly qualified workers predominated in the early sixties (Grazhdan, 1965, p. 67). (For greater detail, see Lane, 1976, p. 341.) They were generally attracted to enterprises or institutions, such as hospitals, which are weakly organised and have a lax work discipline. Pentecostalists try to work with fellow believers in a separate work brigade (ibid., p. 30).

These findings on social position are partly contradicted by Grazhdan's statement that Pentecostalists have recruited heavily from former *kulaks*, small businessmen, officials and other representatives of the bourgeoisie and petty bourgeoisie (Grazhdan, 1965, p. 30). Members of these classes were surely not characterised by a lack of literacy. Perhaps the author was referring mainly to the leading members of congregations.

Unfortunately we have no information to judge whether Soviet Pentecostalists, like early Western recruits, perceived and felt anguish about their discrepantly low status or whether the more egalitarian structure and ethics of Soviet society did not generate such extreme status anxiety. We cannot, therefore, deal with the often posed hypothesis that recruits to Pentecostalism try to gain superior spiritual qualities to compensate for their lack of secular success and prestige.

Pentecostalists differ from Baptists and Adventists in age and sex characteristics: they tend to have a higher percentage of young and middle-aged members and of men (contrary to Klibanov's 1969, p. 95, claim). Around 20 per cent of members in the various congregations were under 30 years of age and between 25 and 37 per cent were men during the 1960s (Gegeshidze, 1964, p. 10; Grazhdan, 1965, pp. 67, 68; Belov, 1969, p. 31; Eryshev, 1969, p. A41; Gagarin, 1970, p. 380, 1971, pp. 145f.). Unfortunately, it is not always made clear in the literature whether the surveyed Pentecostal groups are of the legal (those in the Union) or illegal kind. Thus it is impossible to find out whether, like the Initsiativniks among Baptists, the illegal groups have a membership with a more dynamic social background.

An analysis of Pentecostal religious commitment shows that this too differs in some significant respects from that of other sectarians and highlights the fact that Soviet Pentecostalists, despite prolonged isolation, are still close to their Western brethren in basic religious orientations but have retained a more sectarian stance than the latter.

*Religious and Social Orientations*

There is widespread agreement among Soviet students of the sect that Pentecostalists are highly committed, if not fanatical, sectarians in the terms of their particular faith. The central experience of Pentecostalism is that men will be sanctified through Baptism of the Holy Spirit, and most of their religious practice is oriented towards this religious experience. Preparations for the reception of the Holy Ghost among Soviet Pentecostals consist of strict fasting and of long and intense prayer sessions. Prayer meetings among Pentecostals take place once or twice daily or, at the least, three times a week, and they are usually of several hours' duration (Chiperis, 1964, p. 79; Grazhdan, 1966, p. 285). One author speaks of Pentecostal believers fasting and praying to physical exhaustion, inducing a state of hallucination (Moskalenko, 1966, pp. 139–40). Evidence on the extent and forms of glossolalia during such prayer meetings is understandably scanty. In one study it is described in the following way: 'In their religious ecstasy, losing control over themselves, they have convulsions, hit themselves, shriek unintelligibly . . .' (*Prichiny* . . ., 1965, p. 143). Several writers suggest that the legal Pentecostalists often violate the agreement on refraining from glossolalia in joint services with Baptists and that, in some areas, their practice and general fervour have influenced Baptist worshippers. Klibanov (1972, p. 53), on the other hand, reports about one congregation in the RSFSR abandoning glossolalia during the last decade, and Mandrygin and Makarov (1966) write about a large Belorussian congregation which gradually turned Baptist after the Second World War. Judging from the many complaints by leading Baptists in the Union about the incidence of glossolalia in joint services, the first trend is probably more common. Ritual footwashing is also a common practice among Soviet Pentecostalists.

Besides the gift of tongues, most Soviet Pentecostalists claim the Spirit gifts of healing, driving out devils and general miracle working (Chiperis, 1964, p. 79; Klibanov, 1969, p. 157). These 'miracles' are particularly performed by travelling Pentecostalists who try to recruit new members, and the 'Sabbatarian' Pentecostalists are especially renowned for these practices (Moskalenko, 1966, p. 169).

Prophetism, both in connection with, and independent of, glossolalia, appears to be widespread. Most congregations have their prophets who both interpret tongues and generally prophesy all sorts of events, usually with strong and vivid eschatological overtones. In many groups the day of Christ's second coming was being expected in the near future (Moskalenko, 1966, p. 126). In some groups the second advent was believed to be so imminent that believers gave away their possessions, and stopped work and even eating (*Prichiny* . . ., 1965, p. 141). Among Kazakhstan Pentecostalists, too, eschatological threats and promises were often made. Thus Pentecostalists were urged to migrate to the Far Eastern town of Nakhodka where an ark would arrive to collect the faithful to take them to the heavenly kingdom. In their native Alma-Ata, however, destruction was imminent and only the Pentecostalists would escape death and destruction by their timely departure (Yakovlev, 1961, p. 24). The destruction of the Soviet state in a future world was also often prophesied, and believers were encouraged to rejoice at this prospect (ibid., p. 34). In general, eschatology among the Pentecostalists described by Yakovlev appears to be as central to their faith as among

Jehovah's Witnesses and more developed than among Adventists. In content, too, it closely resembles that of the former, differing only in the more local colouring and detail. Paradise and Hell, too, are frequently and vividly depicted by prophets and preachers (Yakovlev, 1961, p. 26).

Like the Baptists, Pentecostalists put great stress on Bible reading and, despite their low level of literacy, are said to be keen and knowledgeable in this area (Gagarin, 1971, p. 144). The only other source of religious information accessible to Soviet Pentecostalists is a defunct Pentecostal journal from the twenties from which believers copy out passages by hand (*Prichiny . . .*, 1965, p. 139). It is therefore not surprising that they have remained one of the most fundamentalist and conservative religious organisations in the Soviet Union (Moskalenko, 1966, p. 126; Belov, 1969, p. 49).

Like the Baptists, Pentecostalists are greatly interested in moral questions as well as in problems connected with their relation to a militantly atheist socialist environment. This latter interest, however, is purely theoretical defining the boundaries of the religious group. Pentecostalists take great pains to hold themselves aloof from the rest of society. Besides separation from the socio-political life Pentecostalists also foster a withdrawal from any cultural pursuit and all worldly pleasures.

In contrast to the situation among corresponding Western Pentecostal organisations, ethical rigorism is still commonly accepted. But it is impossible to establish, with the available data, whether Soviet Pentecostalists differ subtly in their moral outlook from other sectarians in the way Schwartz (1970) described it for his American sample. We cannot ascertain whether, like American Pentecostalists, they set aside certain types of behaviour as sinful but are then tolerant towards transgressors, or whether they both teach and practise ethical rigorism. While the literature on Baptists conveyed the distinct impression that the ethical implications of religious belief were clearly specified it was impossible to gain a clear picture on that point in the case of Pentecostalists.

Soviet Pentecostalists isolate themselves not only from society in general but also from believers of other faiths. Among the sects, Pentecostalists seem to have one of the strongest elite conceptions. In a survey of Ukrainian sectarians only 14 per cent of Pentecostalists expressed positive views about other sectarians, in contrast to 24 per cent among Baptists (Eryshev, 1969, p. A47). Applicants for membership are thoroughly examined and only admitted after extensive preparation (Moskalenko, 1966, p. 175).

Hostility to out-groups is allied to cultivation of the religious community. It is held together by both positive and negative sanctions and binds individuals to the group by a common moral code and social orientations incompatible with those of the wider society. The religious community is also strong and pervasive among Baptists but there are some indications that it is even more totalitarian among Pentecostalists. Groups are very hierarchical, and leaders organise rank-and-file members in an authoritarian manner (Moskalenko, 1966, p. 177). For one community nightly patrols of believers, making spot checks on fellow sectarians, were reported (*Prichiny . . .*, 1965, p. 144). In general, the legal Pentecostalists are said to be less fanatic in all their orientations than their illegally existing brethren, although no less committed (ibid., p. 199).

Pentecostalists in the Soviet Union have preserved the 'sectarian' tendency much more strongly than Soviet Baptists or Seventh Day Adventists in several ways: they appear to devote more time and physical energy to religious activity and, more crucially, they set themselves more completely apart from both their surrounding cultural and social environment and from other religious groups. The latter, of course, applies only to the illegal non-affiliated Pentecostalists. Similarities with the above sects are also, however, notable. Like these sectarians, Pentecostalists establish a strong religious sub-community and, in recent years, have turned increasingly to a concern with moral values and ethical questions. While these similarities must be due to the similar constituency from which both sects recruit recent immigrants, divergencies reflect a different degree of social alienation among members of the two sects. In general, Pentecostalists display a much higher degree of hostility to their socio-political environment, although some adaptation to the demands of their society has been noted during the sixties among legal Pentecostalists (Klibanov, 1972, p. 53). Let us now turn to examine in some detail how this alienation expresses itself among believers and how it is articulated by leaders.

Baptist leaders and rank-and-file members (excluding only Initsiativniks) have been generally described in the literature as being politically loyal, as good hard-working citizens and were only accused of social indifference. Pentecostalists are often described as politically hostile, anti-Soviet and are charged with more extreme and consistent withdrawal from general social life. While Baptist national and local leaders frequently urge members to become more involved in public affairs and to make full use of the social and educational provisions of Soviet society, Pentecostal leaders never encourage members in this way. Unlike leaders of the Jehovah's Witnesses, however, Pentecostal leaders also never voice their hostility to the Soviet regime too publicly, nor do they often actively encourage civil disobedience among their members. Their approach is more subtle, and this must account for the fact that illegal Pentecostalists have not been outlawed as drastically as Jehovah's Witnesses.

The position of Pentecostal leaders on members' relations with their social environment is characterised by the tactic of 'silent consent'. It means that leaders give their silent approval to forms of social isolationism but never openly encourage any particular measure conflicting with Soviet ideology. While it is left to the individual's conscience to decide which social or cultural activities he will take part in, it is made very clear to him in general that anything which detracts in the slightest way from his faith ought to be avoided. Spiritually reborn believers, it is urged, cannot have any obligation to a society not reborn (Grazhdan, 1966, pp. 279–81). Conversely, leaders do not generally express any active approval of socialism and the socialist construction of Soviet society. The social and economic advances of socialism are perceived by them to be preludes to the coming end of the world (Moskalenko, 1966, p. 126). These attitudes of silent disapproval, of refusal to voice even rhetorical acclaim, distinguish Pentecostalists from most other religious organisations in the Soviet Union. Not surprisingly, there is general consent in the Soviet literature that Pentecostalists are anti-social.

This tactic of 'silent consent' seems to have been singularly effective as Pentecostalists keep apart from any officially organised activities such as lectures, youth organisations, cultural pursuits, entertainment and military service. None of the children of Pentecostalists in two settlements of the Komi ASSR, for example, joined the Young Pioneers (Gagarin, 1971, p. 153). Although Pentecostal parents have also a negative attitude towards Soviet schools they do, on the whole, comply with Soviet laws in this area. There is no indication in the literature of how widespread is refusal of military service. Among Pentecostalists in Kazakhstan, refusal was commonly advocated by leaders. Believers were even advised against participation in the 1959 census. Members who ignored this and other admonitions to stay aloof from involvement in Soviet social and political life were often said to be ostracised by the group (Yakovlev, 1961, pp. 28, 32–3). Believers have even tried to insulate themselves from mass communication. Many would not have radio points installed in their homes, and one study speaks of Pentecostalists who immediately threw out of the window newspapers to which they had not subscribed (*Prichiny* . . ., 1965, p. 200).

Anti-Soviet feelings also express themselves in another form, namely, in the interpretation of 'unknown tongues'. Such hostile translation of tongues by prophets is usually couched in moral, rather than political language (*Prichiny* . . ., 1965, p. 142). Whether the expression of hostile sentiments in this way can be attributed to a sense of reduced responsibility on the part of the believer (after all, the Holy Ghost has spoken) or to a sense of reduced inhibition in a state of religious ecstasy is difficult to determine. There is no doubt, however, that such denunciations of Soviet moral standards, endowed with supernatural authority, must make a deep impact on believers.

Unlike the Baptists and Adventists, Pentecostalists do not seem to excel in their work attitudes and performance. They are said to see work as punishment, as something to be shirked as much as possible. Thus they do not support rationalisation programmes, socialist competition or shock work and do not attempt to better their qualifications (Grazhdan, 1965, pp. 61–3). Such an orientation, of course, widens the gulf between Pentecostalists and the rest of society still farther.

To sum up, Pentecostalists in the Soviet Union differ from Soviet Baptists and Adventists in the greater depth of their religious commitment, their more complete aversion from worldly things and their hostility to the socio-political order they live in. If we compare Soviet Pentecostalists with those in the West we are also struck by the fact that the latter have departed considerably farther from a 'sect' type. While Soviet Pentecostalists have widely rejected central organisation and have no trained ministers and Bible schools, in the West organisation and professionalisation have gone far. Soviet independent Pentecostalists have preserved a large degree of religious spontaneity, and a widespread belief in prophetism and healing and in the imminence of a second coming, as well as upholding ethical rigorism. Western mainstream Pentecostalists, in contrast, have greatly curtailed spontaneity and have formalised worship, have abandoned the more extreme aspects of faith and practice and have relaxed their ethical standards (Wilson, 1970, pp. 78*f*.; Schwartz, 1970, pp. 167–8; Hollenweger, 1972, pp. 34–5, 199–201). In addition, Soviet Pentecostalists set themselves more apart from, or even in opposition to, the rest of society as well as to other religious bodies.

There is little indication in the Soviet literature why their faith has proved more resilient in the face of the secularising impact of modern industrial society and of militant atheism. We have to draw tentative conclusions from the incidental information we possess.

If it is a general feature, as it was described for Kazakhstan (Grazhdan, 1965, pp. 21, 30) that many Pentecostalists (probably mostly the leaders) come from those social strata whose members were the chief opponents of the Revolution and subsequent social changes, then we have an explanation of why sect leaders have not accommodated themselves to Soviet power in recent decades. Their hostility would have been filtered down to ordinary members who have seen these negative views about Soviet power confirmed by Soviet policy towards the sect and the harsh treatment resulting from it.

In addition, the more 'sectarian' stance of Soviet Pentecostalists is due to the social characteristics of their recruits who are shaped by the particular development pattern of Soviet society. Western societies experienced the social upheaval of industrialisation, and of the attendant processes of large-scale urban–rural migration and immigration,* much earlier than Soviet society. In addition, Western societies accomplished the goal of general secondary education much earlier. This time-lag in the development of Soviet society has meant that a pool of recently uprooted, poorly educated people – the traditional recruiting ground of Pentecostalism – has provided the Soviet Pentecostal movement for much longer with the type of member who is likely to have 'sectarian' rather than 'denominational' orientations.

It must not be forgotten, however, that a large proportion of Pentecostalists have entered the Union with the Evangelical Christian Baptists and must have been exposed to, and influenced by, the accommodative tendencies of Baptist leaders as well as to the religiously and socially more moderate orientations of Baptist rank-and-file members. The chasm between legal and illegal Pentecostalists is bound to have become great and may be likened to the split among Baptists into a legal and an illegal faction. Unlike the breakaway Initsiativniks, illegal Pentecostalists do not vigorously and articulately campaign for their religious rights. Nor have they adopted a completely uncompromising stance *vis-à-vis* the Soviet regime but express their disaffection mainly in passive withdrawal. For an example of active and undisguised hostility to their social environment and political order among the sects of Western origin we have to turn to the sect of Jehovah's Witnesses.

## JEHOVAH'S WITNESSES

Of all the sects in the Soviet Union, the Jehovah's Witnesses must definitely be placed on the extreme left of a 'sect to denomination' continuum. They are in a position of greater tension with society compared with both other extreme sects in the Soviet Union (except, perhaps, True Orthodox Christians) and Jehovah's Witnesses in the West. We shall examine how this radical 'sectarianism' manifests itself as well as consider the factors which have shaped their religious responses. But first of all a short historical description of Jehovah's Witnesses is appropriate.

In the Soviet Union there are two different branches of Jehovah's Witnesses. The Jehovists or Il'intsy (after their founder, Captain Il'in) are an indigenous Russian organisation founded in the twenties, while the Jehovah's Witnesses are a branch of the Brooklyn organisation. The former is a very small and insignificant organisation today, and lack of information about it does not permit us to include it in this study.

---

* The more recent waves of immigration into Britain and the USA have again created a pool of uprooted, underprivileged people. Their attraction to Pentecostalism has revived the more fervent and enthusiastic forms of its early formative years in small separate groups.

Jehovah's Witnesses have been the latest arrival in the Soviet Union among the sects of Western origin. A few groups were established before the Second World War in the western republics by members who had penetrated into the Soviet Union from neighbouring Poland, the Baltic republics and Bessarabia. The sect gained a real foothold only at the end of the war when parts of these countries were incorporated into the Soviet Union (Moskalenko, 1971, p. 65). From these areas the sect expanded into other parts of the western republics and, through migration and deportation, into Siberia, the Far East, and central Asia. Groups in the European part of the RSFSR or in the Caucasian republics are not mentioned in the Soviet literature. Thus the sect started relatively late and under the extremely unfavourable circumstances of illegality and criminal prosecution. According to *Watchtower* (1 April 1956, p. 214) 7,000 Witnesses were deported between 1948 and 1951, and in 1957 another nationwide campaign was staged against them. Nevertheless, the Witnesses have expanded quickly and are supposed to be similar in size to the Pentecostalists (Klibanov, 1969, p. 95) which would give a membership of around 40,000. But as no indication is given of how this estimate is arrived at, and as the size of membership of an illegal conspiratorial sect is difficult to measure, one cannot be too certain about this figure.

Turning to the organisation of Soviet Jehovah's Witnesses, it is noteworthy that, although the sect exists underground, its ties with the Brooklyn head-quarters are strong. It is organised in the same elaborate hierarchical structure as Jehovah's Witnesses in the West, and its policies and religious activity are determined by the American centre. The distinctive Soviet features are conditioned by the necessarily conspiratorial nature of the Soviet branch. The administrative head of the Soviet Witnesses is the branch office in Poland, and the highest organisational organ in the Soviet Union is a 'Regional Committee'.

Besides the groups of ten to fifteen members, which meet regularly to study the content of the American *Watchtower* magazine, there exist underground schools in which all group leaders are instructed for a year (Moskalenko, 1971, p. 193). Schools are said to emphasise particularly techniques for proselytising and countering atheist propaganda (ibid., p. 195). In addition to the schools there is also an elaborate organisational network for supplying and distributing the *Watchtower* magazine to every family (Bartoshevich, 1969, p. 155). Family members will then copy the journal out by hand.

As in the West, members are obliged to distribute the sect's literature. Believers have to keep an account of the number of hours spent on gaining new members, and these accounts are passed on to headquarters in code language (ibid., p. 158). But no indication is given of how the selling is accomplished in view of the sect's illegal status. While it is fairly easy and common to drop literature anonymously into letter boxes in the big impersonal flat blocks, the more important 'call-backs' to consolidate and exploit any initial impact made would be dangerous in the Soviet Union. In the West the activity of publicising the sect and its message in door-to-door calls has become the central concern of the Witnesses, the *raison d'être* of their elaborate organisation and the means to prevent the setting in of frustration about disappointed millennial hopes. It would have been interesting to see how the Soviet branch copes, faced with the severe curtailment of this activity, and in what ways it has adapted. But unfortunately there is no information about this in the Soviet literature.

Organisational principles of conspiracy are elaborated in such detail and observed with such care and zeal that one author feels it appropriate to call the network of communication between leaders at the various levels 'the Holy Okhrana' (name of the secret police under the Tsars) (Bartoshevich, 1969, p. 159). The employment of code language, of watchwords at inter-regional meetings, the great stealth and secrecy with which members cloak their weekly visits to Bible study groups, all emphasise the conspiratorial character of the sect.

## Religious and Social Orientations

The religious teachings of the Soviet Jehovah's Witnesses are those of their American brethren. Not only do they accept the same dogmatic positions, the same religious practice, but they also let themselves be guided by the same centrally devised interpretations of the Bible in their regular Bible study meetings. A study probing the beliefs held by members of the sect in some Moldavian villages found that there was a great fit between them and the official sect ideology (Gazhos, 1969, p. 34; see also Gagarin, 1970, p. 373). No other ideology has as completely and successfully penetrated the 'Iron Curtain' as the religious world-view of the Jehovah's Witnesses shaped in Brooklyn. In a way their religion has even greater saliency for Soviet Witnesses than for Western ones, given the fact that they live in the society through which Satan, according to a 1959 number of *Watchtower*, used to do his work. The start of the Battle of Armageddon, too, has frequently been predicted to come about through some action of the Soviet Union. Since 1964, the Brooklyn line on the Soviet Union has softened. These associations are no longer mentioned, and Soviet members are enjoined to acknowledge the state as a legitimate power. This new line, however, has not yet been fully internalised by rank-and-file members, and many have refused to accept this ideological turnabout.

Like Western Witnesses, members are extremely committed to the sect, its teachings and practice. They know their teachings, are keen proselytisers and arrange their whole life in accordance with their religious beliefs. Where they differ markedly both from their Western brethren and from members of most other Soviet sects is in their stronger elite conception, greater exclusivity and self-identification (see Wilson, 1970, pp. 29–32).

While members of the Western branches and of other Soviet sects also hold to the belief that only their faith enables them to be saved, this belief is not so dominant that it colours all their activities but usually remains at the level of ideology. Among Soviet Jehovah's Witnesses, however, their strong elite conception profoundly influences their relations to other sectarians and to their fellow men in general. They either isolate themselves as much as possible from non-members, or they are very hostile to them. If they find they cannot win a person over to the sect they are reputed to break up relations with that person, even if it is a marriage partner (Gazhos, 1969, p. 71). When attitudes to members of other sects were probed in a Ukrainian survey (Eryshev, 1969, p. A45), it turned out that Jehovah's Witnesses were by far the most hostile (see also Gazhos, 1969, p. 71). Seventy-three per cent of them expressed great hostility to members of other sects, and only 9·6 per cent had anything positive to say about them (Eryshev, 1969, p. A41). The existence of a strong elite conception is also borne out by the fact that of all sectarians, Jehovah's Witnesses least often change over to other sects (ibid.), and those few who do incur the wrath of their former brethren (Gazhos, 1969, p. 71).

Their firm elite conception is allied to a highly developed sense of exclusivity. Many sectarians in the West and the Soviet Union have worked out a compromise between answering the demands of the sect and those of the wider society or only in theory put allegiance to their faith above all other loyalties. English Jehovah's Witnesses, for example, still uphold the principle of exclusivity in theory but in practice have lost that hostility to 'the world' which set them apart from the rest of the society in the sect's earlier period (see Beckford, 1975). Soviet Jehovah's Witnesses, however, have on the whole sustained that deep hostility to secular power and the wider society, which makes it easy for them to put allegiance to the sect above all else.

This hostility, which is fully reciprocated by the state, also assists the development of a clear sense of identity. Partly due to its illegal status and partly to its self-imposed standing aside from society, the sect's boundaries are very clear. Separation from society is not of an 'introversionist' type but is the consequence of conscious rejection rather than passive avoidance. Members are not indifferent to the world outside the sect but Witnesses spend a lot of time (negatively) evaluating Soviet social reality and defining their relationship to it (Eryshev, 1969, p. A47; Bartoshevich, 1969, p. 154). Scientific and atheist literature is read by the more literate members to get to know 'enemy positions' so as to defend the sect and themselves better against challenges (Gazhos, 1969, p. 65).

While still living in the midst of society, Jehovah's Witnesses do their utmost to stay outside that sector of society which is organised and controlled by the state. They rarely take jobs which force them to integrate into a working collective. They seek out either those few occupations which have not been encompassed by nationalisation, or they work in isolation from an industrial or agricultural collective. They have a preference for artisan work, such as house painting and joinery. Besides helping them to avoid contact with officialdom these jobs also provide ideal opportunities for proselytising (Gazhos, 1969, p. 83). They also frequently work as service personnel, choosing such individualist jobs as watchmen or lift operators (Gagarin, 1973, p. 63). Many Witnesses keep their children at school only for an absolute minimum, usually up to the fifth year. In three Moldavian villages studied, for example, only 22, 25 and 33 per cent respectively of members' children stayed to the seventh or eighth year (Gazhos, 1969, pp. 82–3).

Considering themselves citizens of a coming theocracy, Soviet Witnesses do not feel that they have any obligations to Soviet society, or even that they have to observe Soviet laws. While Western Witnesses hold the same position, in practice their obligations to the sect now rarely clash with those to the state. In Soviet society, however, where the state continually tries to mobilise individuals and makes many demands on them, such clashes are frequent and unavoidable. Thus Soviet Witnesses resist demands for participation in military service, elections, and all other political as well as social activities. In 1959 members were even urged not to participate in the census. They were warned that Satan wanted a list of his supporters and that inclusion on that list would lead to destruction in the Battle of Armageddon (*Prichiny . . .*, 1965, p. 154).

But even among Jehovah's Witnesses attitudes to the wider society have been softening, and exclusivity is starting to be undermined. While the majority of long-standing rank-and-file members continue strictly to uphold the 'sectarian' principles of exclusivity, some sections of the sect's leadership and some of the more recently recruited members are beginning to abandon a totally intransigent hostility to Soviet society. Leaders have changed their secular orientations in response to directives from American headquarters. Since 1964, as indicated above, the notion of Satan being at work through the Soviet rulers has been abandoned by Brooklyn leaders, and a generally more accommodative stance to the demands of Soviet society has been urged. While Soviet sect leaders, according to a study of Moldavian Witnesses (Gazhos, 1969, pp. 22–3), have responded with their usual obedience, rank-and-file members have chosen to ignore these new directives or to revolt against them. Thus, for example, when local leaders gave permission for members to join trade unions, the latter did not avail themselves of this opportunity. This has naturally caused some conflict in local groups, but we are given no indication of the seriousness of this rift. New and younger members, however, have generally showed less resentment about this directive and have been following their leaders' advice (ibid., p. 23). They have begun to join trade unions, collective farms, and even to vote in elections (Gazhos, 1975, pp. 101, 102). They have taken a more positive attitude to the Soviet Union and have not kept themselves completely apart from social activity. In one area of Moldavia, for example, children of some Witnesses continued their education, borrowed from the public library and even joined the Young Pioneers (Tabakaru, 1973, p. 4). Decrease of exclusivity is also vividly expressed in the following assorted statistics: of a sample of 128 Witnesses 50 per cent owned a radio, 12·5 per cent had television sets, 72 per cent subscribed to a paper or journal and 30 per cent had some involvement in public affairs (ibid., p. 9). On the part of the Soviet authorities there has been a partial response to the more accommodative stance of American and local leaders. Although the sect is still illegal, there has been no wave of arrests in recent years, and those arrested in the fifties have been released from labour camps.

Despite those indications of some modest change in the relations between Soviet Jehovah's Witnesses and the state, the over-riding image of the sect in the literature is still that of a hostile and, in relation to its size, very effective and influential ideological opponent. The faith of the Witnesses must be considered one of the most clearly articulated and comprehensive counter-ideologies in the Soviet Union, possessing strong political overtones. The secular ethic of the Witnesses, in contrast to that of other sects of Western origin, is not concerned with questions of morality. It does not advocate charity to ameliorate the conditions of individuals but has political orientations and visions of large-scale quasi-political change. While some of the rank-and-file members may not be clearly aware of the politically oppositional element in the religious response of the Soviet Witnesses, there is a large section among leaders and members for whom this feature constitutes its prime attraction. Thus a comparative study of sectarians in the Ukraine brought out clearly that Jehovah's Witnesses had a disproportionately large proportion of socially alienated members. The study concluded that 52 per cent of members chiefly expressed their dissatisfaction with worldly society by joining the sect. In contrast to other sectarians, they looked to their faith primarily in the hope of realising Paradise *on earth*. They pictured the coming kingdom vividly and in glowing colours and juxtaposed it all the time with a picture of Soviet society showing only the negative features and the most drab forms of social reality (Eryshev, 1969, pp. A43–4). Another author, too, points out that a significant section of members are more fanatically anti-

Soviet, both in theory and practice, than religious (Gazhos, 1969, p. 78). When questioned about their motives for joining the sect 19 per cent of respondents in one survey singled out social or political injustice suffered as their prime reason (ibid., p. 79), a motive rarely mentioned by other sectarians. More indirect evidence about the political experiences preceding members' sect affiliation is given by the nature of the sect's expansion in the postwar Soviet Union. Expansion into Siberia and central Asia has been considerable and has, to a large extent, been due to the missionary success of Witnesses in the labour camps of those areas and the subsequent settling of released inmates in those areas. The presence of clearly recognisable groups of deportees – Germans – among Jehovah's Witnesses is also notable (see *Central Asian Review*, 1963, p. 352).

In addition to members with overt political orientations, the sect attracts a large number of socially uprooted people who have migrated from the western to the eastern areas of the Soviet Union, or from the country to the city, for reasons of unspecified dissatisfaction. Thus the sect in the Siberian areas around Irkutsk and Tomsk is said to consist mainly of immigrants, 5,000 having arrived there from the western republics since the Second World War (Kostenko, 1967, p. 35). In the Komi ASSR, too, there were many western immigrants in the sect in the early sixties in addition to people who had only recently taken up industrial work (Gagarin, 1963, pp. 62–3). In a Ukrainian sample of Witnesses, between 63 per cent and 88 per cent of all men in the worker category were migratory workers (Moskalenko, 1971, p. 178). A sociological survey in Sverdlov region (Kolosnitsyn, 1969, p. 134), too, established that *all* the Witnesses in that area had only recently arrived in the towns from the countryside.

Unlike most other religious organisations in the Soviet Union, the sect cannot contain any members wholly unaware of the fact that their religious involvement sets them into opposition to the dominant ideology of their society. The illegal status of the sect and the continual need for conspiratorial organisation makes every member conscious of the fact that he is offending against the rules of his society. Acceptance of this deviant behaviour alone is an indication of a certain degree of social alienation.

*Social Composition*
Which social groups then in Soviet society choose to express their social disillusionment in this form and why? As Witnesses frequently refuse to give interviews to sociologists, there are only limited sources available on social characteristics of Jehovah's Witnesses, but these provide a fairly consistent picture. Compared to other Soviet religious organisations, the sect has a relatively high proportion of men (around 35 per cent in various regions) and of members aged between 30 and 50 years. Around 65 per cent of members were under 50 during the late sixties and early seventies. Their level of education is generally low (see survey data presented by Gagarin, 1963, p. 63; Belov, 1969, pp. 31–3; Eryshev, 1969, p. A41; Gagarin, 1970, p. 380, 1971, p. 145; Moskalenko, 1971, p. 178). But they do have a small proportion of members with complete middle or technical education (Gagarin, 1971, p. 145). They tend to work as independent small artisans, collective farmers or unskilled service workers, preferring jobs in isolation from the collective, such as that of a watchman (Moskalenko, 1971, p. 178), although in the Komi ASSR, they have been said to work more often in production than True Orthodox Christians or Lutherans (Gagarin, 1971, p. 145).

In general, the sect of Jehovah's Witnesses seems to be remarkably similar to the illegal Pentecostalists and True Orthodox Christians on all aspects of its social profile. (For greater detail on social characteristics see Lane, 1976, p. 365.) To sum up, the social group which regards affiliation to a radically 'sect'-like religious organisation as a means to express socio-political disillusionment or alienation has the following characteristics: it predominantly contains persons who were born after the Revolution, grew up during the height of Stalinism, are likely to have experienced the social upheaval attendant on deportation or migration and are too inadequately educated to express their dissatisfaction through other channels.

While in the West Jehovah's Witnesses predominate also in the 30 to 50 years age group, their educational and occupational characteristics place them firmly in the lower middle and the upper working classes (see Rogerson, 1969, p. 175, and Beckford, 1975, p. 136 on British Witnesses). Unlike their Soviet brethren, they are no longer as deeply alienated from their social and political environment although they stand still more aloof from 'the world' than do other sectarians. In the Soviet Union, however, the combined influence of a lesser degree of economic development and an uncompromisingly hostile relation to the Jehovah's Witnesses has served to arrest development of their organisation at the extreme left pole of a 'sect-to-church' continuum. While in many other sects in the Soviet Union movement away from that pole has been induced by partial or complete tolerance of their organisations, the continued illegality of the Witnesses has served to strengthen their sectarian orientations. The relationship of hostile deadlock between state and sect, however, has been partially broken by accommodation initiated by the American leaders of the world organisation. Generally, Jehovah's Witnesses are renowned for their unquestioning acceptance of new directives from their central leadership. Whether, in the case of Soviet Witnesses, loyalty to the sect's international leaders will prove stronger than a resentful response to their local situation remains to be seen.

# Chapter 9

# Religion and Nationality I

## LUTHERANS AND MENNONITES

Lutheranism in the contemporary Soviet Union is represented chiefly by three national groups each having its own church – Estonians, Latvians and Germans. All three churches are or were national churches which have been connected with the history and culture of the group they serve, and the religiosity of their members has been inseparably interwoven with feelings of national consciousness and patriotism. While the Lutheran churches of the Latvians and Estonians are the churches of the dominant nationalities on their home territory, the German Lutheran Church is non-existent as an official organisation and serves an immigrant national minority under conditions of quasi-exile. The different fate of the German group from that of the two Baltic nationalities has decisively influenced the development and present state of its Lutheran Church and faith and must, therefore, be treated separately from the other two. There is a shortage of Soviet sociological data on all three churches but there are some interesting descriptions of the German Lutheran communities by Lutheran visitors from East and West Germany. As the German Lutheran community is also sociologically the more interesting case it will be dealt with in greater length.

The close association of German nationalism with religious affiliation is also evident in the sect of the Mennonites which is here coupled with different religious orientations and modes of organisation. A comparison and contrast between these two religio-national groups will therefore bring out more distinctly the distinguishing features of each. First, however, a short description of the Baltic Lutheran churches and an analysis of the religiosity of their members will be made.

### The Latvian and Estonian Lutheran churches
Although the Latvian and Estonian churches are amongst the oldest Lutheran churches in the world and have served the majority of their respective populations for centuries, a close bond has not developed between these two churches and the national groups they serve. Unlike the Lithuanian Catholic Church or the Russian Orthodox Church, the two churches have not always been true national churches linked closely with the development of national consciousness of their members. Up to the turn of the century the churches were almost exclusively

staffed by their German colonisers as well as being under Scandinavian influence and were thus identified with political and cultural domination by a foreign minority. Only from 1940 onwards could Latvians and Estonians truly call the Lutheran churches their own, although even then the level of nominal member- ship was not very high, being 56 and 78 per cent of the Latvian and Estonian population respectively (Beeson, 1974, p. 109). In 1945 the Baltic states were incorporated into the Soviet Union. The period between 1940 and 1948, after which Soviet militant atheism began to make a strong impact on the life of the two churches, was too short to forge the close link between religion and nation usually developed by national minorities incorporated into a larger political unit. Besides having developed only a weak identification on national grounds in their members, the two Baltic churches had also been unable to evoke a deep religious commitment in their members. This was due to the fact that the churches, like most Protestant national churches, had never tied their members closely to the Church by a multiplicity of bonds. They therefore left them much more vulnerable after 1945 to the onslaught of militant atheism, rapid collectivisation and intensi- fied industrialisation.

It is therefore not surprising to find that both churches suffered a drastic weakening of their organisational structure, a decline of membership and a loss of influence over their members. Although the churches were given a short respite between 1945 and 1948 and could reconstruct and consolidate their disrupted organisations to some extent, two intensive and harsh anti-religious campaigns coming in short succession in 1949–53 and 1959–64 caused great havoc (Veinbergs, 1971). The following statistics contrast pre-communist and post-communist church life. The Estonian Lutheran Church (hereafter ELC) suffered a decline from between 1,000,000 (Beeson, 1974, p. 110) and 800,000 (Russell, 1970) nominal members in 1940 to 350,000 in 1961 (*Current Develop- ments in the Eastern European Churches*, 3, 15, 1962, p. 9). The Latvian Lutheran Church (hereafter LLC) had lost half of its 1941 membership by 1967 when only 500,000 members were left (Beeson, 1974, p. 110).

In 1961, when the LLC and the ELC joined the World Council of Churches, they supplied the following figures on their organisational strength. The LLC claimed 500,000 members or the allegiance of 24 per cent of the total population (*Current Developments in the Eastern European Churches*, 3, 15, 1962, p. 9), but by 1973 total membership had fallen to 350,000 (*Glaube in der 2. Welt*, 11, 1975, pp. 26–7) or 14·4 per cent of the total population. (It must be pointed out, however, that this population figure includes many who are ethnically Russian and would, therefore, not constitute a possible pool for recruitment to the Lutheran Church.) These worship in 214 congregations (ibid.). The number of clergy in 1961 was stated as being 115, i.e. one for every 4,350 members, and twenty candidates for the ministry were studying in evening courses at the one theological establishment in Riga (*Current Developments*, op cit.). By 1964 the number of pastors was slightly reduced to 110 (*Digest des Ostens*, 3, 1965, p. 64), and by 1968 it had fallen to ninety (*Digest des Ostens*, 5, 1968, p. 82).

The picture in the Estonian Church is equally gloomy. In 1961 the ELC was reported to have had 350,000 members (33 per cent of the population), 148 parishes, 114 pastors, i.e. one for every 3,070 members (*Current Developments in the Eastern European Churches*, 3, 15, 1962, p. 9), and one theological institute. By 1964 the number of pastors had declined drastically to sixty, i.e. one for every 5,833 members (*Digest des Ostens*, 3, 1965, p. 64). A further reduction in the size of membership had occurred by 1970 when an English visiting cleric was told that there were only 100,000 members (8 per cent of the population) which may represent actual membership (Russell, 1970), while the higher figure of 250,000 or 18 per cent of the population for 1973 (Beeson, 1974, p. 110) may represent nominal membership. This decline in strength in both Lutheran churches is partly a consequence of administrative interference during the anti-religious campaigns and reflects also a decline in the religious commitment by Lutherans in both countries. A drop in the number of church attenders is partly attributable to the acute shortage of pastors which has necessitated the cessation of *regular* services in the countryside and a gross overburdening of the remaining pastors who may have to serve as many as eight parishes (Veinbergs, 1971). This is not, however, the whole explanation. The Catholic Church in the Baltic republics, which suffered similar persecution, can still rely on churches being consistently full, whereas the Lutheran churches in some areas may be found nearly empty on Sundays, though not everywhere (Veinbergs, 1971, p. 415).

Participation in rites of passage is one index of the extent of religiosity although it is often indicative of only a shallow commitment. Figures collected in one district of Latvia indicate a sharp decline in the extent to which people participated in rites of passage between 1960 and 1964. Baptisms suffered a four-fold, wedding rites a ninefold decline, and the total number of confirmations dropped from thirty-three to two. Only the number of religious funerals stayed constant (Veinbergs, 1971, p. 417). This is also confirmed for other areas (*Stroitel'stvo* . . ., 1966, p. 255). Such a drastic decline may partly have been the result of the anti-religious campaign of those years which either frightened people off temporarily, or drove the performance of these rites underground. Thus in one rural parish of Latvia, where no baptisms or weddings had been performed in the village church during 1964, 25·7 per cent of all babies had nevertheless been christened at home, 7 per cent of all those married during that year had the wedding rites celebrated at their homes and 19·4 per cent of all deceased received a religious burial conducted by an old village woman (Terent'eva, 1966, p. 65). This, however, is not the whole explanation. Statistics collected at a different time indicate a similar decline. Data collected in Estonia for the ten-year interval between 1957 and 1968 also show a sharp drop in the number of participants in rites of passage. Of all those born in 1957, 55·8 per cent were baptised but only 12·3 per cent of the 1968 babies received baptism. The respective figures for weddings are 29·8 and 2·6 per cent and those for funerals 64·5 and 46 per cent (*Osteuropa*, March 1971, p. 195).

Religious commitment has fallen to a particularly low level among young people who have in large numbers turned from religious rites of passage to the newly introduced secular rites. In particular the Day of Maturity, introduced in the Baltic republics in 1959 to replace confirmation, appears to have been widely accepted and responsible for a steadily increasing drop in the proportion of confirmed since that year (Tevent'eva, 1966, p. 71; *Stroitel'stvo* . . ., 1966, p. 225). The number of confirmations is said to have dropped ten times between 1958 and 1963 in both Latvia and Estonia. A similar decrease has been experienced in the number of church weddings. In 1963, 26 per cent more couples than in 1957 opted for the civil ceremony in the Soviet wedding palace (ibid.).

In general, then, it appears as if the combined impact of rapid economic and social change on the one side and of militant atheist activity on the other has eroded the strength of the Baltic Lutheran churches to such an extent that they now have only a very marginal influence over their respective populations and are faced with the prospect of complete decay in the not so distant future. Although Lutheran churches in the West have also experienced a marked reduction in active membership in the postwar period, the Baltic churches appear to have suffered a much stronger decline. They have been subjected to the additional secularising influence of a socialist and militantly atheist society and do not possess a strong social base which would allow them to challenge their ideological enemies.

## The German Lutherans
The German Lutheran Church in the Soviet Union (hereafter GLC) has suffered much longer and more deeply than the Baltic churches under the impact of the anti-religious regime. It is today completely destroyed as an organisation but German Lutheran communities of believers have resurged in the late fifties. They appear to possess a greater religious vitality than their Baltic brethren and have also departed considerably from them in following their faith. A brief review of the history of the Lutheran Church and the German population on Soviet soil is necessary for an understanding of the position of German Lutheranism today.

Lutherans first arrived in Russia at the end of the seventeenth century as artisans and colonists. Their Church recruited predominantly from among the German community, and to a lesser extent from other non-Russian minority groups. As the former were respected and influential at court, the Church was left in peace by the Russian authorities and could expand undisturbed. This relaxed state–church relationship continued for a while under Soviet rule. In 1924 the Lutheran superintendent was even given permission to unite the nearly 1 million members, organised in 212 local churches (Stange, 1963, p. 29), into one all-Russian Church. But after 1929, the German Lutheran Church experienced the same wave of repression and persecution as the other religious organisations, and in 1938 the last German Lutheran church was closed. While the other religious organisations could re-emerge and restore some of their destroyed organisational network in the more relaxed political atmosphere of the war and postwar years, the Lutheran Church with its predominantly German membership was given no such respite. As nominal members of the nation which had subjected the Soviet Union to the destruction and misery of the Second World War they suffered the full burden of the hostility and revenge the Russians felt towards everything connected with Germany. They were driven from their traditional western settlement areas and dispersed into the many labour camps of Siberia and central Asia. Those who survived were cowed into complete submission and refrained from any organised activity which linked them with their German origins and heritage. For a long while it appeared as if the Lutheran Church and faith had been completely extinguished among Soviet Germans.

However, after the 1955 general amnesty for Germans in the Soviet Union and the gradual reconstitution of German communities in central Asia, the Far East and Siberia there also occurred a cautious revival of religious life among the $1\frac{1}{2}$ million or so German survivors. Although the official Church was irrevocably destroyed and most pastors were either dead or unwilling to resume their office, Lutheran faith was not dead. Lutheran groups formed themselves in many places under a devoted and dedicated lay leadership. During that time, according to Stange (1963, p. 30), 'the Lutheran sense of mission seemed to be fervent and fruitful with every church member taking it upon himself to witness to three or four non-believers'. At first these groups worshipped together with other Protestant (mainly Baptist) groups, then they gradually established separate communities. They were not given the right by the Soviet authorities to organise themselves on a nationwide scale into a church.

*Organisation and membership.* An assessment of the number of Lutherans in the non-Baltic parts of the Soviet Union today is difficult, but some estimates of nominal membership, based on the 1959 census material and knowledge about Lutheranism, have been made. Of the 1,619,000 Germans listed in the 1959 census, about half live in the central Asian republics, Siberia, the north and Far East. Of these, about two-thirds are estimated to be nominal Lutherans or members of the Reformed Church (only a small minority). In addition, there are Estonian, Latvian and Finnish Lutherans in these areas, but in much smaller numbers and usually affiliated to German groups. Altogether there are estimated to be 1·25 million nominal Lutherans in these areas, but it is impossible to know how many of these are professing Lutherans (Römmich, 1972, pp. 264–5). The prominent presence of Germans in other religious organisations, especially among the Baptists, and reports about defection into the sects (see *Travel Report . . .*, 1970, p. 3) suggests that many of those formerly Lutheran have joined more active and not nationalistic religious organisations and that the number of professing Lutherans is now very much lower.

Of the many groups which applied for registration with the Soviet authorities, the community in Tselinograd (Kazakhstan) was for a long time the only one to be recognised. In later years several others followed, and today there are said to be registered congregations in the Siberian towns of Omsk, Tomsk and Novosibirsk, in the Kazakh towns of Alma-Ata and Karaganda, in the Uzbek towns of Frunze and Tokmak, the Ural town Chelyabinsk, and in the Volga town Sysran (Römmich, 1972, p. 268). Besides these registered congregations there are hundreds of small unregistered groups. A Christian delegation from Berlin visiting Siberia reported many small (up to 200 members) Lutheran congregations in the environment of Novosibirsk and estimated there to be about 300 such congregations in western Siberia. Of these, eighty had their own, self-built meeting place (*Dein Reich Komme*, March 1970, pp. 13–14). An East German pastor visiting Kirgizia noted in the republic the existence of fifty-nine Lutheran and Reformed congregations with between fifty and eighty people present at the Sunday services of each (*Travel Report . . .*, 1970, Appendix).

These unregistered groups have either been unable to obtain registration or, more commonly, prefer to remain unregistered, and thus preserve anonymity, to the organisational security of legal status (*Travel Report . . .*, 1970, p. 3). This endeavour by the group and its members to preserve anonymity is one of the most distinctive features of Lutheranism in the Russian parts of the Soviet Union and has had far-reaching consequences for organisation and the character of members' religiosity. It is prompted on the one side by the fear of members of this long-suffering national group openly to commit themselves to any position implying some degree of ideological dissent (*Religion und Atheismus in der UdSSR*, 8, 1971, p. 10). On the other side, anonymity and illegality are welcomed because they necessitate the retention of small closely-knit groups. They make the group accessible only to people of the same nationality. This enables the religious community to retain its German religious and general cultural heritage, especially the oldfashioned pietistic form of worship and German as the language to render it. The other distinctive feature of contemporary Soviet Lutheranism is the absence of a clerical hierarchy or even of professional pastors as well as, in most communities, of fixed places of worship. The second feature, although not caused by the first, is bound to be perpetuated by it.

With a few exceptions the groups are headed by lay leaders or elders who acquired their status because of superior religious qualifications. Thus many lay pastors were formerly deacons or teachers (Römmich, 1972, p. 268) or merely particularly keen members of a church before 1937 (see *Travel Report . . .*, 1970, p. 3). They feel qualified to hold reading services (German *Lesedienste*) and to perform rites of passage, while the sacraments are only administered by the occasional visiting ordained pastor or by specially selected 'brothers'. Taken together, the features of lay pastors, lack of formal organisation and small and close-knit groups of members of one nationality have endowed Soviet Lutheranism outside the Baltic republics with characteristics completely removed from the 'church' type and have given it a 'sect'-like organisational pattern.

*Religious Orientations and Nationalistic Involvement.* Although this 'sect'-like organisation has had an influence on the nature of the religiosity of members and has differentiated it from that of Lutherans in the Baltic churches, it has not had the effect of evoking religious and social responses of the type usually associated with sects. Three related features distinguish the religious commitment of German Lutherans: religious and national allegiance are closely and inseparably entwined; they practise a pronounced community Christianity; the style of their worship is archaic. Although the second characteristic is usually associated with 'sect'-like orientations this is not the case with German Lutherans. Among them it is closely related to the first characteristic in that practising a community-style Christianity of an oldfashioned kind is the most appropriate form in which they can express their national allegiance.

The communitarian aspect of religious life does not only come out in the small size, national homogeneity and intimacy of the religious groups but even more in the way they organise their worship. Although groups do have an elected lay pastor, the spiritual life of the community is carried by the pietistic *Betbrüder* and *Betschwestern* (Pray Brothers and Sisters), a feature preserved from the religious Revival movement of the last century in the German Volga communities (see *Travel Report . . .*, 1970, p. 4). The whole religious life of the community is coloured by this rather archaic, pietistic style of worship. Hymns are devotional songs (*Erbauungslieder*) from the last century, sermons are read from nineteenth-century prayerbooks, and communal prayer – in which the Elder begins to speak a prayer and is joined by congregation members speaking their own individual prayers – is the rule (ibid.). Many of their attitudes about social conduct, too, date from that period and appear fossilised to the outside observer (*Dein Reich Komme*, 6, 1973, p. 6). Despite these anti-institutional characteristics, the groups emphasise that they regard themselves as a church and do everything possible to set themselves apart from the Baptists and other sects. Thus, for example, they insist on infant baptism instead of adult conversion. Their 'churchly' character, however, becomes most pronounced in their constant endeavour to equate membership of the Lutheran religious community with that of the German national group. Let us consider how national allegiance expresses itself in religious commitment and what the nature of this nationalism is.

First and foremost, the connection is forged by the practice of conducting worship only in the German language. This excludes all possible converts from other national groups and keeps the groups as German islands in a sea of Soviet Russianism. It has also had the effect of excluding the young generation in the German communities. As a German school education has no longer been uniformly provided since the war, the majority of the postwar generation have grown up with little understanding of German language and feel themselves to be primarily Soviet citizens rather than Germans. Those among the younger people with religious inclinations have preferred to join the multi-national sovietised Baptist sect rather than the nationalistic, inward- and backward-looking group of their fathers and forefathers. Preservation of the German character of the Lutheran groups is also sought by proscribing inter-marriage with Russians. Mixed marriages are, indeed, said to be much more rarely entered by those Germans who have grown up in a Lutheran family than by those who have not. Germans with a Lutheran background, unlike the non-religious ones, are also apt to stress their German origin and set themselves apart from their Russian environment (Gagarin, 1971, pp. 148*ff*.).

The preceding discussion makes it clear that German nationalism is fostered by, and expressed through, allegiance to the Lutheran religious community. It is not an active and aggressive type of nationalism, like that found among Ukrainian Uniates or, in somewhat milder form, among Catholic Lithuanians. It is rather of a passive, expressive kind without explicit political overtones. German Lutherans never seek confrontations with the authorities but, on the contrary, try to express their religious and national sentiments as unobtrusively as possible. The authorities do not seem to find their form of nationalism dangerous. One author describes Germans as being 'to an overwhelming extent loyal to the Soviet state, submitting to its laws and being honest citizens' (Gagarin, 1971, p. 147). Although many individual Germans keep up links with relations and friends in West Germany and would like to emigrate there, their nationalism is not focused on a German nation in the way Hitler's ideology was. It appears to be more a nationalism of a broad cultural kind which looks back to 'the good old times', an attempt to preserve a piece of Russian *Heimat* in the new Soviet settlement areas. The Russian Germans were torn abruptly and completely out of their comfortable and familiar social setting and were transferred into an unfamiliar, socially hostile and climatically harsh environment. Up to 1964, when the wartime accusations of being anti-Soviet spies were lifted, Germans were citizens with restricted rights (Römmich, 1972, p. 274). Such an experience is bound to cultivate nostalgia and an attempt to re-create something of that which shaped their identity for generations. Preservation of religious culture has been the one way in which this could be accomplished. In their effort to preserve some aspects of German identity, which is becoming increasingly more elusive, they have rigidified the religious culture of the community.

Their nationalist focus on their past in Russia and their flight from the present is well expressed in the fact that sermons are read exclusively from prayerbooks dating from the last century so that problems of contemporary Soviet life are never touched upon in sermons. This complete envelopment in the group and its past is also reflected in their complete ignorance of the problems encountered in other parts of the world, even those well propagated by the communist media (*Travel Report . . .*, 1970, p. 6).

The attempt to preserve their religious and national identity has been successful for the middle and old generation. The communitarian character of their religious groups has kept Lutheran religion alive and relevant to its members as well as giving them a focus for expressing their national identity. Although we have no quantitative data on religious commitment among the traditionally Lutheran German population, qualitative information suggests a picture of a high rate of participation in Lutheran worship by members of the older and middle generation. The character of the services, as described above, has ensured the religious involvement of participants along the ideological, intellectual and practice dimensions (Stange, 1968; *Travel Report . . .*, 1970; Römmich, 1972, p. 274; *Heimat im Glauben*, 1, 1973). The religious tradition of the German Lutheran Church, in contrast to that of other churches, is indeed carried and kept alive by its lay members. Unlike other churches, the German Lutheran community does not receive such minimal support for the maintenance of religious culture from the authorities as small editions of Bibles, hymn-books or journals. Yet it has seemingly managed to maintain the flow of religious information to ordinary believers better than the comparatively well-provided Orthodox Church. While Orthodox believers usually had no written information at their disposal and had a low level of involvement along the intellectual dimension of religiosity, German Lutherans had hand-written copies of the relevant religious texts and were familiar with the basics of their faith (Römmich, 1972, p. 274).

Ironically, the very success of the prewar generation of German Lutherans in keeping the national-religious heritage alive at the present time is endangering its survival in the future. The keenness of the religious communities to preserve faithfully religious tradition and to avoid anything which might attract attention from the political authorities has created a spirit of inflexible conservatism, narrowness and timidity. The archaic character of the services, the exclusive use of German language no longer familiar to all the young, the introverted and backward-looking nature of the community, and the resulting absence of a relevant social ethic have all served to alienate many young Germans. The partly complacent and partly fearful (of the state) attitude towards active recruitment among the young has prevented any activity to overcome this alienation. Young Germans with religious interest have instead turned to the more dynamic, multi-national legal Baptist sect (*Travel Report . . .*, 1970, pp. 7–8). The age structure of Lutheran communities is thus imbalanced towards the elderly (see Gagarin, 1971, p. 145), probably no more so than in the Baltic Lutheran churches or the Orthodox Church, but much more so than in the sects.

The foregoing descriptions of the organisation and socio-religious orientations of both Lutheran communities and their members have brought out how the particular historical fate of the German Lutheran Church and national group in the Soviet Union has created a religious type with a peculiar mixture of 'churchly' and 'sect'-like features. While the organisational structure is akin to that of an 'introversionist' sect and has coloured the religiosity of members to some extent, the social responses of the groups and their members are still of the 'church' type. One of the most important features of the 'church' type, according to Troeltsch, is the equation of religious with national allegiance, the identification of the religious organisational unit with the national one. The endeavour of Russian–German Lutherans to forge such a close link dominates their religious life and shapes the character of their communities. While, on the one hand, this has given their religious commitment depth and stability, on the other hand, it has led them to neglect a religious activity usually regarded as an expression of strong religious commitment, namely, proselytising. Thus, paradoxically, the close entwinement of religious and national involvement, which has helped German Lutheranism to survive and gain new impetus against heavy odds, will in the long run destroy it. The inflexible, timid and backward-looking form of nationalism adopted does not appeal to the postwar generation of Soviet Germans, and its repudiation has at the same time become a rejection of the religion so closely allied to it.

### The Mennonites

This complete entwinement of religious and German national allegiance can also be found among the Mennonites, the oldest Western sect in the Soviet Union. In their case, however, both religious and nationalist orientations differ significantly from those of Lutherans. The resulting religious–national combination has had completely different effects on the organisational complexion and religious vitality of the group. Mennonites have had a more complex history manifested in greater internal differentiation. Consequently a much greater variety of social, political and religious responses is found among contemporary Soviet Mennonites, and no such clear unilinear trend can be discerned in the relationship between their responses as in the case of the German Lutherans.

The Mennonites are spiritual descendants of early sixteenth-century German and Dutch Anabaptists. In reaction to the anarchic events at Münster, many Anabaptists united around Menno Siemens, attracted by his call for a disciplined religious group. They were distinguished by the adoption of adult baptism and of high moral principles. The developing concern for the moral purity of the religious group resulted in great emphasis being put on the practice of expelling the unworthy. In search of a tolerant and economically supportive environment, they went from Holland to the eastern parts of Germany, and finally, at the end of the eighteenth century, to Russia. They were founded, and developed their teaching, in Holland and spent the longest span of their organisational life in Russia, though their identification is with the German national group.

Mennonites first arrived in Russia in 1789. They gained special concessions with regard to their economic and religious life as well as being given large expanses of virgin land. Here they settled to form their spatially and culturally segregated communities. Their self-sufficient agrarian communities guaranteed economic independence, and their use of the German language and the creation of their own educational and welfare systems ensured their cultural separation. Both their economic and their religious life flourished. Their level of economic and cultural development soon became superior to that of the surrounding

Russian population as well as surpassing the level of development of Western Mennonite communities (Epp, 1971, p. 285).

The Tsarist government's respect of their pacifist position and their consequent exemption from military service eliminated friction between their communities and the wider society. In 1860, however, internal conflict resulted in a schism of Mennonites into two groups – Church Mennonites and Mennonite Brethren, or Old and New Mennonites – the major difference between them being a different mode of baptism.

Peace and prosperity came to a sudden end with the 1917 Revolution. Their discrepantly high level of economic development made them prime targets of attack during the Civil War. The fact that Mennonites did not regard the new regime favourably contributed to a further deterioration of state–sect relations. Of the 110,000 Mennonites in the country in 1917, 20,000 left for Canada in 1923. A further 13,000 fled in 1928, after an outspoken demand for religious freedom at the last Mennonite conference in 1925 had met with only a negative response (Epp, 1971, p. 291). Further severe disruption of communities and extensive imprisonment and deportation of individual Mennonites followed during the collectivisation period, when Mennonites, because of their high level of economic development, were generally classed as *kulaks* (rich peasants). By 1935, as was the case in other sects, their religious life was seriously undermined, though not completely destroyed. The last blow to their communities occurred during the Second World War when, because of their German origins, whole villages were deported from the western to the eastern parts of the Soviet Union and their inhabitants were dispersed. Religious life was then almost completely destroyed. Thus, at the time when all other religious organisations were suddenly given a relatively large measure of religious freedom and could recover some of their strength, the Mennonites had to face the gravest trials and tribulations in all their long history.

A gradual renewal and consolidation of religious communities occurred only after the general amnesty during the late fifties. Those released from labour camps set about founding new communities in central Asia (mainly Kazakhstan) and Siberia or joined the undisrupted settlements east of the Urals and the Volga (Epp, 1971, p. 295). In Orenburg region of the RSFSR, for example, there were in the late sixties still thirty-six villages inhabited exclusively by German Mennonites who settled there at the end of the nineteenth century (Il'inykh, 1969, p. 201). In 1963, to gain legal status, the majority of the Mennonite Brethren joined the Union of Evangelical Christian Baptists, while the Church Mennonites stayed outside (Epp, 1971, p. 296). The great affinity in religious orientations and practice between Baptists and Mennonites had led to a *rapprochement* between the two sects in many localities before 1963 (Il'inykh, 1969, p. 207), and the Mennonite entry into the Union has caused no problems. The two sects uphold friendly neighbourly relations and often worship together. The Mennonites are not, however, becoming absorbed by the larger Baptist organisation but, due to their national identification, have successfully preserved a separate identity. Since 1967, there have been informal approaches for union between the two Mennonite branches (Epp, 1971, p. 297), and Mennonite leaders have toured the country trying to effect a reconciliation between the two branches (Krest'yaninov, 1967, p. 79). The number of Mennonites left in the Soviet Union in the early seventies has been estimated to be between 40,000 and 50,000. A Canadian

Mennonite writer speaks about 20,000 Mennonite Brethren and 20,000 Church Mennonites (Epp, 1971, p. 296). A 1975 estimate puts the overall number of Mennonites in the Soviet Union at 50,000 (*Dein Reich Komme*, 3, 1975, p. 15).

*Religious Commitment and Organisation.* Mennonites are a radical Protestant sect with slight 'introversionist' tendencies. They differ from other sects merely by their discrepantly strong emphasis on some tenets of Christian faith. The Bible, especially the New Testament, is considered the ultimate source of truth, and avid Bible study is common among them. A further distinguishing feature is their striving for high ethical standards and their pronounced secular ethic. Pacifism is a prominent part of the latter. In all these concerns they differ from the Baptists only by degree of emphasis.

Considering the severe trials and tribulations of the Soviet Mennonites since 1917 they have experienced an astonishing degree of religious revival from the late fifties and are enjoying today a relatively high measure of religious and organisational vitality. Western visitors to Soviet Mennonite congregations have been impressed by the vitality of their religious life and the real fellowship among members (Peters, 1968, p. 3; Epp, 1971, p. 297) which, to them, appeared to be greater than in the Western communities. Although no longer as exclusive and elitist as they were in pre-revolutionary time, Mennonites are still very much oriented towards the religious community, and they live out the greatest part of their lives within its boundaries. Like the Baptists, they are keen proselytisers and utilise every opportunity and means they have to this end. Although they mainly recruit new members from among their own communities, local congregations also have a small percentage of non-German members. New recruits are prepared thoroughly for membership and are only accepted if they have a true conversion experience and have attained a high standard of holy living (Epp, 1962, p. 460). The religious education of children is taken very seriously by both the family and the community, and systematic and wide-ranging provisions are made to that end (see Ipatov, 1974, p. 41).

Mennonites try to express their religious commitment by moral conduct. Christian neighbourly love is given high priority, and extensive mutual help and support rather than material accumulation are practised (Epp, 1971, p. 298). Their work ethic is particularly pronounced. They are generally known as responsible and conscientious workers (Krest'yaninov, 1967, pp. 135–7) and often receive medals or special responsibility in recognition of their work performance (Theodorovitch, 1968, p. 34). They fight drunkenness, hooliganism and thieving.

There is an active congregational life with religious activities taking place on every day of the week, except on Mondays. The mid-week activities are mainly organised for the younger members (Krest'yaninov, 1967, p. 159). Mennonites are particularly adept at overcoming the great shortage of religious literature provided by the state. They distribute a lot of hand-written material and make use of any foreign radio broadcasts or newspapers they can obtain, exchanging taped versions of the former with other congregations. Some Siberian Mennonites, for example, subscribe to an officially permitted newspaper from the communist German Democratic Republic which carries every Sunday an article on a religious theme (Theodorovitch, 1968, p. 34).

The level of devotional involvement also appears to be high with daily prayer and private Bible study being common practice (Ipatov, 1974, p. 41). In general, religious commitment appears to be strongest among the elderly minority and a small section of the middle generation (Krest'yaninov, 1967, pp. 178–9).

But the long period of enforced religious inactivity and the great hardship suffered by Mennonites during the war and postwar period have left their mark on Mennonite religious life. A lot of former members have become indifferent or apostate, and many of the present younger members have an inadequate religious knowledge (Epp, 1962, p. 460). A growing number of the younger people are also no longer content to have their social life confined to the religious community although, in general, Mennonites appear to be particularly successful in retaining their young under their influence (see data on social composition below). It is noteworthy that those eastern communities undisrupted by deportation have retained the religious allegiance of the young and male – those members most vulnerable to secularisation – much better than the resettled groups. A comparison of data on communities in Orenburg region with those of resettled groups brings out that the former have a much higher percentage of male members and of members aged under 50 than the latter.

The organisational framework for congregational life differs between localities. In a few places Mennonite Brethren have their own modest churches, in others they use Baptist churches, and mostly they meet in small groups in private houses. The latter is the norm for the illegal Church Mennonites. Groups of eight to ten members meet in different, prearranged private dwellings (Krest'yaninov, 1967, p. 159). Although there is some informal co-ordination of the many scattered congregations by travelling preachers on a regional level, each congregation is autonomous. The congregation is formally run by a general assembly which elects leaders and is convoked according to need. The untrained lay preachers are tremendously powerful and influential in the communities and know the lives of all the members (Krest'yaninov, 1967, p. 150). Mennonites (probably mainly the illegal branch) are said to be particularly secretive about their meetings and to try to make their many activities inaccessible to outsiders (ibid., p. 159).

*Social Composition.* The relative vitality of Mennonite congregations is expressed in their social composition (see Krest'yaninov, 1967, pp. 176*f*.; Il'inykh, 1969, pp. 202*f*.). They are characterised by having a very high percentage of middle-aged and young members, a medium high proportion of men, and a low percentage of illiterate and well-educated members. The vast majority of their members – an average of 70 per cent – are under 50 years of age. Preachers, too, were found to be much younger than among Baptists. Out of nineteen preachers in one district, fourteen were under 50 years of age. In its age structure the Mennonite sect is thus very similar to the more extreme Pentecostalists and Jehovah's Witnesses and differs significantly from the more closely related Baptists, and even more from the German Lutherans. The sect also attracts a higher percentage of men – an average of 30 per cent – than the latter two, but slightly less than the more radical sects. Mennonites are unique in terms of educational levels. They neither have among themselves a large proportion of illiterate people, like the Pentecostalists and Witnesses, nor do they attract any individuals with full middle or even higher education like the Baptists and Adventists. The vast majority of their members (around 95 per cent) have primary or incomplete secondary education. Consequently, most Mennonites are found in

204 Christian Religion in the Soviet Union

occupations with low qualifications. Specialists, like teachers, doctors, agronomists, are completely absent among them (Il'inykh, 1969, p. 206). (For more detailed data on social characteristics see Lane, 1976, p. 393.)

This social profile of Mennonites is, as in other sects, closely related to historical, social and religious characteristics of the sect. The fact that the sect contains relatively few illiterate people is connected to the fact that Mennonites, up to 1929, had their own schools and had higher educational standards than the Russian population in general. In 1920, they not only had 450 elementary schools but also 27 more advanced schools with around 2,000 pupils (Hein, 1970, p. 108). Although the generation now prominent in the sect did not directly benefit from these schools they did so indirectly by growing up in literate families appreciating the value of education. The absence of better-educated members among Mennonites is more difficult to explain. The explanation by Soviet writers that Mennonites do not value education (e.g. Krest'yaninov, 1967, p. 169) is not convincing when one considers other factors. First, Mennonites had a good educational system before Soviet power abolished it. Secondly, there is a notable presence of well-educated members among the Canadian Mennonites who emigrated from the Soviet Union in the twenties (Epp, 1962, p. 484). It seems more likely that the relatively low level of educational attainment of Mennonites is to some extent due to the disruption caused by deportation and the lack of educational opportunity one associates with deprivation of citizens' rights well into the sixties. A low valuation of *Soviet* education, rather than of education in general, may also have contributed.

The fact that Mennonites have managed to attract such a high proportion of younger people as well as a higher than average percentage of men is related to the fact that they are a communitarian religious organisation with distinctive cultural and social orientations. While the communitarian nature of a sect alone does not ensure its attractiveness to the young (see the example of the Molokans and Dukhobors), its combination with a distinctive socio-religious orientation does. Only when religious organisations offer what is regarded as a clear alternative to the socialist world-view do they attract the younger generation.

*Social and Nationalistic Orientations.* The socio-religious orientation of Mennonites has three components: a socio-political, an ethical and a national-cultural one. While we found in other sects that a younger membership was associated with a socio-political outlook in opposition to Soviet power, this is in general not true of Mennonites. Like the legal Baptists, most Mennonites have gone some way towards accommodating themselves to the political authorities. They appear anxious to express their political loyalty, no longer refuse categorically to join the armed forces and try to keep their religious activity within the framework of legality (Il'inykh, 1969, pp. 204–8; Epp, 1971, p. 299). There are, however, a minority of mainly elderly members who still put allegiance to the religious group and its teachings above everything else and come into conflict with the state (Krest'yaninov, 1967, p. 178). Although this group is fairly small it is said to be influential beyond its number (Il'inykh, 1969, p. 204). A few politically disenchanted people can also be found among the middle-aged sect members. They are extremely embittered about the treatment of Mennonites during and after the Second World War (Krest'yaninov, 1967, p. 179). While most Mennonites of the old and middle generation are politically indifferent and uninvolved there have been a number of younger Mennonites who have joined the communist cause as active participants (Epp, 1962, p. 465).

Most Mennonites, then, accept the general socio-political framework of Soviet society, but very few identify consciously and actively with all its values. The maxim that religion and the state have nothing in common and that believers cannot involve themselves in the political life of society is still widely accepted. In encounters with atheists, Mennonites usually express their position in the following words: 'You read and believe in your books, and we believe what is said in the Bible' (Krest'yaninov, 1967, p. 88). Although the Mennonite secular ethic is very similar to some postulates of the communist moral code, they ignore this similarity of content. Like other sectarian parents they prefer not to send their children to the youth organisations which play a big part in imparting communist moral education (ibid., p. 169; Theodorovitch, 1968, p. 34). But such orientations to the Soviet order which we have discussed are not distinctive enough to account on their own for the marked difference in the age and sex structure of the sect.

The attraction of the sect to a wide cross-section of the traditionally Mennonite communities is largely due to its close identification with a particular German national and cultural heritage. To be a Mennonite does not just stand for belonging to a religious organisation but signifies membership of a national-cultural group which has come to be regarded as an ethnic group. Centuries of spatial and linguistic segregation as well as endogamy have set the Mennonites apart from the rest of society and have given them a distinct identity of their own. It is expressed by the wide use of German spoken and written language for religious worship and in general life and by the preservation of a folk culture of music and handicraft (Krest'yaninov, 1967, p. 161; Theodorovitch, 1968, p. 34). A recommendation to militant atheist fieldworkers that only someone with a knowledge of the Mennonites' language and culture should be sent in to 'proselytise' for atheism (Il'inykh, 1969, p. 210) shows how much Mennonites are regarded by their Russian countrymen as a separate national–cultural group.

While a strong German national orientation among Lutherans had the effect of alienating the younger generation from the religious group, it has had the opposite effect among Mennonites. There are several ways to account for this. First, having always been a more communitarian religious group, Mennonites have a much more distinctive cultural heritage to pass on to the younger generation. German language has been kept alive by the family or, sometimes, by special private lessons organised for Mennonite children (Krest'yaninov, 1967, p. 170). Mennonite religious and folk culture has been preserved by the family unit. Secondly, being a sect-type organisation, religious and secular culture have traditionally been much more closely entwined than among Lutherans. Particularly the linking of religion to secular pursuits by a distinctive secular ethic has kept religion relevant. Thirdly and lastly, the nationalism of the Mennonites appears to be less introverted and backward-looking than that of the Lutherans. Mennonites are not only open to other Soviet religious organisations, particularly to the Baptists, but also maintain extensive ties with Mennonites in the West, especially with German and Canadian ones, on an organisational and personal level. Thus 90 per cent of Siberian Mennonites received religious literature from abroad (Kostenko, 1967, p. 37), and 30 per cent of the inhabitants of one village in Orenburg region of the RSFSR corresponded with relatives abroad (Il'inykh,

1969, p. 210). The younger Mennonites have also become gradually acculturated, and marriage out of the national group has been reported as becoming more frequent (Epp, 1962, p. 465).

Although Mennonite cultivation of their national heritage is, like that of the Lutherans, mainly expressive and not explicitly oppositional, there are among the Mennonites some groups and individuals advocating a more aggressive and chauvinistic kind of nationalism. Some preachers foster among the members of their congregation an attitude of exclusivity and superiority to the surrounding Russian population. They forbid inter-marriage with Russians and agitate for emigration to 'the paradise in the West' (Krest'yaninov, 1964, pp. 138, 139, 1967, p. 127; Ipatov, 1974, p. 41). These attitudes are usually linked with general political disenchantment and hostility. When links with Germany were mentioned they were always ties with West Germany rather than the communist Democratic Republic. One wonders whether this reflects an absence of desire among Mennonites to make contact with East Germany, or whether it is simply politically inopportune for communist writers to mention such a desire as such contacts are usually officially referred to in a deprecating manner. The fact that some Siberian Mennonites have subscribed to an East German paper makes one think that there is at least some unacknowledged contact with the German Democratic Republic.

We have no information on whether these social and political orientations are common among both legal and illegal Mennonites and cannot check whether, as in other sects, illegality has radicalised the responses of members to their society and has reverted a trend towards denominationalisation.

Mennonites, it has been argued in this chapter, are distinguished by a high degree of religious and organisational vitality. Particularly noteworthy has been their success in keeping the middle-aged and young members of the communities in the sect. In this they differ markedly from the other old communitarian sects in the Soviet Union – the Molokans and Dukhobors. Their vitality has been due to the fact that they have offered their members a clear ideological alternative. Although fairly accommodative in their general socio-political response, their national-cultural identification, coupled with a distinctive secular ethic, offers members a satisfying focus around which a severely disrupted religious community can rally. Study of the German Lutherans has shown that a nationalistic orientation may sap rather than strengthen religious vitality in the long run if it is of an introverted and backward-looking nature. The case of the Mennonites brings out that cultivation of a national culture woven into the whole fabric of the community, and kept alive and relevant to all its members, will greatly enhance the religious vitality of the group.

Chapter 10

# Religion and Nationality II

## THE ROMAN CATHOLIC CHURCH

Roman Catholicism* has been the religion of non-Russian national minorities in both Tsarist Russia and the Soviet Union. Whereas before the Revolution the Catholic Church catered mainly for groups of German, Poles and Lithuanians dispersed over the Russian Empire and had a well-established organisational network, today it is virtually destroyed in that area, its presence being reduced to a small number of unco-ordinated churches in a few big towns and some more informal groups in Siberia and central Asia served by itinerant priests (Gagarin, 1971, p. 142; Read, 1975, p. 11). At the present time Catholics are found in large concentrations only in the western territories acquired by the Soviet Union during the Second World War – in the western parts of the Ukraine and of Belorussia and in the Baltic republics – Estonia, Latvia and Lithuania. Only in the latter two areas does the Catholic Church now have a formal diocesan organisation and only in Lithuania is it the dominant organisation.

Being the religion of non-Russian national minorities in the Soviet Union there has been a virtually complete absence of sociological work by Russians on Catholicism and its believers, and work by non-Russian sociologists – with one or two exceptions – either does not exist or has not been made accessible. This circumstance severely limits what we can say about the impact of Soviet society on Catholic believers. We are inadequately informed about who the believers are, what proportion of the population they amount to in the different republics, and what constitutes the nature of their religiosity. To compensate slightly for the dearth of information on these aspects we can draw on a comparatively rich *samizdat* literature on the relations between the state and the Catholic Church and its believers. This has been issued in recent years by Lithuanian Catholics. In the following we will therefore confine our attention mainly to developments in the Lithuanian Catholic Church stepping only outside these boundaries to draw in sociological data on Catholics in other republics when certain topics cannot be adequately covered from Lithuanian material. Information about the organisational strength of Catholicism outside Lithuania, as far as available, will

---

* Greek Catholicism or Catholicism of the Eastern Rite is practised illegally at the present time in parts of the western Ukraine but lack of sociological information prevents its discussion here.

be presented in Appendix B at the end of the book. We shall focus on the fact that the Lithuanian Catholic Church has maintained its influence over the population much better than other churches in the Soviet Union and examine how much this is due to its identification as a symbol of the Lithuanian nation.

## THE LITHUANIAN CATHOLIC CHURCH

It is difficult to fit the Lithuanian Catholic Church (LCC) into a typology of religious collectivities. Despite being part of a supra-national religious organisation it is very much a national church at the same time. As such it has many features of a 'church'-like organisation but lacks one of the prime characteristics of that type. It is not closely allied to the state nor is it in any way supportive of secular power. Being the national church of a smaller political unit within a larger state – the Soviet Union – it sets itself in opposition to the state almost by definition. It is this opposition which permits the LCC to maintain another important 'church'-type feature much better than other national churches, namely, achieving a much closer approximation to the notion of a church of the whole nation and the whole population.

The LCC has been under Soviet influence only since the Second World War when Lithuania became incorporated into the USSR. At that time the Church was strong and flourishing counting more than 80 per cent of the population as its members (*Die Katholische Kirche* . . ., p. 5). It was organised in six dioceses with 1,035 churches and chapels which were served by 14 bishops and 1,480 priests. Besides the 4 seminaries and 118 monasteries, many Catholic lay organisations and media spread the religious and social teachings of the Church all through the population (ibid.).

Although the LCC was not subjected to the worst excesses of Stalinist religious policy during the thirties it has not been spared disruption of church life through state interference. At first the state concentrated its efforts on making the Church break with Rome. In the terrorisation campaign towards this end most bishops and a large number of clergy were imprisoned or deported. Although seriously weakened, the resistance of the Church was not broken.

In the period under consideration here the state policy towards the LCC has been more cautious and subtle, though still hostile. On the one hand the Soviet political authorities have regarded the Catholic Church with particular suspicion and hostility because of its ties with the Vatican and would have liked to reduce its influence as much as possible; but, on the other hand, they have recognised the close relationship in Lithuania between religious and national allegiance and fear that too much interference would stir up nationalist feelings. Instead of antagonising ordinary believers by direct interference through large-scale closure of churches and dismissal of priests, the authorities have proceeded in a more subtle way. They have attempted to undermine the Church slowly by severely limiting the renewal of priests, by restricting the number of bishops and by trying to isolate the young generation from the Church.

Thus, although the stock of churches and the number of priests and bishops have been reduced in Lithuania and state interference in the internal life of the Church is common, the LCC has not been as badly affected as the Russian Orthodox Church. In 1970 the LCC was said to have six dioceses with 630 working churches, served by 850 priests (Rimaitis, 1971, p. 18) as against 708 churches in

1940 and 1,000 priests in 1944–6 (Vardys, 1971, pp. 395–6). Not all of these priests, however, are able to perform their duties. A more severe curtailment has occurred in the number of bishops and of training places in the one remaining seminary. Thus in 1970 the six dioceses were administered by only four apostolic administrators (as against fourteen bishops in 1940), and two of these had been appointed only in that year (Simon, 1972, p. 6). Two bishops are still confined to remote rural areas. Until very recently the seminary provided only 30 places as against four seminaries offering 450 places in 1940. Since 1973 this quota has been increased to 48 (*Chronicle of the Lithuanian Catholic Church*, 8, 1974, p. 26). The Church has no journal nor catechetic literature, and none of the many monastic institutions are left today.

The political authorities have also tried to limit the renewal of church membership by shielding children from the influence of the Church. Since the early sixties it has been illegal for the priest to prepare children for first communion in their home. Involvement of children and young people in any church activity leads to trouble for the priest responsible.

The general *détente* between the Soviet government and the Vatican since the early sixties has affected the LCC in both positive and negative ways. The LCC is now able to have fairly normal relations with the Vatican. The spiritual life of the LCC is guided by directives from the Vatican, and the Pope is formally responsible for the appointment of bishops, although these appointments have to have the prior approval of the Soviet government. Since the *détente* a few new appointments of bishops have been made, and permission was gained for the publication of small editions of religious literature. The LCC was represented at the Second Vatican Council, and many of its recommendations have been implemented in Lithuania (Rimaitis, 1971, pp. 19–21). Among the changes inspired by Vatican II were a liturgical reform aiming at a greater use of the Lithuanian language, a wider and more conscious involvement of believers in rituals, a new initiative towards ecumenism, attempts to turn believers into missionaries among non-believers, the opening of a dialogue between priests and atheists (Anichas, 1971b, pp. 87–93) and a general modernisation of the Church's political, social and philosophical doctrines (Barkauskas, 1970, p. 163). In order to maintain diplomatic relations with Moscow, however, the Vatican has forfeited the opportunity to protect the Catholic Church in the Soviet Union by making public the restrictive and discriminatory measures against the Church and its believers by the Soviet state. In addition it has had to accept the appointments to the hierarchy as suggested by the Soviet authorities and thus has aided the infiltration of the Church with politically subservient religious leaders. These developments have been noted with alarm by contributors to the *Chronicle of the Lithuanian Catholic Church*, and it appears as if the LCC is powerless to represent its real interests to the Vatican. The facts that relations with the Vatican have only been established in recent years and that there has never been a permanent head of the Church for any length of time has put the LCC in a weak position *vis-à-vis* the Vatican, in contrast to the situation in the neighbouring Polish Catholic Church.

The better survival of the LCC than other churches in the Soviet Union does not just reflect a slightly more lenient treatment by the political authorities but is in large measure due to the greater vigour, vigilance and militancy of the Church and its believers in the face of efforts to destroy it. Although we have little direct quantitative evidence to document the vitality of Church life in the contemporary LCC we have much indirect and qualitative information which shows its vigour.

The number of church members has been stated by an East German church paper to be around 2 million, i.e. about two-thirds of the total population (*Begegnung*, 1967, 10, p. 14, quoted by Simon, 1972, p. 8). This represents a slightly lower level of involvement by the population than in the neighbouring Polish Catholic Church where 95 per cent are claimed to be members by a Polish Catholic commentator (Majko, 1972, p. 408). In evaluating these percentages, however, one has to bear in mind that Poland is nationally a much more homogeneous country than Lithuania. While Poland comprises 97 per cent of ethnic Poles and, therefore, traditionally Catholic people, only 79·3 per cent of the Lithuanian republic's population are Lithuanian and a further 8·5 per cent Polish according to the 1959 census (*Itogi* . . ., 1962, Table 54).

*Religious Commitment*

There are few additional statistics that would enable us to examine the reliability of this estimate and what church membership actually means for these 2 million Lithuanians. The few available figures on participation in rites of passage in the Catholic Church, being an index of membership in a loose sense, indicate a much lower level. Thus in 1964, the last year of Khrushchev's anti-religious campaign, 58 per cent of all newly born babies were baptised, 38 per cent of weddings were solemnised by the Church, and 61 per cent of the deceased were given a Catholic funeral. In Kaunas, the second largest town, the corresponding proportions were 42 per cent, 13 per cent and 50 per cent (Pomerantsev, 1966, p. 6). Figures supplied by a party official, derived from statistics on participation in the equivalent civil rites in 1968, indicate a lower level of participation in rites of passage: of all those eligible for the three rites of passage, 30 per cent participated in the marriage rites, 51 per cent in the baptismal rites and 48 per cent received religious funeral rites. Comparable figures for 1958, giving the much higher proportions of 64, 81 and 79 per cent respectively (Barkauskas, 1970, pp. 161, 162), indicate a significant decline in nominal church membership during the sixties. The national average indicated by the 1964 and 1968 figures is roughly equal to the level in many rural traditionally Orthodox areas of the RSFSR, except for wedding rites, but the Kaunas figures are considerably higher than those given for large towns of the RSFSR. But one would require more statistics about rites of passage, collected in different years, to get a reliable impression of membership in a loose sense. Qualitative accounts point to a high rate of participation in rites of passage. A Soviet sociological survey reports that rites of passage are still being widely observed (Bauzhis, 1965, p. 274), a Western observer of Lithuanian Catholics claims that there are hardly any unbaptised children in Lithuania (*Die Katholische Kirche* . . ., p. 5), and a Soviet study of Belorussian Catholics states that they participate much more in rites of passage than do Orthodox in the same area (*Prichiny* . . ., 1965, p. 172).

The rite of first communion, involving children at a very impressionable age, has led to bitter conflict between the political authorities and the Church and its believers. Participation in this rite can be regarded as an act of political defiance by parents of communicants, and statistics on such participation would be particularly revealing. Unfortunately we are not provided with any precise data. All we learn is that in large parishes between 100 and 120 children and in small parishes between 15 and 30 children receive first communion every year (*Chronicle . . .*, 1973, 5, p. 7). In one parish with 8,000 Catholics, however, as many as 300 children participated annually in the rite (*Chronicle . . .*, 1971, 1, pp. 1–4).

Indicative of a deeper and more regular religious commitment are a great demand by believers for receiving the sacraments (*Die Katholische Kirche . . .*, p. 5), comparatively high rates of church attendance (Veinbergs, 1971, p. 415) and thorough religious instruction of children by the family (Bauzhis, 1965, p. 272). In Kleipeda, a big coastal town with 85,000 inhabitants, for example, 8,000 people were reported to have received communion during Lenten Retreat (*Chronicle . . .*, 1972, 2, p. 10). Belorussian Catholics were said to contain a much higher percentage of what Soviet sociologists call 'fanatical' and 'convinced' believers than did Orthodox in that area (*Prichiny . . .*, 1965, pp. 167, 168).

The data tell us nothing about the consequential dimension of Catholic religiosity. We do not know what impact the distinct Catholic teaching on morality, especially on such matters as birth control or divorce, has made on Lithuanian Catholics. We come across expressions of concern about the deterioration of moral standards since the assumption of Soviet rule and the adoption of militant atheism (see *Chronicle . . .*, 2, p. 5) but we met this concern among members of many faiths in the Soviet Union.

Some observers also note a weakening of religious commitment among Catholics in recent years. A study of one rural Lithuanian area concluded that many of the community-based religious rituals and traditions had faded or disappeared completely. Singled out were communal family evening prayer, putting crosses on the farmstead, wearing crosses and observance of fast (Bauzhis, 1965, p. 273).

To get a more comprehensive picture of the meaning of church membership to Lithuanian Catholics we have to utilise the indirect evidence on this subject contained in the rich *samizdat* literature produced in recent years by Lithuanian Catholics.* While this gives us little information on either the general nature or the constituent dimensions of individual religiosity, it provides us with some evidence about the strength of ties of Catholics to their church and about their degree of involvement in the life of their local churches.

*Religious Protest*
*Samizdat* literature reveals that from the late sixties onwards both priests and ordinary believers in LCC have been roused to protest against the restrictive measures taken against their church by the state. In particular the restriction on religious instruction of children for first communion and on the training of priests have caused Catholics to rally to the defence of their church on a mass scale. The shortage of religious literature and of church buildings, and the arrest of dissident priests, are also singled out as issues for complaint. Protests were expressed in letters sent to persons in authority in both the Soviet Union and the West. As the letters had appended to them the signatures of all the people voicing

* *Samizdat* literature produced by Lithuanian Catholics came to the West from around 1970 onwards. At first, only isolated documents appeared but from 1972 onwards, information came in the form of a journal entitled *Chronicle of the Lithuanian Catholic Church*. This has appeared every year since then. Extracts from the early documents and the *Chronicle* are reproduced in *Religion in Communist Lands* (4 and 5, 1973, pp. 47f. and 4 and 5, 1974, pp. 39f.) and the full text of most documents as well as the signatures are held at the CSRC which produces the journal.

their protest they provide us with a good measure of the scope of the protest movement among Lithuanian Catholics. When evaluating the figures revealed by these letters one has to bear in mind what it means to put one's signature on a protest letter in the Soviet Union. In the West such a signature may be given without any risk to the signatory and does not necessarily express any *deep* commitment to the cause in question. In the Soviet Union, however, such signatures are both collected and given at great personal risk. Lists are frequently confiscated and collectors arrested, and signatures constitute concrete and permanent evidence of political dissent and may be held against the signatories in all sorts of situations. In such a political context signatures are not given lightly but may be taken as symbolising considerable commitment to the cause in question.

*Samizdat* documents and the *Chronicle of the Lithuanian Catholic Church* contain dozens of such letters from priests and believers from various regions, districts and towns, composed from 1969 up to the present day. In 1971, for example, there were among them three letters from believers of a town with roughly 8,000 Catholics signed by altogether 2,450 people (*Chronicle* . . ., 1972, 1, pp. 1–6) and a letter with 1,344 signatures from believers of several parishes in one district (ibid., pp. 36ff.). In 1972, the protest movement gathered greater momentum. A letter to Brezhnev contains 17,000 signatures (*Chronicle* . . ., 1973, 2, pp. 1–5). A letter from a town with 85,000 inhabitants is signed by 3,023 persons (ibid., p. 15), another from a district by 1,026 (ibid., pp. 30f.), and one parish appended 190 signatures to its protest letter. In May 1972 protest erupted into the well-known Kaunas revolt. Sparked off by the self-immolation of a young Catholic as a gesture of protest against Russian disregard of Lithuanian national and religious sensitivities, the revolt became a popular protest against Russian domination. In 1973 protest reverted to peaceful means but the number of protesters swelled steadily. Two letters composed in that year are signed by 30,782 and 16,498 people respectively (*Chronicle* . . ., 6, 1974, pp. 1–10).

These protest letters tell us several things about Catholic believers in Lithuania. They convey the impression that a large number of believers have an attachment to their church which goes far beyond what is implied by nominal membership. They are concerned about their own religious rights and about the rights of priests to satisfy religious needs without state interference. Not only are they fighting for freedom of religious activity in the present but they are worried about the survival of their religious world-view and their church in years to come. While the protests are certainly indicative of deep commitment, we cannot from the limited evidence be sure that this commitment is necessarily of a wholly religious nature. Two alternative forms of commitment may be involved. First, protests may either express an orientation towards the values of Western liberal democracy, i.e. an insistence on religious rights as one of cherished *civil* rights. The Catholic Church's connection with a Western organisation and world-view then makes it an obvious focus of such civil rights activity. Secondly, protests may be inspired by anti-Soviet and Lithuanian nationalist sentiments which see the Church as a symbol of national identity. These possibilities will be explored in more detail below.

*Social Composition of Membership*
These protest letters also give us some indication about believers' social characteristics. The wide scope of protest conveyed in the *samizdat* literature tells us that

believers are active and committed in rural and urban areas and that they must come from a variety of social strata and educational and age groups. We learn from several sources that, in contrast to the situation in the other churches in the Soviet Union, the young are well represented among believers. According to a report in *Chronicle* . . . (5, p. 24), one survey in the ninth grade of a secondary school revealed that 90 per cent of children were believers. A survey among sixth formers in Kaunas, however, established that only a minority of the pupils were religious. As the size of the minority is not revealed one must assume that it was a fairly large one. This assumption receives support from the fact that nearly half of the pupils said that one or both of their parents were religious and more than two-thirds ranked their parents highest in a hierarchy of authority (*Kommunist Litvy*, 1973, pp. 61–2). Such an assumption would be borne out by another sociological survey in one district which found that 22 per cent of young people between the ages of 16 and 25 were religious, though only a small proportion were convinced believers (Barkauskas, 1970, p. 162). The exceptionally active atheist campaign against the involvement of the young in church life and the intensity of anti-religious indoctrination in schools are further evidence of this fact (see *Chronicle* . . . nos 4 and 5). In their anxiety to keep children away from church, local authorities go as far as organising compulsory school activities on Easter Sunday (*Chronicle* . . ., 6, 1974, p. 36).

If we compare some Belorussian data on the social characteristics of members of a Catholic church *dvadtsatka* with those about Orthodox activists in their local church (see p. 48), it is evident that the Catholic Church attracts a socially less marginal section of the population for the performance of special duties. While Orthodox members of the church council are mainly elderly, retired, female and poorly educated, Catholic activists are predominantly male, middle-aged, employed and slightly better educated than Orthodox (see data in *Prichiny* . . ., 1965, p. 176).

We have no information on whether there are groups of Catholic intellectuals as in neighbouring Poland, or whether the harsher and more rigorous anti-religious policy of Soviet rulers has succeeded in isolating the intelligentsia from the Catholic Church as has been the case in other religious organisations in the Soviet Union.

In general, then, the Catholic Church in Lithuania has managed much better than other churches in the Soviet Union to retain the allegiance of a wide cross-section of the population, and Catholic Church members, on average, have a much stronger tie to their church than members of other churches. How can we account for this? An explanation of these facts has to refer both to the special characteristics of the Catholic Church and its faith in general and to the particular historical and socio-political context in which the Catholic Church has found itself in Lithuania.

*The Catholic Priests and their Parishes*
In nearly all modern industrial societies the Catholic Church has been more successful in retaining the allegiance of the population in its traditional constituencies than have the Protestant or Orthodox churches. This has been due to the teaching of the Church and to the special relation between clergy and lay implied by it. Orthodox churches have developed mainly the ritual and experiential dimensions of religiosity among their members and the Protestant churches

have stressed an intellectual orientation to faith and church as well as giving the individual considerable autonomy in society. The Catholic Church, in contrast, has cultivated all dimensions of religiosity and has attempted to gain a total hold over its members. Consequently Catholic priests, unlike Orthodox and Protestant clergy, have made it their task to develop multiple ties with their parishioners and have traditionally had a much closer and intimate relationship with them.

The data on the Lithuanian Catholic Church and its members are insufficiently detailed to allow us to examine whether the above generalisation about the influence of the Roman Catholic Church on the nature of believers' religiosity also applies in the Lithuanian case. We do, however, have considerable evidence to show the existence of a close relationship between clergy and lay and can demonstrate the crucial role priests have played in maintaining the vitality of the Catholic Church in Lithuania.

Catholic priests are said to be more involved and more active than Orthodox priests or Lutheran pastors. In contrast to the latter two they are still influential and respected figures in local communities. Catholic priests show great concern about the spiritual welfare of their flock and do not hesitate to make home visits to remind laggards of their religious obligations (*Prichiny* . . ., 1965, p. 115). They make an effort to go out into the community to involve its more influential members in the life of the church or, at least, to win them over to their side. Thus Belorussian Catholic priests are said to recruit on to church committees people like collective farm team leaders, farm managers and local Soviet deputies and to try to establish social relations with leading employees of local organisations (*Stroitel'stvo* . . ., 1966, p. 62). They write and distribute their sermons, memoirs, essays, tracts on theological themes and religious verse. The general activism of Lithuanian priests is said to have increased markedly since Vatican II. This greater activism may be partly due to the fact that they have smaller parishes than do most Orthodox priests, but more important are their greater community orientation and their higher level of education. The fact that most Catholic priests in Lithuania, Latvia and Belorussia have higher education (see Balevits, 1972, p. 2, on Latvian priests; *Stroitel'stvo* . . ., 1966, p. 60, on Catholic priests in other republics) must make it much easier for them to gain the respect of their parishioners than it is for the generally much worse educated Orthodox priests. They maintain ritual prescriptions and general church rules much more strictly and put more demands on believers than is common among Orthodox priests (*Stroitel'stvo* . . ., 1966, p. 190). They are particularly anxious to fulfil their religious duties in relation to the young and often put themselves at considerable personal risk to prepare children for first communion and involve them generally in church life. Thus, for example, forty priests of one diocese protested in 1969 to Kosygin about the restrictions placed on them in executing their religious duties with regard to children (*Religion in Communist Dominated Areas*, 1970, pp. 34–6). Several priests have been arrested for their work with children.

Lithuanian priests do not only display a greater dedication in the execution of their religious duties to their flocks but also show more awareness of the threat militant atheism poses to their church or, at least, a greater courage and preparedness to act on that realisation than do the clergy in other churches. The widespread readiness on the part of believers to profess allegiance to their church publicly must be sparked off to a large extent by the courageous example put to them by their priests. Between 1969 and 1971 groups of priests from several dioceses issued a number of protests about various restrictions on the life of their church. Altogether 291 priests, i.e. more than a third of all priests, were involved (see Simon, 1972, pp. 9–15). Severe censure from their bishops (pronounced under pressure from the political authorities) and waves of arrests hardened rather than weakened their determination.

All these protests by believers and priests convey a strong sense of solidarity between the various sections of the Church. Priests defend the rights of believers as well as those of their bishops (e.g. the 1971 protest on behalf of the deposed Bishop Stepanovichius) and of their own colleagues. Believers agitate for the release of their arrested priests, and bishops, although not engaging in open protest, often refrain from censuring protesters. Both the wide scope of the protests and the amount of solidarity between clergy and lay they reveal are in great contrast to development in the Orthodox Church in recent years.

The only breach of that solidarity in the LCC occurred in April 1972 when bishops responded to Soviet pressure and publicly censured those involved in recent protest activities. Unlike Orthodox hierarchs, however, they have never expelled protesting priests from the Church. Bishops are the one weak link in the Church defences for they are few in number and are extremely exposed and vulnerable. They can be manipulated by the threat of arrest or dismissal and by playing on the fear of leaving the Church without leadership. Future developments will depend on the way the Vatican responds to diplomatic pressure from the Soviet government.

If the present strength of the LCC is, as was shown above, to a large extent due to the dedication and courage of its functionaries, its vitality in the future will depend on the continued availability of this leadership. Such continuity, however, is gravely threatened at the present time. Lithuanian priests, as a body, have a high average age (for details of the age structure see Vardys, 1971, p. 396), and their depletion by declining health and death is not balanced by an equivalent infusion of new young priests. In 1971, for example, twelve priests died and only six new ones were consecrated in 1972 (*Religion und Atheismus in der UdSSR*, 1973, 6, p. 16). If this development is allowed to continue the stock of priests will eventually become too low to continue providing the heroic example which has inspired believers so far. Developments in the Catholic Church in the RSFSR have borne this out. But it would be an oversimplification to say that the Catholic Church in Lithuania has survived much better because it has experienced militant atheism only for a relatively short time. The Lutheran churches in neighbouring Latvia and Estonia have had the same length of exposure but have not preserved the same degree of vitality as the LCC.

## Catholicism and Nationalism

The LCC's strong persistence, we said above, is due not only to the characteristics generally associated with the better survival rate of the Catholic Church in all modern industrial societies but also to the specific historical and political context in which it has functioned in Lithuania. There is a strong consensus between Soviet and Western observers of the LCC that its strength at the present time owes a good deal to its close association with the idea of a Lithuanian nation. To become a member of the LCC expresses as much a national as a religious commitment and sometimes merely the former. The Catholic Church and its world-view provide a strong link with the independent Lithuania of the past and form the main differentiating feature of Soviet Lithuania from Soviet Russia. Consequently the Church has become the focus of nationalist sentiments and aspirations. Unlike the Polish Catholic Church, the Church in Lithuania has not been for centuries a depository of national culture and neither has it always been the main bulwark in the fight for national independence. Lithuanian nationalism is a fairly recent phenomenon. Only from the end of the nineteenth century has the LCC become a bearer of national consciousness directed against both Poland and Russia. Today it is nourished only by anti-Russianism. The fact that this connection between church and nation has been neither as long nor as deep in Lithuania as in Poland is reflected in the more limited influence of the LCC over the population and, to some extent, in its much less powerful position *vis-à-vis* the state.

How has this close association between Lithuanian nationalism and the Catholic Church manifested itself? In the early years of Soviet occupation it found a very concrete expression in the widespread involvement of Lithuanian priests in the partisan struggle for national independence from the Soviet Union. Although the Church was not officially associated with the partisans, most bishops and priests did not succumb to Soviet pressures to condemn Catholic participation in the struggle. In more recent years the connection between Catholicism and nationalism has become much more intangible, expressing itself mainly in the Church's efforts to link religion and nationalism in its services of worship. The liturgy has been adapted to national peculiarities, old religious traditions and holidays are presented as Lithuanian custom (Anichas, 1971b, pp. 89–90; Bauzhis, 1971, p. 23), and many priests try to convince believers that to be a good Lithuanian means to be a good Catholic. Both among priests and believers, nationalism expresses itself mainly through inchoately held sentiments. The Kaunas events, however, have shown that these sentiments can in certain circumstances be activated into a more clearly focused and concrete expression.

What are the aims of this Lithuanian nationalism? Our knowledge about the political orientations of the Church and of individual priests and believers is, by the nature of circumstances, incomplete, and the following description of them may not paint the whole picture. Nationalist striving seems to be mainly for cultural and, perhaps, limited political independence. In general, it does not seem to be directed towards the abolition of the socialist socio-economic framework and towards a return to capitalism.

Soviet descriptions of contemporary priests and believers as fundamentally in support of the social system or, at least, neutral on these issues (Anichas, 1971a, p. 76; *Prichiny* . . ., 1965, p. 107, on Belorussian Catholics) are borne out by the lack of any fundamental criticism of the Soviet system among the protests voiced in the *samizdat* literature. A degree of adaptation to the socialist system is manifested in some minor adjustments of the Church's social teachings, such as instilling a regard for *public* property, good work attitudes, condoning a striving for this-worldly wellbeing and promising the heavenly kingdom for work done for the good of society (Anichas, 1971a, pp. 76f.).

On the other hand, Catholic priests are said not to be particularly forthcoming in expressing support for the system in their sermons. They either denigrate worldly matters or declare themselves to be politically neutral. An analysis of 300 sermons found that only three of these contained any positive references to socialism and socialist institutions (Bauzhis, 1971, p. 6). As always, there is some variation in political orientation among priests. While a majority are said to have adjusted to socialism, small minorities both strongly in favour of, and violently hostile to, socialism are mentioned. There is said to be a small group of 'leftist' Catholics comparable to such Western figures as H. Johnson, E. Fuchs and A. Beretskii. The hostile minority consists mainly of older priests but also of a few former monks and some members of the younger clergy. This latter group combines a strong nationalist leaning with a complete rejection of everything Soviet.

Thus, in general, nationalism among Lithuanian Catholics is mainly of an expressive kind and contains at the present time little potential for basic political transformation. There is a possibility, though, that the large body of those who have merely adjusted to the Soviet order or are politically indifferent may be swayed in a time of crisis by the hostile minority. The widespread cultural nationalism may then become a lever to arouse more basic and active protest. The Kaunas events have shown this to be a possibility, and Soviet political authorities are constrained by such an eventuality in their treatment of the LCC.

The Lithuanian Catholic Church, it has been argued in this chapter, although not the church of the vast majority of the population, is still very influential among Lithuanians of all social groups. The Church can count on the firm allegiance of a large proportion of members. How much this allegiance is based on deep religious commitment and how much it is given for non-religious reasons is impossible to decide with the limited data at our disposal. The strength of the LCC is due partly to the distinctive supra-national Catholic tradition of close and total relations between clergy and lay also preserved in Lithuania. In addition, the LCC derives extensive support from the fact that it is closely identified with the idea of a Lithuanian nation and uniquely suited to serve as a focus of nationalist aspirations. It has proved difficult to pinpoint how this connection between Catholic religion and nationalism manifests itself in concrete ways. There is little evidence at present to show that the Catholic Church, or even some section within it, will in the near future become the instigator of, or driving force in, a nationalist revolt or separatist movement. However, the presence of a large body of men with nationalist aspirations and a relatively weakly developed loyalty to the Soviet order forces the political authorities into a position of cautious restraint.

The case of the LCC illustrates the fact that in a militantly atheist society a national church has a much better chance to retain that status if it remains firmly oriented towards that national minority and does not strive for a close association with the state. Even if political circumstances do not permit the adoption of an active oppositional position *vis-à-vis* the state, it can become the focus for the expression of more passive and inchoately held sentiments of disaffection, and thus retain the allegiance of wide sections of the national group it caters for.

# Chapter 11

# Conclusion

Religious change in the postwar Soviet Union has been in the same general direction as that in the West but differs significantly in many details of its mode and tempo of change. While it is not possible to determine with certainty to what extent different characteristics of Soviet society have initiated and directed change one can nevertheless say that similarities in the pattern of religious change between Western and Soviet society are due to the similar stage of industrial development reached. The marked differences in the Soviet pattern of religious transformation are attributable to four different, but related aspects of Soviet society: (a) its pace of development, (b) its socialist organisation, (c) its political style, especially during the Stalin era, and (d) its militantly atheist character.

Several discrete, though related, areas of religious change have been examined and will be discussed below. These are:

Changes in religious collectivities.
Changes in the distribution of religiosity in Soviet society.
Some qualitative changes in religious ideology, organisation and activity as well as in individual religiosity.

## TYPES OF RELIGIOUS COLLECTIVITIES AND THEIR DEVELOPMENT

It was found that Soviet society contained a much wider spectrum of religious collectivities than contemporary Western societies, except, perhaps, the USA. The wide range of religious groupings may be ascribed to a number of factors. First, the existence in one political unit of socio-geographical areas with widely differing levels of development, such as Latvia at one end and the extreme northern territories at the other end of the scale, has preserved various types of sects, some of which have been long extinct in the relatively more evenly advanced industrial societies of the West. The archaic character of these religious collectivities is further reinforced by their total isolation. They have no contact with similar organisations outside the Soviet Union and often little with others in their own country. Thus they are completely untouched by any modernising theological or ecumenical ideas. Secondly, an aspiration to total ideological control, coupled with a ruthless political style, has called forth sects equally totalitarian and hostile in their worldly responses, such as are no longer prevalent in the pluralist and religiously tolerant Western societies but were frequently found in Troeltsch's late medieval society dominated by the Catholic Church. Thirdly, strong political manipulation of religious organisations and their consequent greater dependence on the benevolence of the state has resulted in types of collectivities retaining many of the features associated with the 'church' type. The Orthodox Church is the prime example here.

Among the sects in Soviet society, the great preponderance of some sub-types (as defined by Bryan Wilson) and the virtual absence of others can also be explained by reference to particular features of Soviet society. To explain why Soviet social conditions have generated thriving 'conversionist' sects we can do no better than refer to Wilson's general explanation:

'Conversionist sects appear to arise most readily in circumstances in which a high degree of individuation occurs. This happens through atomization of social groups in a process of profound social upheaval. Stable social structures are destroyed or impaired, communities disrupted and individuals forcibly detached from their kinsfolk. Then many individuals seek spiritual and social accommodation in an alien social context. Likeness of circumstance overcomes other differences and welds communities together on a religious basis.' (Wilson, 1973, p. 38)

This description of social circumstances is tailor-made to describe the effects of the Revolution, the Civil War, rapid industrialisation and collectivisation, and of the purges, on two generations of Soviet citizens.

Sects of the 'revolutionist' type have arisen in response to the political style with which these social changes were accomplished and have served, as we shall see below, as avenues for the expression of political protest in a society which offers no other channels for its expression. Sects of the 'introversionist', 'utopian' and 'reformist' type flourish only in ideologically diverse and religiously tolerant societies. It is therefore hardly surprising that none have arisen in the Soviet Union and that those dating from pre-revolutionary time – the Molokans and Dukhobors – are now held together as communities by the force of tradition rather than that of religion. Although there are no sects at the present time of the three above types there are still some religious groups with strong 'introversionist' tendencies. Most notable are the Maksimisty, the Old Believer *Stranniki* and the True Orthodox Christian Wanderers. Even in a supposedly totalitarian society some groups manage to escape state control. Nor can 'Manipulationist' sects, which greatly depend on written communication, flourish in a militantly atheist society. But their absence may also be due to the fact that those strata from which they usually recruit – the well-to-do, urban, middle-status groups – are generally well integrated into the socialist collective and thus not so open to religious teaching. There are also no sects of the 'thaumaturgical' type in the Soviet Union although many believers of the Orthodox tradition frequently adopt a thaumaturgical response to the world.

Turning from the question of the presence in Soviet society of certain types of religious collectivities to that of their development we have raised the following more central issues. How does religious change occur and what direction does it take? Religious collectivities, we said earlier, may be assigned to a certain type according to the religious orientations of members at a given point in time. It is, however, rare to find that only one religious orientation is held by members, and most established religious organisations accommodate a variety of religious orientations. It is then preferable to describe a collectivity in terms of a balance between conflicting orientations rather than assigning it rigidly to one type. Religious collectivities in Soviet society contain more complex combinations of these orientations than their Western counterparts. In Western society the nature and development of religious organisations is influenced mostly by the relations between only three factors – the religious teaching of the group, the social composition of its members and the inevitable process of institutionalisation. In Soviet religious organisations an additional factor – the state policy towards the organisation in question – exerts a powerful intervening influence on religious orientations. As a result many organisations are characterised by an incongruous mixture of religious orientations existing in a more or less peaceful coexistence.

The balance between these conflicting orientations determines whether there will be religious change and what direction it will take. Due to the greater number of influences and the resulting higher complexity in the balance of religious orientations in Soviet religious collectivities, religious change also follows more complex paths. The overall direction of change is, as in the West, towards the 'denominational' type, but change in the USSR is less often linear but an oscillation between conflicting tendencies and therefore follows a less predictable path. Thus a predominantly 'church'-like organisation such as the Russian Orthodox Church has been injected with some as yet weakly developed 'sect'-like orientations. Whether the latter will increase in future and change the existing balance decisively would depend on how the third factor – state intervention – will turn out in times to come. The study of Evangelical Christian Baptists uncovered an on-going process of confrontation between opposing religious orientations and analysed the resulting changes. While religious teaching and social composition of membership propelled the sect strongly towards a denominational position, state intervention in its internal life reduced this denominational striving to a considerable extent.

Religious change as the outcome of a new balance between religious orientations can take two forms. It may be contained within one collectivity which merely moves along the continuum from 'sect' or 'church' to 'denomination', or it may lead to schism. If the latter is the case each of the formerly conflicting orientations may assert itself in a purer form in a separate collectivity and continue the struggle from there. Often, though, the existence of the schismatic group keeps the parent organisation religiously 'on its toes' and thus inserts sectarian impulses. The prime example of this is the relationship which has evolved between the legal Baptists and its schismatic brethren, the Initsiativniks.

Given this more complex path of religious change in general, we also found that generalisations on sect development derived from a study of sects in Western society were not always apposite in the Soviet context. Sects in general retained their status much longer than is suggested by sociologists of Western society, and 'conversionist' sects in particular, which are deemed to denominationalise most quickly, displayed reversals to radical sectarian positions. Having said this it must also be emphasised that from the late 1960s onwards denominational trends have become apparent even in those sects which earlier gave the impression of being staunchly and solidly 'sect'-like in their orientations. Even such hitherto intransigently hostile sects as the Jehovah's Witnesses or the True

Orthodox Christians show signs of mellowing in their stance towards Soviet society and of accepting compromises between their religious ideology and the demands of their social environment. These as yet timid denominational leanings appear to be held by the more recent recruits to these sects who are usually younger and better educated people. Having had no experience of either pre-socialist norms and values or of the political violence of the Stalinist period they find it easier to adjust to Soviet society than their older embittered brethren.

In general, however, 'sect'-like orientations predominate. They are continually being revived by the intervention in religious affairs of the militantly atheist state. Such intervention has ranged from restriction on organisation (e.g. refusal of a national co-ordinating centre or of a regular publication or training facilities) over direct interference in internal matters (e.g. prescription of what can be preached to whom and by whom or of who administers the local church) to religious persecution (e.g. victimisation or arrest of religiously particular active individuals, dismissal of priests, closure of churches). The first set of measures has acted to preserve sectarian forms of organisation which would otherwise have been cast off and thus indirectly shaped religious orientations. The second and third set of policies have had a direct impact on members' responses to the world, provoking a 'sect'-like protest.

Inquiry into the social composition of the various religious collectivities established how their believers differ in their social characteristics. We found no simple relation between socio-economic status and religious orientations as suggested by Dynes (1955) and Demerath (1965) although distinct differences in membership between the various religious organisations were established. In general, collectivities in which a 'church'-like orientation predominates, such as the Russian Orthodox Church, the Old Believer churches of the Popovtsy, and the German Lutheran community, have a higher percentage of old, female, retired and rural members than do collectivities with 'sect'-like and 'denominational' tendencies. Among the sects in the USSR there are again clear differences between the three major groupings of sects. The rapidly declining sects of pre-revolutionary origin, which were found to be cultural, quasi-ethnic rather than religious communities, have a membership similar in social status to that of the Orthodox Church, except that members have a slightly higher average age. The sects of the Orthodox period, Jehovah's Witnesses, and the small illegal schismatic groups of Pentecostalists, Reform Adventists, and Initsiativniks, all little touched by denominational striving, have the biggest contingent of young to middle-aged and male members. The members of the legal Protestant sects, which are characterised by denominational leanings, fall in between the members of the more 'church'-like and the more 'sect'-like collectivities as far as age and sex is concerned.

The matter becomes more complicated when educational and occupational status are considered. The sects with only very slight denominational striving have a much lower percentage of members with complete secondary or higher education, of white-collar and *skilled* workers than those with more pronounced denominational leanings. In this they closely resemble Orthodox believers, except that they are more likely to be low-status urban than rural inhabitants and more likely to be still in employment.

There are, however, some collectivities which do not fit into this pattern. The

Initsiativniks, a particularly radical sectarian group, have a high concentration of young and male members like the other collectivities approximating closely to the 'sect' type. But unlike the latter, they contain a very high proportion of relatively well-educated and qualified urban members. This striking difference may be due to the fact that the 'protest against the world' of this sect contains a very large element of *political* in addition to the religious activism, i.e. it is based on a clear realisation of the source of trouble and is characterised by purposeful and effective action (e.g. protest letters and demonstrations) to eliminate the trouble. Also difficult to fit into these continua are those religious collectivities shaped by a strong element of political nationalism. These organisations, like the Lithuanian Catholic Church, have a membership which is socially more representative of the population as a whole than those of other collectivities.

Discounting these two exceptions, we found that 'sect'-like orientation is related to low socio-economic status (i.e. low educational and occupational qualifications) but to high age-sex status (i.e. younger age and male sex), 'denominational' striving to higher (though not high) socio-economic status but lower age-sex status. A 'church'-like orientation, however, is allied to a low status on both counts. The differences in our findings from those of Dynes and Demerath are largely due to the differences in structure and ideology between a capitalist and a communist society which will be examined in some detail below.

The positing of a distinct hierarchy among Soviet religious collectivities in terms of the strength of 'sect'-like orientations receives support from the finding that recruitment of new members to these collectivities follows a clearly graduated pattern. Besides gaining new members from former non-believers and members' children, Baptists recruit predominantly from former Orthodox, Adventists from former Baptists, Pentecostalists from former Adventists or Baptists, and Jehovah's Witnesses from former Pentecostalists. Defection from one to another collectivity rarely goes in the opposite direction, and joining the sect of the Witnesses is the last step for an individual in his quest for religious satisfaction (for precise figures collected in the Ukraine, see Eryshev, 1969, p. A41).

While these differences in membership between collectivities have been made explicit in the preceding chapters, other more general empirical and theoretical issues on the question of religiosity have only been implicitly touched upon and need to be drawn out here. First, I shall give a general overview of both the incidence of religiosity and its distribution among the various strata and socio-demographic sectors of Soviet society. Secondly, to put these findings into perspective, I shall bring out the differences in these patterns from those found in Western capitalist societies and explain them by reference to the distinguishing features of Soviet society.

## THE INCIDENCE AND SOCIAL DISTRIBUTION OF RELIGIOSITY IN SOVIET SOCIETY

It must be said straight away that an attempt to estimate the number of those committed to Christian religion in contemporary Soviet society is bedevilled by various difficulties. These difficulties are due to the absence of reliable data on a national scale and to the various inadequacies in the quantitative data collected at local level as described in the introductory chapter and at various points throughout the book. In addition, the task is complicated by the great internal differentiation of the Soviet Union in terms of history, religion and level of economic and cultural development. This makes it meaningless to look at an overall national average of religiosity. Consequently, estimates of the level of religiosity put forward in the following will be for different social and historical units within the USSR and are no more than rough approximations based on a careful appraisal of the more detailed data available to us. I shall define as religious all those who are *regularly* committed to a religious organisation *or* faith along any one index of religiosity as outlined in Chapter 3. It will thus exclude those only episodically connected with religion through participation in rites of passage or the social customary aspects of religious holidays.

In the RSFSR, where the Russian Orthodox Church and the Old Believers still have their stronghold but where the sects of Western origin are relatively weak, around 25 per cent of the population can be said to be religious. Such an estimate fits in which the various figures cited in the book for separate areas and with the more reliable general estimates given by Soviet specialists. Okulov, the director of the Institute of Scientific Atheism (AON) under the Party's Central Committee, has estimated the percentage of religious in various parts of the RSFSR to be around 15 per cent in urban and around 30 per cent in rural areas (Okulov, 1967, p. 16). A thorough study of a whole, fairly typical region of the RSFSR (Voronezh) puts the proportion of religious at 22·4 per cent of the region's total population (Teplyakov, 1972, p. 121), and a study of another region (Penza) gives the figure of 30·3 per cent (archive material of the Institute of Scientific Atheism, quoted by Teplyakov, 1972, p. 121). The extent of religiosity varies significantly between rural and urban areas (see details below) and between the geographical areas west and east of the Urals. Whereas the level of religiosity is moderately high in most areas (excluding large industrial towns) west of the Urals, it is often very low among European settlers in some parts of Siberia and the Far East. In these latter areas the sects have a larger relative weight.

A similar relationship can be found in the central Asian republics where, in addition, Muslims form a large proportion of the population. We possess no data to determine the level of religiosity among the European population of these republics.

Yet a different picture prevails in the western republics. The Ukraine must have one of the highest levels of religiosity among the Union republics, with around 40 per cent of the population being religiously committed. This percentage is higher in the western, more recently (1945) incorporated and more rural parts and lower in the eastern industrial parts. In addition to a sizeable proportion of Orthodox there are in the Ukraine a discrepantly large proportion of the membership of the Western sects, particularly of the Baptists. In the western parts of the Ukraine we find also sizeable concentrations of Catholics of both the Eastern and the Latin rite. In Belorussia and Moldavia, a similar picture prevails, though the level of religiosity is somewhat lower here, involving, according to one source (Duluman, Lubovik and Tancher, 1970, p. 33), 16 per cent of the urban and 40 per cent of the rural population of Belorussia. In the Baltic republics, Catholic Lithuania has a much higher proportion of religious people in the population (between 50 and 60 per cent) than Latvia and Estonia, where the Lutheran Church has retained only around 15 per cent of the population as members. The level of religiosity in these two republics is slightly increased by the large proportion of Baptists and Adventists as well as by the significant concentrations of Catholics and Old Believers found here. To evaluate all these different figures, it has to be borne in mind that in 1972 more than half of the 248 million strong Soviet population (132 million) lived in the RSFSR, and 48 million in the Ukraine, while most of the other Union republics had relatively small (European) populations (between 1 and 7 million). It is also relevant to any overall evaluation to consider that in 1972 59 per cent of the Soviet population lived in urban areas (*Narodnoe khozyaistvo SSSR v 1973 g.*, pp. 9, 11).

While it has been very difficult to speak in quantitative terms about the level of religiosity in the contemporary Soviet Union, it is even more problematic to discuss trends in the number of religious believers during the whole Soviet period. The statistics on membership of religious organisations collected by the Tsarist regime at the eve of the Revolution are generally considered too unreliable to form a baseline. Sociological surveys conducted by Soviet atheist activists and social scientists during the relatively free years of the 1920s provide us with a better starting point. According to an evaluation of various regional surveys by Lunacharskii in 1930, the number of religious in the late twenties was put as 80 per cent of the population (A. V. Lunacharskii, *Stenograficheskii otchet o Vtorom Vsesoyuznom s'ezde SVB*, Moscow, 1930, p. 164, quoted by Kobetskii, 1973, p. 126). By the middle thirties this proportion had sunk to 50 per cent (Em. Yaroslavskii, cited in Kobetskii, 1973, p. 126). No figures are available for the war and immediate postwar years. If we make a rough general estimate from the figures mentioned above for the present time that around 30 to 35 per cent of the total Soviet population are religious we get an overall approximate decline by two and a half times during the Soviet period.

Turning from the geographical spread of religiosity to its social distribution among various strata of the Soviet population we need to bring together data on age, sex, urban–rural location, educational and occupational status of believers. Believers in the Soviet Union are now predominantly concentrated on the periphery of society, among those strata which are marginal to its functioning. These strata have become marginal through lack of involvement in the processes of industrialisation and technical development. This trend has gone considerably farther than in Western European societies where, in varying degrees, sections of the middle class are still involved in church-oriented religious activity. Apart from a certain similarity in general trend there are a number of differences between Soviet and Western societies due to differences in ownership and ideology.

While in Western European societies both the old and the young are more frequently religious than the middle-aged, in the Soviet Union only the old show a higher propensity to be religious. Among both Orthodox and sectarians an average of around 50 per cent are over 60 years of age, particularly in the RSFSR. Another sizeable proportion of believers is between 50 and 60 years old, and only a minority (generally not over 15 per cent) are between 30 and 50. Young believers, i.e. those under 30 years of age, are rare among Orthodox and a little more frequent among sectarians (see data in the relevant chapters). Estimates of the number of believers among young people in general range around 3 per cent (Sytenko, 1967, p. 126; Galitskaya, 1969, p. 392; Troyanovskii, 1975,

p. 77). This percentage is higher in rural and lower in urban areas, particularly in and around Moscow and Leningrad (Galitskaya, 1969). This skewed age structure is the result of a number of factors. Thorough atheist indoctrination and legal sanctions against the involvement of minors in religious activity have kept children and youths isolated from religion. This absence of religious instruction in both religious and educational institutions is not being compensated for by a religious upbringing in the family. The larger degree of religious indifference among the parent generation has meant that only a small proportion of children in traditionally Orthodox families come into contact with religion at home. Even in families with self-identified Orthodox believers only 16 per cent gave their children a religious upbringing (Duluman, Lobovik and Tancher, 1970, p. 94). Only in three-generation households – a phenomenon decreasing with urbanisation and the development of housing and public child care services – are children still being religiously influenced by grandmothers.

The preponderance of old people (especially women) among believers is due to a number of factors. This generation contains people born before the Revolution or in the early post-revolutionary period (data were collected in the sixties) who are thus likely to have grown up in church-oriented families and to have received a religious education at school and/or in the family. One survey established that 90 per cent of Orthodox believers had begun believing in early childhood (ibid., p. 93). The available evidence does not permit us to determine what percentage of them have remained religious all through their lives and what proportion have returned to religion in old age. Some evidence suggests that a turning or returning to religion in old age is now not such a frequent phenomenon as is generally supposed by Western writers (see below). It is likely, though, as is the case in the West, that some have turned or returned to religion in old age because it usually induces a preoccupation with death and the meaning of life as well as increasing ill-health and loneliness. The latter is a particular problem among old women in the Soviet Union as a very high proportion of that generation were widowed in the Second World War. This latter explanation for increased religiosity among the old is frequently advanced by Soviet sociologists and well documented by empirical evidence which shows a great preponderance of single people among believers. Significantly, an increased concern with spiritual life among old people is never singled out by sociologists. The official ideology stresses a this-worldly orientation and claims to give meaning to individual life by linking it to the collective endeavour for the building of full communism. Another explanation of the connection between religiosity and old age lies in the fact that old age, being synonymous with retirement, also means invulnerability to discrimination in career advancement because of religious commitment. This explanation, of course, is also never mentioned by Soviet sociologists, as the official ideology claims complete religious tolerance.

From a review of plausible explanations for the preponderance of the old among religious people, let us now turn to examine the implications this age structure has for the incidence of religiosity in the future. While Soviet sociologists generally deduce that the skewed age structure points to the decline of religion in the near future, when the old generation has died, some Western religious writers write off this prediction with the triumphant assertion of the truism that there will always be many people who return to religion in old age. The latter, however, neglect to consider the sociological fact that religious conver-

H

sion in middle or old age usually presupposes a close contact with religion in childhood or youth (e.g. Thouless, 1971, p. 115). This early religious education, we have noted above, is now provided only on a very small scale, particularly among Orthodox. Another factor facilitating a return to religion, the easy availability of places of worship or religious leaders, is also considerably reduced in Soviet society. Lastly, the excessively high number of widows and spinsters among the religious is, one hopes, a unique historical phenomenon due to the Second World War and will be absent as a strong predisposing factor towards religiosity for future generations of Soviet citizens. Indeed we possess one set of statistics which indicate that turning to religion in old age is not the rule among Orthodox. It was shown on the basis of one survey that the overwhelming majority of Orthodox (88·5 per cent) became active members of the Church before 1941. Baptists, in contrast, joined the sect more often (55·5 per cent) after 1941 (Klibanov, 1970, p. 73). This striking contrast may simply reflect the different conceptions of membership among members of churches and sects. One cannot be sure whether Orthodox respondents cited the date of their childhood involvement with Orthodox religion and disregarded long lapses during their middle years, or whether the year named really reflects the beginning of active adult membership. If the latter were the case these data, together with the statistics on the age structure, would indicate a further general numerical decline of religiosity in the Soviet Union in years to come provided present trends continue. But more data would be needed to substantiate this point conclusively.

As regards the distribution of religiosity between the sexes, women outnumber men in all Soviet religious organisations. Their proportion of believers ranges between 76 and 86 per cent in most of the legal religious organisations and decreases to an average of 60 per cent in the illegal sects and among Catholics.

The greater involvement of women in religious organisations, due to their greater exclusion from paid skilled or professional work in industrial society, is common to all Western societies and to the Soviet Union, despite greater efforts by the latter to involve women in the economy. As yet this involvement has meant, to a greater extent than among men, employment in low-skill occupations, i.e. occupations peripheral to the functioning of an advanced industrial society. An additional predisposing factor towards religiosity for Soviet women may be seen in the hardship resulting from the double burden of employment and house and child care in the absence of adequate provisions to lighten their burden (see Teplyakov, 1972, p. 162). For many women of the older generation this hardship is aggravated by the absence of moral and practical support from a husband.

In both Western and Soviet society, religiosity is more prevalent in rural than in urban areas. (The difference is much slighter in the USA than in Western Europe.) Estimates for the RSFSR put the proportion of believers in rural areas as twice or just under twice that in urban areas (Okulov, 1967, p. 16; Teplyakov, 1972, p. 123), and statistics collected in Belorussia indicate an even higher differential between urban and rural areas (Duluman, Labovic and Tancher, 1970, p. 33). In the Soviet Union this picture is conveyed because of the numerical predominance of Russian Orthodox. The Orthodox Church has its support overwhelmingly in rural areas. While in some rural areas the proportion of Orthodox in the population may be as high as 45 per cent, in some large industrial towns it may fall as low as 5 per cent. Members of the Protestant sects, however, once also predominantly rural, are now to an equal or perhaps even greater extent urban. In recent years particularly, there has occurred a process of concentration of believers, leading to a virtual translocation of the sects from the villages to the towns and settlements of an urban type (Russ. *poselki gorodskogo tipa*) (see Filimonov, 1974, pp. 25–6).

Apart from this basic similarity between the USSR and the West concerning the location of religion, there are important differences. The most important concerns the social status of the carriers of religiosity. In the rural areas of the West they are the farmers and small artisans whereas in Soviet society they are the low-skilled and, therefore, technically unsophisticated collective farmers, or those removed from the core economic processes by female sex and old age, who are much more concentrated in the countryside. The incidence of religiosity among collective farmers decreases markedly as level of skill increases (see, for example, Alekseev, 1970, pp. 230–40). Thus, in the Soviet Union, it is a low level of technical sophistication, rather than membership of the rural bourgeoisie as in the West, which determines religious involvement.

In the towns in Western European society, membership of religious organisations is much more prevalent among the middle class than the working class, particularly among those groups which are survivors of the traditional bourgeoisie and petty bourgeoisie. In the USA religion is more evenly embraced by all classes, although there, too, the working class is somewhat less involved in religious organisations. In the Soviet Union, in contrast, the traditional capitalist middle class is extinct and the nearest contemporary equivalent, the white-collar strata with higher and middle education, are widely estranged from organised religion. Their employment is neither in the 'free' professions nor in independent business but they are economically and ideologically closely integrated into the socialist core of the economy and the political apparatus. It is impossible to determine with our present knowledge to what degree communist ideology has replaced religion as a satisfying alternative world view for them and to what extent religious non-affiliation is merely prompted by fear of state reprisal among those 'who have a lot to lose'. There is some indication that sections of the intelligentsia have turned to religion in recent years, but there is no evidence to suggest that this is a very widespread phenomenon. Industrial workers are slightly more involved in organised religion than the middle and upper white-collar strata but still only in very small proportion. According to one study, believers form between 1 and 4 per cent of industrial workers (Ol'shanskii, 1965, p. 492). Of these, few are skilled workers or employees of large enterprises in heavy industry. The bulk of urban believers are unskilled workers in smaller light industry factories or in service jobs, as well as those not employed because of age, infirmity or family ties. There is, however, a marked difference between those affiliated to 'church'- and 'sect'-type collectivities. The sects, especially those in the AUCECB, have in recent years increased their share of skilled and better-educated manual workers and of the lower and middle ranks of white-collar employees.

The predominance among believers in employment of people in low-status occupations is paralleled by a very high proportion of believers with very low educational qualifications. The proportion among believers of people with only primary education or less ranges between 75 and 90 per cent, the number of illiterate and semi-literate people being highest among Orthodox. This exceptionally low level of educational attainment is not, however, quite as strikingly different from that of the general Soviet population as it appears at first sight. The difference will decrease in magnitude if we consider the fact that believers are predominantly in that generation of Soviet citizens which grew up during the first difficult years of Soviet power and thus has generally a low level of education.

The question arises whether the predominance of believers in the lowest occupational and educational strata is a cause or the result of their religiosity. In general, the data have shown that their low status precedes their affiliation to a religious organisation. The fact that in a number of cases social advancement through education or occupation has been blocked because of religious allegiance does not affect the general picture of low social status prior to religious affiliation. It could only account for the small number of believers with higher education and in high-status occupations but not for a preponderance of people with primary education or less and, consequently, low-status occupations. It is also a possibility that the number of believers in the highest educational and occupational categories would have been slightly higher if the fear of discrimination did not prevent these people from declaring their belief. But we have at present no reliable evidence that such a phenomenon is very widespread and would significantly alter the data presented.

Besides hastening religious decline by increasing those strata in Soviet society which are religiously indifferent or atheist, the process of socialist industrial development has also retarded secularisation. It has created a large new pool of individuals who are easily drawn into religious collectivities. These are the new recruits to industrialism uprooted from their stable rural communities and lifestyle and thrown into an urban industrial environment for which they are ill equipped with their low educational standard and lack of experience. This industrialisation process occurred much more rapidly and much later than in Western industrial societies. Consequently this pool of uprooted individuals has been much larger and probably more severely disoriented and has only just been assimilated or is still in the process of being integrated into urban industrial life. As in Western societies at an earlier period, these anomic individuals are predominantly attracted by the sects. The strict moral code and tight-knit community they are able to provide give these new recruits a link to their rural past and ease the transition into the alien urban–industrial environment. This integrating function of the sects in general explains the relatively great vitality and stability of sects in present Soviet society. The overwhelming popularity of the Evangelical Christian Baptists in particular may be attributable to their strong emphasis on moral standards and a moral community. This preoccupation with morality has often been more or less consciously related to a rejection of the Soviet claim that communist ideology provides a philosophy of life.

Communality has also been sought for the general psychological satisfactions derived from belonging to a clearly defined group, being sure of its support in times of need and playing a valued part in its maintenance. Soviet religious communities, which are constantly counterposed to a hostile wider society, appear to develop community to a much higher degree than their present-day Western equivalents. This general quest for, and cultivation of, community has been perceived in all sects but has figured little in the ROC. In some of the older Russian sects striving to maintain a valued community it has completely overshadowed the religious functions of the group.

As the first generation of migrants have been assimilated into their urban–industrial environment and have acquired some of the skills valued in an industrial culture, some of the sects are finding themselves with an increased share of better-educated and qualified manual and white-collar workers. This applies particularly to Baptists and Seventh Day Adventists.

To sum up, there has been some convergence between Western capitalist and Soviet society in the way that secularisation has proceeded. In both types of society religious commitment is now least frequent among those employed in the technologically advanced sector of industrial society. (It must be noted that this process is less complete and less uniformly developed in different Western societies. The USA does not conform to this pattern at all.) Besides this similarity in general trend, there are numerous divergencies caused by differences in the tempo, scale and timing of the industrialisation process as well as by the differences between the socialist and the capitalist mode of industrialisation. The first is manifested in a relatively stronger and more persistent 'sect' component in the Soviet religious scene, while the second comes out in a different social distribution of religiosity due to a difference in social structure.

Further divergencies from the pattern in Western capitalist society are due to the differing political ideology and culture of the Soviet Union and especially the basic ideological orientation towards religion. The availability of communist ideology, which poses a firm, clear and comprehensive alternative to a religious world-view, has had a differential impact on various social strata. Among those social groups actively engaged in the core economic and political processes and modern industrial occupations it appears to have been embraced as a comprehensive world-view, though it is difficult to know how deeply this acceptance goes. Among those socially marginal or new to these processes, communism as an ideology is either totally rejected or has failed to make an impact as a philosophy of life.

The other factor shaping the Soviet religious scene in a distinctive way has been the Soviet political system and the political culture it has created. The political system has been determined partly by Marxist–Leninist ideology, partly by the political strain which resulted from building the economic foundations of socialism in a hostile world, and partly by the personality of the nation's leader in these formative years. It has been characterised by a political style of extreme ruthlessness which inspired a chain of actions characterised by complete disregard for the rights of individuals. Examples of such forms of activity are the violence of the class war during the collectivisation period of the late twenties and early thirties, the purges and deportations of the thirties, and the many affronts to human dignity carried out in the name of Marxism–Leninism against religious and political dissenters in more recent times. For many of the victims political upheaval was accompanied by extreme social upheaval, such as geographical relocation or disruption and destruction of family ties. These events created widespread political disillusionment, anomie and hostility. Among many of the simple and unsophisticated victims this state of anomie and/or hostility to the system could only find expression in religious terms. Here the sects rather than the churches benefited. While the industrialisation process had led to the strengthening of sects with strong moral orientations, the above events of political violence fostered the growth and persistence of sects with distinct political overtones, such as the Jehovah's Witnesses and the Orthodox sects of the Soviet period.

Besides accommodating political dissent based on a total rejection of the Soviet order, religious collectivities are also avenues for the expression of more limited disaffection about the Soviet claim to total ideological control. This manifests itself in nationalistic dissent and is more common in the churches than in the sects. This type of dissent was seen to be mainly cultural but had political overtones in some collectivities. Sometimes it was just an expressive nationalism serving more to assert national identity than to challenge the political status quo as, for example, among Lutherans. In some instances, however, it assumed a more aggressive character as in the Lithuanian Catholic Church. In churches of national minorities, the cultural or political rights of the minority against the Russian majority were upheld. In the churches catering for the Russian majority – the ROC and Old Believer churches – the Russian cultural heritage was asserted against Soviet culture.

The militantly atheist, as opposed to the tolerant and/or supportive attitude by the state to religion in the West, has caused further divergencies and complexities in the religious pattern of Soviet society. Rather than causing basic changes of direction it has acted to hasten and to retard the process of religious decline. It has hastened the decline of religion among those strata with an initially weakly developed religious commitment and has retarded it by deepening commitment even further among those who had a strong allegiance to their faith anyway. Thus it has influenced the balance between those with 'sect'-like and those with 'church'-like orientations, giving mainly vitality to the sects but radicalising also sections within the churches who had previously held 'church'-like orientations. Unlike the other influences described, the militantly atheist orientation towards religion has not brought new strata or individuals to religion but has held back the process of denominationalisation.

In the discussion so far we have laid particular stress on the impact on religion of social forces external to the collectivities rather than on characteristics internal to them. This approach is based on the conviction that these have been the more decisive factors in influencing religious change. But it must be pointed out that religious characteristics have mediated their impact in important ways. Bryan Wilson's findings on this in relation to sect development may be extended to cover development towards a more accommodating stance towards state and society of all types of religious collectivities. A religious collectivity is much less likely to be accommodated in a militantly atheist environment if it possesses a distinctive ideology, practice or organisation which are in opposition to aspects of the secular ideology and/or social practice. The underdevelopment of the ideological dimension in Orthodox religion provides Orthodox believers with no theoretical perspective from which to resist the pressures of the wider society to accommodate while Catholic religion equips believers well for such confrontations. Distinctive practices diverging sharply from general social custom, such as the keeping of the Sabbath by Adventists, the practice of glossolalia by Pentecostalists, or the avoidance rituals of Old Believers and True Orthodox Christians, are equally effective in maintaining barriers between the religious collectivity and socialist society. A clear-cut form of organisation also contributes considerably to the maintenance of effective boundaries. The extent to which the religious group has succeeded in establishing a distinct community is closely related to the degree of accommodation. Consequently the sects are much more insulated than the churches. Those churches which have generated a community out of the association, like Lithuanian Catholic churches, are better able to resist accommodation than those which are only associational, like Orthodox churches.

QUALITATIVE CHANGES IN RELIGIOUS IDEOLOGY, ORGANISATION AND INDIVIDUAL RELIGIOSITY

It is impossible to determine to what degree the present incidence and distribution of religiosity has been due to one rather than the other factors described above as having had an impact on religion in Soviet society. Thus the crucial question whether the socialist nature of Soviet society or its developmental course towards, and present status as, an advanced industrial society have been more important in influencing religious change cannot at present be answered. Again it is easier to deal with qualitative rather than quantitative changes in this area.

Among the qualitative changes which have taken place I shall describe those created by the impact of communist ideology and Soviet social order and those which have occurred in response to militantly atheist measures. But it is often difficult in practice to determine where the normative power of communist ideology or the manipulatory power of socialist achievement stops and the coercive power of militant atheism begins. In the field of religious ideology we noted a growing adaptation to political ideology. This expresses itself in adjusting the emphasis on existing Christian norms and values to achieve greater congruence with political ideology, in responding more readily to political demands, in minimising the ideological dimension of religion in favour of the practice dimension or in the mere cultivation of tradition and community. The first tendency was shown to be particularly prominent at the leadership level in the Orthodox Church and among Baptists, but has also gained ground at the lower level in most religious collectivities. The second tendency is particularly marked in the Orthodox Church and among Baptists, Molokans and Dukhobors, but is also becoming noticeable among the sects which have traditionally been very hostile to the Soviet order. The recent recommendation to members by leading Jehovah's Witnesses to join trade unions is a case in point. The third trend is marked among Orthodox believers and in the Old Russian sects of the Molokans and Dukhobors. All these adaptations are more or less consciously carried out to bridge the much greater and more publicised ideological gap between the political and the religious sector in Soviet compared to that in Western society. But this drawing together is also motivated by an awareness of basic similarity between religious and political norms, values and goals on the part of the religious organisations. In some respects this similarity is much greater than in the West. Besides affinities at a very general level between the goals of communism and of Christian religion there is also an uncanny similarity between the communist moral code and the more fundamentalist Christian secular ethic. This is evident not only in their content but also in the inflexible and moralistic way the postulates are stated. Both codes are reminiscent of a bygone age and type of community. The similarities at the level of general goals were made particularly evident in our study of the Molokan sect, while affinities at the level of moral postulates and general prescriptions for living were highlighted when we described the Baptists and the Adventists. It is worth mentioning that any such similarities are usually stressed by believers but hotly disputed by militant atheists.

Militant atheist measures, both in premeditated and in unforeseen ways, have also caused far-reaching changes in the organisational structure of collectivities, in the ways they perform their religious functions and in which believers satisfy their religious requirements. In the field of organisation, most measures have had the effect of weakening or destroying central organisation and strengthening local independence and spontaneity. Notable exceptions have been the cases of the ROC and the AUCECB where central organisation, in recent decades, has been strengthened at the expense of local initiative. In some cases such restrictive measures have fostered the formation of an underground conspiratorial organisation, as in the cases of the Orthodox sects, the True Orthodox Christian Wanderers or the Witnesses. Enforced isolation from contact with Western brethren has preserved in some of the smaller organisations an introverted and backward-looking spirit, an unawareness of the theological changes which have engulfed their Western counterparts. The theological literature of the independent Pentecostalists, for example, consists only of material written in the early twenties, while many Old Believer groups often depend entirely on pre-revolutionary literature. Even the larger organisations, which have had much contact with Western religious organisations in recent years, have absorbed remarkably little of the Western modernising trend. The result of all this has been an enhancement of 'sect'-like orientations and the retardation of the denominationalisation process.

The impact of militant atheist measures on the performance of religious duties and the satisfaction of religious requirements has been of a different kind. To counteract or circumvent the impact of anti-religious activities both religious leaders and believers have displayed great creativity. They have found ways to circumvent restrictions or have devised alternative means to achieve religious satisfaction. This process has been particularly evident in the ROC where religious activity is much more open to scrutiny than in the more informally organised sects. These developments have included changing ancient religious traditions to avoid state sanctions, granting greater anonymity to socially vulnerable believers, and the transference of some religious duties from clergy to lay in areas where the official organisation has been destroyed.

In conclusion, it is necessary to discuss the applicability of our findings to the religious situation in other societies. The approach adopted throughout this study has been to compare and contrast developments in organised Christian religion in one communist society with those in Western capitalist societies. The questions arise of whether the theoretical conclusions are also applicable to other communist societies of the Soviet pattern and how far the book is intended as a contribution to the sociology of religion of communist society. As has been made clear repeatedly, religion in Soviet society has been shaped not just by the socialist element of that society but equally by its distinctive course of development, its present status as an advanced, though unevenly developed, industrial society, by its political culture and history and by its militantly atheist character. Other communist societies have modelled themselves on the Soviet pattern but have modified it to fit their own circumstances and requirements. In addition, there is considerable variation between these societies both on the level of social and economic development at the time of the communist rise to power and in religious heritage. Consequently assertions about the level of generality of the theoretical findings have to be much more modest. All I wish to claim here is that some of the findings are also relevant to other communist societies for which a similar concurrence of influences on aspects of religious change can be demonstrated. Only in this limited sense may the present work be regarded as a contribution to the sociology of religion of communist society. A more general claim can only be advanced after a comparative study of several state socialist societies, each representing a distinctive sub-type within the general type. Although the social phenomena and processes singled out as having had an impact on religion are more likely to be prevalent in communist societies of the Soviet type they may also be found in other kinds of society. Our findings about the relationship between religion and society would thus not be limited to communist societies but would apply to all modern industrial societies characterised by the adoption of a total ideology as well as by the experience of extensive social and/or political upheaval.

# Appendix A

LIST 1: REGISTERED URBAN CONGREGATIONS OF AUCECB IN THE SOVIET UNION, 1959–74

The names of these congregations are drawn mainly from the reports of senior presbyters about visits to congregations in various areas between 1959 and 1972. These reports are printed in issues of the AUCECB journal *Bratskii Vestnik* of that period. The list gives only the names of congregations affiliated to the AUC. In addition to these there are a large number of unregistered congregations, but systematic information about them is lacking. Although I must have assembled a fairly full sample of registered urban congregations by this method, it may not be complete. Other information collected has shown that the reports in *Bratskii Vestnik* are very incomplete on rural congregations so that I have felt obliged to omit rural congregations completely from my list. The list may also contain a few congregations that have dissolved in the meantime. The congregations are ordered by republics and, for the RSFSR (except Siberia), the Ukraine and Belorussia, again sub-divided by regions. Congregations in settlements of an urban type, *poselki gorodskogo tipa (PGT)* are considered as urban congregations. The list is supplemented with information drawn from the sociological literature. Figures in brackets behind a region or town denote the number of congregation members. Unfortunately only a few of such membership figures have been disclosed by sociological writers or foreign visitors. 'Lg. congr.' implies that membership is at least around a thousand members.

## I  RSFSR

Arkhangelsk region: Arkhangelsk; Astrakhan region: Astrakhan (200 members in 1965); Bryansk region: Bezhitsa, Bryansk (lg. congr.), Karachev, Kletnya (PGT), Klintsy, Pochep, Sevsk, Unecha; Belgorod region: Belgorod, Borisovka (PGT), Graivoron; Chelyabinsk region: Chelyabinsk, Magnitogorsk; Gorky region: Gorky; Ivanovo region: Furmanov, Ivanovo; Kalinin region: Kalinin, Kuvshinovo, Leninabad, Rzhev; Kaluga region: Kamyshin, Kaluga, Kirov, Maloyaroslav, Volgograd; Kostroma region: Kostroma; Kuybyshev region: Kuybyshev, Syzran; Kursk region: Kursk, Ryl'sk; Leningrad region: Leningrad (3,500 members); Lipetsk region: Lipetsk; Moscow region (12 congregations): Dedovsk, Klin, Moscow (5,000 in 1967), Serpukhov, Voskresensk, Kubinka; Murmansk region: Murmansk; Novgorod region: Borovichi; Orenburg region: Orenburg, Orsk; Orel region (20 congregations altogether): Grimma (PGT), Khotynets, Livny, Maloarkhangelsk, Mtsensk, Orel (400 members in 1973), Verkhov'e (PGT); Penza region: Penza (522 members in 1963); Perm region: Berezniki, Gubakha; Pskov region: Pechory, Pskov; Rostov region: Bataisk, Gukovo, Novoshakhtinsk, Novocherkassk, Pervomaisk, Rostov (over 1,000 members), Shakhty, Taganrog (lg. congr.), Tselina (PGT), Tsimlyansk; Ryazan region (560 members in 1961): Ryazan (250 members in 1963), Kazimov (40 members in 1963); Saratov region: Saratov; Smolensk region: Elnya, Smolensk; Tambov region: Michurinsk (99 members in 1961), Morshansk (121 members in 1961), Rasskasov (60 members in 1961); Tula region: Novomoskovsk, Plavsk, Tula; Ul'yanov region: Novoul'yanovsk, Ul'yanovsk; Vladimir region (several congregations); Volgograd region: Leninsk, Ramyshin, Uryupinsk, Volgograd (700 members); Voronezh region (2,376 members in 1970 in 8 registered and 20 unregistered congregations as well as in 103 smaller groups): Ostorozhsk, Pavlovsk, Petropavlovsk, Rossosh, Peski, Voronezh; Yaroslav region: Yaroslav (100 members in 1967); Siberia (around 9,500 members in western Siberia in 1970s) and Altai region: Barnaul, Slavgorod, Abakan, Cheremkhovo, Irkutsk (400 members in 1973), Kemerovo, Krasnoyarsk, Kupina, Leninsk-Kuznetskii, Minusinsk Noril'sk, Novo-Kuznetsk, Novosibirsk (1,500 members in 1973), Omsk (over 1,000 members), Osinniki, Taishet, Tomsk (250 members in 1973), Tyumen (90 members in 1963), Tuvin ASSR (sev. congrs); Far East: Blagoveshchensk (261 members in 1962), Khabarovsk (423 in 1973), Krasnaya, Rechka (PGT), Nakhodka, Sakhalin, Ussuriisk, Vladivostok, Zavatinsk, Belogorsk, Komsomol'sk na Amure; Stavropol region or Karachai – Cherkess ASSR: Cherkess, Essentuki, Georgievsk, Inozemtsevo (PGT), Karachaevsk, Kislovodsk, Minvodsk, Nevinnomyssk, Nikolaevsk, Novopavlovsk, Novoselitsk, Prikumsk, Pyatigorsk, Stavropol, Ust' Dzhegatinskaya (PGT), Vorontsovo, Aleksandrov, Zelenokumsk; Krasnodar region: Anapa, Apsheronsk, Belorechensk, Krasnodar (950 members in 1975), Kropotkin (132 in 1963), Labinsk, Maikop, Neftegorsk (PGT), Novorossisk, Psebai (PGT), Tikhorets; Bashkir ASSR: Birsk, Davlekanovo, Ufa, Sterlitamak; Chechenо – Ingush ASSR: Grozny; Chuvash ASSR: Cheboksary, Gudermes; Kalmyk AR: Elista; Karbadino – Balkar ASSR: Dokshukina, Nalchik, Maiski; Komi ASSR: Achim (PGT), Inta, Trakt (PGT), Madmas (PGT), Mezhog (PGT), Pechory, Sosnogorsk, Syktyvkar, Ukhta, Lemty (PGT), Vorkuta, Zhelezno – Dorozhny (PGT); Putovo (PGT); Mari ASSR: Yoshkar – Ola (60 members in 1970); Northern Osetian ASSR: Mozdok Ordzhonikidze (lg. congr.); Tatar ASSR: Chistopol, Kazan; Udmurt ASSR: Izhevsk, Sarapul.

## II  Armenia
Echmiadzin, Leninakan, Erevan.

## III  Azerbaidzhan
Baku (600 members in 1961), Kirovabad.

## IV  Belorussia
Brest region: Baranovichi (lg. congr.), Brest (380 members in 1960), Kamenets (PGT), Kobrin, Malorita (PGT), Pinsk (lg. congr.), Ol'shany (429 members); Gomel region: Buda – Koshelevskaya, Gomel (lg. congr.); Grodno region: Grodno, Mosty, Novogrudok, Pervomaiskii (PGT), Slonim, Volkovysk (lg. congr.), Zel'va (PGT); Minsk region: Berezino (PGT), Krasnoye, Minsk (620), Molodechno, Slutsk (lg. congr.), Stolbtsy, Volozhin; Mogilev region: Cherikov, Gorki, Krasnopol'e (PGT), Mogilev (lg. congr.), Osipovichi; Vitebsk region: Berezino (PGT), Bogushevsk, Orsha, Vitebsk.

## V  Estonia (63 congrs with 8,500 members)
Kekhra (PGT), Khaapsalu, Kingisep, Kiviyli, Kokhila (PGT), Kokhtla – Yarve, Kuressare, Narva, Rakvere, Pyarnu, Saaremaa island has 12 congrs, Tallin (2,000), Tapa, Tartu, Valga.

## VI  Georgia
Batumi, Gagre, Tbilisi (1,200), Sukhumi (150), Suchan.

## VII  Kazakhstan
Alma-Ata region has 61 congregations with 15,000 members. Alma-Ata town (2 congregations with at least 1,000 members), Balkhash, Chimkent, Dzhambul (900 in 1963), Dzhetygara, Dzhezkazgan, Issyk, Karaganda (lg. congr. with over 1,000 members), Kaskelen, Kustanai, Pavlodar, Petropavlovsk, Saran, Shchuchinsk, Tselinograd, Ush-Tobe, Ust'-Kamenogorsk.

## VIII  Kirgizia
Dzhalal-Abad, Fergana (lg. congr.), Frunze (1,800 in 1970), Kant (PGT), Kyzyl-Kiya, Osh, Przhevalsk, Tokmak.

*IX   Latvia (66 congrs with 6,000 Baptists)*
Elgave, Liepaya (big congr.), Riga (2,000), Sloka, Ventspil (lg. congr.), Yauneglava,
Sigulda.

*X   Lithuania*
Vil'nyus.

*XI   Moldavia (over 70 congrs)*
Bel'tsy, Bendery, Chadyr-Lunga, Dubossary, Kishinev, Tarakliya (PGT), Tiraspol.

*XII   Tadzhikistan*
Dushanbe, Kurgan-Tyube, Leninabad.

*XIII   Turkmenistan*
Ashkhabad (70 in 1961), Bairam-Ali, Mary, Nebit Dag, Krasnovodsk (40 in 1961).

*XIV   Uzbekistan*
Bukhara, Kokand, Samarkand, Tashkent (at least 1,000 members), Yangi-Yul.

*XV   Ukraine*
Cherkassy region: Cherkassy, Gorodishche, Smela, Uman, Zhashkov, Zolotonosha;
Chernigov region (24 congrs): Bakhmach, Shchorsk, Varva (PGT), Netyazh, Radom;
Chernovitsy region: Chernovitsy, Khotin; Dnepropetrovsk region: Apostolov,
Amuro – Nizhnedneprovsk, Chaplina (PGT), Dneprodzershinsk, Dnepropetrovsk,
Krinichki (PGT), Lotsmano – Kamenka (PGT), Nikopol, Novomoskovsk, Marganets,
Pyatikhatki, Sinel'kikovo, Taromskoe (PGT), Verkhovtsevo, Zheltye Vody,
Vasil'kovka (PGT), Dubovaya Balka; Donets region (at least 35 congrs): Donetsk
(1,464 members in 1968), Druzhkovka, Enakievo, Gorlovka, Khanzhenkov, Khart-
syzsk, Kirov (PGT), Konstantinovka, Kramatorsk, Makeevka (905 in 1968), Niko-
laevka (PGT), Novo-Ekonomicheskoe, Petrovka (PGT), Shakhtersk, Slavyansk,
Snezhnoe, Yam (PGT) (32 members in 1968); Ivanovo – Frankovsk region: Iva-
novo – Frankovsk; Kharkov region (40 congrs): Andreevka (PGT), Berezovka (PGT),
Dergachy (PGT), Kharkov (over 1,000 members), Kolomak (PGT), Kupyansk, Lozo-
vaya, Mereta, Olshany (PGT), Orel'ka (PGT), Pechenegi (PGT), Pervomaiskii (PGT),
Rogan (PGT), Sakhnovshchina (PGT), Vasishchevo (PGT), Volchansk, Yasnaya Pol-
yana, Zmiev, Zolochev (PGT); Kherson region: Kakhovka, Novoalekseevka (PGT),
Novotroitskoe (PGT), Partisany (PGT); Khmelnitsa region: Dunaevtsy, Smotrich (PGT),
Shepetovka, Volkovintsy (PGT); Kiev region: Boguslav, Kiev (at least 1,000 members),
Skvira, Tarashcha, Vorzel' (PGT); Kirovograd region: Aleksandriya, Bobrinets, Dolin-
skaya, Kirovograd, Novoukrainka, Pomoshnaya, Znamenka; Krym region: Azovskoe
(PGT), Bakhchisarai, Dzhankoi, Evpatoriya, Kerch, Nizhnegorskii (PGT), Saki, Sevasto-
pol, Simferopol (at least 400 members), Sochi, Yalta (at least 140); Lugansk region:
Gorodishche, Kadievka, Kommunarsk, Krasnodon (PGT), Krasnyi Luch, Lisichansk,
Lugansk, Mikhailovka (PGT), Ol'khovka (PGT), Pereval'sk, Proletarsk, Rovenki,
Rubezhnoe, Sverdlov; Lvov region: Borislav, Lvov, Nikolaev, Rava-Russkaya, Stryi,
Zokochev; Nikolaev region: Nikolaev, Pervomaisk, Voznesensk; Odessa region:
Artiz, Balta, Belaya Tserkov (over 100 members), Fastov, Izmail, Odessa, Tarashche,
Tatarbunary (PGT), Vilkovo; Poltava region (18 congrs): Kremenchug, Kryukov,
Likhvitsa, Piryatin, Poltava, Reshetilovka (PGT); Rovno region (45 congrs): Alek-
sandriya, Dubno, Kostopol, Ostrog, Sarny, Zdolbunov; Sumy region: Akhtyrka,
Belopol'e, Buryn, Chupa-Khovka (PGT), Konotop, Lebedin, Romny, Trostyanets;
Ternopol region: Ternopol, Shumskoye (PGT), Vishnevets (PGT); Vinnitsa region:
Gaisin, Kazatin, Khmel'nik, Vinnitsa; Volynsk region: Kovel', Lutsk; Zakapartskii
region: Beregovo, Khust, Mukachevo, Uzhgorod, Vinogradov, Zolotvina (PGT);

Zaporozhe region: Berdyansk, Kamenka, Melitopol, Molochansk, Pologi, Primorskoe, Prishib (PGT), Zaporozhe (1,000 members); Zhitomir region: Grural Korostyshev.

LIST 2: GEOGRAPHICAL DISTRIBUTION OF INITSIATIVNIKS
IN THE SOVIET UNION 1961–74 BY REGIONS AND TOWNS

The list is based on the above-mentioned sample of 826 Initsiativniks (see Chapter 7) and on the Appeals of Initsiativnik mothers (1969) and of the Congresses of the Council of Baptist Prisoners' Relatives in November 1969 and December 1970 (all documents are kept at the CSRC in Keston, Kent). It is supplemented by information from the sociological literature. It is probably incomplete and may also contain groups which have, in the meantime, returned to the legal Baptist congregations.

*I RSFSR*
Arkhangelsk region: Arkhangelsk; Belgorod region: Nikitovka; Bryansk region: Bryansk; Chelyabinsk region: Chelyabinsk, Kopeisk, Magnitogorsk; Gorky region: Arzamas, Gorky, Kulebaki, Shakhtunya, Vyksa; Kaniningrad region: Kaliningrad; Kemerov region: Kemerovo, Kiselevsk, Mezhdurechensk, Prokopevsk, Tashtagol, Yurga; Kirov region: Kirov, Sosnovka, Vyatskie–Polyaniy; Kursk region: Dmitriev, Kursk, Zheleznogorsk; Leningrad region: Leningrad; Moscow region: Dedovsk, Elektrostal', Moscow, Mtsensk, Noginsk, Podolsk, Zhukov; Orel region: Dmitrovsk, Naryshkino, Orel; Orenburg region; Penza region: Penza; Perm region: Kizel, Perm; Rostov region: Bataisk, Novocherkassy, Novoshakhtinsk, Rostov, Shakhty, Taganrog; Ryazan region: Rubnoe, Ryazan; Smolensk region: Demidov, Smolensk; Sverdlov region: Kirovgrad, Nizhny-Tagil, Sverdlov; Tambov region: Michurinsk, Morshansk, Tambov; Tula region: Novomoskovsk, Plekhanovo, Shchekino, Tula, Uzlovaya; Voronezh region: Voronezh; Siberia, Altai Krai and Far East: Barnaul, Blagoveshchensk, Irkutsk, Kansk, Krasnoyarsk, Kulunda, Novopavlovka (PGT), Novosibirsk, Omsk, Tomsk; Stavropol region: Cherkess, Karachaevsk, Kislovodsk, Prikumsk, Pyatigorsk, Zelenchuk; Krasnodar region: Apsheronsk, Krasnodar, Kropotkin, Kurganinsk, Maikop, Mogilev, Novorossisk, Tikhoretsk, Timashevsk; Bashkir ASSR: Davlekanovo; Chuvash ASSR: Cheboksary; Karbadino – Balkar ASSR: Nartkala; Komi ASSR: Sosnovka, Syktyvkar, Vorkuta; Mari ASSR: Oshkar-Ola, Volzhskii; Northern Osetian ASSR: Mozdok, Ordzhonikidze; Tatar ASSR: Kazan, Yclabuga.

*II Armenia*

*III Azerbaidzhan*
Baku, Kirovabad, Sumgait.

*IV Belorussia*
Brest region: Baranovichi, Brest, Kamenets (PGT), Malorita (PGT); Gomel region: Gomel, Khoiniki Svetlogorsk; Grodno region: Grodno, Volkovysk; Minsk region: Berezino (PGT), Minsk, Soligorsk, Slutsk; Mogilev region: Mogilev, Osipovichi; Vitebsk region: Verkhnedinsk, Vitebsk.

*V Georgia*
Sukhumi.

*VI Kazakhstan*
Aktyubinsk region, Alma-Ata, Dzhambul, Dzhezkazgan; Issykulsk region; Kara-

ganda; Kokchetov region: Pavlodar, Saran, Semipalatinsk, Syryanovsk, Trofimovka, Tselinograd.

*VII   Kirgizia*
Frunze, Kant.

*VIII   Moldavia (10 congrs with around 380 members)*
Bendery, Chadyr-Lunga, Dubossary, Kaushany, Kishinev, Kulebaki, Orgeev, Strasheny, Tiraspol.

*IX   Tadzhikistan*
Dushanbe, Ordzhonikidzeabad.

*X   Uzbekistan*
Fergana, Namangan, Tashkent, Yangi-Yul.

*XI   Ukraine*
Cherkassy region: Cherkassy, Smela; Chernigov region: Chernigov; Chernovitsy region: Chernovitsy, Khotin; Dnepropetrovsk region: Dnepropetrovsk, Krivoi Rog, Zheltiye Vody; Donets region: Druzhkova, Enakievo, Gorlovka, Khartsyk, Kramatorsk, Makeevka, Novossovsk, Volnovakhi, Zhdanov; Kharkov region: Dergachy (PGT), Kharkov, Merefa, Protopovka, Zmieva; Kherson region; Khmelnitsa region: Khmelnitsa, Shepetovka, Slavuta; Kiev region: Kiev; Kirovograd region: Kirovograd; Krym region: Kerch; Lugansk region: Brody, Khorinsk, Krasnodon, Lisichansk, Lugansk, Rubezhnoye; Lvov region: Lvov, Sosnovka; Nikolaev region: Nikolaev, Voznesensk; Odessa region: Odessa, Izmail'; Poltava region: Mirgorod, Piryatin, Poltava; Rovno region: Chervonoarmeisk, Rovno, Zdolbunov; Sumy region: Seredina-Buda, Shostka, Sumy; Vinnitsa region: Vinnitsa; Volynsk region; Zaporozhe region: Zaporozhe; Zhitomir region: Zhitomir.

# Appendix B

## I   Russia in 1917
1,600,000 Catholics, 912 priests and monks, 980 churches and chapels (Beeson, 1974, pp. 112–13).

## II   RSFSR, Central Asia, Georgia
No central organisation, no hierarchy, no seminary. Churches functioning in Moscow, Leningrad, Tbilisi, Frunze. Congregations organised by laymen and visited by itinerant priests reported in Siberia and central Asia (Gagarin, 1971, p. 142; Read, 1975, pp. 9 and 11; *RiCL*, 3, 1974, p. 32; Beeson, 1974, p. 113).

## III   Moldavia
A church in Kishinev.

## IV   Ukraine
No central organisation, no seminary, no hierarchy. Around 10 functioning churches of which 4 are said to be in Vinnitsa region and 4 in the towns of Odessa, Kiev, Lvov and Stryi (*Lyudina i Svit*, January 1974).

## V   Belorussia
Over 100 churches and a big staff of priests (*Prichiny* . . ., 1965, p. 107) concentrated mainly in Grodno and Brest regions (*Stroitel'stvo* . . ., 1966, p. 59).

## VI   Estonia
1939: 3,000 Catholics, 1 diocese, 1 bishop, 6 parishes and 14 priests (Beeson, 1974, p. 114).
1967: 2,500 Catholics, 2 churches looked after by 2 Latvian priests (ibid.).

## VII   Latvia
1939: 500,000 Catholics, 2 dioceses, 4 bishops, 207 priests, 160 parishes with 250 churches and chapels, 1 theological faculty, 1 seminary (*Die Katholische Kirche* . . ., p. 4).
1964: 178 parishes, 157 priests, 1 bishop, 1 seminary (ibid.).
1967: 380,000 Catholics, 2 dioceses, 1 bishop, 149 priests (ibid.).
1972: 178 parishes, 147 priests (Beeson, 1974, p. 114).

# References

I. A. Aleksandrovich, G. E. Kandaurov and A. I. Nemirovskii (1961), 'Sektantstvo v Voronezhskoi oblasti i rabota po ego preodoleniyu', *Ezhegodnik muzeya istorii religii i ateizma*, 5, Moscow–Leningrad, pp. 59ff.

N. P. Alekseev (1967), 'Metodika i rezul'taty izucheniya religioznosti sel'skogo naseleniya na materialakh Orlovskoi oblasti', *Voprosy nauchnogo ateizma*, 3, pp. 131–50.

N. P. Alekseev (1970), 'Prichiny sokhraneniya religioznosti v psikhologii kolkhoznogo krest'yanstva i puti ee preodoleniya', in V. N. Kolbanovskii (ed.), *Kollektiv kolkhoznikov*, pp. 227–49.

A. P. Andreev (1973), 'Ideologiya i praktika sovremennogo baptizma', Moscow, dissertation summary.

N. P. Andrianov, R. A. Lopatkin and V. V. Pavlyuk (1966), *Osobennosti sovremennogo religioznogo soznaniya*, Moscow.

N. P. Andrianov (1972), 'Evolyutsiya nravstvennogo oblika sovremennogo veruyushchego', *Ateizm, religiya, nravstvennost'*, Moscow, pp. 170ff.

N. P. Andrianov (1974), *Evolyutsiya religioznogo soznaniya*, Leningrad.

I. Anichas (1971a), 'Evolyutsiya sotsial'no-politicheskoi orientatsii katolicheskoi tserkvi v Litve v usloviyakh sotsialisticheskogo stroya', *Katolitsizm v SSSR i sovremennost*, Vil'nyus.

I. Anichas (1971b), 'Realizatsiya reshenii P. Vatikanskogo sobora v katolicheskoi tserkvi Litvy', *Katolitsizm v SSSR i sovremennost*, Vil'nyus.

L. A. Anokhina and M. N. Shmeleva (1966), 'Religiozno-bytovie perezhitki u kolhoznogo krest'yanstva i puti ikh preodoleniya', in N. P. Krasnikov (ed.), *Voprosy preodoleniya religioznykh perezhitkov v SSSR*, Moscow–Leningrad, pp. 115–28.

D. M. Aptekman (1965), 'Prichiny zhivuchesti religioznogo obryada kreshcheniya v sovremennykh usloviyakh', *Voprosy filosofii*, 3, pp. 83ff.

A. Ardabaev and D. Plotkina (1970), 'Religiya sevodnya', *Narodnoe obrazovanie*, 2, pp. 55ff.

Yu. V. Arutyunyan (1966), 'Sotsial'naya struktura sel'skogo naseleniya', *Voprosy filosofii*, 5, pp. 51ff.

Yu. V. Arutyunyan (1968), *Opyt sotsiologicheskogo izucheniya sela*, Moscow.

Yu. V. Arutyunyan (1970), *Sotsial'naya struktura sel'skogo naseleniya*, Moscow.

V. P. Arzamazov (1964), *Podlinnoe litso Iegovizma*, Irkutsk.

Z. V. Balevits (1972), *Katolicheskaya tserkov' v Latvii posle P. Vatikanskogo sobora*, Riga.

P. G. Baltanov (1973), *Sotsiologicheskie problemy v sisteme nauchno – ateisticheskogo vospitaniya*, Kazan.

A. S. Barkauskas (1970), 'Osushchestvlenie Leninskikh idei ob ateisticheskom vospitanii v prakticheskoi deyatel'nosti partiinykh organizatsii', *Voprosy nauchnogo ateizma*, 10, pp. 151f.

E. M. Bartoshevich and E. I. Borisoglebski (1969), *Svideteli Iegovy*, Moscow.

V. N. Basilov (1967), 'Etnograficheskoe issledovanie religioznykh, verovanii sel'skogo naseleniya', in A. I. Klibanov (ed.), *KISRV*, Moscow, pp. 152ff.

Yu. Yu. Bauzhis (1965), 'K voprosu o prichinakh sushchestvovaniya religioznykh predrassudkov v soznanii kolkhoznikov', *Trudy A. N. Litovskoi SSR*, Seriya A, 2, 19, Vil'nyus, pp. 271ff.

Yu. Yu. Bauzhis (1971), 'Ideologiya i deyatel'nost' Katolicheskoi tserkvi v Litovskoi SSR v sovremennykh usloviyakh', Moscow, dissertation summary.

H. Becker (1932), *Systematic Sociology on the Basis of the Beziehungslehre and Gebildelehre of Leopold von Wiese*, New York.

J. A. Beckford (1975), *The Trumpet of Prophecy*, Oxford.

T. Beeson (1974), *Discretion and Valour*, London.

A. F. Belimov (1972), 'Kritika filosofskikh i sotsial'no-eticheskikh kontseptsii ideologii baptizma i mennonitstva', Tashkent, dissertation summary.

A. V. Belov (1968), *Adventizm*, Moscow.

A. V. Belov (1969), *Sovremennoe sektantstvo*, Moscow.

A. V. Belov (1973), *Adventizm*, Moscow.

B. R. Bociurkiw (1971), 'Religion and Atheism in Soviet Society', in R. H. Marshall *et al.* (eds), *Aspects of Religion in the Soviet Union*, Chicago–London.

B. R. Bociurkiw (1974), 'Soviet Research on Religion and Atheism since 1945', *Religion in Communist Lands*, 1, pp. 11–16.

B. R. Bociurkiw and J. W. Strong (eds) (1975), *Religion and Atheism in the USSR and Eastern Europe*, London.

B. R. Bociurkiw (1975), *Catholics in the Soviet Union Today*, symposium paper sponsored by Radio Liberty, Munich.

E. Ya. Bograd (1961), 'Opyt izucheniya sovremennogo sektantstva v Michurinskom raione', *Voprosy istorii religii i ateizma*, IX, pp. 113*ff.*

V. D. Bonch-Bruevich (1922), *Iz mira sektantov*, Moscow.

V. D. Bonch-Bruevich (1959), *Izbrannye Sochineniya*, Vol. I, *O religii, sektantstve i tserkvi*, Moscow.

M. Bourdeaux (1968), *Religious Ferment in Russia*, London.

M. Bourdeaux (1969), *Patriarch and Prophets*, London.

M. Bourdeaux (1971), *Faith on Trial in Russia*, London.

M. Bourdeaux (1970), 'The Russian Orthodox Church and its Offshoots', *Religious Minorities in the Soviet Union*, Minority Rights Group, No. 1.

M. Bourdeaux and K. Matchett (1975), 'The Russian Orthodox Church in Council 1945–1971', in B. R. Bociurkiw and J. W. Strong (eds), *Religion and Atheism in the USSR and Eastern Europe*, London, pp. 37–57.

I. I. Brazhnik (1969), 'Genezis i sotsial'naya sushchnost' dvizheniya Baptistov-'Initsiativnikov'', Moscow, dissertation summary.

I. I. Brazhnik (1974), *Sotsial'naya sushchnost' sektantstvogo ekstremizma*, Moscow.

V. A. Bryanov (1965), 'Kritika ideologii i deyatel'nosti sovremennogo baptizma (Kazakhstan)', Alma-Ata, dissertation summary.

V. R. Bukin (1968), *Psikhologiya veruyushchikh i ateisticheskoe vospitanie*, Moscow.

E. H. Carr (1959), *Socialism in One Country*, Vol. 5 of *A History of Soviet Russia*, London.

A. Z. Chernov (1960), *O religioznykh sektakh Tomskoi oblasti*, Tomsk.

V. A. Chernyak (1965), *O preodolenii religioznykh perezhitkov*, Alma-Ata.

V. A. Chernyak (1967), 'O demograficheskikh osobennostyakh obshchin EKhB goroda Alma-Aty i Alma-Atinskoi oblasti', in A. I. Klibanov (ed.), *KISRV*, Moscow, pp. 209*ff.*

V. A. Chernyak (1969), *Formirovanie nauchno-materialisticheskogo ateisticheskogo mirovozzreniya*, Alma-Ata.

V. A. Chernyak and D. Kapparov (1967), 'O prichinakh i usloviaykh zhivuchesti religioznykh perezhitkov', *Voprosy filosofii*, 6, Moscow.

V. E. Chertikhin (1965), *Ideologiya sovremennogo pravoslaviya*, Moscow.

A. M. Chiperis (1964), 'Sovremennoe sektantstvo v Turkmenskoi SSR', *Izvestiya AN Turkmenskoi SSR* (Seriya obshchestvennykh nauk), 5, Ashkhabad.

N. Cohn (1970), *The Pursuit of the Millennium*, London.

Conference Report of a British Delegation of Members of the World Council of Churches to the AUCECB, London, 16 June 1969 (unpublished, held at the CSRCS in Keston, Kent).

R. Conquest (1968), *The Great Terror, Stalin's Purge of the Thirties*, London.

F. Conybeare (1962), *Russian Dissenters*, New York.

N. J. Demerath (1965), *Social Class and American Protestantism*, Chicago.

A. I. Dem'yanov (1974), 'K voprosu o sovremennom sostoyanii religioznogo techeniya "istinno pravoslavnykh khristian" ', *Voprosy nauchnogo ateizma*, 16, pp. 103–24.

*Die Katholische Kirche in der Sowjetunion 1917–67* (unsigned and unpublished report held by the CSRCS in Keston, Kent).

V. Druzhinin (1930), *Dukhobory* (pamphlet), Leningrad.

V. Druzhinin (1930), *Molokane*, Leningrad.

A. Dubrov (1974), 'Father Alexander Men', *Religion in Communist Lands*, 4 and 5, pp. 8–11.

A. Duluman, B. Lobovik and V. Tancher (1970), *Sovremennyi veruyushchii*, Moscow.

E. Duluman (1973), 'Narushenie pravoporyadka i koshchunstvo', *Pravda Ukrainy*, 11 March, p. 3.

E. Dunn (1967), 'Russian Sectarianism in New Marxist Scholarship', *Slavic Review*, 1.

E. Dunn (1971), 'The Importance of Religion in the Soviet Rural Community', in J. R. Millar (ed.), *The Soviet Rural Community*.

S. Durasoff (1969), *The Russian Protestants; Evangelicals in the Soviet Union: 1944–64*, New York.

R. R. Dynes (1955), 'Church-Sect Typology and Socio-economic Status', *American Sociological Review*, 20, 5, pp. 555ff.

A. Eister (1967), 'Towards a Radical Critique of Church-Sect Typologizing', *Journal for the Scientific Study of Religion*, 1, pp. 85–90.

F. H. Epp (1971), 'Mennonites in the Soviet Union' in R. H. Marshall *et al.* (eds), *Aspects of Religion in the Soviet Union*, Chicago–London, pp. 285ff.

F. H. Epp (1962), *Mennonite Exodus*, Altona–Manitoba.

I. M. Ermakov (1973), 'Ob otdel'nykh proyavleniyakh religioznosti nekotoroi chasti molodezhi', *Filosofskie Nauki*, 3, pp. 102–6.

A. O. Eryshev (1967), 'Opyt konkretno-sotsiologicheskikh issledovanii religioznosti naseleniya na Ukraine', in A. I. Klinabov (ed.), *KISRV*, Moscow.

A. O. Eryshev (1969), 'Ergebnisse soziologischer Untersuchungen' (translated from the Ukrainian), *Osteuropa*, July, Munich, pp. A38ff.

P. N. Evdokimov (1967), 'Grundzüge der Orthodoxen Lehre', R. Stupperich (ed.), *Die Russisch-Orthodoxe Kirche in Lehre und Leben*, 2nd edn, Witten/GFR, pp. 62ff.

*Ezhegodnik Rossii za 1914*, St Petersburg.

F. Fedorenko (1965), *Sekty: ikh vera i dela*, Moscow.

E. G. Filimonov (1966), 'Traditsii religioznogo liberalizma v sovremennom Baptizme, *Voprosy nauchnogo ateizma*, 2.

E. G. Filimonov (1974), 'V usloviyakh krizisa', *Nauka i religiya*, 8, pp. 24–6.

W. C. Fletcher (1967), 'Protestant Influences on the Outlook of the Soviet Citizen Today', in W. C. Fletcher and A. J. Strover (eds), *Religion and the Search for New Ideals in the USSR*, New York–Washington–London, pp. 62ff.

W. C. Fletcher (1971), *The Russian Orthodox Church Underground*, Oxford.

Yu. V. Gagarin (1963), *Sekta 'Svideteli Iegova' v Komi ASSR*, Syktyvkar.

Yu. V. Gagarin (1966), *Evangel'skie Khristiane-Baptisty*, Syktyvkar.

Yu. V. Gagarin (1970), 'The Abandonment of Sectarianism in the Komi ASSR', *Soviet Sociology*, pp. 358ff.

Yu. V. Gagarin (1971), *Religioznye perezhitki v Komi ASSR*, Syktyvkar.

Yu. V. Gagarin (1973), *Staroobryadtsy*, Syktyvkar.

T. G. Gaidurova (1969), 'Zavisimost' obydennogo religioznogo soznaniya veruyushchikh ot uslovii ikh zhizni', in I. D. Pantskhava (ed.), *KSISRiOAV*, Moscow, pp. 12ff.

I. A. Galitskaya (1969), 'K voprosy ob izuchenii religioznosti molodezhi', *Voprosy nauchnogo ateizma*, pp. 389ff.

B. I. Gal'perin (1970), 'Osobennosti ideologii i deyatel'nosti soyuza tserkvei Evangel'skikh Khristian-Baptistov', Moscow, dissertation summary.

V. F. Gazhos (1969), *Osobennosti ideologii Iegovizma i religioznoe soznanie sektantov* (Na materialakh Moldavskoi SSR), Kishinev.

V. F. Gazhos (1975), *Evolyutsiya religioznogo sektantstva v Moldavii*, Kishinev.

A. V. Gegeshidze (1964), 'Sekty Baptistov i Pyatidesyatnikov, reaktionnaya sushchnost ikh deyatel'nosti i ideologii', *Tbilisi*, dissertation summary.

P. A. Gladkov and G. Ya. Korytin (1961), *Khristianskie sekty bytuyushchie v Azerbaidzhane*, Baku.

V. S. Glagolev (1969), 'Illyuzornoe udovletvorenie v religii esteticheskikh potrebnostei veruyushchikh', in I. D. Pantskhava (ed.), *KSISRiOAV*, Moscow, pp. 107ff.

A. I. Glassl' (1971), 'O Veruyushchei Molodezhi v SSSR', *Religiya i ateizm v SSSR*, 2, Munich.

A. Glezer, 'Religion and Soviet Non-conformist Artists', *Religion in Communist Lands*, 3, 1976, p. 16.

C. Y. Glock and R. Stark (1965), *Religion and Society in Tension*, Chicago.

C. Y. Glock and R. Stark (1968), *American Piety: the Nature of Religious Commitment*, Los Angeles.

E. Goode (1967), 'Some Critical Observations on the Church-Sect Dimension', *Journal for the Scientific Study of Religion*, 6, pp. 77ff.

N. S. Gordienko (1962), 'Pravoslavnoe dukhovenstvo o nravstvennosti', *Ezhegodnik muzeii religii i ateizma*, Moscow–Leningrad.

N. S. Gordienko (1968), *Sovremennoe pravoslavie*, Moscow.

V. D. Grazhdan (1965), *Kto takie Pyatidesyatniki?*, Alma-Ata.

V. D. Grazhdan (1966), 'Pyatidesyatnichestvo i sovremennost', *Voprosy nauchnogo ateizma*, 2, pp. 270ff.

Paul Gustafson (1967), 'UO-US-PS-PS: A Re-statement of Troeltsch's Church-Sect Typology', *Journal for the Scientific Study of Religion*, 6, pp. 64ff.

P. Hauptmann (1963), *Altrussischer Glaube*, Göttingen.

P. Hauptmann (1967), 'Das Moskauer Patriarchat und die anderen Kirchen und Religionsgemeinschaften innerhalb der Sowjetunion', in R. Stupperich (ed.), *Die Russisch-Orthodoxe Kirche in Lehre und Leben*, Witten/GFR, pp. 256ff.

G. Hein (1970), 'Die Mennonitengemeinden und -siedlungen in Russland und in der Sowjetunion', *Die Evangelische Diaspora* (Yearbook of the Gustav-Adolf Society).

W. J. Hollenweger (1972), *The Pentecostals*, London.

L. M. Ignatenko and E. S. Prokoshchina (1971), 'Opyt konkretnykh issledovanii psikhologii Baptistov v BSSR', *Voprosy nauchnogo ateizma*, 11, pp. 250f.

G. L. Il'ina (1960), 'Ob izuchenii sovremennogo byta "semeiskikh"', *Etnograficheskii Sbornik*, 1, Ulan-Ude.

N. I. Il'inykh (1968), *O sovremennom mennonitstve*, Moscow.

N. I. Il'inykh (1969), 'Osobennosti organisatsii i deyatel'nosti Mennonitskikh obshchin', in I. D. Pantskhava (ed.), *KSISRiOAV*, Moscow, pp. 200–12.

A. Ipatov (1974), 'Mennonity: proshloe i nastoyashchee', *Nauka i religiya*, 5, pp. 40ff.

E. A. Isichei (1964), 'From Sect to Denomination in English Quakerism, with Special Reference to the Nineteenth Century', *British Journal of Sociology*, 3, pp. 207–22.

M. Iskrinskii (1974), 'Sektantstvo v raionakh sploshnoi kollektivizatsii', *Kritika religioznogo sektantstva*, Moscow.

*Itogi vsesoyuznoy perepisi naseleniya 1959g* (1962), Moscow.

Yu. M. Ivonin (1973), *Staroobryadtsy i staroobryadchestvo v Udmurtii*, Izhevsk.

B. Johnson (1963), 'On Church and Sect', *American Sociological Review*, 4, pp. 539–49.

B. Johnson (1971), 'Church and Sect Revisited', *Journal for the Scientific Study of Religion*, 2, pp. 124–37.

V. M. Kalugin (1962), *Sovremennoe religioznoe sektantstvo, ego raznovidnosti i ideologiya*, Moscow.

N. S. Kapustin (1969), 'O spetsifike nekotorykh religiozno-bytovykh perezhitkov', in I. D. Pantskhava (ed.), *KSISRiOAV*, Moscow, pp. 89–106.

*Katolitsizm v SSSR i sovremennost'* (1971), Vil'nyus.

A. Katunsky (1972), *Staroobryadchestvo*, Moscow.

Ye. Kim (1964), *Za vysokom zabore*, Alma-Ata.

K. Kiselev (1967), 'Gemeindeleben und kirchliche Sitte', in R. Stupperich (ed.), *Die Russisch-Orthodoxe Kirche in Lehre und Leben*, Witten/GFR, pp. 83–95.

A. I. Klibanov (1960), 'Sovremennoe sektantstvo v Tambovskoi oblasti', *Voprosy istorii religii i ateizma*, 8.

A. I. Klibanov (1961), 'Sektantstvo v proshlom i nastoyashchem', *Voprosy istorii religii i ateizma*, 9, pp. 9ff.

A. I. Klibanov (1962), 'Sovremennoe sektantstvo v Lipetskoi oblasti', *Voprosy istorii religii i ateizma*, 10.

A. I. Klibanov (1965), *Istoriya religioznogo sektantstva v Rossii*, Moscow.

A. I. Klibanov (ed.) (1967), *Konkretnye issledovaniya sovremennykh religioznykh verovanii*, Moscow.

A. I. Klibanov and L. N. Mitrokhin (1967), 'Raskol v sovremennom baptizme', *Voprosy nauchnogo ateizma*, 3, pp. 84ff.

A. I. Klibanov (1969), *Religioznoe sektantstvo i sovremennost'*, Moscow.

A. I. Klibanov (1970), 'Razmyshleniya nad stranitsami sotsiologicheskikh issledovanii', *Nauka i religiya*, 11, pp. 70–4.

A. I. Klibanov (1972), 'Po tomu zhe marshrutu: 1959–71', *Nauka i religiya*, 3, pp. 52ff.

A. I. Klibanov (1973), *Religioznoe sektantstvo v proshlom i nastoyashchem*, Moscow.

A. I. Klibanov (1973), 'V mire religioznogo sektantstva–Dukhobory', *Nauka i religiya*, 11, pp. 53f.

A. I. Klibanov (1974), *Iz mira religioznogo sektantstva*, Moscow.

V. D. Kobetskii (1969), 'Obryad kreshcheniya kak proyavlenie religioznosti', in I. D. Pantskhava (ed.), *KSISRiOAV*, Moscow, pp. 162–73.

V. D. Kobetskii (1973), 'Issledovanie dinamiki religioznosti naseleniya v SSSR', *Ateizm, religiya, sovremennost'*, Leningrad.

*K obshchestvu, svobodnomu ot religii* (1970), Moscow.

D. M. Kogan (1964), 'O preodolenii religioznykh perezhitkov u staroobryadtsev', *Voprosy istorii religii i ateizma*, 12, pp. 37ff.

W. Kolarz (1962), *Religion in the Soviet Union*, London.

V. I. Kolosnitsyn (1969), 'Vliyanie sotsial'noy struktury Sovetskogo obshchestva na religioznoe soznanie', *Sotsial'nye razlichiya i ikh preodolenie*, Sverdlovsk, pp. 128–38.

N. V. Kol'tsov (1964), *Staroobryadtsy i starovery*, Tallin.

N. V. Kol'tsov (1965), *Kto takie pyatidesyatniki?*, Moscow.

*Kommunist Litvy* (1973), 9, pp. 61–5.

*Kommunist Moldavii* (1967), p. 70.

D. V. Konstantinov (1967), *Religioznoe Dvizhenie Soprotivleniya v SSSR*, London–Ontario.

Z. Korotkova (1974), *Bogorodichnye prazdniki*, 2nd edn, Moscow.

N. A. Kostenko (1967), *Protestantskie sekty v Sibiri*, Novosibirsk.

N. Kozachishin (1971), 'Nekotorye osobennosti deyatel'nosti katolicheskoi tserkvi v zapadnykh oblastyakh Ukrainskoi SSR', *Katolitsizm v SSSR i sovremennost'*, Vil'nyus.

K. I. Kozlova (1966), 'Izmeneniya v religioznoi zhizni i deyatel'nosti Molokanskikh obshchin', *Voprosy nauchnogo ateizma*, 2.

N. P. Krasnikov (ed.) (1966), *Voprosy preodoleniya religioznykh perezhitkov v SSSR*, Moscow–Leningrad.

N. P. Krasnikov (1968), *V pogone za vekom*, Moscow.

V. F. Krest'yaninov (1964), 'O nekotorykh osobennostyakh i putyakh preodoleniya religioznoi ideologii sektantov – mennonitov', *Uchenye zapiski Tomskogo Gosudarstvennogo Universiteta*, 2, Tomsk.

V. F. Krest'yaninov (1967), *Mennonity*, Moscow.

V. D. Kukushkin (1970), 'Puti vozdeistviya religioznoi ideologii na massovoe religioznoe soznanie', Moscow, dissertation summary.

P. K. Kurochkin (1971), *Evolyutsiya sovremennogo russkogo pravoslaviya*, Moscow.

C. O. Lane (1974), 'Some Explanations for the Persistence of Christian Religion in the Soviet Union', *Sociology*, 2, pp. 233f.

C. O. Lane (1976), 'The Impact of Communist Ideology and the Soviet Order on Christian Religion in the Contemporary USSR (1959–74)', dissertation for PhD at the London School of Economics and Political Science.

D. Lane (1970), *Politics and Society in the USSR*, London.

J. Lawrence (1973), 'Observations on Religion and Atheism in Soviet Society', *Religion in Communist Lands*, 4 and 5, pp. 20–7.

A. A. Lebedeva (1962), 'Nekotorye itogi izucheniya sem'i i semeinogo byta u russkikh Zabaikal'ya', *Etnograficheskii sbornik*, 3, Ulan-Ude, pp. 27–37.

A. A. Lebedev (1970), 'Sekulyarizatsiya naseleniya sotsialisticheskogo goroda', *K obshchestvu svobodnomu ot religii*, Moscow, pp. 132f.

V. I. Lenin (1941–50), *Sochineniya*, 4th edn, Vol. 35, Moscow.

M. Ya. Lensu (1967), *Kto takie 'initsiativniki'?*, Minsk.

V. N. Lentin (1966a), 'Sekta Adventistov Sed'movo Dnya v SSSR', Moscow, dissertation summary.

V. N. Lentin (1966b), 'Adventizm i nauka', *Voprosy nauchnogo ateizma*, 1, Moscow, pp. 30f.

V. N. Lentin (1966c), 'Adventisty Sed'movo Dnya', *Voprosy nauchnogo ateizma*, 2, pp. 288f.

Yu. A. Levada (1965), *Sotsial'naya priroda religii*, Moscow.

D. Lockwood (1964), 'Ideal-type Analysis', in J. Gould and W. L. Kobb (eds), *A Dictionary of the Social Sciences*, London.

J. Majka (1972), 'Poland', in H. Mol (ed.), *Western Religion*, The Hague.

G. G. Maksimilianov (1970), *Baptisty-Raskol'niki – kto oni?*, Donetsk.

I. A. Malakhova (1961), 'Religioznoe sektantstvo v Tambovskoi oblasti v posleoktyabr'skii period i v nashi dni', *Voprosy istorii religii i ateizma*, 9, pp. 77f.

I. A. Malakhova (1968), *O sovremennykh Molokanakh*, Moscow.

I. A. Malakhova (1970), *Dukhovnye Khristiane*, Moscow.

L. V. Mandrygin (1963), 'Sekta Evangel'skikh Khristian-Baptistov', *Prichiny sushchest-vovaniya i puty preodoleniya religioznykh perezhitkov*, Moscow.

L. V. Mandrygin (1965a), 'Sotsial'no – psikhologicheskie prichiny sushchestvovaniya baptizma v *SSSR*', Moscow, dissertation summary.

L. V. Mandrygin (1965b), *Vnutrennii mir veruyushchego i prichiny religioznosti*, Moscow.

L. V. Mandrygin and N. I. Makarov (1966), 'O kharaktere i prichinakh sokhraneniya religioznykh verovanii u krest'yan zapadnykh oblastei Belorussii', *Voprosy nauchnogo ateizma*, 1, pp. 223–39.

D. E. Manuilova (1970), 'Religioznaya obshchina v usloviyakh sekulyarizatsii', *K obshchestvu, sovobodnomu ot religii*, Moscow, pp. 189ff.

D. E. Manuilova (1972), 'Evolyutsiya sotsial'nykh funktsii Baptistskoi obshchiny', Moscow, dissertation summary.

R. H. Marshall, T. E. Bird and A. Q. Blane (1971), *Aspects of Religion in the Soviet Union*, Chicago–London.

D. Martin (1962), 'The Denomination', *British Journal of Sociology*, 1, pp. 1–14.

D. Martin (1967), *A Sociology of English Religion*, London.

S. T. Mashenko (1971), 'Osobennosti vnutriobshchinykh otnoshenii Evangel'skikh Khristian Baptistov', Moscow, dissertation summary.

M. P. Mchedlov (1967), *Evolyutsiya sovremennogo Katolitsizma*, Moscow.

M. P. Mchedlov (1970), *Katolitsizm*, Moscow.

M. P. Mchedlov (1970), *Sovremenny Katolitsizm*, Moscow.

V. F. Milovidov (1963), 'Raspad staroobryadchestva v Ryazanskoi oblasti', *Voprosy istorii religii i ateizma*, 11, pp. 126–37.

V. F. Milovidov (1966), 'Staroobryadchestvo i sotsial'ny progress', *Voprosy nauchnogo ateizma*, 2, p. 198ff.

V. F. Milovidov (1969), *Staroobryadchestvo v nastoyashchem i proshlom*, Moscow.

Minority Rights Group (1970), *Religious Minorities in the Soviet Union*, Report No. 1.

L. N. Mitrokhin (1961), 'Reaktsionnaya ideologiya "istinno-pravoslavnoi tserkvi" na Tambovshchine', *Voprosy istorii religii i ateizma*, 9, pp. 144ff.

L. N. Mitrokhin and E. Ya. Lagushina (1964), 'Nekotorye cherty sovremennogo baptizma', *Voprosy filosofii*, 2.

L. N. Mitrokhin (1965), 'O metodologii konkretnykh issledovanii v oblasti religii', *Sotsiologiya v SSSR*, V. I., Moscow.

L. N. Mitrokhin (1966), *Baptizm*, Moscow.

L. N. Mitrokhin (1967), 'O metodologii issledoveniya sovremennoi religioznosti', in I. D. Pantskhava (ed.), *KISRV*, Moscow, pp. 35ff.

L. N. Mitrokhin (1968), 'Chelovek v Baptistkoi obshchine', *Voprosy filosofii*, 8.

L. N. Mitrokhin (1974), *Baptizm*, Moscow.

H. Mol (ed.) (1972), *Western Religion*, The Hague–Paris.

*Molodezh i Ateizm* (1971), Moscow.

V. A. Molokov (1968), *Filosofiya sovremennogo pravoslaviya*, Minsk.

I. Morozov (1931), *Molokane*, Moscow–Leningrad.

A. T. Moskalenko (1966), *Pyatidesyatniki*, Moscow.

A. T. Moskalenko (1971), *Sovremenny Iegovizm*, Novosibirsk.

A. N. Mukhin (1969), 'Dinamika religioznosti veruyushchikh i ideologicheskaya deyatel'-nost' pravoslavnoi tserkvi', Moscow, dissertation summary.

W. Mykula (1969), *The Gun and the Faith: Religion and Church in the Ukraine under the Communist Russian Rule* (pamphlet), London.

*Narodnoe khozyaistvo SSSR v 1965g* (1966), Moscow.

*Nauchny ateizm* (1973), Moscow.

*Newsletter of the Missionary Society 'Licht im Osten'*, Sept. 1974, Korntal/GFR.

R. Niebuhr (1929), *The Social Sources of Denominationalism*, New York.

Metropolit Nikodim (1968), 'Russkaya – Pravoslavnaya Tserkov' i ekumenicheskoe dvizhenie', *Zhurnal Moskovskoi Patriarkhii*, 9, pp. 46ff.

Z. A. Nikol'skaya (1961), 'K kharakteristike techeniya tak nazyvaemykh istinno-pravoslavnykh khristian', *Voprosy istorii religii i ateizma*, 9, pp. 161ff.

K. I. Nikonov (1969), 'O nekotorykh tendentsiyakh v propovednicheskoi deyatel'nosti sovremennogo baptizma', in I. D. Pantskhava (ed.), *KSISRiOAV*, Moscow, pp. 174ff.

G. A. Nosova (1969), 'Bytovoe pravoslavie na materialakh Vladimirskoi oblasti', Moscow, dissertation summary.

G. A. Nosova (1970), 'Opyt etnograficheskogo izucheniya bytovogo pravoslaviya na materialakh Vladimirskoi oblasti' (translated in) *Soviet Sociology*, pp. 343*ff*.

V. I. Nosovich (1962), 'Rol' kul'ta v Pravoslavnoi Tserkvi', *Ezhegodnik muzeya ateizma i religii*, 6, Moscow–Leningrad, pp. 74*ff*.

A. Nove (1969), *An Economic History of the USSR*, London.

M. P. Novikov (1965), *Pravoslavie i sovremennost'*, Moscow.

M. P. Novikov (1973), 'Pravoslavnaya kontseptsiya sotsial'nykh protsessov', *Nauka i religiya*, 3, pp. 47–50.

I. I. Ogryzko (1970), *Deti i religiya*, Moscow.

A. Okulov (1967), 'Nauchno-ateisticheskoe vospitanie segodnya', *Nauka i religiya*, 8.

V. B. Ol'shanskii (1965), 'Lichnost' i sotsial'nye tsennosti', *Sotsiologiya v SSSR*, Vol. 1, Moscow, pp. 492*ff*.

V. B. Ol'shanskii (1967), 'Sotsial'naya psikhologiya i issledovanie religioznykh verovanii', in A. I. Klibanov (ed.), *KISRV*, Moscow.

R. Oppenheim (1974), 'Russian Orthodox Theological Education in the Soviet Union', *Religion in Communist Lands*, 3, pp. 4–8.

V. Osipov (1972), 'The Berdyaev Circle in Leningrad', *Vestnik RSKhD*, 103, Paris–New York, pp. 153–65.

*Osnovnye voprosy nauchnogo ateizma* (1966), Moscow.

I. D. Pantskhava (ed.) (1969), *Konkretno-sotsiologicheskoe izuchenie sostoyaniya religioznosti i opyta ateisticheskogo vospitaniya*, Moscow.

N. A. Pashkov (1969), 'K voprosu o kharaktere obydennogo religioznogo soznaniya pravoslavnykh khristian', in I. D. Pantskhava (ed.), *KSISRiOAV*, Moscow, pp. 148–61.

C. Patock (1966), 'Die Hierarchie der Russisch-Orthodoxen Kirche, Moskauer Patriarchat, special issue of *Ostkirchliche Studien* (Würzburg/GFR).

V. D. Pechnikov (1968), 'Vozdeistvie religii na sotsial'nuyu aktivnost' trudyashchikhsya', *Vestnik Moskovskogo Universiteta* (Filosofiya), 4, pp. 61*f*.

F. Peters (1968), *Mennonites Visit the Soviet Union* (short report in six parts), Mennonite Central Committee, 20 December.

S. Petropavlovsky (1973), The Orthodox Church, *Religion in Communist Lands*, 4 and 5.

W. S. F. Pickering (1974), 'The Persistence of Rites of Passage', *British Journal of Sociology*, 1, pp. 63*ff*.

V. G. Pivovarov (1968), 'Religioznaya gruppa prikhozhan v sisteme tserkovnogo prikhoda', in A. S. Ivanov *et al.* (eds), *Chelovek, obshchestvo i religiya*, Moscow, pp. 130–67.

V. G. Pivovarov (1974), 'The Methodology of Collection and Processing of Primary Sociological Information in the Study of Problems of Religion and Atheism', *Social Compass*, 2, pp. 191*ff*. (translated from an article in *K obshchestvu, svobodnomu ot religii*, Moscow 1970).

G. N. Plechov (1970), 'Obektivnye usloviya izzhivaniya religioznosti', *K obshchestvu svobodnomu ot religii*, Moscow, pp. 65*ff*.

A. A. Podmazov (1967), 'O sovremennom staroobryadchestve v Latvii', *Kommunist Sovetskoi Latvii*, 1, Riga.

A. A. Podmazov (1970a), 'Staroobryadchestvo i ego evolyutsiya v sovremennykh usloviyakh', Moscow, dissertation summary.

A. A. Podmazov (1970b), *Staroobryadchestvo v Latvii*, Riga.

A. A. Podmazov (1970c), Staroobryadchestvo v Latvii', *Nauka i religiya*, 4, pp. 57*ff*.

V. Pomerantsev (1966), 'Vchera i sevodnya', *Nauka i religiya*, 4, pp. 2*ff*.

Z. I. Porakishvili (1970), *Dukhobory v Grusii*, Tbilisi.

*Prichiny sushchestvovaniya i puti preodoleniya religioznykh perezhitkov* (1963), Moscow.

*Prichiny sushchestvovaniya i puti preodoleniya religioznykh perezhitkov* (1965), Minsk.

E. S. Prokoshchina (1967), 'Iz opyta issledovaniya religioznosti naseleniya v Belorusskoi SSR', in A. I. Klibanov (ed.), *KISRV*, Moscow, pp. 72*ff*.

E. S. Prokoshchina and M. Y. Lensu (eds) (1969), *Baptizm i Baptisty*, Minsk.

N. I. Puchkov (1972), 'Vliyanie vnutriklassovykh izmenenii v sotsialisticheskom obshchestve na rasvitie ateizma', *Voprosy nauchnogo ateizma*, 13.

F. M. Putintsev (1928), *Sektantstvo i antireligioznaya propaganda*, Moscow.

F. M. Putintsev (1974), *'Dukhobor'e'* (extracts from), *Kritika religioznogo sektantstva*, Moscow.

G. A. Rahr (1973), 'Combien D'Orthodoxes y a-t-il en Russie?', *Catacombes*, Paris.

C. Read (1975), 'Soviet Roman Catholics', *Religion in Communist Lands*, 1–3, pp. 8*ff*.

248    *Christian Religion in the Soviet Union*

'Reestr osuzhdennykh ili zaderzhannykh v bor'be za prava cheloveka v SSR s 5 marta 1953 po fevral' 1971', *Sobranie dokumentov samizdata*, Vol. I, AS84.

J. Rimaitis (1971), *Religion in Lithuania* (pamphlet), Vil'nyus.

H. Römmich (1971), 'Evangelische Gemeinden in Russland nach einem halben Jahrhundert Sowjetherrschung', *Kirche im Osten*, Vol. 14, Göttingen, pp. 135*ff*.

H. Römmich (1972), 'Die Evangelisch-Lutherische Kirche in Russland in Vergangenheit und Gegenwart', *Die Kirchen und das Religiöse Leben der Russlanddeutschen*, Heimatbuch, 1969–72, ed. Landsmannschaft der Deutschen aus Russland, Stuttgart/GFR, pp. 217*ff*.

A. Rogerson (1969), *Millions Now Living Will Never Die*, London.

J. Rothenberg (1971), 'The Legal Status of Religion in the Soviet Union', in R. H. Marshall *et al.* (eds), *Aspects of Religion in the Soviet Union*, Chicago–London, pp. 61–102.

R. Rozova (1968), 'Seminary i . . . zhivoe delo', *Agitator*, June.

D. Russell (1970), 'My Visit to Russia', *Baptist Times*, 22 October.

Yu. Safronov (1967), 'Chto pokazali otvety?', *Kommunist Belorussii*, 3, pp. 66*ff*.

M. Sapiets (1976), 'Monasticism in the Soviet Union', *Religion in Communist Lands*, 1, pp. 28*f*.

V. V. Sapronenko (1969), 'Kharakter proyavleniya i puti preodoleniya religioznosti selskogo naseleniya', Leningrad, dissertation summary.

V. A. Saprykin (1970), 'Rol' sub'ektivnogo faktora v preodolenii religii v usloviyakh sotsializma', *K obshchestvu svobodnomu ot religii*, Moscow, pp. 100*ff*.

V. A. Saprykin (1970), 'Ateisticheskaya rabota partiinoi organizatsii v usloviyakh goroda', *Voprosy nauchnogo ateizma*, 9, pp. 216*f*.

W. Sawatsky (1975), 'Russian Evangelicals Hold a Congress', *Religion in Communist Lands*, 1–3, pp. 12*ff*.

J. Scanzoni (1965), 'Innovation and Constancy in the Church-Sect Typology', *American Journal of Sociology*, 71, pp. 320*ff*.

G. Schwartz (1970), *Sect Ideologies and Social Status*, Chicago.

L. A. Serdobol'skaya (1963), 'Reaktsionnaya sushchnost' Adventizma', *Ezhegodnik muzeya istorii religii i ateizma*, 7, pp. 113*ff*.

L. A. Serdobol'skaya (1971), 'Kritika sotsial'nykh vozzrenii sovremennogo baptizma v SSSR', Leningrad, dissertation summary.

A. Shamaro (1968), 'Zateryanny mir', *Nauka i religiya*, 9, pp. 17*ff*.

M. M. Sheinman (1966), 'Obnovlencheskoe techenie v Russkoi pravoslavnoi Tserkvi posle Oktyabrya', *Voprosy nauchnogo ateizma*, 2, pp. 41*ff*.

M. D. Shevchenko (1966), 'Rol' semeinykh traditsii v nasledovanii religioznykh perezhitkov det'mi i podrostkami', *Vestnik Moskovskogo Universiteta*, 2, pp. 33*ff*.

G. Simon (1969), 'Staatlicher Druck und Kirchlicher Widerstand. Die Abgespaltene Baptistische Gruppe der Sogenannten Initsiatiwniki', *Osteuropa*, Stuttgart, July, pp. 500*ff*.

G. Simon (1969), 'Der Sowjetische Staat und die Kirche', *Das Parlament* (supplement to), February.

G. Simon (1970), *Die Kirchen in Russland*, Munich.

G. Simon (1972), 'Die Unruhe in der Katholischen Kirche Litauens', *Berichte des Bundesinstituts fur Ostwissenschaftliche und Internationale Studien*, 19, Cologne.

V. E. Soldatenko (1972), *Pyatidesyatniki*, Donetsk.

I V. Sosnina (1962), *Pravda ob Amurskikh sektantakh*, Blagoveshchensk.

D. C. Stange (1963), 'The Case of the Missing Million', *The National Lutheran*, 9 November.

D. C. Stange (1968), 'When Lutherans Came to Russia', *The Lutheran Standard*, 5.

R. Stark (1964), 'Class Radicalism, and Religious Involvement in Great Britain', *American Sociological Review*, 5, pp. 698*ff*.

Yu. I. Stel'makov (1969), 'O sootnoshenii ratsional'nogo i emotsial'nogo v soznanii veruyushchikh', in I. D. Pantskhava (ed.), *KSISRiOAV*, Moscow.

*Stroitel'stvo kommunizma i dukhovny mir cheloveka* (1966), Moscow.

*Stroitel'stvo kommunizma i preodolenie religioznykh perezhitkov* (1965), Moscow.

W. P. Stroyen (1967), *Communist Russia and the Russian Orthodox Church 1943–1962*, Catholic University of America Press.

N. Struve (1967), *Christians in Contemporary Russia*, London.

R. Stupperich (ed.) (1967), *Die Russisch-Orthodoxe Kirche in Lehre und Leben*, Witten/GFR.

R. Stupperich (1969), 'Neue Formen der Frömmigkeit und die Russisch-Orthodoxe Kirche', *Osteuropa*, July, pp. 493*ff*.

A. Sulatskov (1966), *Na iskhode nochi*, Alma-Ata.

L. T. Sytenko (1967), 'O nravstvennom oblike sovremennogo veruyushchego', *Voprosy nauchnogo ateizma*, 3, pp. 113*ff*.

D. N. Tabakaru (1968), 'Kritika religioznykh vzglyadov i deyatel'nosti Evangel'skikh Khristian-Baptistov', Kishinev, dissertation summary.

D. N. Tabakaru (1970), abstract in English by Cosmos Translations, New York, from *Strannitsy istorii religii i ateizma v Moldavii*, Kishinev.

D. N. Tabakaru (1973), 'O nekotorykh yavleniyakh v religioznom sektantstve', *Izvestiya AN Moldavskoi SSSR* (seriya obsh. nauk), 2, pp. 3–12.

V. K. Tancher and E. K. Duluman (1964), 'Opyt konkretnogo issledovaniya kharaktera religioznykh predstavlenii', *Voprosy Filosofii*, 10.

Z. A. Tazhurizina (1969), 'Mistifikatsiya obydennykh otnoshenii v sueveriyakh', in I. D. Pantskhava (ed.), *KSISRiOAV*, Moscow.

M. K. Teplyakov (1967), 'Pobeda ateizma v razlichnykh sotsial'nykh sloyakh Sovetskogo obshchestva', *Voprosy nauchnogo ateizma*, 4, pp. 130*ff*.

M. K. Teplyakov (1972), *Problemy ateisticheskogo vospitaniya v praktike partiinoi raboty*, Voronezh.

L. N. Terent'eva (1966), 'Rasprostranenie ateisticheskogo mirovozzreniya sredi Latyshei', in N. P. Krasnikov (ed.), *Voprosy preodoleniya religioznykh perezhitkov v SSSR*, Moscow–Leningrad.

N. Theodorovich (1968), 'Mennonites in the USSR', *Bulletin, Institute for the Study of the USSR*, 10, 1 October, pp. 31*ff*.

R. H. Thouless (1971), *An Introduction to the Psychology of Religion*, 3rd ed., Cambridge.

I. P. Tinyakova (1969), 'Sotsial'nye izmeneniya i preodolenie religii sredi zhenshchin?', *Voprosy nauchnogo ateizma*, 7.

V. E. Titov (1967), *Pravoslavie*, Moscow.

*Travel Report by an Anonymous East German Pastor*, untitled and undated, in German, held at the CSRCS in Keston, Kent.

E. Troeltsch (1931), *The Social Teaching of the Christian Churches*, Vol. I, London.

M. Troyanovskii (1975), 'Traditsiya ideinoi beskompromissnosti', *Molodoy kommunist*, 8, pp. 76–80.

A. Trubnikova (1964), 'Tainik v taburetke', *Oktyabr'*, 9, pp. 173*ff*.

L. A. Tul'tseva (1969), 'Evolyutsiya starykh Russkikh sekt', *Voprosy nauchnogo ateizma*, 7.

V. A. Tul'tseva (1970), 'Kalendarnye religioznye prazdniki v bytu sovremennogo krest'yanstva', *Sovetskaya etnografiya*, 6, pp. 111–18.

D. M. Ugrinovich (1967), 'O kriteriyakh religioznosti i ikh primenenii v protsesse sotsiologicheskikh issledovanii', *Vestnik Moskovskogo Gosudarstvennogo Universiteta* (Filosofiya), 4, pp. 20*ff*.

L. N. Ul'yanov (1970), 'Izmenenie kharaktera religioznosti', *K obshchestvu svobodnomu ot religii*, Moscow, pp. 160*ff*.

L. N. Ul'yanov (1971), 'Opyt issledovaniya motivatsii religioznogo soznaniya', *Voprosy nauchnogo ateizma*, 11, pp. 219*f*.

V. St. Vardys (1971), 'Catholicism in Lithuania', in R. H. Marshall *et al.* (eds), *Some Aspects of Religion in the Soviet Union*, Chicago–London.

N. S. Vasil'evskaya (1972), 'Opyt konkretno-sotsiologicheskogo issledovaniya otnosheniya k religii v sovremennoi gorodskoi sem'e', *Voprosy nauchnogo ateizma*, 13, pp. 383*ff*.

A. Veinbergs (1971), 'Lutheranism and Other Denominations in the Baltic Republics', in R. H. Marshall *et al.* (eds.), *Aspects of Religion in the Soviet Union*, Chicago–London, pp. 405*ff*.

M. F. Verbit (1970), 'The Components and Dimensions of Religious Behaviour: Toward a Reconceptualization of Religiosity', in P. E. Hammond and B. Johnson (eds), *American Mosaic. Social Patterns of Religion in the United States*, New York, pp. 24–38.

A. Veshchikov (1975), 'V chem vred religii sevodnya', *Molodoy kommunist*, 8, pp. 81–7.

N. N. Volkov (1930), *Sekta skoptsov*, Leningrad.

R. Wallis (1975), 'Relative Deprivation and Social Movements: A Cautionary Note', *British Journal of Sociology*, 3, pp. 260*ff*.

R. Wesson (1963), *The Soviet Communes*, New Brunswick.

G. Wetter (1967), 'Communism and the Problem of Intellectual Freedom', in W. C. Fletcher and A. J. Strover (eds), *Religion and the Search for New Ideals in the USSR*, pp. 1*ff*.

R. H. White (1970), 'Toward a Theory of Religious Influence', in P. E. Hammond and B. Johnson (eds), *American Mosaic. Social Patterns of Religion in the United States*, New York, pp. 14*ff*.

B. Wilson (1959), 'An Analysis of Sect Development', *American Sociological Review*, 1, pp. 3–15.

B. Wilson (1966), *Religion in Secular Society*, London.

B. Wilson (1967), 'The Pentecostalist Minister: Role Conflicts and Contradictions of Status', in B. Wilson (ed.), *Patterns of Sectarianism*, London.

B. Wilson (1970), *Religious Sects*, London.

B. Wilson (1973), *Magic and the Millennium*, London.

B. Wilson (1976), *Contemporary Transformations of Religion*, Oxford.

G. Woodcock and I. Avakumovic (1968), *The Dukhobors*, London.

I. N. Yablokov (1969), 'Transformatsiya religioznoi morali v soznanii veruyushchikh v usloviyakh sotsializma', in I. D. Pantskhava (ed.), *KSISRiOAV*, Moscow, pp. 127*ff*.

I. N. Yablokov (1972), *Metodologicheskie problemy sotsiologii religii*, Moscow.

I. N. Yablokov (1967), 'Ob opyte konkretnykh issledovanii religii', *Vestnik Moskovskogo Gosudarstvennogo Universiteta* (Filosofiya), 4.

I. N. Yablokov (1965), 'Vliyanie nekotorykh psikhologicheskikh faktorov na religioznost' ', *Vestnik Moskovskogo Gosudarstvennogo Universiteta* (Filosofiya), 2, pp. 43*ff*.

I. N. Yablokov (1969), 'Obshchenie veruyushchikh kak faktor formirovaniya psikhologii religioznoi gruppy', in I. D. Pantskhava (ed.), *KSISRiOAV*, Moscow, pp. 47–67.

V. G. Yakovlev (1961), *Kritika ideologii i deyatel'nosti sekty Pyatidesyatnikov v Kazakhstane*, Alma-Ata.

V. G. Yakovlev (1963), *Kto takie sektanty i chto oni propoveduyut?*, Alma-Ata.

Z. A. Yankova (1963), 'Sovremennoe pravoslavie i antiobshchestvennaya sushchmost' ego ideologii', *Voprosy istorii religii i ateizma*, 11, pp. 79*ff*.

A. F. Yarugin (1971), 'Kharakter sovremennoi Baptistkoi propovedi', *Voprosy nauchnogo ateizma*, 12, pp. 149*f*.

P. P. Yashin (1969), *Krizis sovremennogo baptizma*, Kharkov.

V. Yevdokimov (1968), 'Konkretnye sotsiologicheskie issledovanya i ateizm', *Nauka i religiya*, 1, pp. 22–5.

I. M. Yinger (1957), *Religion, Society and the Individual*, New York.

I. M. Yinger (1970), *The Scientific Study of Religion*, London.

B. Zelenkov (1968), 'Chelovek roditsya', *Molodoy kommunist*, 11, p. 95.

N. Zernov (1963), *The Russian Religious Renaissance of the Twentieth Century*, London.

N. S. Zlobin (1963), 'Sovremenny baptizm i ego ideologiya', *Voprosy istorii religii i ateizma*, 11, pp. 100*ff*.

A. G. Zolotova (1962), 'Reaktsionny Kharakter Molokanstva', *Ezhegodnik muzeya istorii religii i ateizma*, 6, pp. 152*ff*.

V. A. Zots (1974), *Dukhovnaya kul'tura i pravoslavie*, Moscow.

'Zur Lage der Evangelisch-Lutherischen Kirche in Russland vor und nach der Revolution' (1971), *Religion und Atheismus in der UdSSR*, 8, 46.

'Zur Situation der Evangelischen Lutherischen Kirche in Estland und Lettland' (1972), Wissenschaftlicher Dienst für Ostmitteleuropa, 22, pp. 338–40.

# Index

Action Group, *see Initsiativniks*

Adventists of the True Remnant, *see* Reform Adventists

Alexei (Patriarch) 34

All-Union Council of Evangelical Christian Baptists (AUCECB) 15, 28, 139n, 140, 141, 143, 144, 146, 148, 157, 158, 161, 178, 185, 201, 232; *see also* Baptists

American Christians 56, 58, 69, 71, 74

Amendment of Statutes in 1961 34

Anabaptists 85, 200

Anti-Christ 84, 85, 86, 118, 121, 126, 128, 131

Anti-religious campaigns 28, 33, 34, 159, 167, 193, 208, 210

Apocalypse, Coming of 82, 84, 88, 90

Asceticism 87, 94

Assemblies of God 175

Atheism 16, 26, 28, 29, 98, 213, 221, 230, 231; in Western society 45

Avoidance Ritual 131, 132, 133

Avvakum (Protopop) 112

Baptism: in the ROC 44, 60–3; of Baptists 141; of Lutherans, 198

Baptists 74, 104, 110, 138–66, 169, 173, 175, 177, 178, 180, 181, 182, 184, 201, 220, 222, 223, 226, 229, 231; English 145; Free 140, 157; German 145; of the Old Faith 140; Political opinions of 161; Pure 140, 157; *see also* All-Union Council of Evangelical Christian Baptists and Baptist sect.

Baptist sect: History of 139–40; Membership of 139, 140–1; Organisation of 142; Training of 142; Geographical distribution of 148–9; Urban/rural distribution of 149; Social composition of 149–51

Baturin 155

*Beglopopovtsy* 115, 116

*Beguny* 118

Beliefs: of Russian Orthodox 56, 73; Magical 57; Saliency of 58; Implementing 57, 58, 125; Purposive 57, 58; Warranting 57; of Old Believers 125f

Belokrinitsa Church (also Old Believer Church of the Belokrinitsa Hierarchy 114, 115, 116, 122, 128, 129

Berdyaev Circle 37, 49, 77

Beretskii, A. 217

*Bespopovtsy* 113, 114, 115, 116–20, 125, 126, 129, 130, 132, 134, 136

Bible Study: in the ROC 69; among Baptists 142; among Pentecostalists 182

Bishops, *see* under relevant churches

Bolsheviks 98, 103, 122

Borovoi (Professor-Archpriest) 37

*Bratskii Listok* 146

*Bratskii Vestnik* 177, 178

Brezhnev 161

*Buevtsy* 82

Bultmann 144

Catherine the Great 94, 113

Catholic Church, *see* Roman Catholic Church *and* Greek Catholic Church

Catholic Church of the Eastern Rite 33, 206, 223

Catholic priests: in the Soviet Union 207; in Lithuania 213–15, 216; in Belorussia 214; in Latvia 214

Catholics, in Belorussia 210, 211, 213, 216, 240; in Estonia 240; in Latvia 240; in Lithuania, *see* Lithuanian Catholic Church; in Moldavia 240; Religious commitment of 210–11, 212, 214; in the RSFSR 240

Centrality 72, 73

Centre for the Study of Religion in Communist Lands 151, 211n

Chalidze 34

*Cherdashniki* 80, 82

Christian socialism 100, 121

Christians of the Seventh Day 168

Chronicle of the Lithuanian Catholic Church 209, 211n, 212

'Church', definition of 18

Church attendance: in the ROC 64, 65f; of Old Believers 128, 129; of Baltic Lutherans 194

'Church'-like tendencies 21, 22, 43, 138, 200, 222, 230; *see also* Religious Orientations

Church Mennonites 201; *see also* Mennonites

Church of England 44, 60, 67

'Church' type 17, 18, 19, 22, 30, 33, 34, 40, 75, 191, 200, 208, 217, 219, 221

Communion: in the ROC 67; among Old Believers 129; among Catholics 211

Communist Molokans 101, 102

Communist moral code 165, 174, 231

Concilium 50

Confession: in the ROC 67; among Old Believers 129

Consequential dimension 71f; definition of 71

Constant Molokans 101, 105, 107, 108, 109

'Conversionist' type of sect 138, 139, 219

Council for the Affairs of the ROC 34
Council for the Affairs of Religious Cults 146
Council of Baptist Prisoners' Relatives 151, 163
Council of Churches of Evangelical Christian Baptists 139n, 146; *see also* Initsiativniks
cults: Agricultural 64, 65; Magical 70

Decree on Religion: in 1918 27; in 1928 27, 28
Demerath 22, 148, 221
'Denomination' 17, 20, 21, 22, 138; Definition of 20, 21
'Denominational' tendencies, 138, 148; *see also* Religious Orientations
Denominationalisation 166, 171, 172, 220, 232
Deprivation, and religion 75, 76
Devotional practice: among Orthodox 68; among Old Believers 130, 131; among Mennonites 202
Dimensions of religiosity 73
Dissenters, *see* Old Believers
Domestic churches 42
Dukhobors 91, 92, 93, 94, 95–100, 204, 206, 219, 231
*Dvadtsatka* 27, 48, 213
Dynes 22, 148, 221

Economic and political development; after 1917 24, 25; before 1917 24
*Edinovertsy* 116
*Edinstvenniki, see Smorodintsy*
Elite conception; among Baptists 143; among Adventists 172; among Pentecostalists 182; among Jehovah's Witnesses 187
Ermogen (Archbishop) 34
Eschatological notions 83, 84, 85, 90, 125, 126, 171, 181
Eshliman 35
Estonian Catholics 240
Estonian Lutheran Church 192–5; Membership of 193–4
Evangelical Christians 139, 157, 175; *see also* under Baptists and AUCECB
Evangelical Christians in the Apostolic Faith; *see* Smorodintsy
Exclusivity: among Baptists 143, 147; among Adventists 169, 171; among Jehovah's Witnesses 188, 189
Experiential dimension, definition of the 69, 70

*Fedorovtsy* 80, 82
*Fedoseevtsy* 116, 117, 120, 132
*Filipovtsy* 116, 117, 120
First Five Year Plan 24
Flavian (Archbishop) 35

Folk religion 57
Fuchs, E. 217
Fundamentalism: among Old Believers 126; among Pentecostalists 182
Funeral rite: in the ROC 60, 61; 'by correspondence' 41, 42

German Lutherans 192, 195–200, 205, 221, 230; History of 195–6; Membership of 196; Nationalism of 197–200; Organisation of 196–7; Political responses of 198; Sermons of 199; Age of 199
Glossolalia 176, 181, 184
Greek Catholic Church, *see* Catholic Church of the Eastern Rite *and* Uniate Church
Gubanov 97

Harnack 144
Hartmann 144
Holy Synod 50; in 1961n, 33

Icons 68, 77
ideological dimension, definition of 55
ideological domination 159, 161
*Il'intsy* 185
Illegal religious organisations and groups 16, 105, 113, 140, 176, 186, 190, 197, 226
Implementing beliefs 57, 58, 125
*Imyaslavtsy* 82
Initsiativniks (Council of Churches of Evangelical Christian Baptists) 22, 83, 139, 139n, 140, 146, 147, 150, 151–63, 172, 178, 180, 185, 220; Geographical distribution of 152; Imprisonment of 163; Social Composition of 153–6; Teachings of 147; Urban-Rural distribution of 153
*Innokenty* 80, 81
intellectual dimension, definition of the 55
Intellectuals: in the ROC 37; in the LCC 213
Intelligentsia in the ROC 48, 49
'Introversionist' type of sect 200, 219
*Ioannity* 80, 81
Isichei 21, 22
Ivanov, N. I. 175

Jehovah's Witnesses 81, 85, 86, 161, 169, 172, 182, 183, 185–91, 220, 221, 222, 231, 232; History of 186; Organisation of 186–7; Social composition of 190; in the West 185, 186, 188, 191; and the Brooklyn centre 186, 189
Jehovists, *see* Il'intsy
Johnson, H. 217

Kalmykova Lukeriya 97
Kaunas revolt 212, 216, 217
Khlysts 91, 92–4, 175
*Khristovoverie* 91, 93, 94
Khrushchev 28, 159, 161
Klibanov 158
Kolarz 151

Kolchak (General) 120
Komsomol 61, 98
Kopylov 92
Kronstadt, John of 81
Kryuchkov 155, 161
Kudinov 103

Laicisation 42, 127, 197, 199
'Latter Rain' movement 179
Latvian Catholic Church 207, 240
Latvian Lutheran Church 192–5; Membership of 193
Leapers 101, 105, 106, 107, 108, 109, 175
Lenin 98; Views on religion of 26, 27
Lithuanian Catholic Church 192, 207, 208–17, 222, 230; Bishops of 215; History of 208; Membership of 210; Nationalism in 212, 215–17; Organisation of 208–9; Priests of 213–15; Relation to state of 208–9, 216; Religiosity of membership 214; Social composition of membership 212–13; and the Vatican 208, 209, 214
Living Church, *see* Renewal movement
Lutheran Church, before Revolution 26; *see also* under name of nationality, e.g. Latvian

Magical beliefs 59
Magical cults 70
Magical practice 86
*Maksimisty* 101, 104, 105, 106, 107, 108, 109, 219
'Manipulationist' type of sect 219
Marx on religion 26, 27
Medieval sects 20, 85, 86
Mennonite Brethren 201, 203; *see also* Mennonites
Mennonites 139, 192, 200–6; History of 200; in the West 201, 202, 205; Nationalism of 197–200; Number of 201–2; Organisation of 203; Political responses of 204–5; Social composition of 203–4
'Men of God' 86, 92
Metropolitan Nikodim 36, 37, 38
Metropolitan Petrovykh 82
Metropolitan Seraphim 35
Midnight Christians 48
Militant atheism, *see* Atheism
Milky Waters 97
*Mirootrechniki, see* World Renouncers
Mitrokhin 141
*Mol'chal'niki* 83, 84, 85, 90
*Molodaya Gvardiya* 49
Molokans 91, 92, 93, 94, 100–11, 204, 206, 219, 231; and socialism 103, 105, 108, 109, 110; Social composition of 106–7; Social orientations of 108f; Religious orientations of 108f; Membership of 101, 104, 105, 106, 107
Molokons of the Don 101

Monasteries: in the ROC 50; in LCC 209
Morozov, S. 122
Mysticism 70, 81, 83, 86

New Economic Policy 24
*New Israel* 91, 92, 93, 94
Niebuhr 21
Nikon (Patriarch) 112
Nikonian reforms 131

October Revolution 23, 24, 98
Okulov 223
Old Believer Church of Ancient Orthodox Christians, *see* Beglopopovtsy
Old Believers 26, 83, 84, 112–37, 223, 230, 232; after the Revolution 113–14; before the Revolution 112–13; Church services of 135; Number of 114; Parishes 135; Political responses of 120f; Social composition of 122f; Socio-geographical distribution of 123
*Old Israel* 91, 92, 93
Orthodox, *see* Russian Orthodox
Orthodox sects 26, 80f, 232
Oscillation between 'sect' and 'church'-like tendencies 21, 22

Pavel (Archbishop) 34
Pentecostalists 139, 142, 143, 157, 161, 169, 172, 174–85, 186, 190, 221, 222, 230, 232; History of 175; Organisation of 177–8, 182; Social composition of 179–81; Socio-demographic distribution of 177; in the West 174, 177n, 178, 179, 180, 182, 184
Perfectionists 176
Peter the Great 117, 118
Pimen (Patriarch) 50
*Pomortsy* 116, 117, 120, 125, 126, 128, 129, 130, 132
*Popovtsy* 113, 114, 115–16, 120, 125, 128, 129, 134, 136, 221
*Postniki* 91, 92, 93
practice dimension, definition of the 59
Prague Peace Conference 35
Prayer: among Russian Orthodox 69; among Old Believers 130
Preobrazhenskii cemetery 107
Priestless Old Believers *see Bespopovtsy*
Priests *see* under relevant churches
*Priguny, see* Leapers
Progressive Movement 103
Prokoviev 155
Prophetism 181
Protestant sects 26, 115, 221, 226
Purges 25
Purposive beliefs 57, 58

*Radenie* 92, 93, 94
*Raskol* see Old Believers
Rasskazov 94, 106

Reform Adventists 168, 170, 174, 221
Reform Baptists, *see* Initsiativniks
Reformed Church 196
Religion: before the Revolution 26; in Britain 58, 60, 67; and anomie 165; and children 27, 162–3, 214, 225; and collectivisation 25, 93, 98, 99, 104, 110; and communist ideology 23, 99, 109, 110, 170, 229, 231; and community 76, 109, 125, 136, 163–5, 172, 182, 197, 202, 228, 230; and culture 76, 77, 78, 99, 136; and deprivation 75, 76, 77; and economic behaviour 87, 88, 93, 95, 96, 98, 104, 106, 134, 169, 180, 184, 188; and identity 136, 199; and industrialisation 24, 25, 165, 185, 228; and migration 122, 165, 179, 190; and monarchism 81, 82, 84; and morality 161–5, 182, 183, 228; and nationalism 77, 78, 134, 197–200, 205–6, 212, 215–17; in Poland 186, 210, 213; and political alienation 88, 121, 158, 160, 183–4, 185, 188, 189–90, 191, 206, 217, 229; as political protest 82, 85, 90, 136, 147, 159; and psychological rewards 78; and public opinion on 45; and Second World War 25, 28, 225; and social insulation 87, 88, 108, 109, 110; and social isolation 118, 119, 120, 121, 123, 182, 183, 218; and socialist society 183, 216–17; in the West 17, 23, 75, 226, 227, 229
Religiosity 22; and social conduct 72; Dimensions of 73; Latent 74; of RO before 1917 31; Future trends in 225; and socio-economic status 228; *see also* Religious Commitment
religious believers: Age of 224–6; education of 227–8; Proportion in the population of 222–4; Sex of 226; Socio-economic status of 227; Urban–rural distribution of 223, 226
Religious chain letter 84
Religious change 17, 21, 22, 166, 219
religious collectivities 13, 21, 22, 218–22; Social composition of 221; Characteristics of 230
Religious commitment 19, 55f, 74, 75, 194, 199, 202, 210f; among rural believers 59; among urban believers 59; *see also* religiosity
Religious Communes 103, 104
Religious education 225; among Orthodox 45, 57; among Baptists 45, 144; among Mennonites 202; among Catholics 211, 214
Religious emotions 70
Religious holidays: in the ROC 63, 64, 77; among Old Believers 128
Religious knowledge: among Russian Orthodox 56; among American Christians 56; among Soviet sectarians 56; among Baptists 141, 142; among Lutherans 199; among Mennonites 203
Religious modernisation 38, 218, 232
Religious orientations 17, 22, 23, 174, 219–20; of Molokans 108, 109; of Baptists 141–6; of Seventh Day Adventists 168–73; of Pentecostalists 175, 181–5; of Jehovah's Witnesses 187–90; of German Lutherans 197, 198
Religious policy 26, 27; in Lithuania 208
Religious protest, of Orthodox 35; of Pentecostalists 178; of Lithuanian Catholics 211–12, 215
Religious tendencies, *see* Religious orientations
Renewal movement 31, 32, 33, 38, 40
'Revolutionist' type of sect 80, 81, 84, 85, 88, 169, 171, 174, 219
Rites of Passage: in Britain 60; among Catholics 210; among Dukhobors 100; among Lutherans 194; Motivations for participation in 61, 62, 128; among Old Believers 127; in the ROC 60f
ritual: Avoidance 131, 132, 133; Modernisation of 38; practice 59f, 73, 127, 141; Religious 38, 39, 60, 61, 79, 211; Sacrificial 81; Secular 42, 61, 79, 194
Rogozhskii cemetery 115
Roman Catholic Church: in Lithuania, *see* Lithuanian Catholic Church; Medieval 20; in Poland 210, 216; in the Soviet Union 207, 215, 240; in Tsarist Russia 26, 207, 240
Rudometkin Maksim 101
Russian Orthodox Academies, *see* Theological Training Institutes
Russian Orthodox belief 56; content of 56
Russian Orthodox believers 37, 38, 39, 40, 42, 82, 134, 135, 151, 199, 210, 211, 222, 225, 226, 230; Definition of 45; Geographical distribution of 46; Number of 46; Political opinions of 37, 72; Social activity of 72; Social characteristics of 47f
Russian Orthodox Bishops 34, 40, 50, 51; Social characteristics of 52
Russian Orthodox Church 15, 19, 28, 175, 192, 215, 220, 221, 223, 230, 231, 232; Baptism in 44; Easter in the 63; Foreign policy of 33, 35; History of 26, 27, 30–3; Income of 47; Membership of 31, 43f, 46, 47–9, 50; and Old Believers 115, 134; Organisation of 50; Political accommodation by 34, 35; Schism in 32; and sectarians 93, 94, 101; Social Teaching of 36, 37
Russian Orthodox churches: Closure of 33, 47; Number of 50
Russian Orthodox church service 78, 101

Russian Orthodox dogma 39; Modernisation of 38; Knowledge of 56
Russian Orthodox monasteries 82
Russian Orthodox parishes 41, 72
Russian Orthodox parishioners, *see* Russian Orthodox believers
Russian Orthodox priests 37, 38, 40, 41, 53, 54, 56; Education of 53, 54, 82, 164; in the parish 54; Status of 53
Russian Orthodox seminaries, *see* Theological Training Institutes
Russian Orthodoxy; and communism 40; and socialism 37

Sabbatarian Pentecostalists 176, 181
Saints' Days 64
Saliency of belief 58
*Samizdat* 15, 120, 178, 206, 211, 212, 216
Schism 22, 97, 138, 220; among Adventists 168; among Baptists 138, 146–8, 156f; in the ROC 32
Schwartz 21
'sect', definition of 19, 20
'sect-church' typology 17, 18, 22
Sect development 21; *see also* Religious Change
Sect leaders: of Adventists 173; of Baptists 142, 153, 155, 156, 161, 164, 173; of Jehovah's Witnesses 189; of Mennonites 203; of Pentecostalists 182
'Sect'-like tendencies 21, 22, 43, 138, 148, 200, 221, 222, 230; *see also* Religious Orientations
Sects, after Revolution 27; before Revolution 92
'Sect-to-church' continuum 191, 220
'Sect-to-church' hypothesis 17, 18, 22
'Sect' type 17, 19, 20, 22, 75, 197, 221
Secular conduct 71f
Secular ritual 42, 61, 79, 194
Secular ethic 71f, 99, 100, 102, 202, 204, 205, 231
Selivanov 94
Sergei (Patriarch) 32, 34, 82
Sermons: among Baptists 161, 162; in the ROC 56
Seventh Day Adventists 81, 86, 167–74, 180, 182, 184, 222, 223, 229, 230; Education of 173–4; on education 169–70; History of 167–8; Membership of 168; Organisation of 172; Social composition of 173–4; in the West 168, 170
Shaker Pentecostalists 176
Shpiller 33, 35
Siemens, Menno 200
*Skoptsy* 91, 92, 94–5
Smorodin N. P. 175
*Smorodintsy* 175, 177
Social activity: of Adventists 170; of

Jehovah's Witnesses 188; of Pentecostalists 182; of RO believers 72
Social distribution of believers in general 22
Society for the Preservation of Historical and Cultural Monuments 49, 77
Society of Educated Molokans 103
Social Orientations, *see also* secular ethic; of Adventists 168–73; of Baptists 158; of Jehovah's Witnesses 187–90; of Mennonites 204–6; of Molokans 108, 109, 110, 111; of Pentecostalists 175, 181–5
Sociology and sociologists of religion in the Soviet Union 15, 16, 17, 59, 74, 139, 158, 207
Sokolovsky (Archpriest) 31
Solzhenitsyn 35
Stalin, on religion 27
Stranniki 116, 118, 119, 120, 121, 123, 125, 126, 129, 134, 219
Synod, *see* Holy Synod

Taborites 85
Talantov 37
'Thaumaturgical' type of sect 80, 86, 219
Theological Training Institutes 37, 51; Students in 51, 215; Syllabus of 51; Libraries of 51
*Theological Works* 37
Tikhon (Patriarch) 32
Traditionalism 74, 78
Troeltsch 17, 18, 19, 20
True Orthodox Christians 83f, 185, 190, 191, 220, 230; Attitude towards ROC of 85; Social and Political orientation of 87; Social composition of 88; Numerical strength of 89
True Orthodox Christian Wanderers 116, 118, 119, 121, 123, 125–6, 129, 130, 134, 219, 232
True Orthodox Church 80, 82
Tsar Peter III 94
Typology of sects 20, 21

Uklein, Simon 101
Uniate Church 198; *see also* Catholic Church of the Eastern Rite *and* Greek Catholic Church
Union of Evangelical Christian Baptists, *see* All-Union Council of Evangelical Christian Baptists
'Utopian' type of sect 102, 110

Venyamin (Archbishop) 34
Verigin, Petr 97
Vil'nyus Highest Council 117
Vins 155, 161
Voronaev 175, 176
*Voronaevtsy, see* Pentecostalists
Voronov (Professor-Archpriest) 37

Wanderers, *see Stranniki*

War Communism 24

Warranting beliefs 57

*Watchtower* 186, 187

Wedding rite, in the ROC 60, 61

White, Ellen 168

Wilson 17, 19, 20, 21, 80, 81, 103, 110, 138, 178, 230

World Council of Churches 35, 140, 143, 193

World Renouncers 118, 119, 124, 130

Yakunin 35

Young believers 44, 150, 173, 213, 225

Zabolotsky (Professor) 37

Zagorsk Peace Conference in 1969 118

Zheludkov 35

Zionists 176

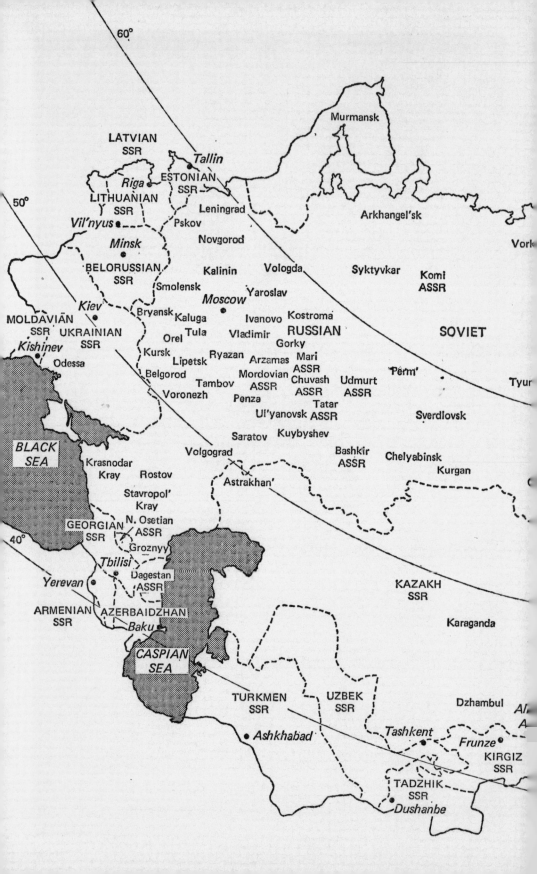

60°

Murmansk

LATVIAN
SSR

*Tallin*

*Riga*    ESTONIAN
          SSR

Arkhangel'sk

50°

LITHUANIAN
SSR

Leningrad

*Vil'nyus*

Pskov

Novgorod

Vork

*Minsk*

BELORUSSIAN
SSR

Kalinin

Vologda

Syktyvkar

Komi
ASSR

Smolensk

Yaroslav

*Kiev*

Bryansk

*Moscow*

Ivanovo

Kostroma

RUSSIAN

SOVIET

MOLDAVIAN
SSR      UKRAINIAN
         SSR

Kaluga

Orel    Tula

Vladimir

Gorky

*Kishinev*

Odessa

Kursk

Lipetsk

Ryazan

Arzamas

Mari
ASSR

Perm'

Tyur

Belgorod

Tambov

Mordovian
ASSR

Chuvash
ASSR

Udmurt
ASSR

Voronezh

Penza

Tatar
ASSR

Sverdlovsk

Ul'yanovsk ASSR

BLACK
SEA

Krasnodar
Kray

Rostov

Volgograd

Saratov   Kuybyshev

Bashkir
ASSR

Chelyabinsk

Kurgan

Stavropol'
Kray

Astrakhan'

GEORGIAN
SSR

N. Osetian
ASSR

40°

*Tbilisi*

Groznyy

Dagestan
ASSR

KAZAKH
SSR

*Yerevan*

ARMENIAN
SSR      AZERBAIDZHAN

Karaganda

*Baku*

CASPIAN
SEA

TURKMEN
SSR

UZBEK
SSR

Dzhambul

*Al*
*A*

*Ashkhabad*

*Tashkent*

*Frunze*

KIRGIZ
SSR

TADZHIK
SSR

*Dushanbe*